"It is not often that a book in apologetics can claim to stand squarely in the historic Reformed tradition while offering new insights into how to do apologetics in the contemporary world, but this one can. Fesko's book demonstrates a deep understanding of the plight of hypermodernity and boldly suggests that historic Christian orthodoxy offers answers to the despair of a post-Christian society. Fesko is not limited by the method of presuppositionalism, but he is not shy about critiquing false presuppositions. He is not limited to evidentialist method but makes judicious use of evidence. He is not afraid to employ metaphysical arguments that have never been proven wrong but just ignored since Kant. He exposes the religiosity of supposedly secular modernity. And he does a masterful job of showing how all his moves are based on scriptural teaching. This is the best single book on apologetics that I know."

—**Craig A. Carter**, Tyndale University; author of *Contemplating God with the Great Tradition*

"J. V. Fesko's *An Introduction to Reformed Apologetics* is a breath of fresh air in the world of Reformed apologetics. After almost a century of captivity to a novel method of apologetics that produced far more interest in talking about itself than in talking to lost and dying sinners, Reformed Christians are gradually becoming aware that the old biblical paths of traditional Reformed apologetics are far superior. Traditional Reformed apologetics, as Fesko explains in this book, is grounded in love of God and love of neighbor, utilizes both of God's books (nature and Scripture), and knows that its goal of turning sinners from idols to Christ depends on the regenerating work of the Holy Spirit."

—**Keith Mathison**, Reformation Bible College

"As the psalmist says, 'The heavens declare the glory of God, and the sky above proclaims his handiwork' (Ps. 19:1). Apologists in the Reformed tradition do not always agree about the grounds and ways for using evidence, but we all know that we cannot escape questions about these matters. While attempting to mediate some of the disagreements about method, J. V. Fesko walks us through some astounding examples of how the reality of God directly confronts every human being and holds us accountable. We should all appreciate his call to see that God's goodness and majesty tear down all objections, summoning everyone to reckon with where they stand before their Maker."

—**Harrison Perkins**, pastor of Oakland Hills Community Church (OPC)

"Dr. Fesko's *An Introduction to Reformed Apologetics* offers a wise layman's guide to understanding and defending the biblical Christian faith. Positing twelve theses grounded in the faithful Word of God (and not Enlightenment pride or psychology's gnosticism), this book offers faithful guidance for witnessing to our neighbors and friends. Dr. Fesko presents a fruitful analogy: like an orchestra's conductor, an apologist employs and coordinates the truths of Scripture, creation, history, philosophy, literature, science, and nature. This book will provide wisdom for all Christians."

—**Rosaria Butterfield**, author of *Five Lies of Our Anti-Christian Age*

An Introduction to REFORMED APOLOGETICS

An Introduction to REFORMED APOLOGETICS

Warring with Idols

J. V. Fesko

B
Baker Academic
a division of Baker Publishing Group
Grand Rapids, Michigan

Published by Baker Academic
a division of Baker Publishing Group
Grand Rapids, Michigan
BakerAcademic.com

Printed in the United States of America

Library of Congress Cataloging-in-Publication Data
Names: Fesko, J. V., 1970– author
Title: An introduction to Reformed apologetics : warring with idols / J. V. Fesko.
Description: Grand Rapids, Michigan : Baker Academic, a division of Baker Publishing Group, [2026] | Includes bibliographical references and index.
Identifiers: LCCN 2026002788 | ISBN 9781540971388 cloth | ISBN 9781493456970 ebook | ISBN 9781493456987 pdf
Subjects: LCSH: Apologetics | Reformed Church—Doctrines
Classification: LCC BT1103 .F47 2026
LC record available at https://lccn.loc.gov/2026002788

Baker Publishing Group publications use paper produced from sustainable forestry practices and postconsumer waste whenever possible.

26 27 28 29 30 31 32 7 6 5 4 3 2 1

To
David Strain

Contents

Preface

Apologetics, or defending the claims of the Christian faith, was the theological discipline that first caught my attention when I had no interest in pursuing ordained ministry. I was minding my own business when I wandered into a Christian bookstore in the mall one day when I was on my lunchbreak. Ever since I was a child, I have always loved books and reading, but I had never read a theology book other than the Bible, of course. That day as I perused the books on the shelf, my eye caught the title of a book: *Evidence That Demands a Verdict* by Josh McDowell.[1] I picked it up and thumbed through its pages and was drawn in. At the time, my budget was quite tight, though my mindset was like that of Desiderius Erasmus (1466–1536), the sixteenth-century humanist scholar: "When I have a little money, I buy books; and if I have any left, I buy food and clothes."[2] So, I bought the book, read it, and it fueled my desire to attend seminary and pursue ordination for the gospel ministry.

Throughout my pastorate I studied apologetics issues because I knew that after worship services people often asked questions about the sermon and the truths of Scripture. I wanted to be prepared to answer those questions. As I moved into full-time teaching, I studied apologetics more in depth because I had to teach courses on the topic. I presently teach an introductory apologetics course at Reformed Theological Seminary. I likewise have used portions of this material to teach introductory apologetics at International Reformed Baptist Seminary.

1. Josh McDowell, *Evidence That Demands a Verdict*, vol. 1, *Historical Evidences for the Christian Faith* (Thomas Nelson, 1979).

2. As cited in William Barker, *Erasmus of Rotterdam: The Spirit of a Scholar* (Reaktion Books, 2021), 63–64.

The first step in offering students a biblical and confessional understanding of apologetics was presented in my book *Reforming Apologetics: Retrieving the Classic Reformed Approach to Defending the Faith*, which consisted of setting the stage for retrieving historic confessional apologetics: scriptural, historical, theological, and philosophical ground clearing. This book represents a second stage in my efforts to "reform apologetics" by setting forth a basic introduction. I present this book both for seminary students studying apologetics for the first time and also for people in the church. In fact, some of the material presented herein was first developed for lectures I delivered at church conferences held at Tenth Presbyterian Church (Philadelphia, PA) and Grace Baptist Chapel (Hampton, VA). I also created some of it for lectures that I presented for the launch of Southern Baptist Theological Seminary's New Center for Christian Apologetics and the Evangelical Theological Society's Northeast Region annual meeting. I have engaged the Scriptures from Genesis to Revelation, conversed with theologians throughout the history of the church (patristic, medieval, Reformation, and post-Reformation), and done my best to infuse aesthetic and imaginative ideas throughout. My hope and prayer is that this book would give readers the basic theological tools they need to defend the Christian faith.

Acknowledgments

Friendship is a gift from God, which is a truth that even unbelievers have acknowledged. The Latin orator Cicero (106–43 BC) once wrote, "For friendship is nothing less than an accord in all things, human and divine, conjoined with mutual goodwill and affection, and I am inclined to think that, with the exception of wisdom, no better thing has been given to man by the immortal gods."[1] Solomon writes upon the theme of friendship, "Faithful are the wounds of a friend" (Prov 27:6) and "The sweetness of a friend comes from his earnest counsel" (Prov 27:9). I am grateful, above all else, that Jesus Christ calls me his friend and that he has given me friends in his body to help me with the endeavor to write this book (John 15:13–15). I am grateful to Bill Challener, an MIT-trained physicist, who read through the whole book and offered helpful suggestions; he especially assisted me in the places where I touch upon astrophysics. I am thankful to Levi Berntson, my former TA and now a professor at Reformation Bible College. He offered insightful comments that have enabled me to hone my arguments in places. My thanks also go to Keith Mathison, professor of theology at Reformation Bible College and fellow Tolkien devotee. Keith and I have been talking about apologetics in person and over email for many years, so I am thankful for his comments and feedback. I am also grateful to Harrison Perkins, Jonathan Cruse, and Bulut Yasar, fellow ministers in the Orthodox Presbyterian Church. They have helped me think through issues and refine my arguments. Thank you for taking the time to read through my manuscript and offer me your thoughts. Thank you to my current TA, Ethan Tucker, for proofreading through the manuscript

1. Cicero, *De Amicitia*, VI.20, in *De Senectute, De Amicitia, De Divinatione*, trans. William Armistead Falconer, Loeb Classical Library (Harvard University Press, 1964), 131.

and for creating the bibliography. Thank you for your careful and attentive work. I am grateful to all these men for their friendship—for taking the time to come alongside me and assist me in writing this book. They are a gift of God, have given me earnest counsel, and have critiqued my work in places in the interest of helping me be a better writer and student of God's word.

Friends, however, do not merely exist outside of the walls of my home. Aristotle (384–322 BC) once wrote that perfect friendship is difficult to find because it is like love, and one cannot love many people at the same time. "Love," writes Aristotle, is "naturally felt towards one person only." You cannot love all people with the same degree of intensity. Moreover, "for perfect friendship you must get to know a man thoroughly, and become intimate with him, which is a very difficult thing to do."[2] These are the marks of the friendship of virtue—the type of friendship where people motivate one another to pursue virtue and be a better person: "For these friends which each alike the other's good in respect of their goodness, and they are good in themselves; but it is those who wish the good of their friends for their friends' sake who are friends in the fullest since they love each other for themselves and not accidentally."[3] These are things that undoubtedly mark my wife and her friendship and love for me, for which I am grateful. Not only does she want to make me a better person, but she also helps me strive to be a better Christian, husband, father, preacher, professor, and writer. Over the years we have discussed the ideas in this book, and she has helped me think through the issues and encouraged me along the way. And like Christ's love for me, she has laid down her life for me and for our family in many ways (John 15:13). Thank you to my children, John Jr., Robert, and Carmen, who give me great love and encouragement. In truth, you are one of the big reasons I write. Among the many reasons I write, I write for the glory of the Triune God, the betterment of the church, and for you. I hope in the years to come, when I am long gone, that you will be able to pick up my books and still hear the voice of your father pointing you to Christ. In this case, I hope you hear my voice as I teach, remind, and embolden you to defend and own the faith once delivered to the saints (Jude 3).

Thank you to Todd Hains and Jessi Strong for their work on earlier drafts of this book. Thank you to the whole team at Baker Academic. I am grateful for your support, encouragement, and diligent labor to see this book to press. I pray that the Lord continues to bless all of you as you seek to edify the church and glorify Christ through publishing works of theology.

2. Aristotle, *Nicomachean Ethics*, VIII.vi.2–3, trans. H. Rackham, Loeb Classical Library (G. P. Putnam's Sons, 1926), 473.

3. Aristotle, *Nicomachean Ethics*, VIII.iii.6 (461).

I dedicate this book to Pastor David Strain, the senior minister at First Presbyterian Church, Jackson, Mississippi. David is a friend, but he is also my family's shepherd and the voice of Christ. I have been able comfortably and confidently to serve in various pulpits knowing that my family sits under his faithful preaching. I am grateful for your love for Christ, his word, and his church, and for your courageous, careful, and convicting preaching week in and week out. Thank you for feeding my family Christ, the manna from heaven, and for defending the truth each and every week. I pray the Lord's continued blessings upon you, my friend, as you serve Christ and his church.

A Prayer for the Study of Apologetics

Blessed be the Lord, my rock,
who trains my hands for war,
and my fingers for battle;
he is my steadfast love and my fortress,
my stronghold and my deliverer,
my shield and he in whom I take refuge.
—Psalm 144:1–2a

Eternal God, who dwells in unapproachable light and who is of purer eyes than to behold evil, cleanse me of my sin that clouds my understanding. Shine the light of your truth upon the sin-darkened corners of my heart to make me aware of my sin; by your grace in Christ through the Spirit, enable me to repent and see clearly. Train my hands for war and my fingers for battle as I confront my own doubts and fears about your faithfulness and truthfulness. Dispel the arrogance and pride in my heart and fill it with a love and concern for those who do not yet believe. Give me courage to speak the truth in love, patience to suffer the slings and arrows of insult, and humility to endure ridicule for the sake of Christ and his gospel. Plant my feet upon the rock of Christ, and use my feeble words to show people your truth, to shine your light upon their path, so that they too may walk in the path of everlasting life. I pray these things to you, oh heavenly Father of lights, through Christ, the Great Shepherd of the Sheep, and in the power of the Holy Spirit, the Lord and giver of life. Amen.

Introduction

Always be "prepared to make a defense to anyone who asks you for a reason for the hope that is in you" are words that the apostle Peter wrote to the church amid suffering persecution (1 Pet 3:15). Christians throughout the ages have heard and read these words and have thus sought to explain what they believe and why in the face of questions, criticism, and hostility toward the Christian faith. At the same time, being prepared to defend one's faith has also served the important purpose of answering questions of doubt in our own hearts and minds. Defending the faith, or apologetics, serves both personal and wider communal purposes. Christians have sought shelter in the truth in the face of their personal doubts, against the criticisms of unbelievers, or even against officially state-sanctioned persecution of the church. Over the centuries there have been many different efforts to defend the faith, such as Augustine's (354–430) *City of God*, a defense of Christianity against the claims that the church had brought about the collapse of the Roman Empire.[1] Anselm (1033–1109) wrote his *Proslogion*, a work in which he encouraged his fellow monks to believe in order to understand that God is the greatest being—no being greater than him can be conceived of.[2] Thomas Aquinas's (1225–1274) *Summa Contra Gentiles* was an apologetics manual to equip Dominican monks as they engaged Muslim philosophers.[3] William Paley's (1743–1805) *Natural Theology, or Evidences of the Existence and Attributes of the Deity* toured the creation to show its design and

1. Augustine, *The City of God*, 2 vols. (New City Press, 2012).

2. Anselm, *Proslogion*, in *The Major Works*, ed. Brian Davies and G. R. Evans (Oxford University Press, 2008), 82–104.

3. Thomas Aquinas, *Summa Contra Gentiles*, trans. Anton Pegis (University of Notre Dame Press, 1975).

purpose that points to the existence of a designer—namely, God.[4] C. S. Lewis (1898–1963) wrote many apologetic works in both didactic and narrative form that communicated Christian truth for a wide range of people, from children to intellectuals.[5] With the myriad of apologists and their works, where can a person go to learn the basics of how to defend the Christian faith?

One of the best approaches to any discipline is to go back to basics—revisit fundamental principles to lay a solid foundation for future labors. While there are numerous biblical passages that showcase defending the faith, perhaps the most iconic is Paul's presentation of the gospel before the Epicurean and Stoic philosophers at Mars Hill (Acts 17:16–33). To be clear, Paul's defense is not normative in the sense that Christians are restricted to Paul's methods and arguments; however, they are certainly instructive and provide a helpful example both in form and content. Paul's Mars Hill address contains at least seven principles that present essential elements for any effort to defend the faith. The apostle Paul

1. was angered by the rampant idolatry in Athens, which tells us that humanity's problem is not unbelief but the worship of everything else but God (Acts 17:16, 29). Humans are hardwired for worship.
2. "reasoned in the synagogue with the Jews" (Acts 17:17). Apologetics involves employing reasoned arguments.
3. connected with his audience by observing their practices (Acts 17:23).
4. appealed to the creation and providence as evidence of God's existence (Acts 17:24–27).
5. was familiar with pagan literature so that he could quote it to his audience and show how it contained kernels of truth that only made sense within a larger Christian context (Acts 17:28).
6. segued from creation and general revelation to special revelation, Christ, the gospel, and the resurrection (Acts 17:31–32).
7. was motivated by love for God and for unbelievers, which drove him to preach and teach the gospel among the Jews and gentiles (Acts 17:16; cf. Eph 4:26–27; 1 Cor 13:4–8).

4. William Paley, *Natural Theology, or Evidence of the Existence and Attributes of the Deity, Collected from the Appearances of Nature*, ed. Matthew D. Eddy and David Knight (Oxford University Press, 2006).

5. E.g., C. S. Lewis, *Mere Christianity* (HarperOne, 2017); *The Space Trilogy* (Harper Collins, 2013); *The Abolition of Man* (HarperOne, 2015); *The Chronicles of Narnia* (Harper Collins, 2004).

These seven principles establish key elements for an introductory approach to apologetics that prepares students of Scripture to defend the faith. This book traces the lines of Paul's address at Mars Hill to provide a biblical and theological introduction to apologetics in the Reformed tradition.

In the light of Paul's address to the philosophers at Mars Hill, this book presents the thesis that apologetics is the art and discipline of engaging idolatry for the sake of promoting and defending the Christian faith. The chief tools for defending the faith are the books of nature and Scripture, or natural and supernatural theology. In our use of the book of nature, we appeal to God's truth and wisdom embedded in the creation, both in the world and innately in humans. Only the regenerating work of the Spirit through the gift of faith resting upon the special revelation of the gospel of Christ, however, saves sinners. Apologetics does not save sinners but instead clears obstacles from the hearts and minds of unbelievers so that the gospel has a clear path forward.

The Twelve Theses

Thesis 1: Humans are hardwired for worship and thus will either worship the one, true God or an idol.

Thesis 2: Reformed apologetics rests on the authority of God's revelation in creation and Scripture, and God has given humans the capacity to know truth through their senses.

Thesis 3: Acts 17 provides an illustrative blueprint for apologetics that Christians can employ as an outline for their own defense of the Christian faith as they seek a meeting of the minds with unbelievers.

Thesis 4: Acts 27 shows that sometimes there is not a meeting of the minds as in Acts 17 but a head-on collision with unbelief.

Thesis 5: Historic Reformed apologetics has followed the apostle Paul's approach to defending the faith, evident in the opening chapters of John Calvin's (1509–1564) *Institutes of the Christian Religion*.

Thesis 6: The book of Scripture shows how God has planted evidence of his being, wisdom, and power in the creation. Scripture warrants the teleological argument, or the argument from design.

Thesis 7: Since God has imbedded knowledge of his being, wisdom, and power in the creation, Christians can appeal to teleological argument as they read the book of nature through the corrective lenses of Scripture.

Thesis 8: The teleological argument should include the microcosmos of the human body, which means that Christians should appeal to it in their apologetics.

Thesis 9: As Paul appealed to the pagan literature of his day, Christians can likewise employ literature written by unbelievers as they defend the faith.

Thesis 10: The resurrection of Christ rests in both the books of nature and Scripture; as Paul appealed to the resurrection, so Christians can appeal to this doctrine in defending the faith.

Thesis 11: As Paul appealed to the book of nature by invoking the doctrine of providence, Christians can appeal to this doctrine as they explain why evil exists and how the book of Scripture points us to the cross of Christ as God's answer to evil.

Thesis 12: A love for the Triune God and for sinners must be the driving force for apologetics and is the greatest apologetic tool in an age when rationalism has given way to irrationalism.

Tracing the lines of Paul's address at Mars Hill, this book consists of two parts: a groundwork for apologetics followed by apologetic arguments. Part 1 begins with a chapter on establishing our cultural context for defending the faith and presents the following theses.

Thesis 1: Humans are hardwired for worship and thus will either worship the one, true God or an idol.

Presently, philosophers and theologians have popularized two key ideas: (1) we used to live in an enchanted world where people believed in angels, demons, and magical things, but, among other factors, the Protestant Reformation disenchanted the world, which has made belief in God more difficult than it was in pre- and early modern times. Within the newly disenchanted world, (2) Western culture became secular as it pushed religion out of the private and public squares. As popular as the disenchantment and secularization thesis is, much like Paul's appraisal of first-century Athens, the world has never been disenchanted or secular. Secularism is a religious myth. Recognizing the irresistibly religious nature of humanity, the world's problem is not unbelief but idolatry. Understanding that idolatry is the world's chief problem equips Christians to interface with the world around them and ably present and defend the gospel.

Thesis 2: Reformed apologetics rests on the authority of God's revelation in creation and Scripture, and God has given humans the capacity to know truth through their senses.

Chapter 2 establishes meta-principles for apologetics from the standpoint of classic Reformed theology. In other words, what chief theological commitments does Reformed apologetics require? This chapter sets forth three key requirements: (1) resting on the authority of Scripture, (2) using the book of nature, or general revelation, and (3) a realistic epistemology. While some approaches to apologetics lean almost exclusively on Scripture, such as the presuppositional approach of Cornelius Van Til (1895–1987), with even some of his disciples saying it is sinful to use historical evidence, historic Reformed apologetics employs both of God's books, creation and Scripture, in the defense of the faith.[6] Reformed apologetics is also committed to a realistic epistemology, which means that humans can perceive the world around them through their senses: taste, touch, smell, sight, and hearing. To put this in theological terms, God has designed and created humans to be able to read the book of nature even though they are fallen and corrupted by sin. Apologists can appeal to both the books of nature and Scripture in their defense of the faith.

Thesis 3: Acts 17 provides an illustrative blueprint for apologetics that Christians can employ as an outline for their own defense of the Christian faith as they seek a meeting of the minds with unbelievers.

Thesis 4: Acts 27 shows that sometimes there is not a meeting of the minds as in Acts 17 but a head-on collision with unbelief.

Chapters 3 and 4 take a closer look at Paul's ministry by first exploring the apostle's Mars Hill address to study the seven principles that appear in his apologetic method. Why does Paul point to creation and invoke the doctrine of providence? Why does he positively quote pagan Stoic poets? In short, this

6. See, e.g., Greg Bahnsen, "The Impropriety of Evidentially Arguing for the Resurrection," *Synapse* 2 (1972), https://answersingenesis.org/apologetics/the-impropriety-of-evidentially-arguing-for-the-resurrection/. To see the roots of Bahnsen's views, see Cornelius Van Til, *An Introduction to Systematic Theology* (P&R, 1974). I believe that this work rather than his apologetics works is a clearer presentation of his presuppositional method. Nevertheless, readers may want instead to consult Cornelius Van Til, *The Defense of the Faith* (P&R, 1967); *Christian Apologetics* (P&R, 1992). In principle, Van Til is not opposed to using evidence, but it rarely features in his apologetics to the point that his disciples and critics have often assumed that he was opposed to its use, which spurred one author to write a book defending Van Til's favorable attitude toward evidence (see Thom Notaro, *Van Til and the Use of Evidence* [P&R, 1980]).

chapter explains how, in a sense, Paul had a meeting of the minds with the philosophers. This is not to say that he agreed *in toto* with their philosophy. Rather, it explains how he used kernels of truth from their literature in his defense of the gospel. The following chapter shows a different side of defending the faith—namely, the head-on collision. Luke includes Paul's shipwreck narrative (Acts 27) to show that the God of the Scriptures is utterly unlike the Epicurean notions of fate and chance. These two chapters establish a bedrock of biblical truth for a foundation. Apologetics must rest in the authority of Scripture.

> ***Thesis 5: Historic Reformed apologetics has followed the apostle Paul's approach to defending the faith, evident in the opening chapters of John Calvin's (1509–1564) Institutes of the Christian Religion.***

Chapter 5 looks to the opening chapters of John Calvin's *Institutes of the Christian Religion* to see how one Reformed theologian traces the same biblical lines of truth that appear in Paul's Mars Hill address. Calvin is not normative for Reformed theology but rather illustrative of general Reformed practice. Like Paul's appeal to creation, Calvin opens his *Institutes* with an appeal to the creation and uses positive citations to pagan literature, most notably *De Natura Deorum* ("On the Nature of the Gods") by the Roman orator Cicero (106–43 BC). Even though many contemporary Reformed theologians claim Calvin as the patron of their apologetic method, such as Van Til's presuppositionalism, Calvin stands in the catholic and historic Reformed tradition by employing the books of nature and Scripture to defend the Christian faith.

Part 2 moves beyond the biblical, theological, and historical foundation to establish apologetic arguments that trace Paul's Mars Hill defense by appealing to creation, providence, the resurrection, and Paul's love for sinners. Part 2 defends the following theses.

> ***Thesis 6: The book of Scripture shows how God has planted evidence of his being, wisdom, and power in the creation. Scripture warrants the teleological argument, or the argument from design.***

> ***Thesis 7: Since God has imbedded knowledge of his being, wisdom, and power in the creation, Christians can appeal to teleological argument as they read the book of nature through the corrective lenses of Scripture.***

Chapters 6 and 7 move beyond the scriptural and historical groundwork of part 1 to the teleological argument for the existence of God, or the argument from design. Just as Paul began his defense of the gospel by appealing to creation, this chapter begins the examination of the evidence for God's design in the cosmos. However, as much as the teleological argument has been criticized as being inconclusive, this chapter looks at the argument through the corrective lenses of Scripture. By beholding the creation through Scripture, Christians can appeal to general revelation, which attests to God's existence, attributes, and wisdom. From a foundation of Scripture (thesis 6), we have the proper footing to consider the specific natural theological evidence for the teleological argument in the following chapter (thesis 7).

Thesis 8: The teleological argument should include the microcosmos of the human body, which means that Christians should appeal to it in their apologetics.

Chapter 8 presses the case for the teleological argument for God's existence by looking to the microcosmic creation of the human body. Calvin followed the ancient philosophers by recognizing that the human body was a cosmos all of its own revealing God's wisdom. Yet in the twentieth century, few apologists applied the teleological argument to the human body. In our present cultural climate, the human body has taken on a renewed importance in the light of anti-Christian claims about sexuality and especially transgenderism. Transgenderism is not biology but an idolatrous religion that makes every effort to deny the general revelation of the human body. If people willfully deny their biology and general revelation, then of course they will deny God's special revelation. Not only must Christians, therefore, press the case for the teleology of the human body in apologetics, but they must also protect the rear flank in the church. Some young people within churches are attracted to the religion of transgenderism, and thus Christians need to be equipped to defend Christian truth claims concerning the body and sexuality both within and without the church.

Thesis 9: As Paul appealed to the pagan literature of his day, Christians can likewise employ literature written by unbelievers as they defend the faith.

Chapter 9 continues to trace Paul's Mars Hill methodology through an examination of the need to use pagan literature in our defense of the gospel. When Paul quoted Stoic poets, he accomplished several things. First, he showed he was familiar with the ideas of the people he evangelized; he was not a remote preacher lobbing truth grenades from afar. Second, he identified the kernels of truth that the pagan philosophers knew by virtue of their image-bearing status. Paul did not use pagan philosophy but rather rested upon the truth of God present in pagan thought. Third, he employed this truth to his advantage to show and tell his audience the rest of the story, a story that appears only in Scripture. Literature is a part of the book of nature and thus constitutes a vital tool for apologetics.

> ***Thesis 10: The resurrection of Christ rests in both the books of nature and Scripture; as Paul appealed to the resurrection, so Christians can appeal to this doctrine in defending the faith.***

Chapter 10 traces the lines of Paul's methodology at Mars Hill by discussing the biblical and historical evidence for the resurrection of Christ. Just as Paul preached the resurrection, so apologists must make every effort to move their arguments from general to special revelation. In this case, we need to be familiar with the extrabiblical historical evidence that confirms Jesus existed, performed miracles, was not found in the tomb, and that his followers worshiped him as God. The average Christian is likely unfamiliar with these facts. This is not to say that we should rest our faith only on historical evidence, which is why the chapter also examines the biblical evidence. The Scriptures are the chief authority with matters pertaining to Christ's ministry, but we impoverish our faith and apologetics if we turn away from history. God is the God of Scripture and history; thus, we do well to employ them both in our defense of the faith.

> ***Thesis 11: As Paul appealed to the book of nature by invoking the doctrine of providence, Christians can appeal to this doctrine as they explain why evil exists and how the book of Scripture points us to the cross of Christ as God's answer to evil.***

Chapter 11 explores in greater detail the doctrine of providence, a teaching that Paul invoked at Mars Hill. But the chapter examines the doctrine by dealing with one of the most common objections to Christianity—namely, if God is good, how can he allow evil to exist in the world? Scripture answers this question but perhaps not in a way that we expect. The short of it is, God is sovereign over all of history, and humans are responsible for their actions. Humans introduced sin into the world through their disobedience, but, stunningly, the Son of God subjects himself to his Father's providence and will and suffers at the hands of sinful men to save sinners from Satan, sin, and death. Just as in Paul's Mars Hill address, the doctrine of providence leads us to the gospel and the cross of Christ. God's presence with sinners is the ultimate answer to the question of why God allows evil. It may not be an answer that we seek or want, but Christ is the answer that we need.

Thesis 12: A love for the Triune God and for sinners must be the driving force for apologetics and is the greatest apologetic tool in an age when rationalism has given way to irrationalism.

Chapter 12 digs further into special revelation by showing how apologetics must always be wedded to love. Our culture has imbibed deeply from the well of Enlightenment rationalism, which has led people to embrace irrationalism. Content with their idols, they build fortresses of irrationalism and hide behind embattlements of contradiction. Many see their irrationalism as a weapon that allows them to believe whatever they want despite evidence to the contrary. People want to protect their freedom at any cost, and thus rationality and truth are casualties of idolatrous desire. In such a context, we might think that apologetics is doomed because people are no longer willing to engage in rational discourse. How can Christians present rational arguments for truth if people reject reason itself as a tool of oppression? Even if the world is unwilling to listen to rational dialogue, this does not mean Christians are helpless. Rather, we may not be able to defend the faith with arguments, but we can demonstrate it through acts of love. Extending someone a cup of water can often melt through the walls of cold irrationalism so that we earn the trust and opportunity to share the gospel with our neighbors. God is love, and his love overflows from heaven into the hearts of sinners so that they too can share God's love with others. Too often apologetics can devolve into a quest to win arguments rather than grow into an opportunity to love sinners. Love was at the core of the apostle Paul's motives when he addressed the philosophers at Mars Hill, and so love must be at the heart of our apologetics.

Conclusion

Apologetics is not the discipline of a select few highly trained theological scholars. If the apostle Peter exhorted the early church that they always had to be ready to give an answer for the hope within, then every Christian should be familiar with the fundamental principles of defending the faith. As we defend the faith, we must remember that we engage idolatry just as Paul confronted the idols of Athens. Just as Paul was courageous in his address, we too must pray for courage. But as we stand for truth, our prayer must be that we would defend the faith in love for God and for our neighbor. Apologists must always remember three simple yet profound words: "God is love" (1 John 4:8). Christians know true love because God's love abides in them through Christ by the Spirit (1 John 4:16). The Father eternally loves the Son, the Son eternally loves the Father, and the Holy Spirit is the eternal bond of love between Father and Son (John 3:35; 5:20; 14:26, 31; 15:26; Rom 5:5). God is love, and his love overflows in both creation and redemption. "For God so loved the world that he gave his only begotten Son" (John 3:16, translation mine). "Christ loved us and gave himself up for us" (Eph 5:2). And "God's love has been poured into our hearts through the Holy Spirit who has been given to us" (Rom 5:5). We who have been redeemed by the love of God through Christ and the Spirit become streams of that eternal, heavenly love of God to sinners in a lost and dying world.

That we are streams of God's love in the world means that our apologetics is all about re-ordering the disordered love of sinners back to God. When Augustine (354–423) was a young man and he arrived in Carthage to study, he described the city as a hissing "cauldron of illicit loves."[7] This description is emblematic of the nature of unbelief as what Augustine calls "disordered love." The Triune God is love and thus the source of all love, but rather than be ordered to God's love in Christ, Augustine instead "sought pleasure, sublimity, and truth not in God but in his creatures," and in himself "and other created things," and this disordered love plunged him into "miseries, confusions, and errors."[8] And "the punishment of every disordered mind is its own disorder."[9] In short, our disordered loves give birth to idols. As C. S. Lewis has astutely observed, when we do not love God as he designed and created us to do, we turn good things, such as love, affection (*storge*), friendship (*philos*), and romance (*eros*) into demons.[10] Lewis explains: "We may give our human loves the unconditional allegiance which we owe only to God. Then they become gods: then they become demons. Then they will destroy us, and also destroy themselves. For natural loves that are allowed to become gods do not remain loves. They are still called so, but can become in fact complicated forms of hatred."[11] Our loves emanate from our hearts, and as Scripture teaches, "Keep your heart with all vigilance, for from it flow the springs of life" (Prov 4:23). In apologetics, therefore, we defend the truth

7. Augustine, *Confessions*, trans. Henry Chadwick (Oxford University Press, 1991), III.i.
8. Augustine, *Confessions*, I.xx (31).
9. Augustine, *Confessions*, I.xii (19).
10. C. S. Lewis, *The Four Loves* (HarperOne, 1960), 8, 28, 141, 152–53.
11. Lewis, *Four Loves*, 10.

and dismantle unbelief to show sinners that they can only find deliverance from judgment, forgiveness from their sins, and true love in God's promise of salvation in Christ through the Spirit. We seek to align the sinner's love with God's revealed will in Christ—to follow Christ and focus our love first and foremost on him.[12] Or in the powerful and insightful words of Augustine, "You stir man to take pleasure in praising you, because you have made us for yourself, and our heart is restless until it rests in you."[13] We point restless hearts adrift on a sea of idolatry to the peaceful haven of God's love in Christ.

At the same time, if apologetics is all about calling people to re-order their loves, then the love of God must indwell our labors from first to last. In today's digital, disconnected, and destructive narcissistic culture, defending the gospel often devolves to online shouting matches, meme mêlées, and even at times real-world violent exchanges. Or in football terms, Christians want to throw a lightning-strike, Hail-Mary pass to the endzone to win an argument in one play rather than patiently ply a more demanding, grinding, and costly ground game that advances a few yards at a time. In a world that preaches a gospel of instantaneous gratification for every desire in life, Christians unknowingly condition themselves to impatience as they feast at the table of immediacy and then have little patience to love their enemies. Moreover, in a world that gives us cameras that point back at ourselves, encourages self-promotion, and provides easy access to branding and platform-building, Christians can be lured into the culture of narcissism and defend the faith out of an idolatry of self rather than a love for God and neighbor.[14]

At its best, apologetics is a stream of eternal love that flows from the Triune God through the words and actions of the apologist. As God loved his enemies (sinners like us) by sending his own Son to die for those who hated him, so we channel God's love in Christ to our enemies (Matt 5:43–48; Rom 5:6–9). We therefore bless and do not curse those who persecute us, and if our enemy is hungry, we feed him; if he is thirsty, we give him something to drink (Rom 12:14, 20). While God may do mighty things through our apologetic labors, we should never ignore our local, embodied place, and we should remember that when we talk with unbelievers, we look into the eyes of a fellow image bearer. This is why when Christ teaches us to love our neighbors, we have to remember that a neighbor can be anyone. And rather than trumpeting our efforts across the World Wide Web, we must seek to

12. James K. A. Smith, *You Are What You Love: The Spiritual Power of Habit* (Brazos, 2016), 1–2.

13. Augustine, *Confessions*, I.i.

14. For an analysis of this trend, see Tara Isabella Burton, *Self-Made: Creating Our Identities from Da Vinci to the Kardashians* (Public Affairs, 2023).

roll back the tide of unbelief through small acts of kindness and love as we defend the faith. Emily Dickinson (1830–1886) penned this mindset with these simple yet profound words:

> If I can stop one heart from breaking,
> I shall not live in vain;
> If I can ease one life the aching,
> Or cool one pain,
> Or help one fainting robin
> Unto his nest again,
> I shall not live in vain.[15]

Dickinson captures the importance of kindness shown to even *one* breaking heart and even helping a creature as insignificant as a robin. While helping robins does not typically play a part in apologetics, Dickinson reveals that kindness and love pay attention to the smallest of details, even to those things that ordinarily pass by the notice of most people. This is the same kind of attention that marks the love of Christ.

Christ reminds us that lilies of the field neither toil nor spin, but God arrays them in garments more glorious than Solomon's finest raiment (Matt 6:28; Luke 12:27). God pays attention to small and seemingly insignificant things. When Jesus speaks of Christian love, he describes the most ordinary and pedestrian actions: welcoming the stranger, clothing the naked, tending to the sick, and visiting those in prison (Matt 25:31–46). Many Christians undoubtedly find inspiration in the apostle Peter's exhortation to defend the faith: "In your hearts honor Christ the Lord as holy, always being prepared to make a defense to anyone who asks you for a reason for the hope that is in you." However, how many of us remember the words that immediately follow: "Yet do it with gentleness and respect" (1 Pet 3:15)? Apologetics is not the disembodied clash of rational rapiers in the effort to subdue rebels but the humble and embodied defense of the truth in loving words, thoughts, and deeds. If we forget the humility and love of Christ as we defend the faith, no matter how true our arguments, no matter how powerful our logic, no matter how solid our evidence, without love we are "a noisy gong or a clanging cymbal" (1 Cor 13:1). Our arguments for truth are not themselves the goal but only signposts to the Triune God himself. Lewis poignantly reminds us that we must always pray for humility as we seek to defend the faith, lest we forget that the love of our Triune God in Christ is the road and goal of our

15. Emily Dickinson, *The Complete Poems of Emily Dickinson*, ed. Thomas H. Johnson (Little, Brown and Company, 1961), 919.

efforts. In a poem titled "The Apologist's Evening Prayer," he prays that God would deliver him not only from defeat but also from victory, from his own cleverness and proofs and ideas—even his ideas of God, which will always fall short of God himself. "Take from me," he prays, "all my trumpery lest I die."[16] Apologetics wears not the triumphal crown of gold but Christ's crown of thorns.

16. C. S. Lewis, "The Apologist's Evening Prayer," in *Poems*, ed. Walter Hooper (Harcourt Brace Jovanovich, 1964), 129.

PART 1

GROUNDWORK FOR REFORMED APOLOGETICS

1

Our Present Context

A Disenchanted and Secular Age?

> **Thesis 1:** Humans are hardwired for worship and thus will either worship the one, true God or an idol.

Now while Paul was waiting for them at Athens, his spirit was provoked within him as he saw that the city was full of idols.

—Acts 17:16

"If you tell a big lie and tell it frequently enough, it will be believed." This is a statement often attributed to Joseph Goebbels (1897–1945), the chief propagandist of the Nazi Party and Reich Minister of Propaganda for Adolf Hitler's Third Reich. The frequency with which we hear of living in a disenchanted and secular world gives me the impression that, knowingly or unknowingly, people are regularly repeating a big lie—the world has moved past the ability to believe in God. There is a small cottage industry of decrying, lamenting, and warning of the secular age in which we live.[1] We supposedly live in an age of unbelief. Some have argued that the Protestant Reformation

1. E.g., James K. A. Smith, *How (Not) to Be Secular: Reading Charles Taylor* (Eerdmans, 2014); Mike Cosper, *Recapturing the Wonder: Transcendent Faith in a Disenchanted World* (IVP Books, 2017); Collin Hansen, ed., *Our Secular Age: Ten Years of Reading and Applying Charles Taylor* (The Gospel Coalition, 2017); R. W. L. Moberly, *The Bible in a Disenchanted Age: The Enduring Possibility of Christian Faith* (Baker Academic, 2020).

brought the unintended consequence of the Enlightenment that stripped away belief in an enchanted world, magic, and the possibility of God.[2] As common as this idea is, the opposite is true. The world in which we live is still as enchanted as ever—people still believe in magic and in god(s). Moreover, the Enlightenment as an intellectual and cultural force was a failure. The Enlightenment tried to strip the world of religion but flopped miserably.[3] Why are these claims important for apologetics? Why must we recognize that we live in an enchanted world and that the Enlightenment was a failure? The claims are important because in order to defend the Christian faith, we always need to know where we stand historically and culturally. We have to know our audience, the people with whom we share the gospel and against whom we defend its claims. We can stand on a street corner and shout the gospel and make little effort to connect relationally with the people around us. Such a method is a monologue and easily ignored. If we follow the apostle Paul's example, we should engage in intelligent and biblically informed dialogue. Conversely, we do not want to let the surrounding culture dictate the terms of the discussion lest unbelievers deem the gospel irrelevant. Neither do we want to ignore the opportunity to challenge unbelief at the specific intellectual and moral pressure points in order to present the gospel's truth and beauty more clearly to our culture.

This chapter argues that, contrary to the popular claim that we live in a secular and disenchanted age, the exact opposite is true. This chapter's thesis is: *Humans are hardwired for worship and thus will either worship the one, true God or an idol.* We live in a mystical and enchanted age, and knowing this is vital to engaging unbelief through defending and presenting the gospel. Humanity's problem is not scientific atheism but idolatry. A failure to recognize this feature of our historical and cultural context unnecessarily hobbles our apologetics. God can and still uses our flawed efforts at defending the gospel, but why not eliminate intellectual, philosophical, and theological inaccuracies so we can more clearly present the gospel? Clearing intellectual debris from our path is conducive both to our own faith so we can keep doubts at bay but also advantageous in our defense of the faith. To demonstrate this chapter's thesis, it proceeds by answering the following four questions: (1) Do we live in a disenchanted age? (2) What did the Reformation accomplish? (3) In what ways is our present age both mystical and enchanted? And (4) what is the significance of living in an enchanted age for apologetics? In short, the

2. Brad Gregory, *The Unintended Reformation: How a Religious Revolution Secularized Society* (The Belknap Press, 2015).

3. Jonathan I. Israel, *The Enlightenment That Failed: Ideas, Revolution, and Democratic Defeat* (Oxford University Press, 2020).

Protestant Reformation did not contribute to the disenchantment of the world because the world never was, is not now, and never will be disenchanted or secular. All people are religious by nature because God has hardwired humans for worship. We will always worship something, either the one true God or an idol of our making. The idolatrous age in which we live presents no more of an obstacle to proclaiming and defending the gospel than the age of the apostolic church. Understanding that our culture is idolatrous rather than simply atheistic, disenchanted, and full of secularism will equip us better to defend the claims of Christianity and testify to the truth of the gospel.

A Disenchanted Age?

There are intellectual headwaters that have produced the disenchantment thesis, which supposedly brings along with it the rising tides of secularity. If the world is no longer a place inhabited by God, then there is no place for religion in the public square. There are three key pillar figures that have promoted the disenchantment thesis: Charles Taylor, Max Weber, and Sigmund Freud.

Charles Taylor

Philosopher Charles Taylor argues in his popular work *A Secular Age* that we live in a "disenchanted world." He writes, "The enchanted world in this sense is the world of spirits, demons, and moral forces which our ancestors lived in." But he asks, "What happened between 1500 and 2000?" He argues that the Protestant Reformation promoted the "disenchantment" of the world.[4] "In a disenchanted world only the locus of thoughts, feelings, spiritual élan is what we call minds; the only minds in the cosmos are those of humans."[5] People once believed they lived in a world of good and evil spirits, Satan and demons, God, his angels, and saints, but now these outdated entities violate the principle of the disenchanted world because only human minds inhabit the cosmos.[6] The enchanted world was a place of magical and spiritual power that resided in things—the burial place of saintly relics, pieces of their remains, of the cross, or the sacraments where ordinary bread and wine become the literal body and blood of Christ. In the enchanted world, the lines between personal and divine agency are blurry, such as was the case of the magical power of relics.[7] Meaning, therefore, resided both in the mind

4. Charles Taylor, *A Secular Age* (The Belknap Press, 2007), 26.
5. Taylor, *A Secular Age*, 30.
6. Taylor, *A Secular Age*, 30.
7. Taylor, *A Secular Age*, 30.

but also in things. "In the enchanted world, the meaning exists already outside of us, prior to contact; it can take us over, we can fall into its field of force. It comes on us from the outside."[8] Relics, for example, can affect things: cure illnesses, save ships, or steer lightning away. Relics possess magical power.[9]

Inhabitants of the enchanted world were *porous*—magic could take them over. The porous person stands in contrast to the modern *buffered* person—the individual isolated from the cosmos and dominated by her mind.[10] According to Taylor, one of the contributing factors to the onset of disenchantment was Newtonian physics, which described the world in a mechanical manner rather than attribute natural phenomenon to divine agency.[11] How do all of these things relate to the conditions of belief?[12] Unbelief is difficult in an enchanted world, and thus going against God in such a context is not an option. By way of contrast, "The buffered self can form the ambition of disengaging from whatever is beyond the boundary, and of giving its own autonomous order to its life. The absence of fear can be not just enjoyed, but seen as an opportunity for self-control or self-direction."[13] In the present, people buffer themselves from the external world and look only to the inner cosmos of their own minds. Key to Taylor's claims about disenchantment is the analysis of German sociologist Max Weber (1864–1920).[14]

Max Weber

Weber coined the now popular term "disenchantment" in his well-known "Vocation Lectures," delivered in November of 1917. He argued that the modern scientific outlook stripped enchantment out of the world:

> It means that in principle, then, we are not ruled by mysterious, unpredictable forces, but that, on the contrary, we can in principle *control everything by means of calculation*. That in turn means the disenchantment of the world. Unlike the savage for whom such forces existed, we need no longer have recourse to magic in order to control the spirits or pray to them. Instead, technology and calculation achieve our ends. This is the primary meaning of the process of intellectualization.[15]

8. Taylor, *A Secular Age*, 34.
9. Taylor, *A Secular Age*, 35.
10. Taylor, *A Secular Age*, 38.
11. Taylor, *A Secular Age*, 40.
12. Taylor, *A Secular Age*, 41.
13. Taylor, *A Secular Age*, 38–39.
14. Taylor, *A Secular Age*, 25.
15. Max Weber, *The Vocation Lectures*, trans. Rodney Livingstone, ed. David Owen and Tracy B. Strong (Hackett Publishing Co., 2004), 13, emphasis added.

Weber believed that Western culture launched a rational experiment as a way of reliably controlling life because without such an approach, modern empirical science would be impossible.[16] Given Weber's perceived progress between the past and present, the pre-modern versus the modern, the enchanted versus the disenchanted, he submits that there is a "vast gulf here between past and present."[17] What was the chief cause of the world's disenchantment? Weber lays the blame at the feet of the Protestant Reformation.

Weber contended how the apologetics of his day, such as trying to prove God's existence from the design of the anatomy of an insect, gained its impetus from the influence of Protestantism and Puritanism. Under these twin influences, Protestants believed that science was the way to God—he could no longer be found where the Middle Ages had looked for him, such as in the magical sacraments.[18] In other words, the Reformation turned away from mysticism and enchanted objects and instead looked for God through the scientific study of nature.[19] Weber maintained that if you go back far enough, this penchant for rationalization originated in Greek thought: "It was the Greek spirit that produced this effect, and all the theology of the West can be traced back to Greece, just as all theology of the East (obviously) goes back to Indian thought. All theology is the intellectual *rationalization* of sacred religious beliefs."[20] These developments started a war between science and religion:

> St. Augustine's assertion holds good: "Credo non quod, sed *quia* absurdum est" ["I believe nothing, except that which is absurd"]. The talent for this virtuoso achievement of "sacrificing the intellect" is a crucial characteristic of men with positive religion. And the fact that this is to show that despite (or rather as a result of) the theology (that after all reveals this fact) the tension between the value spheres of "science" and religious salvation cannot be overcome. Properly speaking, it is only the disciple who makes a sacrifice of the intellect to the prophet.[21]

The consequence of these developments is that rationalization and intellectualization, and chiefly, above all, disenchantment, marks the modern world. "Its resulting fate," writes Weber, "is that precisely the ultimate and most

16. Weber, *Vocation Lectures*, 15.
17. Weber, *Vocation Lectures*, 14.
18. Weber, *Vocation Lectures*, 15–16.
19. Weber, *Vocation Lectures*, 16.
20. Weber, *Vocation Lectures*, 28.
21. Weber, *Vocation Lectures*, 29. Note, Augustine never said this, though the saying has been attributed to Tertullian. Even then, Tertullian never said it (see Peter Harrison, "'I Believe Because It Is Absurd': The Enlightenment Invention of Tertullian's Credo," *Church History* 86/2 [2017]: 339–64, esp. 361–62). I am grateful to Bill Challener for alerting me to Weber's error.

sublime values have withdrawn from public life."[22] But Weber was not alone in his claims of disenchantment.

Sigmund Freud

Another of the other key promoters of the disenchantment thesis was Sigmund Freud (1856–1939): "If we accept the evolution of man's conceptions of the universe, according to which the *animistic phase* is *succeeded* by the *religious*, and this in turn by the *scientific*, we have no difficulty in following the fortunes of the 'omnipotence of thought' through all the phases."[23] Freud argued that people could influence the world through their thoughts alone. People conjure illusions to explain the world, so things like guilt play a role in what the world looks like. Whether a person's illusions agree with external reality is inconsequential. Freud's description of the mind's power sounds a lot like Taylor's *buffered self*. Nevertheless, Freud believed that the illusory power of the mind led people to animistic thinking but that humans eventually progress beyond animism to religion, and then from religion eventually to science. Thus, the three stages of cultural life are: the infancy of animism, the childhood of religion, and the adulthood of science. In short, mature scientific cultures outgrow their fondness for magic.[24]

Taylor, Weber, and Freud present a small cross-section of intellectuals who claim that the world is disenchanted, though Taylor and Weber argue this has come about largely due to the Protestant Reformation—Protestants unwittingly sawed the very branch upon which the world sat and unleashed the genie of large-scale unbelief into Western culture. Others have argued similar versions of the disenchantment thesis, such as church historian Ernst Troeltsch (1865–1923), who claimed that the Reformation was an indirect agent of modernization.[25] Historian Keith Thomas does not invoke the specific claims of the disenchantment thesis, but he argues along similar lines in his book *Religion and the Decline of Magic*.[26] And most recently, Roman Catholic

22. Weber, *Vocation Lectures*, 30.

23. Sigmund Freud, *Totem and Taboo: Resemblances of the Psychic Lives of Savages and Neurotics*, trans. A. A. Brill (Moffat, Yard and Co., 1918), 145–46; Jason Ā. Josephson-Storm, *The Myth of Disenchantment: Magic, Modernity, and the Birth of the Human Sciences* (The University of Chicago Press, 2017), 193–94.

24. Josephson-Storm, *Disenchantment*, 194.

25. Ernst Troeltsch, *Protestantism and Progress: The Significance of Protestantism for the Rise of the Modern World*, trans. W. Montgomery (G. P. Putnam's Sons, 1912); Alexandra Walsham, "The Reformation and 'The Disenchantment of the World' Reassessed," *The Historical Journal* 51/2 (2008): 497–528, here 498.

26. Keith Thomas, *Religion and the Decline of Magic* (Penguin, 1991); Walsham, "The Reformation," 498.

historian Brad Gregory contends that one of the unintended consequences of the Reformation was the secularization of the world.[27] What are the repercussions of the disenchantment thesis? Is the world truly secularized and disenchanted? Asking this question is crucial because it impacts the nature of our apologetics. Are we fundamentally dealing with the problem of the scientific impossibility of believing in God? And when it comes to the remedy—namely, the Protestant and Reformed understanding of the gospel—are we administering a solution that is doomed to fail because it is poisoned with unbelief in the very heart of its message? To answer these questions, we need to turn to the next question: What did the Reformation actually accomplish?

What Did the Reformation Accomplish?

The simple answer is, the Reformation neither disenchanted nor secularized the world. We can provide a more detailed answer to this question on two levels. Contrary to the claims that we live in a disenchanted world, Reformation theology taught and still teaches that we live in an enchanted world. The Westminster Confession of Faith (1647), a confession professed by Protestants today, speaks of Satan in six places (1.1; 5.6; 6.1; 17.3; 20.1, 25.5) and angels in seven places (2.2; 3.3, 4; 5.4; 8.4; 21.2; 33.1). Contrary to the claims of historian Keith Thomas, the Protestant doctrine of providence was not a rear-guard effort to retain and protect an enchanted world. Reformed works such as the *Synopsis Purioris Theologiae* (1624) demonstrate the catholicity of the Reformed understanding of the doctrine by positively citing and agreeing with patristic and medieval authorities.[28] French Reformed theologian Pierre DuMoulin (1548–1658) similarly defends the Reformed doctrine of providence.[29] In its articulation of the doctrine of providence, the Westminster Confession affirms that God "is free to work without, above, and against" means "at his pleasure" (5.3). If Reformation and medieval understandings of providence are the same, then how can the Reformation be guilty of disenchanting the world? What, then, did the Reformers seek to do?

The Reformers wanted to remove "magic," or superstition, from the hands of the church and put the supernatural back into the hands of God. In

27. E.g., Gregory, *The Unintended Reformation*, 21.

28. Johannes Polyander et al., *Synopsis Purioris Theologiae / Synopsis of a Purer Theology*, vol. 1, ed. Dolf te Velde et al. (Brill, 2014), disp. XI.i, xi, xxiv, xxv (pp. 261, 269, 281).

29. Pierre DuMoulin, *The Anatomie of Arminianisme, or The Opening of the Controversies of These Times (Formerly Handled in the Low-Countries), Concerning the Doctrine of Providence, Predestination, and the Death of Christ, of Nature and Grace, etc.* (London: Nathanael Newberry, 1635), esp. 5–18.

technical terms, there is a difference between anti-sacerdotalism (being against the idea that priests wield the grace of God) and disenchanting the world. Taylor, Thomas, and others equate an enchanted world with a magical one—that is, where the possibility of the supernatural and miraculous still exist.[30] But they argue as if the removal of magic was only a Protestant phenomenon and fail to see that an anti-magic theme appears in both the Scriptures and the early church. The prophet Ezekiel rebuked the Israelites for their use of enchanted wristbands (Ezek 13:18, 20), and the apostles confronted Simon the magician (Acts 8:9, 11).[31] As a result of the conversion of many to Christianity in Ephesus, converts burned their magic books at great personal cost (Acts 19:19).[32] The Didache also warns against the practice of magic (§2).[33]

The Reformation's rejection of magic was not an effort to disenchant the *world* but to take superstition out of the hands of the *church*. John Calvin (1509–1564), for example, wrote about relics:

> Now let us consider how many relics of the true cross there are in the world. An account of those merely with which I am acquainted would fill a whole volume, for there is not a church, from a cathedral to the most miserable abbey or parish church, that does not contain a piece. Large splinters of it are preserved in various places, as for instance in the Holy Chapel at Paris, whilst at Rome they show a crucifix of considerable size made entirely, they say, from this wood. In short, if we were to collect all these pieces of the true cross exhibited in various parts, they would form a whole ship's cargo. The Gospel testifies that the cross could be borne by one single individual; how glaring, then, is the audacity now to pretend to display more relics of wood than three hundred men could carry![34]

In short, Calvin's objection to relics is that they are instruments of superstition—there were enough splinters of the cross that one could build Noah's ark from them. Calvin's objections go back to similar protestations by Saint

30. Taylor, Thomas, and others also fail to account that especially within the Lutheran Reformation, theologians such as Philip Melanchthon appealed to and promoted scientific astrology, a means by which people could read and even predict God's providence in the stars. Scientific astrology, as related to natural philosophy, stands in contrast to religious astrology. In contrast, the Reformed wing of the Reformation was against all forms of astrology (see Robin B. Barnes, *Astrology and Reformation* [Oxford University Press, 2016]).

31. Daniel I. Block, *The Book of Ezekiel: Chapters 1–24*, NICOT (Eerdmans, 1997), 414; C. K. Barrett, *Acts 1–14*, ICC (T&T Clark, 2006), 407.

32. C. K. Barrett, *Acts 15–28*, ICC (T&T Clark, 2006), 912–13.

33. Michael W. Holmes, ed., *The Apostolic Fathers: Greek Texts and English Translations*, 3rd ed. (Baker Academic, 2007), 347.

34. John Calvin, *Treatise on Relics*, 2nd ed., trans. Valerian Krasinski (Johnstone, Hunter, & Co., 1870), 233; see also *Inventory of Relics*, in *Tracts and Treatises*, vol. I, trans. Henry Beveridge (Eerdmans, 1958), 289–341.

Augustine (354–430) and the relic salesmen who hawked the bones of martyrs.[35] Augustine acknowledged the existence of magic and sorcery but was opposed to it. He believed that Christians should have nothing to do with magic. Augustine writes:

> They [miracles] were wrought by simple faith and godly confidence, not by the incantations and charms composed under the influence of a criminal tampering with the unseen world, of an art which they call either magic, or by the more abominable title necromancy, or the more honorable designation theurgy. . . . Both classes are slaves of the deceitful rites of the demons whom they invoke under the names of angels.[36]

Augustine likewise opposed astrology.[37] Thus, the Reformation was in continuity with the early church in its opposition to magic in the hands of Christians.

Where criticisms against the Reformation often land regarding the disenchantment thesis concerns the rejection of transubstantiation—namely, that the bread and wine of the sacrament become the literal body and blood of Christ.[38] At first glance, this may seem like a smoking gun, but upon closer examination, a fair observer can see that the gun is a plastic toy replica and has been planted. The Reformers objected to two things in the Roman Catholic doctrine of the Lord's Supper: (1) the notion of *ex opere operato*, that the sacraments function "by the work performed" regardless of whether faith is present or absent in the recipient, and (2) the idea of transubstantiation. They believed that with the Supper, a person had to have a mouth by which to consume Christ—that is, *faith*—and that transubstantiation was "repugnant to Scripture" and "even to common sense, and reason" and overthrew "the nature of the sacrament," and was the cause of "manifold superstitions" and "gross idolatries" (WCF 29.6). But just because they rejected transubstantiation does not mean Reformed theologians were opposed to the spiritual and otherworldly Communion that believers enjoy through the sacrament. The Westminster Confession maintains that "worthy receivers" who partake of the outward elements do inwardly by faith "really and indeed" "spiritually,

35. Augustine, *Of the Works of Monks*, §36, in *The Fathers of the Church*, vol. 16, ed. Roy J. Deferrari (The Catholic University of America Press, 1952), 331–96, here 384.

36. Augustine, *City of God*, trans. Marcus Dods (Random House, 1993), X.ix; see also XXI.vi for Augustine's explanation of how magicians work, either by deception or demonic power; Lynn Thorndike, "The Attitude of Origen and Augustine Toward Magic," *The Monist* 18/1 (1908): 46–66.

37. Augustine, *Confessions*, trans. Henry Chadwick (Oxford University Press, 1991), IV.iii (pp. 54–55).

38. Gregory, *Unintended Reformation*, 40, 42, 45, 165; Taylor, *Secular Age*, 802n21.

receive, and feed upon, Christ crucified" even though the body and blood of Christ are not physically present. Christ's body and blood are "spiritually, present to the faith of believers" (29.7). This hardly sounds like a disenchanted description of the sacrament. In contrast to transubstantiation, Calvin argues that Christ does not descend from heaven but rather lifts the souls of participants to heaven where he is seated at the Father's right hand so the faithful can sup upon his body and blood. When asked to explain how this happens, Calvin replies: "I will not be ashamed to confess that it is too high a mystery either for my mind to comprehend or my words to express; and to speak more plainly, I rather feel than understand it."[39]

The Reformers therefore did not disenchant the sacrament but rather objected to the Roman Catholic view because they believed Rome replaced biblical truth with superstition with its claims about transubstantiation. Elizabethan Reformed theologian William Perkins (1558–1602), for example, did not reject the existence of witchcraft or magic but instead taught that Christians should have nothing to do with them as Augustine had counseled long before him: "Witchcraft (or magic) is that sin whereby men renounce the true God and betake themselves to the aid, counsel, and help of the devil, either by himself or in his instruments. This is a large sin, and a great part of atheism, and many are tainted with this sin, either because they are practitioners of witchcraft or else do seek help of such."[40] Magic exists in the world, but Perkins believed "if a man will but take a view of all popery, he shall easily see that a great part of it is mere magic."[41] Thus, the Reformers did not try to disenchant the world but rather sought to leave enchantment in the hands of God. Anti-sacerdotalism is not disenchantment. Rejecting transubstantiation as contrary to Scripture disenchants neither the sacrament nor the world.

How Is Our Age Mystical and Enchanted?

If the Reformation did not disenchant the world, then who is to blame for its disenchanted state? Who or what is to blame for the secular age in which we now live? Such questions likely arise because of the prominence and popularity of the disenchantment thesis, yet I contend that the world is still as mystical and enchanted as it has ever been. We can demonstrate this by explaining

39. John Calvin, *Institutes of the Christian Religion*, trans. Henry Beveridge (Calvin Translation Society, 1845), IV.xvii.32.

40. William Perkins, *The Damned Art of Witchcraft*, in *The Works of William Perkins*, 10 vols., ed. Joel Beeke and Derek Thomas (Reformation Heritage Books, 2020), IX:200.

41. William Perkins, *A Golden Chain*, in *Works*, VI:85.

how all people are religious: all human beings are hardwired for worship. Edmund Burke (1729–1797) long ago observed that we are by our very nature religious animals:

> We know, and it is our pride to know, that man is by his constitution a religious animal; that atheism is against, not only our reason, but our instincts; and that it cannot prevail long. But if, in the moment of riot, and in a drunken delirium from the hot spirit drawn out of the alembic of hell, which in France is now so furiously boiling, we should uncover our nakedness, by throwing off that Christian religion which has hitherto been our boast and comfort, and one great source of civilization amongst us, and amongst many other nations, we are apprehensive (being well aware that the mind will not endure a void) that some uncouth, pernicious, and degrading superstition might take place of it. . . . On these ideas, instead of quarrelling with establishments, as some do, who have made a philosophy and a religion of their hostility to such institutions, we cleave closely to them.[42]

Burke makes an important twofold observation: (1) humans are hardwired for religion. Or, to put things theologically, we are all hardwired for worship. (2) The implied consequence of our worship-oriented nature is that we will either worship the one, true, living God, or we will worship an idol.

French psychologist Gustave Le Bon (1841–1931) offers a sociological rather than theological description of religion that helpfully diagnoses the human condition. He contends that a person is not religious only when they worship a god, but rather when they put all the resources of their mind, the complete submission of their will, and the whole-souled ardor of fanaticism to the service of a cause or individual through their thought and actions. Intolerance and fanaticism are the necessary corollaries of this type of religious sentiment. They are the inevitable fruit of those who believe they alone possess the secret of earthly happiness. We can find these two characteristics (intolerance and fanaticism) in groups of people when they unite in a common conviction of any kind. During the French Revolution (1789–1799), the Jacobins of the Reign of Terror, for example, were just as religious as the Roman Catholics of the Inquisition, and their cruel ardor flowed from the same source.[43] The Roman Catholics and the French revolutionaries were both very religious. No matter how much people promote disenchantment and secularization, human beings are inescapably religious because God has designed us for worship. Even though it is bad grammar, the double negative puts an exclamation on

42. Edmund Burke, *Reflections on the Revolutions in France and Other Writings*, ed. Jesse Norman (Alfred A. Knopf, 2015), 504–5.

43. Gustave Le Bon, *The Crowd: A Study of the Popular Mind* (The Macmillan Co., 1896), 64.

this point: we cannot *not* worship. The Bible recounts the history of humanity's continual struggle between worshiping the one true God and worshiping idols of their own making, whether in the garden of Eden, as Adam and Eve sought God-like powers, or on the plains of Shinar, as the inhabitants built a temple to their own might (Gen 11:4), or even in Israel, as God's covenant people continually collapsed into idolatry throughout the book of Judges, which began with Israel's impatience at the foot of Sinai leading to the creation of the golden calf (Exod 32:4). More examples could be easily adduced, but this list sufficiently makes the point.

What Are the Implications for Apologetics?

If all human beings are religious, what are the consequences for apologetics? How does humanity's hardwired condition for worship undermine the disenchantment thesis? The two short answers to these questions are: (1) since all human beings are hardwired for worship, our task in apologetics is not about confronting unbelief but rather idolatry. And (2) for all the claims that we live in a disenchanted and secular world, humanity's worship-oriented nature means that disenchantment and secularity are religious myths. Moreover, contrary to the claims of disenchantment and secularization, religious faith has only grown in the present. These short answers call for greater exposition and clarification.

Disenchantment Is a Religious Myth

As defenders of the Christian faith, we should not fall prey to the religious myth that we live in a disenchanted and secular world. Calvin observed that "the human mind is, so to speak, a perpetual forge of idols." He explains the nature of this idolatry:

> The human mind, stuffed as it is with presumptuous rashness, dares to imagine a god suited to its own capacity; as it labors under dullness, nay, is sunk in the grossest ignorance, it substitutes vanity and an empty phantom in the place of God. To these evils another is added. The god whom man has thus conceived inwardly he attempts to embody outwardly. The mind, in this way, conceives the idol, and the hand gives it birth.[44]

44. Calvin, *Institutes*, I.xi.8.

Calvin makes these observations in his discussion of Rachel's theft of her father's idols (Gen 31:19), but the pattern still applies to the broader practice of idolatry outside the covenant community. Key in Calvin's analysis is the claim that the sinful human mind "substitutes vanity and an empty phantom in the place of God." In other words, people fill the empty space that belongs to God with something else—they worship a god of their own making. How does this idolatry appear in our supposedly disenchanted and secular world?

A 2012 study revealed that a quarter of American adults say they have no religion, and if you include millennials (anyone born after 1981), that number climbs to 40 percent. Sociologists have labeled this demographic as the "nones," since they claim they have no religion. Some may cite this as evidence of the secularization of the culture, yet the fact that nones claim no religious affiliation does not mean they reject enchantment and spirituality. Among the nones,

- 72 percent claim they believe in God, either the God of the Bible or a deity of some kind.
- 55 percent believe in a higher power.
- 46 percent talk to God.
- 47 percent believe in the presence of "spiritual energy" in physical objects.
- 42 percent believe in psychics.
- 38 percent believe in reincarnation.
- 32 percent believe in astrology.[45]

With these statistics, how disenchanted and secular can the world be? In fact, one of the characteristics of our present cultural moment is DIY religion.[46] In the age of the internet, people find their own sources of information and mix and create their own religious belief systems. Such a pattern is natural in this era. If people can personalize their own social media pages, why should they not curate their own religions?[47] While institutional religions might be suffering decline, individual religiosity is thriving.[48]

45. Tara Isabella Burton, *Strange Rites: New Religions for a Godless World* (Hachette Book Group, 2020), 16–17.

46. Burton, *Strange Rites*, 23.

47. Burton, *Strange Rites*, 24.

48. What explains this phenomenon is that even if people identify as nones, they nevertheless still retain scattered religious beliefs about God, higher powers, and transcendent beings (Stephen Bullivant, *Nonverts: The Making of Ex-Christian America* [Oxford University Press, 2022], 64–69).

If we examine religion as a social rather than a theological phenomenon, then we can say that religion is a set of rituals and beliefs that people affirm to reinforce their purpose as a group. In the assessment of sociologist Emile Durkheim (1858–1917), religion is "a unified system of beliefs and practices which unite in one single moral community, called a Church, all those who adhere to them."[49] In other words, *religion* and *churches* are not just Christian things; sociologically defined, we can apply these concepts to all sorts of beliefs and activities in life. As Durkheim notes: "A religion is a unified system of beliefs and practices relative to sacred things, that is to say, things set apart and surrounded by prohibitions—beliefs and practices that unite its adherents in a single moral community called a church."[50] Religions provide people with three key elements:

1. Meaning—explanations of why the world is the way it is.
2. Purpose—direction with which individuals can shape their lives.
3. Community—belonging, connection to a group of people committed to the same meaning and purpose.[51]

Defined in this manner, religion is no longer the property of institutional groups (as in Christianity, Islam, Buddhism, e.g.); rather, it belongs to individuals, movements, and even corporations. The Gillette razor company, for example, in 1989 created an ad campaign called "The Best a Man Can Get," which featured handsome men playing sports and interacting with beautiful women. They were selling appeal: "Use our razors, and your life will look like this!" In 2019 Gillette created a new campaign called "The Best a Man Can Be," in response to the #MeToo movement. Gillette was encouraging men to step up when women were being mistreated. By sharing and liking the ad or buying the razors, consumers were joining a unified tribe, a Durkheimian church: Gillette customers care about women.[52] Gillette was selling religion and ethics and trying to encourage customers to join their "church."

These same Durkheimian patterns unfold in other quarters of culture with fandoms, where people immerse themselves in the fantasy worlds of Harry Potter, Star Wars, Star Trek, or the Lord of the Rings. The internet has propelled these franchises to greater cultural heights and has created for many people a sacred canon of texts. People then take the mythos of these fictional

49. Burton, *Strange Rites*, 27.

50. Émile Durkheim, *The Elementary Forms of Religious Life*, trans. Carol Cosman (Oxford University Press, 2001), 46.

51. Burton, *Strange Rites*, 30–31.

52. Burton, *Strange Rites*, 59–60.

worlds and infuse them into their own curated collection of religious beliefs. Tara Isabella Burton explains this phenomenon:

> Why force our beliefs into a narrow category of organized religion, with its doctrines and creeds, when we can cobble together a metaphysical system that demands of us no moral, ethical, spiritual, or aesthetic compromises? Why not combine meditation with sage cleansing with the odd Christmas service and its aesthetically pleasing carols? Why not use the language of Hogwarts houses to talk about good and evil, alongside the rhetoric of social justice and metaphors garnered from *Star Wars*?[53]

There is no set menu of beliefs; people instead come to the salad bar of theological, philosophical, and mythical ideas to create their own religions. This practice is not new, however, as Thomas Jefferson (1743–1826) took this same approach when he created his own cut-and-paste Bible by removing the portions that he found unbelievable.[54]

Common Religions: Social Justice, Politics, Money, and Technology

People are as religious as ever, and the cacophony of competing claims clamor and course through the culture. A few examples illustrate this point: social justice, politics, money, and technology. Cultural commentator David French insightfully assesses the nature of the social justice movement: "The campus culture war is a religious war, a so-far largely peaceful counterpart to the violent purges and revolutions of jihad. One faith has been expunged, relegated to the margins of the academy, and now another fills the vacuum. Out with the Christianity that spawned American higher education, in with a ferocious new faith—a social-justice progressivism unrestrained by humility and consumed with righteous zeal."[55] Others such as John McWhorter have argued that "woke racism" is not merely *like* a religion, it *is* a religion. He calls "woke anti-racists" the "elect" and explains that they have clergy such as Ta-Nehisi Coates and Robin DiAngelo, there is "original sin" (namely, "white privilege"), they have their sacred texts (such as DiAngelo's *White Fragility*), they are evangelistic as they spread their message of anti-racism, they have an eschatology of creating a world without racism, and they practice

53. Burton, *Strange Rites*, 88.
54. Burton, *Strange Rites*, 90.
55. David French, "The Ferocious Religious Faith of the Campus Social-Justice Warrior," *National Review*, November 23, 2015, https://www.nationalreview.com/2015/11/religious-zealots-campus-social-justice-warriors/; Burton, *Strange Rites*, 177.

excommunication by banning those who disagree.[56] Burton comes to similar conclusions when she writes: "Like its Marxist antecedents, from which it draws much of its imagery and inspiration, modern social justice culture has managed to create a thoroughly compelling, eschatologically focused account of a meaningful world, in which every human being has a fundamental purpose in a cosmic struggle, all without including, well, God."[57]

Marxism is an inherently religious movement that has its roots, at least according to Friedrich Engels (1820–1895), in sixteenth-century Anabaptist theology. Engels drew inspiration from Thomas Müntzer (ca. 1489–1525) and the Peasants' Revolt (1524) and his efforts to usher in the kingdom of God through violent revolt. Engels believed that people had to bring about the kingdom's advent: "Heaven is, therefore, not a thing of another world, and is to be sought in this life and it is the task of believers to establish this Heaven, the kingdom of God, here on earth."[58] This is not to say that those interested in social justice and fighting racism have no genuine concerns but rather that these movements are inherently religious in nature.

Similar religious configurations emerge in the political arena even though Enlightened politics was supposed to create a space for religious neutrality where no one religion could claim to be authoritative. Going back to the ideology of Jean-Jacques Rousseau (1712–1778) and his *Social Contract*, he argued for the need of a civil religion:

> There is thus a profession of faith which is purely civil and of which it is the sovereign's function to determine the articles, not strictly as religious dogmas, but as expressions of social conscience, without which it is impossible to be either a good citizen or a loyal subject. Without being able to oblige anyone to believe these articles, the sovereign can banish from the state anyone who does not believe them; banish him not for impiety but as an antisocial being, as one unable sincerely to love law and justice, or to sacrifice, if need be, his life to his duty. If anyone, after having publicly acknowledged these same dogmas, behaves as if he did not believe in them, then let him be put to death, for he has committed the greatest crime, that of lying before the law. . . . The dogmas of the civil religion must be simple and few in number, expressed precisely and without explanations or commentaries. . . . As for the negative dogmas, I would limit them to a single one: no intolerance. Intolerance is something which belongs to the religions we have rejected.[59]

56. John McWhorter, *Woke Racism: How a New Religion Has Betrayed Black America* (Portfolio/Penguin, 2021), 23–60.

57. Burton, *Strange Rites*, 177.

58. Karl Marx and Friedrich Engels, *On Religion* (Dover Publications, 2008), 111.

59. Jean-Jacques Rousseau, *The Social Contract*, trans. Maurice Cranston (Penguin Group, 1968), 186.

Rousseau's theory of politics has all the markers of a religion: there is a profession of faith, dogmas that express the social conscience, and the sovereign's power to excommunicate the faithless. To institute an immanent political sphere, Rousseau believed he needed transcendent ideas to make it effective.[60]

The Roman Empire employed this transcendence principle especially with its emperor cult.[61] As English philosopher Simon Critchley remarks, "Whether liberal democracy, fascism, soviet communism, national socialism and the rest have to be grasped as new articulations and mutations of the sacred, as *metamorphoses of sacralization*?"[62] In this case, rather than God giving laws to the people through the monarch, the people become God.[63] Politics becomes the manifestation of the collective being and will of the people.[64] Yet, one of the dangers of this type of democratic authority structure is that if the people are the source of the laws, then government ends up as an expression of collective narcissism, or even collective idolatry.[65] Religious language appears in various political campaigns such as President Barack Obama's 2008 raft of religious language: hope, change, and reconciliation of a "house divided," an echo of Abraham Lincoln's (1809–1865) invocation of Matthew 12:22–28, a "house divided against itself shall not stand" (KJV).[66] In his most recent book, *A Promised Land,* President Obama continues to use religious language.[67] Politicians are not the sole promoters of civil religion; ordinary citizens say the pledge of allegiance, take a vow of membership, venerate the sacrament of the American flag, and celebrate the cult of the war dead, the nation's coterie of saints.[68] Within this enchanted framework, politicians create a doctrine of original sin that can only be healed through political authority. There are antichrists to be conquered, which requires violence. Politicians seek to create a utopian new Jerusalem or return us to the garden of Eden.[69] Thus, Critchley rightly concludes that "modern politics is a chapter in the history of religion" and that "secularism, which denies the truth of religion, is a religious myth."[70]

60. Simon Critchley, *Faith of the Faithless: Experiments in Political Theology* (Verso, 2014), 23, 67.

61. Critchley, *Faith of the Faithless*, 24.

62. Critchley, *Faith of the Faithless*, 25, 78.

63. Critchley, *Faith of the Faithless*, 52, 55.

64. Critchley, *Faith of the Faithless*, 56.

65. Critchley, *Faith of the Faithless*, 60.

66. Critchley, *Faith of the Faithless*, 69.

67. Barack Obama, *A Promised Land* (Crown, 2020).

68. Critchley, *Faith of the Faithless*, 78–79.

69. Critchley, *Faith of the Faithless*, 108, 118.

70. Critchley, *Faith of the Faithless*, 111.

Religion likewise appears in the worship of money, or what the Scriptures call "Mammon" (Matt 6:24; Luke 16:9, 11, 13 KJV). The idolatry of money is one of the most formidable pieces of counterevidence against the secularization thesis given what the book of Revelation has to say about Mammon. Far from God's judgment falling on a secularized world, Christ returns to judge a world in the throes of the worship of Mammon. The famous words of judgment fall upon Babylon, the symbol for the universal city of the world, a "great industrial and commercial metropolis": "Fallen, fallen is Babylon the great! She has become a dwelling place for demons, a haunt for every unclean spirit, a haunt for every unclean bird, a haunt for every unclean and detestable beast" (Rev 18:2).[71] God strips away Babylon's luxurious façade to reveal its demonic frame. The demonic—that is, its spiritual and religious forces—have been the driving factor behind Babylon's idolatry.[72]

Beyond its demonic frame, for what specific sins does God judge Babylon? "For all nations have drunk the wine of the passion of her sexual immorality, and the kings of the earth have committed immorality with her, and the merchants of the earth have grown rich from the power of her luxurious living" (Rev 18:3). She has led the nations to drink the wine of her immoral sexual passion. But what is the immorality? John echoes Isaianic language here in Revelation 18:3 that reveals the worship of Mammon lies behind Babylon's sin: "At the end of seventy years, the Lord will visit Tyre, and she will return to her wages and will prostitute herself with all the kingdoms of the world on the face of the earth" (Isa 23:17). In particular, the Septuagint renders Isaiah as saying, καὶ ἔσται ἐμπόριον πάσαις ταῖς βασιλείαις τῆς οἰκουμένης ("and she will be a market for all the kingdoms of the earth").[73] Babylon is the city that "worships economic prosperity and cultural achievement."[74] But we should note the alliance between the two religious forces.

The kings of the earth have committed immorality with Babylon. The kings represent the political powers of the earth.[75] In Revelation 17, Babylon the great prostitute rides the beast, which is representative of earthly political power: "And he carried me away in the Spirit into a wilderness, and I saw a woman sitting on a scarlet beast that was full of blasphemous names, and it had seven heads and ten horns" (Rev 17:3).[76] The fact that Babylon's economic

71. William Hendriksen, *More Than Conquerors: An Interpretation of the Book of Revelation* (Baker Book House, 1967), 154, 168.

72. G. K. Beale, *The Book of Revelation*, NIGTC (Eerdmans, 1999), 894.

73. Beale, *Revelation*, 895.

74. Dennis E. Johnson, *Triumph of the Lamb* (P&R, 2001), 243–44.

75. Beale, *Revelation*, 896.

76. Beale, *Revelation*, 853.

activities have a religious facet is evident from the clothing she wears: purple and scarlet garments decorated with gold, jewels, and pearls (Rev 17:4; 18:6). This is the same language that the Septuagint uses to describe the high priest's clothing and portions of the sanctuary. Moreover, Babylon's clothing is an imitation of the church's garments, revealing Babylon's desire to mimic the church's ecclesiology (Rev 21:10–23).[77] The worship of Mammon apes the worship of the one, true, living God, but she is an imposter who worships a false god and persecutes the church. Or, in the words of historian Eugene McCarraher, "Under capitalism, money occupies the ontological throne from which God has been evicted."[78]

Technology might seem to be the very antithesis of religion, especially in the light of Weber's and Taylor's claims that the manipulation of the creation has given humans the impression that there is no longer room for God in the world because technology and science has pushed him out. Prophetic futurist and science fiction author Arthur C. Clarke (1917–2008) has popularly opined, "Any sufficiently advanced technology is indistinguishable from magic."[79] Ever since the fall, humans have sought to harness the power of the divine through technology. Cain built a city (Gen 4:17), and his descendants, among other activities, forged instruments of bronze and iron (Gen 4:22). However, technology does not merely push God out of the picture but is itself a manifestation of the divine. Rather than disappear, religion has modernized itself and transformed into a new form of enchantment.[80] Unlike in the past, where gods and idols were the work of human hands that had mouths but did not speak, eyes but did not see, ears but did not hear, noses but did not smell, hands but did not feel, and feet but did not walk (Ps 115:4–7), machines are the new gods—but they speak, hear, and see. The high priests of the religion of technology are gurus like Apple co-founder Steve Jobs (1955–2011), and the new monuments to transcendence are the mini-cathedrals of our smart phones.[81] Advertisements for these devices are the new stained-glass windows that express aspirations of transcendent devotion.[82] Smart phones and tablets are sacramental objects that mediate transcendence. Like rosaries and relics, they are powerful mediation devices

77. Beale, *Revelation*, 854–57, 912.

78. Eugene McCarraher, *The Enchantments of Mammon: How Capitalism Became the Religion of Modernity* (The Belknap Press, 2019), 11.

79. Arthur C. Clarke, *Profiles of the Future: An Inquiry into the Limits of the Possible*, rev. ed. (Harper & Row, 1973), 21n1.

80. Brett T. Robinson, *Appletopia: Media Technology and the Religious Imagination of Steve Jobs* (Baylor University Press, 2013), 7.

81. Robinson, *Appletopia*, 8, 10.

82. Robinson, *Appletopia*, 43–44.

of the seemingly infinite digital realm. When one technology reviewer assessed the latest version of the iPhone, he said it was "mind-blowing," "unbelievable," and something that felt "like magic."[83] Perhaps unaware of Clarke's opinion that technology is indistinguishable from magic, the lead designer of the iPad introduced the device by saying, "[W]hen something exceeds your ability to understand how it works, it . . . becomes magical. And that's exactly what the iPad is."[84]

However, as new and advanced as technology always appears, technology taps into deeper, more ancient religious aspirations and ideals. In Apple's early and groundbreaking advertisement, "1984," which plays off George Orwell's (1903–1950) famous dystopian novel by the same name, a female runner carrying a large sledgehammer sprints into a meeting hall where mindless people sit watching a large screen broadcasting the latest missive from Big Brother. She runs to the front of the hall and hurls the hammer at the screen, shattering it and releasing a bright, piercing light. This idea finds precedence in gnostic literature. A "calling" passage from a gnostic Peratae sect recorded by Hippolytus (ca. 170–ca. 235), the bishop of Rome, states: "They bestowed upon the guardians a sublime call, to shake up and make to rise those that slumber. They were to awaken the souls that had stumbled away from the place of light. They were to awaken them and shake them up, that they might lift their faces to the place of light."[85] The female runner in the Apple commercial is a symbol for self-divinization whereby the person achieves gnosis through her own magical and intellectual efforts. By breaking through the bounds of this earthly realm, she peers into the mind of God, the realm of light, and gains access to the seemingly infinite body of knowledge granted by the technology of the computer. By means of the computer, she gains the omniscience of God.[86]

The idea of self-divinization runs throughout gnostic literature, a point captured in the *Hermetica*, a body of texts attributed to the mythical gnostic Egyptian Hermes Trismegistus:

> Having conceived that nothing is impossible to you, consider yourself immortal and able to understand everything, all art, all learning, the temper of every living thing. . . . Collect in yourself all the sensations of what has been made, of fire and water, dry and wet; and be everywhere at once, on land,

83. Robinson, *Appletopia*, 69.
84. Robinson, *Appletopia*, 93.
85. Hippolytus as cited in Hans Jonas, *The Gnostic Religion: The Message of the Alien God and the Beginnings of Christianity*, 3rd ed. (Beacon Press, 2001), 80; Robinson, *Appletopia*, 23.
86. Robinson, *Appletopia*, 23.

> in the sea, dead, beyond death. And when you have understood all these at once—times, places, things, qualities, quantities—then you can understand god.[87]

Technology presents the possibility of omniscience, thus making the user almost divine. In the Middle Ages, theologians produced great summas of doctrinal knowledge in the effort to explain God, creation, and redemption. In the Enlightenment, philosophers produced encyclopedias, which were purported to organize all knowledge under rational categories, in alphabetical order, and in indices. In the information age, knowledge has migrated to the internet—an infinite network of documents, images, and knowledge.[88] But even more than omniscience, the chimera of technology holds out the promise of disembodied eternal life, the ultimate gnostic paradise. Devotees to the religion of technology now speak of uploading their consciousness to the infinite web of knowledge. In the words of Yuval Noah Harari, "For modern people death is a technical problem that we can and should solve."[89] Death is not the consequence of sin but a technical glitch: "And every technical problem," writes Harari, "has a technical solution. We don't need to wait for the Second Coming in order to overcome death. A couple of geeks in a lab coat can do it. If traditionally death was the specialty of priests and theologians, now the engineers are taking over."[90] The chief project of humanity in the twenty-first century is to acquire the divine powers of creation and destruction and upgrade *Homo sapiens*, "man the wise," to *Homo deus*, "man as god."[91] The Enlightenment, argues Harari, was not about losing faith in God but about gaining faith in humanity.[92] For some, the world is still enchanted, but rather than resting in the hands of an all-knowing, all-seeing, all-powerful God, enchantment has migrated to humans. Why believe in the transubstantiation of bread and wine into the flesh and blood of Jesus Christ when you can instead transubstantiate yourself from a mortal, human to a god? Despite the thousands of years, the serpent still calls out to the children of Adam, "You

87. As cited in Erik Davis, *TechGnosis: Myth, Magic and Mysticism in the Age of Information* (North Atlantic Books, 2015), 94. For a brief history of Hermes Trismegistus, see Florian Ebeling, *The Secret History of Hermes Trismegistus: Hermeticism from Ancient to Modern Times* (Cornell University Press, 2011).

88. Davis, *TechGnosis*, 292.

89. Yuval Noah Harari, *Homo Deus: A Brief History of Tomorrow* (Vintage, 2016), 23.

90. Harari, *Homo Deus*, 26.

91. Harari, *Homo Deus*, 53.

92. Harari, *Homo Deus*, 259. Harari is part of an emerging transhumanism movement that seeks to overcome the limitations of human existence through technology. For analysis and biblical critique of transhumanism, see Jacob Shatzer, *Transhumanism and the Image of God: Today's Technology and the Future of Christian Discipleship* (IVP Academic, 2019).

will not surely die. . . . You will be like God" if only you eat of the forbidden fruit (Gen 3:4–5).

The Persistence of Religion and the Occult

As much as enchantment has migrated and continues to migrate throughout history, there is other significant counterevidence that presents problems for the secularization thesis. Despite the popularity of the secularization thesis, the world is more religious than ever. Evidence of pervasive religion appears in both commitment to traditional institutional faiths as well as belief in the occult. A 2015 survey found that in Russia there are more occult healers than medical physicians. Thirty-eight percent of the French believe in astrology, and 35 percent of the Swiss agree that some fortune tellers can truly see the future. And despite Japan's rejection of Christianity, many people in Japan seek the blessing of a Shinto priest when they purchase a new car.[93] According to sociologists of religion, Iceland is among one of the most secularized nations, and yet 34 percent of Icelanders believe in reincarnation, and 16 percent are undecided. In a 2015 national survey, 55 percent of surveyed Icelanders reported that they believe in the existence of *huldufolk*, or hidden people, such as elves, gnomes, and trolls. When Icelanders build highways, they sometimes must route them around hills and rocks wherein such *huldufolk* are reputed to dwell. And Icelanders sometimes hire "elf spotters" when they build a new house to ensure they do not disturb *huldufolk* settlements.[94] In a survey of more than a million people living in 163 different countries, 81 percent claim to belong to an organized religious faith, 74 percent say that religion is an important part of life, 50 percent attend worship once a week, and 56 percent believe God is directly involved in daily affairs; only 5 percent claim to be committed atheists.[95] Far from a faithless, secular world, commitment to religions around the world shows no signs of abatement. Based on the statistical data, Baylor University sociologist Rodney Stark concludes, "A great religious awakening has taken place around the world."[96]

Among the manifestations of religious activity is the irrepressible, pronounced presence of the occult in the so-called disenchanted age. One of the more infamous examples is the occult roots of Adolf Hitler's

93. Rodney Stark, *The Triumph of Faith: Why the World Is More Religious Than Ever* (ISI Books, 2015), 1.

94. Stark, *Triumph of Faith*, 6.

95. Stark, *Triumph of Faith*, 11. See pages 21–35 for statistical tables on this data.

96. Stark, *Triumph of Faith*, 35.

(1889–1945) Third Reich. Many people falsely assume that the atrocities committed by Hitler's regime were acts of violent atheists. And yet, ample historical evidence demonstrates that the Nazi party in part grounded its manufactured history in an amalgamation of a twisted form of Christianity and the occult, a state religion filled with myths, magic, and enchanted relics.[97] In Taylor's supposed disenchanted age, the Nazi government appealed to occultism, gnosticism, Rosicrucianism, cabalism, and Freemasonry to create a *völkisch* ("folkish") ideology to propel Hitler's government and fuel a religious crusade to conquer Europe.[98] The spiritual mood of Germany was fertile ground for the occult, and Hitler capitalized on this atmosphere. Christian Rosenkreutz (1378–1484) founded the Rosicrucian sect, which developed the aim of uniting Protestantism, magic, alchemy, cabbalism, and scientific knowledge to provoke a reformation of the whole world.[99] Within this milieu, the Nazi government prized relics such as the holy lance, the relic that supposedly pierced Christ's side, and even Thor's mythological hammer.

In the Nazi mythology, an Aryan soldier pierced Christ's side with the holy lance as he hung upon the cross, and this soldier carried the message of Christianity into Europe.[100] The lance had been passed down from Emperor Constantine (ca. 272–337) to various rulers in Europe; it was cherished for its mystical powers until it finally arrived in Nürnberg, Germany.[101] A cult following surrounded the lance even after the supposed disenchanting Protestant Reformation. The revered German mystic and Augustinian nun Anna Katherine Emmerich (1774–1824) was renowned for her ability to see into the ancient past and foresee the future. Nürnberg city officials asked her to verify that the spear was authentic. She reportedly touched the tip of the spear, fell into a state of ecstasy, and stigmata appeared on the side of her chest as blood and water flowed out.[102] Later, Nürnberg officials knew that Napoleon Bonaparte (1769–1821) sought the lance, so they moved it to Regensburg, and it eventually came to Vienna along with the crown jewels of the Holy Roman Empire. The holy lance and crown jewels were mythical relics of power and magic and thus held sway with the German population. Hitler believed that these relics had the power to unite a divided Germany. Hitler writes in his *Mein Kampf*: "The insignia of former imperial glory, preserved in Vienna, still

97. Sidney D. Kirkpatrick, *Hitler's Holy Relics: A True Story of Nazi Plunder and the Race to Recover the Crown Jewels of the Holy Roman Empire* (Simon & Schuster, 2010).

98. Nicholas Goodrick-Clarke, *The Occult Roots of Nazism* (Tauris Park, 2004), 5, 17–18, 49, 51, 57, 65, 77, 162–63, 203.

99. Goodrick-Clarke, *Occult Roots of Nazism*, 58–59.

100. Kirkpatrick, *Holy Relics*, 81.

101. Kirkpatrick, *Holy Relics*, 81–89.

102. Kirkpatrick, *Holy Relics*, 90.

seem to cast a magic spell."[103] Heinrich Himmler (1900–1945) was also deep into the occult, to the extent that, among other religious pursuits, Himmler expended government resources to locate other magic relics. He created a think tank, the *Deutsches Ahnenerbe* (German Ancestral Heritage Research and Teaching Society), to search for things like Thor's hammer, the holy grail, and the ark of the covenant—an endeavor popularized by Hollywood in the Indiana Jones movies series. Thor was a well-known figure from Norse mythology, the god of thunder who wielded a hammer called *Mjölnir*; he was more recently made popular in movies based on Marvel Comics. The purpose of finding these relics was to validate Hitler's ideas about the superiority of the Aryan race.[104] In short, in the supposed disenchanted modern age, the entire apparatus of the Nazi government was fueled by myths, magic, and enchanted relics.

Defending the Faith in a World of Idolatry

Whether social justice, politics, money, technology, or the persistence of belief in some sort of transcendent deity, *everything* is ultimately religious in nature because human beings are hardwired for worship. We can multiply examples such as "The Church of CrossFit," where gyms fill the social and spiritual needs of supposedly non-religious people.[105] Related to this are the religious rhythms of sports within various nations as the faithful undertake pilgrimages to their local team's houses of worship to sing songs of devotion, celebrate the cyclical advent calendar of championship games, and worship their idols.[106] Witchcraft, New Age spiritualism, the occult, sexuality, or online communities dedicated to every type of imaginable belief only add mounting evidence that contradicts the claims of disenchantment and secularization.[107] Rather than becoming disenchanted and secularized, what the secularization thesis misses is that enchantment does not dissipate or evaporate but rather

103. Adolf Hitler, *Mein Kampf*, trans. Ralph Manheim (Houghton Mifflin Co., 1999), 13; Kirkpatrick, *Holy Relics*, 91.

104. Kirkpatrick, *Holy Relics*, 103; Eric Kurlander, *Hitler's Monsters: A Supernatural History of the Third Reich* (Yale University Press, 2018).

105. Julie Beck, "The Church of CrossFit," *The Atlantic*, June 24, 2017, https://www.theatlantic.com/health/archive/2017/06/the-church-of-crossfit/531501/.

106. E.g., Joseph L. Price, "From Sabbath Proscriptions to Super Sunday Celebrations: Sports and Religion in America," in *From Season to Season: Sports as American Religion*, ed. Joseph L. Price (Mercer University Press, 2001), 15–38, esp. 34–36.

107. For a history of witchcraft in the contemporary period, see Ronald Hutton, *The Triumph of the Moon: A History of Modern Pagan Witchcraft*, 2nd ed. (Oxford University Press, 2019).

migrates. While Roman Catholics like Taylor may be miffed that Protestants reject transubstantiation and cite this as evidence of disenchantment, the fact that enchantment exists in many other corners of culture is evidence of the "migration of the holy."[108] That we still live in an enchanted and religious world does not mean that the culture has somehow obstructed the church's ability to present the gospel and defend the faith.[109]

On the contrary, now more than ever, our world looks like the first century with its plurality of religious beliefs and practices. Corinth was a place filled with "dumb idols," and the Corinthian Christians regularly had to associate with "idolaters" (1 Cor 5:10; 12:2 KJV). On the east end of the forum with the Acropolis on the left were the ruins of the temples of Demeter, Persephone, Octavia, Hera, and Apollo. There were multiple sanctuaries in the forum that contained statues of Athena, Apollos, Aphrodite, Heracles, Zeus, Hermes, Asclepios, and Dionysius. The Corinthians also worshiped Egyptian gods such as Helius, the Fates, the Maid, Isis, and Serapis.[110] Monotheism was far from the minds of the Corinthians, as Paul writes: "For although there may be so-called gods in heaven or on earth—as indeed there are many 'gods' and many 'lords'—yet for us there is one God, the Father, from whom are all things and for whom we exist, and one Lord, Jesus Christ, through whom are all things and through whom we exist" (1 Cor 8:5–6). Similar religious pluralism marked the city of Ephesus.[111] Competing idolatries are not new but are as old as the garden of Eden and the fall of humans. If the gospel was relevant in such an idol-saturated environment, then it is still relevant in our own enchanted idol-rich culture.

Conclusion

We need not fear that our culture has somehow outrun the Bible: "What has been is what will be, and what has been done is what will be done, and there is nothing new under the sun" (Eccl 1:9). We live not in a secular or disenchanted age, but in an idolatrous world that is ever all too religious.[112]

108. William T. Cavanaugh, *Migration of the Holy: God, State, and the Political Meaning of the Church* (Eerdmans, 2011), 1–6, esp. 4.

109. D. A. Carson, *The Gagging of God: Christianity Confronts Pluralism* (Zondervan, 1996), 270–71.

110. Bruce W. Winter, "Theological and Ethical Responses to Religious Pluralism—1 Corinthians 8–10," *Tyndale Bulletin* 41/2 (1990): 209–26.

111. Clinton Arnold, *Power and Magic: The Concept of Power in Ephesians* (Wipf & Stock, 1989).

112. Peter L. Berger, *The Many Altars of Modernity: Toward a Paradigm for Religion in a Pluralist Age* (De Grutyer, 2014).

Poet Matthew Arnold (1822–1883) once lyrically lamented in his well-known poem "Dover Beach":

> The Sea of Faith
> Was once, too, at the full, and round the earth's shore
> Lay like the folds of a bright girdle furled.
> But now I only hear
> Its melancholy, long, withdrawing roar,
> Retreating, to the breath
> Of the night-wind, down the vast edges drear
> And naked shingles of the world.[113]

Arnold lamented the withdrawing roar of faith in the world, which might have been true of his native Victorian England and the increasingly diminishing tides of Christianity.[114] But the withdrawal of the tides of faith did not leave dry sands behind but the equally loud returning roar of the flood of idolatries. With the retreat of faith in God came the deluges of humanity's ever-ancient, ever-new quest for self-divinization. The hissing serpent's promise to be like God continues to echo in humanity's ears. Thus, within this enchanted and religious context, the Bible's truth claims are still relevant both in how it presents and defends the gospel. Our battle is not against unbelief but against idolatry. We stand in a great line of biblical apologists, including Elijah, who battled the prophets of Baal, Jesus against the Pharisees and Sadducees, and Paul at Mars Hill. In our efforts to defend the faith, we are not merely out to win arguments but to help people see their idolatry and need for Christ. Our goal is to help unbelievers recognize the truth that Augustine expresses so powerfully: "You stir man to take pleasure in praising you, because you have made us for yourself, our heart is restless until it rests in you."[115] We seek to reorient unbelievers' disordered loves away from their idols and aim them toward the Triune God. God made us for worship, and we will either worship the Triune God or an idol of our own making. Our context for defending the faith, then, is not a disenchanted or secular age but a world filled with idols.

113. Matthew Arnold, "Dover Beach," in *Dover Beach and Other Poems* (Dover Publications, Inc., 1994), 86.

114. E.g., Owen Chadwick, *The Secularization of the European Mind in the 19th Century* (Cambridge University Press, 1975).

115. Augustine, *Confessions*, I.i.

2

What Makes Apologetics Reformed

Using the Books of Nature and Scripture

Thesis 2: Reformed apologetics rests on the authority of God's revelation in creation and Scripture and that God has given humans the capacity to know truth through their senses.

> And so far as the intellectual defense of Christianity is concerned, the fact should never be obscured that theism is the logical prius of faith in Christ. "Believe in God," said Jesus, "believe also in me." To reverse that order, is to throw the entire organism of apologetics out of joint.
>
> —J. Gresham Machen

Orchestra conductors helm a myriad of musicians, instruments, and sounds to play the notes on a score so that all the individual parts perform as a unified whole. The task of apologetics stands in a similar relationship as the orchestra conductor to his symphony. The apologist must employ and coordinate the truths of Scripture, creation, history, philosophy, literature, and science to defend the claims of Christianity. But in the twentieth century, the Reformed tradition has had a severe aversion and even antipathy toward one of the key instruments in the theological orchestra—namely, natural theology. Natural theology is the body of truths that a person draws from reading the book of nature. In the apostle Paul's description, "For what can be known about God is plain to them, because God has shown it to them. For his invisible attributes, namely, his eternal power and divine nature, have been clearly perceived, ever since the creation of the world, in the things that have been made" (Rom 1:19–20). When people look at the book of creation and draw conclusions about God's attributes from what they observe, they read natural revelation and making natural-theological conclusions. Alvin Plantinga has summarized the overall negative reception of natural theology as ranging from indifference, suspicion, and hostility, to even accusations of blasphemy.[1] According to Plantinga's claims about John Calvin's (1509–1564) attitudes toward natural theology, "The Christian doesn't need natural theology, either as the source of his confidence or to justify his belief."[2] Natural theology, of course, does not exhaust apologetics, but it has historically played a large role. The largescale rejection of natural theology also prompts the question: What makes apologetics Reformed? Is natural theology excluded, as some Reformed theologians have argued? Or is there a legitimate role for it? What instruments comprise the orchestra in the symphony of Reformed apologetics? *This chapter defends the thesis that Reformed apologetics rests on the authority of God's revelation in creation and Scripture and that God has given humans the capacity to know truth through their senses.* To flesh out this thesis, Reformed apologetics is the defense of theology. Our theology comes from the *principium* (principle or foundation) of Scripture and is our chief, infallible authority for faith and practice. Scripture itself teaches that in defending theology, we ought to use God's revelation in nature to argue for the truthfulness of our theology. And for the sake of the unbeliever who does not accept the authority of Scripture, we can use natural theology to argue for God's existence before we defend the claim that Jesus is God. But when the unbeliever "[holds] the truth in unrighteousness" (Rom 1:18 KJV), we have recourse to the virtue of love to win him over with winsome patience. This means there are three chief elements of Reformed apologetics: (1) the authority of Scripture, (2) use of the book of nature, and (3) a realistic epistemology (or, the basic reliability of the senses). To defend this chapter's thesis, the chapter first examines our present historical context: How did we get to the point where the Reformed church has a tenuous relationship toward natural theology? The chapter then explores some common Reformed opinions regarding natural theology. Finally, the chapter explains the three key elements of Reformed apologetics: Scripture, nature, and realism.

1. Alvin Plantinga, "The Reformed Objection to Natural Theology," in *Philosophy of Religion: Selected Readings*, ed. Michael Peterson et al. (Oxford University Press, 2001), 329–41, here 329.
2. Plantinga, "Reformed Objection," 333.

Our Present Context

Friedreich Schleiermacher (1768–1834) has been called the father of modern liberal theology and thus provides a good starting point for understanding our present context as it relates to apologetics. Schleiermacher proposed that theology is chiefly about a person's feeling of absolute dependence upon God. Where Enlightenment rationalism had erected intellectual barriers to knowing God, Schleiermacher took a common detour through the heart by means of mysticism. This was not an unprecedented move, as medieval mystics had done the same thing before.[3] If theology was no longer based on objective revelation about God in the creation or Scripture, then rational arguments for the existence of God were superfluous. Schleiermacher is clear on the feeling of absolute dependence sidelining proofs for the existence of God: "Doctrines of faith carry the recognition that this feeling of absolute dependence, in that therein our self-consciousness acts as a surrogate for recognizing the finitude of our being in general terms (cf. §8.2), is not something accidental or even some that varies from person to person but is a general feature of life. This recognition completely supplants all the so-called proofs for the existence of God."[4] The proofs supposedly only bring an objective consciousness of God, which is hardly the aim of faith.[5] The subjective feeling one has for God is superior and desirable over the supposed objective nature of the proofs:

> By now, it is self-evident that this appeal is completely useless for the purpose of dogmatics. That is to say, neither in catechesis nor in homiletic communication nor in missionary work is any sort of use to be made of such proofs; moreover, experience also shows how little is accomplished by doing battle with theoretical atheism, as it was described above. Thus, in every part dogmatics must presuppose a condition of immediate surety, faith; and, accordingly, as concerns God-consciousness in general, its task is not to effect recognition of God-consciousness but simply to explicate its content.[6]

Theology is not about proving God's existence but about explaining a person's sense of God-consciousness. Theology does not lie in the world "out there" but in the world "in here," in the human heart.

3. See, e.g., Thomas à Kempis, *The Imitation of Christ: A Spiritual Commentary and Reader's Guide* (Christian Classics, 2005).

4. Friedrich Schleiermacher, *Christian Faith: A New Translation and Critical Edition*, 2 vols., trans. Terrence N. Tice et al. (Westminster John Knox Press, 2016), I:191.

5. Schleiermacher, *Christian Faith*, I:196.

6. Schleiermacher, *Christian Faith*, I:196.

There were additional reasons why Schleiermacher opposed use of the proofs. First, he believed that Scripture and the Reformed confessions did not themselves provide proofs but rather only make assertions, and for a believer such assertions are sufficiently authoritative and require no proof.[7] Second, common uses of the proofs that employ reason with accompanying judgments mistake "philosophy for dogmatics."[8] Third, Schleiermacher claimed that Christianity had a unique epistemological foundation. The only source for "religion" is Scripture. "Theology," on the other hand, draws from the church fathers, reason, and philosophy. Schleiermacher avers: "This view, however, cannot apply to Christian theology, since theology draws directly from Scripture, and Scripture itself first arose through Christian religion, but what draws on reason and philosophy cannot be Christian theology. It is surely a great gain, here and elsewhere, to banish all materials of this kind from the domain of Christian faith-doctrine."[9] In some sense Schleiermacher was part of a trend that set the stage for either the rejection or diminution of natural theology, a significant element of apologetics.

Karl Barth (1886–1968) famously rejected natural theology for similar reasons as Schleiermacher because he believed that one of the chief defining characteristics of theology is the existential encounter with the living Christ. Barth gives expression to this idea early in his career in his commentary on Ephesians when he writes:

> Being *en Christo* ["in Christ"] is the presupposition and goal of our human being, having, and doing—the *beneplacitum Dei* ["good pleasure of God"] on the one hand and the *glorificatio Dei* ["glorification of God"] on the other—in their original relation, not the human creature's existence or anything he might produce or achieve. Paul would never have described his conversion at Damascus as the cause of his being in *en Christo*. He was not *en Christo* because he experienced Damascus; rather, he experienced Damascus because he was *en Christo*.[10]

Because Christ is the elected and rejected man, there is no room for natural categories, such as the covenant of works, natural law, or natural theology.[11] There is only one covenant of grace in Christ.[12] Despite Barth's opposition

7. Schleiermacher, *Christian Faith*, I:196.

8. Schleiermacher, *Christian Faith*, I:196.

9. Schleiermacher, *Christian Faith*, I:197.

10. Karl Barth, *The Epistle to the Ephesians*, ed. David Nelson, trans. Ross Wright (Baker Academic, 2017), 83.

11. Karl Barth, *Church Dogmatics*, 14 vols., ed. G. W. Bromiley and T. F. Torrance (T&T Clark, 1936–1968), II/2:116–18.

12. Barth, *Church Dogmatics*, IV/1:62–63.

to natural theology, he ironically delivered the 1936–1937 Gifford Lectures, which are dedicated to natural theology, "without reference to or reliance upon any supposed special revelation or so-called miraculous revelation."[13] Within this context Barth proudly declared, "I am an avowed opponent of all natural theology."[14] He believed he was standing with the Reformation in his rejection, which stood in contrast to the compromises of modern Protestant and Roman Catholic uses of natural theology.[15] According to Barth, the Reformers rested church and salvation on the word of God alone and on his revelation in Jesus Christ.[16]

Many place Barth on the left side of the Reformed tradition, given the *neo* in his neo-orthodoxy, and might assume that his rejection of natural theology soaked his mind because of the liberal streams of theology in which he swam. Yet the same patterns of rejecting natural theology unfold among twentieth-century conservative Reformed theologians. Scottish Presbyterian theologian James Orr (1895–1987) was fond of Kantian idealism, which posits that systems of thought originate from one single solitary idea. Just as Christology was Barth's central doctrine from which he deduced all others, Orr made the same move. Given that Christology so defines theology, there is no need for the proofs for God's existence: "Neither shall I waste time at this stage by discussing in what sense it is permissible to speak of 'proof' of so transcendent a reality as the Divine existence. We remember there the saying of [Friedrich Heinrich] Jacobi, that a God capable of proof would be no God at all."[17] Another Reformed theologian who makes a similar move in his own theology, especially in relation to his apologetic methodology, is Cornelius Van Til (1895–1987).

We should first note that Van Til was not in principle opposed to the use of evidence or the proofs for the existence of God. At the same time, Van Til makes statements that sound very much like Orr and Barth: "Of course Reformed believers do not seek to prove the existence of their God. To seek to prove or to disprove the existence of this God would be to seek to deny him. To seek to prove

13. Karl Barth, *The Knowledge of God and the Service of God According to the Teaching of the Reformation: Recalling the Scottish Confession of 1560; The Gifford Lectures Delivered in the University of Aberdeen in 1937 and 1938*, trans. J. L. M. Haire and Ian Henderson (Hodder and Stoughton, 1960), 3.

14. Barth, *Knowledge of God*, 6. See, of course, Karl Barth, *Natural Theology: Comprising Nature and Grace by Professor Dr. Emil Brunner and the Reply 'No!' by Dr. Karl Barth* (Wipf & Stock, 2002).

15. Barth, *Knowledge of God*, 8.

16. Barth, *Knowledge of God*, 8–9.

17. James Orr, *The Christian View of God and the World: As Centering in the Incarnation* (Eerdmans, 1947), 94.

or disprove this God presupposes that man can identify himself and discover facts in relation to laws in the universe without reference to God. A God whose existence is 'proved' is not the God of Scripture."[18] Because of statements like this, some have assumed that Van Til was against the use of evidence in apologetics.[19] Nevertheless, John Frame has noted that Van Til's anti-evidential reputation is in part Van Til's own fault because he never spent time explaining detailed Christian evidences but only focused on large-scale philosophical issues.[20] But more importantly, and related to Barth's and Orr's commitment to idealism, is Van Til's own affable stance toward Kant. Robert Knudsen (1924–2000), Van Til's colleague at Westminster Theological Seminary (Philadelphia, PA), noted that Orr's approach to epistemology and apologetics required starting with Jesus.[21] Van Til confirms this point when he writes: "We must really do what Karl Barth has insisted that we must do but has not done, namely, start our interpretation of the whole of life *von oben* ['from above']. We must begin our meditation upon any fact in the world in the light of the Son of God, the light which is as the light of the sun, the source of all other light."[22] Given this christological starting point, and in spite of the significant differences between Barth and Van Til on a host of theological issues, there is a tendency in Van Til's apologetics to downplay evidence, the proofs for God's existence, and natural theology.[23] This point becomes only more pronounced in Van Til's disciples.

Van Tillian apologist Greg Bahnsen (1948–1995) believed he was being faithful to Scripture and Van Til when he argued that the use of evidence in apologetics is unbiblical: "Scripture itself should be enough to dissuade a person from depending upon evidential arguments for Christ's resurrection. . . . The only tool an apologete needs is the word of God, for the sinner will either presuppose its truth and find Christianity to be coherent and convincing (given his spiritual condition and past experience) or he will reject it and never be able to come to a knowledge of the truth."[24] Other Van Tillians

18. Cornelius Van Til, *The Protestant Doctrine of Scripture*, In Defense of Biblical Christianity 1 (Den Dulk Christian Foundation, 1967), 137.

19. C. Stephen Evans, *Faith Beyond Reason: A Kierkegaardian Account* (Eerdmans, 1998), 19; Clark Pinnock, "The Philosophy of Christian Evidences," in *Jerusalem and Athens: Critical Discussions on the Theology and Apologetics of Cornelius Van Til*, ed. E. R. Geehan (P&R, 1971), 421.

20. John Frame, *Cornelius Van Til: An Analysis of His Thought* (P&R, 1995), 182, 184.

21. Robert D. Knudsen, "The Transcendental Perspective of Westminster's Apologetic," *Westminster Theological Journal* 48 (1986): 223–39

22. Cornelius Van Til, *The Reformed Pastor and Modern Thought* (P&R, 1980), 196.

23. Knudsen, "Transcendental Perspective," 236.

24. Greg Bahnsen, "The Impropriety of Evidentially Arguing for the Resurrection," *Synapse* 2 (1972), https://answersingenesis.org/apologetics/the-impropriety-of-evidentially-arguing-for-the-resurrection/.

have made similar blunt claims, as according to Richard B. Gaffin Jr., 1 Corinthians 2:6–16 is supposedly "the death blow to all natural theology," and thus "natural theology may have a place in Roman Catholic and Arminian theologies . . . but not in a theology that would be Reformed."[25] This overview of key figures lends credence to Plantinga's assessment that twentieth-century Reformed theologians view natural theology with indifference, suspicion, and outright hostility. This is not to say that natural theology or the use of evidence exhausts the apologetic task, but it does reveal why the twentieth-century Reformed tradition has downplayed it along with appeals to creation, history, and evidence. Yet, if we go behind the modern period to historic early modern Reformed theology, we can trace a different line of reception from the Reformation into the present day.

Historic Reformed Views

One of the greater canards in discussions about apologetics is that Calvin was opposed to all forms of natural theology. Calvin does not present *a priori* arguments like Anselm's (1033–1109) *Proslogion*, and neither does he argue like Thomas Aquinas (1225–1274), with the latter's five proofs for the existence of God. Calvin does, however, appeal to Cicero's (106–43 BC) *De Natura Deorum* a number of times in the opening chapters of his *Institutes*.[26] He also appeals to the Stoic idea of *prolepsis*, or "common notions," in his commentary on Romans 2:14–15.[27] He agrees with Cicero that the intricacy of the human body is evidence for God's existence.[28] In fact, Calvin does not begin to cite Scripture until the fourth chapter of his *Institutes*, a fact obscured by the Battles edition, which inserts forty-three Scripture citations that do not appear in Calvin's original 1559 edition.[29] All of these facts point in the direction that Calvin stands with the earlier patristic and medieval tradition in its use of natural theology, a belief captured in the French Confession (1559), which Calvin co-wrote: "God reveals himself to men; firstly, in his works, in their creation, as well as in their preservation and control. Secondly,

25. Richard B. Gaffin Jr., "Some Epistemological Reflections on 1 Cor 2:6–16," *Westminster Theological Journal* (1995): 123–24.

26. Egil Grislis, "Calvin's Use of Cicero in the Institutes I:1–5—a Case Study in Theological Method," *Archiv für Reformationsgeschichte* 62/1 (1971): 5–37.

27. John Calvin, *Romans and Thessalonians*, Calvin's New Testament Commentaries, ed. T. F. Torrance and David F. Torrance (Eerdmans, 1996), comm. Rom 2:14–15 (96–97).

28. John Calvin, *Institutes of the Christian Religion*, trans. Ford Lewis Battles, ed. John T. McNeil (Westminster Press, 1960), I.iii.1.

29. Cf. John Calvin, *Institutio Religionis Christianae* (Robert Stephanus, 1559); Calvin, *Institutes*, I.i–v.

and more clearly, in his Word, which was in the beginning revealed through oracles, and which was afterward committed to writing in the books which we call the Holy Scriptures" (II).

Guido de Bres (1522–1567) subsequently took this passage from Calvin's French Confession and amplified it in his own Belgic Confession (1561) by employing a term used by Augustine (354–430) and Raymond Sabunde (ca. 1385–1436)—namely, the "book of nature."[30] Augustine explains: "Some people read books in order to find God. Yet there is a great book, the very appearance of created things. Look above you; look below you! Note it; read it! God, whom you wish to find, never wrote that book with ink. Instead, He set before your eyes the things that He had made."[31] De Bres combines this idea of the book of nature with Calvin's French Confession when he writes:

> We know God by two means: First, by the creation, preservation, and government of the universe, since that universe is before our eyes like a beautiful book in which all creatures, great and small, are as letters to make us ponder the invisible things of God: God's eternal power and divinity, as the apostle Paul says in Romans 1:20. All these things are enough to convict humans and to leave them without excuse. Second, God makes himself known to us more clearly by his holy and divine Word, as much as we need in this life, for God's glory and for our salvation (II).

This trend continues from the early modern to the modern period in Reformed theologians such as Abraham Kuyper (1837–1920) and Herman Bavinck (1854–1921).

Kuyper and Bavinck followed in the path of Augustine, Sabunde, and Calvin, among others, and argued for the importance and necessity of using both books in theology, nature and Scripture. Kuyper, for example, appealed to Calvin's ideas of the *sensus divinitatis* ("the sense of divinity") and the *semen religionis* ("seed of religion"), as well as Belgic Confession article II (quoted above), to support the idea that there are two sources for the knowledge of God: creation and Scripture. Kuyper makes an important observation that bears upon present-day hostility toward appealing to the book of nature through natural-theological arguments:

30. Raymond of Sabunde, *Theologica Naturalis, sive Liber creaturarum specialiter de homine et de natura eius in quantum homo et de his que sunt ei necessaria ad cognoscendum seipsum et Deum et omne debitum ad quod hom tenetur et obligatum tam Deo quam primo* (Martinus, 1496).

31. Augustine, *The Essential Augustine*, ed. Vernon J. Bourke (New American Library, 1964), 123; Alexander W. Hall, "Natural Theology in the Middle Ages," in *The Oxford Handbook of Natural Theology*, ed. Russell Re Manning (Oxford University Press, 2013), 57–74, here 59.

> Modernists deem a *supernatural* knowledge of God unnecessary. They deny it, combat it, and recommend the *natural* knowledge of God as the only true one. They do not hold that the Bible or internal illumination is of no value, but they include both Bible and illumination among the class of *natural* givens and deny that either of them have any *supernatural* character. The Christian Church counters by emphasizing that the supernatural knowledge of God is of vital importance. The more it is assailed, the more she is inclined to proclaim that it can be attained *only* supernaturally. She does not deny that nature declares the glory of God, that history testifies to His providence, and that God speaks into man's conscience. However, she mentions these sources of knowledge of God only "for the sake of completeness."[32]

Kuyper believed that the conservative church pushed the book of nature away, however unintentional the move, because liberal theologians scuttled Scripture and claimed nature was all-sufficient: "This furnished natural theology the occasion to unfold its wings ever more broadly; to expand itself and lessen the importance of special theology; until finally it succeeded in stepping forth as a monarch and in contesting all right of utterance to special theology."[33] Yet, Kuyper was unpersuaded that the church should only rest upon Scripture as a source of theological knowledge. The two sources, natural and supernatural revelation, work in concert. In fact, "That special revelation (*revelatio specialis*) is not conceivable without the hypothesis of natural theology, is simply because *grace* never creates one single new reality."[34]

Bavinck argues similarly when he pinpoints a problem with natural theology: it becomes compromised only when someone separates natural from supernatural theology. Together, however, natural and supernatural theology are powerful witnesses that demonstrate and reveal the existence of God. Bavinck writes:

> There is not an atom in the universe in which [God's] everlasting power and deity are not clearly seen. Both from within and from without, God's witness speaks to us. God does not leave himself without a witness, either in nature or history, in heart or conscience, in life or lot. This witness of God is so powerful, accordingly, that almost no one denies its reality. All humans and peoples have heard something of the voice of the Lord. The consent of all peoples is confirmation

32. Abraham Kuyper, "The Natural Knowledge of God," trans. Harry Van Dyke, *The Bavinck Review* 6 (2015): 73–112, here 73.

33. Abraham Kuyper, *Principles of Sacred Theology*, trans. J. Henrik de Vries (Eerdmans, 1963), 372–73.

34. Kuyper, *Principles of Sacred Theology*, 373.

> of the fact that God does not leave himself without a witness; it is humanity's response of the voice of God.[35]

Other early twentieth-century Reformed theologians have held similar beliefs regarding the necessity of natural theology. Geerhardus Vos (1862–1949) believed that natural theology has an apologetic function and value: "Natural theology owes its position in science to its use in apologetics, for refuting those who have rejected the supernatural revelation of God."[36]

Like Calvin and Kuyper, Vos was favorable toward the idea of the innate knowledge of God in all human beings.[37] Vos promoted a number of the various arguments for the existence of God in his lectures on natural theology, though he preferred the teleological argument to others, such as the ontological or cosmological arguments, because he believed it was clearer and weightier.[38] In his *Reformed Dogmatics*, for example, Vos writes: "We can certainly reason from the world up to God, but we cannot by logic descend from God to the world."[39] Vos works out his commitment to natural theology in his biblical theology where he insists on the need for both faith and history:

> To join in the outcry against dogma and fact means to lower the ideal of what the Christian consciousness ought normally to be to the level of the spiritual depression of our own day and generation. How much better that we should all strive to raise our drooping faith and to reënrich our depleted experience up to the standard of those blessed periods in the life of the Church, when the belief in Bible history and the religion of the heart went hand in hand and kept equal pace, when people were ready to lay down their lives for facts and doctrines, because facts and doctrines formed the daily spiritual nourishment of their souls. May God by His Spirit maintain among us, and through our instrumentality revive around us, that truly evangelical type of piety which not merely tolerates facts and doctrines, but draws from them its strength and inspiration in life and service, its only comfort and hope in the hour of death.[40]

35. Herman Bavinck, *Reformed Dogmatics*, 4 vols., trans. John Vriend, ed. John Bolt (Baker Academic, 2003–2008), II:90.

36. Geerhardus Vos, *Lectures on Natural Theology*, ed. J. V. Fesko, trans. Albert Gootjes (Reformation Heritage Books, 2022), §12.d.

37. Vos, *Lectures*, §91.d.

38. Vos, *Lectures*, §132ff.

39. Geerhardus Vos, *Reformed Dogmatics*, vol. 1, ed. Richard B. Gaffin Jr. (Lexham, 2012), 157.

40. Geerhardus Vos, "Christian Faith and the Truthfulness of Bible History," *Princeton Theological Review* 4/3 (1906): 304–5.

Biblical faith and history, facts embedded in the soil of creation, facts such as the empty tomb, go hand in hand.

Another twentieth-century Reformed voice is J. Gresham Machen (1881–1937), who argues for the need for both nature and Scripture in apologetics, whether in the creation, in the human conscience, or in Scripture. All three give witness to the truths of Christianity. Machen asks how people can know God. Interestingly, Machen first turns his attention to liberal preachers who claim that we can only know God through Jesus. Such a claim, opines Machen, has the appearance of piety but is highly derogatory to him. Machen writes:

> For Jesus Himself plainly recognized the validity of other ways of knowing God, and to reject those other ways is to reject the things that lay at the very center of Jesus' life. Jesus plainly found God's hand in nature; the lilies of the field revealed to Him the weaving of God. He found God also in the moral law; the law written in the hearts of men was God's law, which revealed His righteousness. Finally, Jesus plainly found God revealed in the Scriptures. How profound was our Lord's use of the words of prophets and psalmists! To say that such revelation of God was invalid, or is useless to us today, is despise things that lay closest to Jesus' mind and heart. But as a matter of fact, when men say that we know God only as He is revealed in Jesus, they are denying all real knowledge of God whatever. For unless there be some idea of God independent of Jesus, the ascription of deity to Jesus has no meaning. To say, "Jesus is God," is meaningless unless the word "God" has an antecedent meaning attached to it. And the attaching of a meaning to the word "God" is accomplished by the means which have just been mentioned.[41]

It may surprise some, but Machen opposed the Christocentricism that was common in the nineteenth and twentieth centuries, an approach popular with Barth, Orr, and Van Til.

Machen fleshes out his opposition to Christocentric approaches of apologetics by appealing to the relationship between theology (proper) and Christology:

> And so far as the intellectual defense of Christianity is concerned, the fact should never be obscured that theism is the logical prius of faith in Christ. "Believe in God," said Jesus, "believe also in me." To reverse that order, is to throw the entire organism of apologetics out of joint. The old order of apologetics is correct: First, there is a God; second, it is likely that He should reveal

41. J. Gresham Machen, *Christianity and Liberalism* (Eerdmans, 1999), 55–56.

> Himself; third, He has actually revealed himself in Christ. It is a very serious fault when the last of these points is put first.[42]

In today's biblically illiterate culture, Machen's observation is especially relevant. To begin apologetics with Christ is not fatally wrong, but when we say that he is God incarnate, many might respond with befuddlement, "What do you mean by *God*?" Machen, therefore, wanted to begin with nature and creation to say that everything that we see in the cosmos is temporal, finite, contingent, and is separate from the eternal, infinite, necessary being of God. We can fill out what it means to be God by pointing to the creation so that when we say that Jesus is God incarnate, the term "God" has meaning and significance. In theological terms, Christology presupposes theology (proper). In biblical terms, Genesis 1:1, "God created the heavens and the earth," precedes John 1:1, "In the beginning was the Word." Likewise, Romans 1:19, "What can be known about God is plain to them . . . his eternal power and divine nature, have been clearly perceived . . . in the things that have been made," precedes Romans 3:21, "But now the righteousness of God has been manifested apart from the law . . . the righteousness of God through faith in Jesus Christ." Or, in the simple words of Jesus, "Believe in God; believe also in me" (John 14:1). This collective witness of the Reformed tradition from Calvin, the French Confession, the Belgic Confession, Kuyper, Bavinck, Vos, Machen, and a whole host of others abundantly proves that the historic Reformed tradition has been committed to using both the books of nature (natural theology) and Scripture (supernatural theology) in theology and apologetics.[43] This historic witness sets the stage for answering the question: What makes apologetics Reformed?

What Makes Apologetics Reformed?

To answer the question of what makes apologetics Reformed, we cannot merely appeal to the majority report from the tradition to settle the debate. However, the historic tradition's congenial relationship to natural theology does press the question of how it fits within the overall discipline

42. Machen, "Religion, Science and Philosophy," *Princeton Theological Review* 24/1 (1926): 59.

43. See, e.g., J. V. Fesko and Guy Richard, "Natural Theology and the Westminster Confession of Faith," in *The Westminster Confession into the 21st Century*, vol. 3, ed. J. Ligon Duncan (Mentor, 2009), 223–66; Wallace W. Marshall, *Puritanism and Natural Theology* (Pickwick Publications, 2016); Richard A. Muller, "Was It Really Viral? Natural Theology in the Early Modern Reformed Tradition," in *Crossing Traditions: Essays on the Reformation and Intellectual History*, ed. Maria-Cristina Pitassi and Danieal Solfaroli Camillocci (Brill, 2017), 507–31.

of apologetics. There are three fundamental pieces for an apologetics that is Reformed: (1) the authority of Scripture, (2) the book of nature, and (3) a realistic epistemology.

Scripture

First and foremost, any Reformed, or Christian for that matter, apologetics must rest on the authority of Scripture. The "word of God is living and active, sharper than any two-edged sword, piercing to the division of soul and of spirit, of joints and of marrow, and discerning the thoughts and intentions of the heart" (Heb 4:12). Only the word of God working in concert with the sovereign regenerative work of the Spirit gives us a clear picture of who the Triune God is. Apart from the Spirit's work, a person will never embrace special revelation or the gospel, because "the natural person does not accept the things of the Spirit of God, for they are folly to him, and he is not able to understand them because they are spiritually discerned" (1 Cor 2:14). In the words of the Westminster Confession,

> We may be moved and induced by the testimony of the church to an high and reverent esteem of the Holy Scripture. And the heavenliness of the matter, the efficacy of the doctrine, the majesty of the style, the consent of all the parts, the scope of the whole (which is, to give all glory to God), the full discovery it makes of the only way of man's salvation, the many other incomparable excellencies, and the entire perfection thereof, are arguments whereby it doth abundantly evidence itself to be the Word of God: *yet notwithstanding, our full persuasion and assurance of the infallible truth and divine authority thereof, is from the inward work of the Holy Spirit bearing witness by and with the Word in our hearts.* (1.5, emphasis added)

Only the Spirit makes sinners receptive to the word of God. As the rain waters the earth and makes it fruitful, so the word of God and the outpoured Spirit waters the human heart to produce the fruit of faith and repentance (Isa 55:11). God's Spirit-empowered word fulfills its content and transforms that content into reality. The word of predication creates the future, and the word constitutes the beginning of the fulfillment of God's will.[44] We must remember, then, that Scripture is the *sine qua non* of apologetics and, as B. B. Warfield (1851–1921) once observed, "We are not absurdly arguing that Apologetics has in itself the power to make a man a Christian or to conquer

44. Herman Bavinck, *Saved by Grace: The Holy Spirit's Work in Calling and Regeneration*, trans. Nelson Kloosterman (Reformation Heritage Books, 2008), 157.

the world to Christ."[45] Arguments do not save people—the Spirit through the word saves people. This fact does not render apologetics useless. Rather, we clear obstacles to faith, answer objections, and even buttress our own faith as we dispel doubt and answer questions in our own hearts. But we do these things resting on the authority of God's word.

The Book of Nature

Just because we rest our apologetics upon the book of Scripture does not mean that the book of nature is irrelevant or unnecessary or at risk of contaminating a faithful apologetic. The book of nature and reading that book (i.e., natural theology) has a place in Reformed theology and apologetics, as the historic Reformed tradition attests. Dorothy Sayers (1893–1957) astutely observes: "The whole material universe is an expression and incarnation of the creative energy of God, as a book or a picture is the material expression of the creative soul of the artist."[46] As theologians going back to Augustine have argued, we can and should make *a posteriori* arguments from the creation and reason back to the creator. The criticism against natural theology has been that Enlightenment philosophers such as David Hume (1711–1776) and Immanuel Kant (1724–1804) supposedly subjected the proofs for the existence of God to devastating critique and rendered them impotent in a modern world. Or, as others have argued, the theistic proofs at best only lead to a general theism and not the Christian theism of Scripture. But as Kuyper and Bavinck pointed out, the problem has been that theologians divorced natural and special revelation from each other. Kant and Hume abstracted the proofs (more properly demonstrations) from the larger context of Aquinas's *Summa Theologica*, wherein he employed general and special revelation working in concert. Aquinas's *Summas* do not present a general theism but rather his full-fledged picture of the Triune God of Scripture. The same is true of Van Til's criticism of Warfield, whose apologetics supposedly could only lead to general theism, yet Warfield himself wrote: "The function of Apologetics is not performed until it has placed in our hands God, Religion, Christianity and the Bible, and said to us, Now go on and explicate these fundamental facts in all their contents."[47]

45. B. B. Warfield, "Introduction," in Francis R. Beattie, *Apologetics: or The Rational Vindication of Christianity*, vol. 1, *Fundamental Apologetics* (The Presbyterian Committee of Publication, 1903), 19–32, here 25.

46. Dorothy Sayers, *Letters to a Diminished Church: Passionate Arguments for the Relevance of Christian Doctrine* (Thomas Nelson, 2004), 63.

47. Warfield, "Introduction," 31; cf. Cornelius Van Til, *Defense of the Faith*, 3rd ed. (P&R, 1966), 220.

The books of nature and Scripture give us the complete divine library from which we can know God and defend the faith. We always give interpretive priority, of course, to special revelation—the corrective lenses of Scripture, as Calvin once called it:

> For as the aged, or those whose sight is defective, when any book, however fair, is set before them, though they perceive that there is something written, are scarcely able to make out two consecutive words, but, when aided by glasses, begin to read distinctly, so Scripture, gathering together the impressions of Deity, which, till then, lay confused in our minds, dissipates the darkness, and shows us the true God clearly.[48]

Unbelievers can know of God's existence and his attributes unaided by the regenerative work of the Holy Spirit, but they are, as Calvin explains, like bleary-eyed old men trying to make out the words in a book. They can read some of the words, but others are indiscernible apart from the Spirit affixing the corrective lenses of Scripture before their eyes so they can see the truth clearly. Must we include the book of nature in every apologetic effort? Can we restrict ourselves to the word of God? A soldier need not employ every weapon in his arsenal to fight the enemy, but neither should he prejudicially ignore or leave some weapons behind when he travels to the field of battle. There are advantages to carrying and using the full panoply of truth in the divine armory.

There are at least three reasons why we should employ both books in the divine library, nature and Scripture. First, the book of nature (or creation) is the revelatory stage for the word of God and places human beings in their proper context. We are not abstract beings, minds floating in a disembodied sea of subjectivity in virtual worlds of our own making. Rather, we are creation-conditioned creatures planted amid a world filled with revelatory truth: "The heavens declare the glory of God, and the sky above proclaims his handiwork," exclaims the psalmist (Ps 19:1). Second, when we read in Scripture that God created the heavens and earth, we must look away from the page of holy writ and gaze upon the book of nature. Scripture's God is the same God who has created the cosmos—nature and Scripture speak with one voice, and we foolishly ignore the heavens if we turn a deaf ear to their message.

Third, the creation reveals our insignificance and God's greatness. In this technologically idolatrous age in which we live, so many of our devices give us

48. John Calvin, *Institutes of the Christian Religion*, 2 vols., trans. Henry Beveridge (Calvin Translation Society, 1845), I.vi.1.

the impression that we have mastered the creation. In the analysis of Wendell Berry (1934–), "We became less and less capable of sensing ourselves as small within Creation, partly because we thought we could comprehend it statistically, but also because we were becoming creators, ourselves, of a mechanical creation by which we felt ourselves greatly magnified."[49] But when we point to the immensity and seeming infinity of the cosmos, then unbelievers have an immediate sense of their insignificance and a better idea of the power and wisdom of the God who has created it all. Berry writes: "Seeking enlightenment or the Promised Land or the way home, a man would go or be forced to go into the wilderness, measure himself against the Creation, recognize finally his true place within it, and thus be saved both from pride and from despair. Seeing himself as a tiny member of a world he cannot comprehend or master or in any final sense possess, he cannot possibly think of himself as a god."[50] The creation can fill unbelievers with a sense of despair. In the words of Blaise Pascal (1623–1662), "When I consider the span of my life absorbed into the eternity which comes before and after—as the remembrance of a guest that tarries but a day—the small space I occupy and which I see swallowed up in the infinite immensity of spaces of which I know nothing and which know nothing of me, I take fright."[51]

The creation filling unbelievers with despair is much like the pedagogical use of the law, accusing sinners of their sin. Assuming the Spirit both convicts and opens the sinner's eyes, apologists can point to the cosmos and then pivot to the book of Scripture: "In the beginning, God created the heavens and earth," and "What is man that you are mindful of him, and the son of man that you care for him" (Gen 1:1; Ps 8:4). We can turn unbelievers to the one true Son of Man, the one who came to seek and save the lost (Luke 19:10). After conversion, the creation can serve like the third use of the law (the normative use), that which informs us of the will of God. The creation declares God's glory and places his wisdom on display throughout, from things as small as the ant all the way to the glorious heavenly bodies (Prov 6:6; Ps 19:1–4). Thus, "A sanctified sensibility, formed not on the visible and material splendors of the universe alone, but on its divine origin and spiritual significance, is what our Savior himself and all his inspired servants exemplify and commend. The works and the word of God should never be dissociated in our thoughts. Every Christian should assiduously cultivate in himself the habit of hallowed association."[52]

49. Wendell Berry, "The Body and the Earth," in *The Art of the Commonplace: The Agrarian Essays of Wendell Berry*, ed. Norman Wirzba (Counterpoint, 2002), 95.

50. Berry, "The Body and the Earth," 95.

51. Blaise Pascal, *Pensées*, trans. A. J. Krailsheimer (Penguin Books, 1995), 19.

52. Joseph Atkinson, "Moral Æsthetics; or the Goodness of God in the Ornaments of the Universe," *The Biblical Repertory and Princeton Review* 24 (1852): 38–52, here 50.

A Realistic Epistemology

Scripture and nature are necessary for apologetics as they reveal God's truth, but what good are they if humans are incapable of receiving their message? Yes, unregenerate humans are incapable of believing in special revelation for their salvation, but such a positive reception of divine revelation presupposes the basic reliability of the senses. In other words, God designed human beings to receive general and special revelation through their senses: taste, touch, smell, sight, and hearing. Why is the basic reliability of the senses important for apologetics? Because our present cultural moment has challenged the idea of the goodness of the body and even expresses a complete rejection of scientific truth in the pursuit of its idols. The Enlightenment hens of René Descartes (1596–1650) and Kant have come home to roost.[53] Descartes's desire to distrust his senses and argue that doubt and his mind alone were a firm foundation for knowledge set the modern age on a course of conflict between body and mind, where the senses are untrustworthy. With Kant's elevation of the individual as the measure of all things and the one who shapes reality, added to Descartes's distrust of the senses, we have come to a point where people believe they are isolated minds existing in a world of subjectivity. Descartes's and Kant's rationalistic idealism are a snare according to Bavinck, who writes: "This misstep has already been taken with the claim that we know nothing immediately beyond our own sensations and representations. Whosoever speaks this way has already been caught in the snares of idealism and cannot free himself by any reasoning."[54] In other words, do we form the objective world in our minds, or does the world around us impress itself upon our minds?

Uncoupled from the authority of Scripture, creation is no longer legible revelation. Why? Because unfastened from the authority of Scripture, humans fancy themselves as gods of their own worlds. Since creation is a part of God's book of nature, we should seek to exegete it rightly just as we exegete God's other book, the Bible. To exegete rightly the creation, we must use the God-given means—namely, our senses. Bavinck explains, "We know the external world only through our sensations and can never approach it from

53. For detailed arguments, see Carl R. Trueman, *The Rise and Triumph of the Modern Self: Cultural Amnesia, Expressive Individualism, and the Road to Sexual Revolution* (Crossway, 2020). This is not to say that our present context arises purely from the philosophy of Descartes and Kant, as there are undoubtedly other political, economic, societal, and historical issues at play. Rather, this point presses Descartes's and Kant's influence on epistemology as it relates specifically to the bodily senses.

54. Herman Bavinck, *Christian Worldview*, trans. and ed. Nathaniel Gray Sutanto et al. (Crossway Publishing, 2019), 34.

beyond them."[55] "Knowledge of truth is possible," writes Bavinck, "only if we begin with the fact that subject and object, and knowing and being correspond to each other."[56] Or, in Berry's simpler analysis, "By understanding accurately his proper place in Creation, a man may be made whole."[57] This realistic epistemology is a concomitant of the doctrines of creation *ex nihilo* and humanity's special creation in the image of God. We can know God and the creation through our senses because God has created us to receive his revelation. But the capacity to know God through the senses, even as fallen human beings, rests not in the raw power of human reason but in the reality of God's creation, which reveals his truth. Bavinck explains: "Thus, all intellectual knowledge begins with sense perception. To acquire knowledge, Scripture refers man not to his own reason but to God's revelation in all his works. Lift up your eyes, and see the one who has created all things; [lift them up] to the teaching and the testimony; otherwise, they shall perish."[58] In his argument, Bavinck draws upon Augustine: "We know the things because they are, but they are because God has known them. The doctrine of the creation of all things by the Word of God is the explanation of all knowing and knowing about, the presupposition behind the correspondence between subject and object."[59] Or as Augustine expresses it, "As for ourselves, we see the things you have made because they are. But they are because you see them."[60] A realistic epistemology is not the idea of philosophers but the teaching of Scripture, as "For 'what is seen' did not come to be 'out of the visible' (Heb 11:3); the 'invisible attributes of God' can be 'perceived' through his works, becoming beheld by the 'mind' (Rom 1:18)."[61] In other words, the only way people can know that the "heavens declare the glory of God," and behold the sun as it "runs its course with joy," and discern the "invisible attributes" of God "clearly" through the "things that have been made" is if their senses (even in a fallen state) function sufficiently well (Ps 19:1, 5; Rom 1:20). A realistic epistemology sounds technical, philosophical, and complex, but it is not. Bavinck beautifully illustrates the simplicity of a realistic epistemology when he writes:

> It is the human who has to conform his perception and thinking to God's revelation in nature and grace: "Reality does not have to make itself comply with

55. Bavinck, *Christian Worldview*, 35.
56. Bavinck, *Christian Worldview*, 38.
57. Berry, "The Body and the Earth," 94.
58. Bavinck, *Christian Worldview*, 39.
59. Bavinck, *Christian Worldview*, 46.
60. Augustine, *Confessions*, trans. Henry Chadwick (Oxford University Press, 1991), XIII. xxxviii (53).
61. Bavinck, *Christian Worldview*, 46.

> our reason, but rather, on the basis of the whole experience of the whole age, our thinking must seek to lay bare the metaphysic that God has woven it into reality." To enter the realm of truth, we must become children: "It is of nature to bring forth, and freedom, the freedom brought from truth." All knowledge consists in the conformity of our consciousness to the objective truth.[62]

A realistic epistemology means that we use our senses to read the book of nature and Scripture, and consequently we submit to the truths that God publishes in each book.

Conclusion

This chapter has surveyed historic voices to see what doctrinal commitments are common to Reformed apologetics, such as Calvin, Kuyper, Bavinck, Vos, Machen, and confessions such as the Belgic and Westminster. Seeing how Reformed theologians in the past have addressed apologetic issues helps us to retrieve lost tools and concepts for apologetics today. For example, although many twentieth-century Reformed theologians have derided and decried natural theology, it serves a crucial role in apologetics, has solid footing in Scripture, and has experienced widespread use in the historic Reformed tradition. Natural revelation (the book of nature) exists and proclaims the truths of God's existence and his being and invisible attributes. When human beings, created after his image, read this book, they do natural theology. However, natural theology should not function independently apart from supernatural theology, which finds its basis in Scripture. That natural and supernatural theology work in concert does not mean that apologists can never make stand-alone arguments from natural theology for the sake of discussion, but it does require that as they formulate these natural arguments, they do so with an eye on Scripture to guide them. As Warfield pointed out, the goal of apologetics is never to bring people merely to a vague notion of theism but to the Triune God of Scripture, which means that whatever natural theological stand-alone arguments an apologist presents, he must eventually and necessarily pivot to special revelation in order to point people to Christ. Employing both the books of nature and Scripture presupposes the necessary truth of the basic reliability of the senses, or a realistic epistemology. Humans do not form the world according to their idolatrous whims, but rather God impresses truth through creation and Scripture upon human minds. Therefore, Scripture, nature, and a basic reliability of the senses comprise the three key elements necessary for Reformed apologetics.

62. Bavinck, *Christian Worldview*, 48.

3

Paul at Mars Hill

Paul's Use of the Books of Nature and Scripture

Thesis 3: Acts 17 provides an illustrative blueprint for apologetics that Christians can employ as an outline for their own defense of the Christian faith as they seek a meeting of the minds with unbelievers.

For the wrath of God is revealed from heaven against all ungodliness and unrighteousness of men, who hold the truth in unrighteousness; Because that which may be known of God is manifest in them; for God hath shewed it unto them. For the invisible things of him from the creation of the world are clearly seen, being understood by the things that are made, even his eternal power and Godhead; so that they are without excuse.

—Romans 1:18–20 (KJV)

So Paul, standing in the midst of the Areopagus, said: "Men of Athens, I perceive that in every way you are very religious. For as I passed along and observed the objects of your worship, I found also an altar with this inscription: 'To the unknown god.' What therefore you worship as unknown, this I proclaim to you."

—Acts 17:22–23

Worship and apologetics might seem like an odd combination of topics, but in truth they are closely connected. If we recall that apologetics is about unseating idols from the human heart, then apologetics and worship are a perfect pair. If God has hardwired humans for worship, then we either worship the one, true God or we worship idols of our own making. The connection between worship and apologetics appears prominently in Acts 17, where Paul addresses the Epicurean and Stoic philosophers at Mars Hill. In his address, Paul presents the gospel. But in his gospel presentation, he employs an apologetic methodology where he appeals to both general and special revelation—the books of nature and Scripture. In his defense of the faith, the motivating factors are for both evangelism and worship, love for God and for fallen sinners. Paul saw that the philosophers were mired in unbelief and idolatry and thus sought to turn them to Christ so that they would worship God in Spirit and truth. In his address, the apostle argues that the God of Scripture is also the God of nature—the God of Scripture is no local deity or merely one divine being within a greater pantheon of gods. He therefore appealed to the book of nature but gave the philosophers the corrective lenses of Scripture so they could read it aright. This is the pattern of argumentation that Abraham Kuyper (1837–1920) lamented had been lost in his day.[1] Modernists set aside the supernatural knowledge of God (Scripture) and claimed that natural knowledge was true, valuable, and sufficient. In response to modernist claims, the church leaned heavily on supernatural knowledge and virtually ignored the natural knowledge of God in the creation. And yet, Herman Bavinck (1854–1921) has noted that general revelation provides the church with "a firm ground on which they can meet all non-Christians."[2]

Paul's use of nature and Scripture in his engagement with the idols at Mars Hill provides us with a good paradigm for learning how to do apologetics. *This chapter defends the thesis that Acts 17 provides an illustrative blueprint for apologetics that Christians can employ as an outline for their own defense of the Christian faith as they seek a meeting of the minds with unbelievers.* Acts 17 shows us how to use the books of nature and Scripture in tandem. This chapter therefore starts with Paul's evangelism among the Jews to show how he begins with Scripture because they were familiar with the Old Testament. Second, the chapter examines how Paul's methodology shifts when he evangelizes the gentiles; he begins not with Scripture but with an appeal to the book of nature because he and the gentiles had the creation in common. Finally, the chapter examines the relationship between apologetics and worship to prove that apologetics is about engaging the idols of unbelief.

1. Abraham Kuyper, "The Natural Knowledge of God," trans. Harry Van Dyke, *Bavinck Review* 6 (2015): 73–112, here 73; also Richard A. Muller, "Kuyper and Bavinck on Natural Theology," *Bavinck Review* 10 (2019): 5–35, here 9.

2. Herman Bavinck, *Reformed Dogmatics*, ed. John Bolt, trans. John Vriend (Baker Academic, 2003–2007), I:318; Muller, "Kuyper and Bavinck," 27.

Paul and the Jews

Paul conducted his missionary labors in Thessalonica, where he approached a "synagogue of the Jews" (Acts 17:1). Luke records this contextual fact, which immediately tells us that Paul's recipients were familiar with the Old Testament: "And Paul went in, as was his custom, and on three Sabbath days he reasoned with them from the Scriptures, explaining and proving that it was necessary for the Christ to suffer and to rise from the dead, and saying, 'This Jesus, whom I proclaim to you, is the Christ'" (Acts 17:2–4). There are several noteworthy elements in this observation that set the stage for Paul's address to the philosophers at Mars Hills. First, the passage focuses on worship. Paul went to the synagogue on three consecutive Sabbath days, a day dedicated to the worship of God. Second, he "reasoned with them from the Scriptures" (Acts 17:2). Paul's starting point was the commonly shared Old Testament Scriptures. That Luke mentions "the Christ" shows us that the Jews with whom he spoke knew the meaning and significance of the title. They would have been familiar with passages such as Psalm 2, a chapter shot through with themes of worship. But we should note the specific point of conflict—namely, that Paul was "proving that it was necessary for the Christ to suffer and to rise from the dead" (Acts 17:4).

In proving that Jesus was the Christ, Paul did two things: (1) He followed in the footsteps of Christ as he taught his disciples on the road to Emmaus that "the Christ should suffer and on the third day rise from the dead" (Luke 24:46). (2) Paul could have simply presented the claims of Christ apart from proving from the Scriptures that Jesus was the Messiah. Instead, he *proved* (παρατίθημι) and made an apologetic argument that Jesus is indeed the Messiah. In other words, apologetic arguments neither contradict nor diminish the authority of Scripture.[3] Paul merely followed Jesus's example, but Jesus did not only appeal to the Old Testament Scriptures to demonstrate he was indeed the Messiah. Rather, Jesus appealed both to Scripture and to created reality: Jesus encouraged his disciples to touch him when they doubted his resurrection (Luke 24:39–40); he ate fish with them (Luke 24:42–43). He used the books of Scripture and nature, appealing to their senses (sight, taste, touch, and hearing), but he also opened their minds through the Spirit so that they would understand (Luke 24:45). Thus, Paul did not simply demand obedience to the gospel but "reasoned with [the Jews] from the Scriptures" (Acts 17:2).

3. Contra, e.g., James Orr, *The Christian View of God and the World: As Centering in the Incarnation* (Eerdmans, 1947), 94; Cornelius Van Til, *The Protestant Doctrine of Scripture*, In Defense of Biblical Christianity 1 (Den Dulk Christian Foundation, 1967), 137.

Paul's work in Thessalonica sets the stage for the events that unfold among the gentiles in Athens.

Paul and the Gentiles

Just as in the Jewish synagogue, Paul arrives at Athens in a worship-charged environment because what spurred Paul to deliver his apologetic and evangelistic message is that the "city was full of idols" (Acts 17:16). Paul spoke to the philosophers at the Areopagus and said, "Men of Athens, I perceive that in every way you are very religious. For as I passed along and observed the objects of your worship, I found an altar" (Acts 17:22–23). But this is not the first time that one inspired by God confronted gentiles for their idolatry. The book of Isaiah forms much of the backdrop for Luke-Acts in general, just as it does here in Acts 17, a background indebted to an anti-idol polemic prominent in the book of Isaiah.[4] Here in Athens Paul followed the same method that he employed at Thessalonica and "reasoned in the Synagogue with the Jews" (Acts 17:17). But when the audience changed and "some of the Epicurean and Stoic philosophers also conversed with" Paul (Acts 17:18), he changed his tack. He changed his approach because Paul no longer had a commonly shared knowledge base in Old Testament revelation. Moreover, he could not assume that they knew of the recent events surrounding Jesus's public ministry, crucifixion, and resurrection. These two facts reshape Paul's approach where he pivots to the book of nature rather than employ the book of Scripture as his opening argument.[5] Another subtle layer that Luke highlights is that he characterizes Paul's summons to the Areopagus by the gentile philosophers in language evocative of the trial of Socrates (ca. 470–399 BC), an appeal to history, or the book of nature.[6]

When Paul arrived at the Areopagus and began his address, he appealed first to general revelation because this was a point of contact between him and his audience. There is a sense in which the Athenian philosophers knew God but also a sense in which they did not know him.[7] Imagine sitting in a darkened room looking through a doorway and seeing a large figure standing in the doorframe. Without light you can make out some of the person's features—you

4. Flavien Pardigon, *Paul Against the Idols: A Contextual Reading of the Areopagus Speech* (Pickwick Publications, 2019), 89.

5. Pardigon, *Paul Against the Idols*, 82–83; Francis J. Beckwith, *Never Doubt Thomas: The Catholic Aquinas as Evangelical and Protestant* (Baylor University Press, 2019), 27–29.

6. Pardigon, *Paul Against the Idols*, 119–20.

7. Pardigon, *Paul Against the Idols*, 142–43.

can tell that he is over six feet tall, has broad shoulders, and holds nothing in his hands. You know *something* of the man, but apart from greater light there is much that you do not know about him. We can switch illustrations and apply John Calvin's (1509–1564) imagery of bleary-eyed people trying to read a book and being able to make out some of the words but unable to read the book's entire message.[8] The apostle Paul begins with an appeal to the creation because "what can be known about God is plain to [the Athenians] because God has shown it to them" (Rom 1:19). The Athenians knew of God's "invisible attributes, namely, his eternal power and divine nature" because they were "clearly perceived" truths known by all people "ever since the creation of the world, in the things that have been made" (Rom 1:19–20). So, Paul draws the philosophers' attention to an inscription on one of the idols, to the "unknown god," and he declares, "What therefore you worship as unknown, this I proclaim to you" (Acts 17:23).

Paul begins with the "things that have been made" (Rom 1:20) and tells the philosophers: "The God who made the world and everything in it, being Lord of heaven and earth" (Acts 17:24). Yes, Paul appeals to the creation but he also alludes to words that Isaiah the prophet summoned in his indictment against the gentile nations: "Thus says God, the Lord, who created the heavens and stretched them out, who spread out the earth and what comes from it, who gives breath to the people on it and spirit to those who walk in it" (Isa 42:5). In fact, Isaiah 42:1–9 is the first of the Servant Songs in which the prophet depicts the call of the servant in relation to the nations in God's judgment against the nations in his polemic against false gods and idols.[9] In other words, Paul echoes Isaiah's appeal to the creation in order to indict the gentiles. Rather than appeal first to Scripture, Isaiah and Paul turn to the book of nature because "the heavens declare the glory of God," and "there is no speech, nor are there words, whose voice is not heard" (Ps 19:1–3).

Paul takes another step further into the creation by quoting the gentiles' own poets, their own literature:

> The God who made the world and everything in it, being Lord of heaven and earth, does not live in temples made by man, nor is he served by human hands, as though he needed anything, since he himself gives to all mankind life and breath and everything. And he made from one man every nation of mankind to live on all the face of the earth, having determined allotted periods and the boundaries of their dwelling place, that they should seek God, and perhaps

8. John Calvin, *Institutes of the Christian Religion*, 2 vols., trans. Henry Beveridge (Calvin Translation Society, 1845), I.vi.1.

9. Pardigon, *Paul Against the Idols*, 147.

> feel their way toward him and find him. Yet he is actually not far from each one of us, for
> "In him we live and move and have our being";
> as even some of your own poets have said,
> "For we are indeed his offspring." (Acts 17:24–28)

Paul tours the creation and explains that God has created all things, a move that distinguishes God's self-existent being from the contingent, temporal, finite existence of humans.[10] Paul caps his appeal to the creation with two quotations, the first from Epimenedes (ca. seventh century BC), a philosopher-poet, from his now lost work *Cretica*. The fuller quotation, from Epimenedes, states:

> They fashioned a tome for you, holy and high one,
> Cretans, always liars, evil beasts, idle bellies
> But you are not dead: you live and abide forever
> For in you we live and move and have our being.[11]

In its original context these are lines of poetry dedicated to the god Zeus. Zeus was the thunder god in ancient Greek mythology. He ruled the other gods on Mount Olympus and was known as Jupiter in the Roman pantheon. For what was Zeus known?

Zeus created women, "From her, the first woman, comes the race of women, who are an evil to men, with a nature to do evil."[12] Zeus abhorred human sacrifice and thus sent a flood to destroy the world. He called upon Poseidon, god of the sea, to overwhelm the earth with water.[13] Zeus was very much a "human" god given his emotions, actions, and ethos. He appears, for example, in Homer's (ca. eighth century BC) *Iliad* as a chief character where he interacts with the protagonist, Odysseus. In Homer's *Odyssey*, Odysseus was journeying home to Ithaca and his wife Penelope after the Trojan war. Along the way he was stranded on an island by the goddess Calypso, who had fallen in love with him. Poseidon wanted him to remain stranded on the island, but Odysseus's divine patroness, Athena, was able to persuade the other gods in Poseidon's absence to intervene on his behalf. The Olympian gods opposed Poseidon and so Zeus sent the messenger god, Hermes, to tell Calypso that she must release Odysseus and allow him to resume his journey

10. Geerhardus Vos, *Reformed Dogmatics*, 5 vols., ed. Richard B. Gaffin Jr. (Lexham, 2015–2016), 1:160.

11. As cited in Gerald L. Bray, *The Pastoral Epistles*, ITC (T&T Clark, 2019), 490.

12. Edith Hamilton, *Mythology* (Little, Brown and Co., 2013), 88.

13. Hamilton, *Mythology*, 92.

home.[14] This is the murky thought-world to which Paul appealed when he drew upon the quotation from Epimenedes, "In him we live and move and have our being" (Acts 17:28).

Paul's second quotation from the pagan poets, "For we are indeed his offspring" (Acts 17:28), comes from a line in a poem written by Aratus (ca. 315–240 BC) where he states: "It is with Zeus that every one of us in every way has to do, for we are also his offspring." This poem explains the nature of the stellar constellations and that they all depend on Zeus:

> Let us begin with Zeus, whom we men never leave unspoken. Filled with Zeus are all highways and all meeting places of people, filled are the sea and harbors; in all circumstances we are all dependent on Zeus. For we are also his children [τοῦ γὰρ καὶ γένος ἐσμέν], and he benignly gives helpful signs to men, and rouses people to work, reminding them of their livelihood, tells when the soil is best for oxen and mattocks, and tells when the seasons are right both for planting trees and for sowing every kind of seed.[15]

This same line "for we are also his children" also appears in a *Hymn to Zeus* by the Stoic poet Cleanthes (331–232 BC), where he writes:

> Most glorious of Immortals, mighty God,
> Invoked by man a name, O sovereign King
> Of universal Nature, piloting
> This world in harmony with Law—all hail!
> Thee it is meet that mortals should invoke,
> For we Thine offspring are, and sole of all
> Created things that live and move on earth
> Receive from Thee the image of the One.[16]

In these two quotations pulled from Epimenedes, Aratus, or possibly Cleanthes, Paul appeals to poems dedicated to and written about Zeus. How and in what way do these two quotations from pagan poets advance Paul's argument? Appealing to the creation is understandable, as God has written the book of nature. But how does Paul draw from literature written by unbelievers?

To answer these questions, we do well to remind ourselves of the relationship between general and special revelation, and natural and supernatural theology. Kuyper observed that supernatural theology does not exist for a single moment without natural theology, but conversely, natural theology in

14. Hamilton, *Mythology*, 286–86.
15. Aratus, *Phaenomena*, ed. Douglas Kidd (Cambridge University Press, 1997), 1–5 (73).
16. Cleanthes, *The Hymn of Cleanthes*, trans. E. H. Blakeney (SPCK, 1921), 8.

a fallen world in and of itself is incapable of supplying a pure knowledge of God. Kuyper explains, "That special revelation (*revelatio specialis*) is not conceivable without the hypothesis of natural theology, is simply because *grace* never creates one single new reality."[17] In other words, "One simple confession, that *without the basis of natural* theology there is no *special* theology."[18] In the contemporary period such statements may seem out of place, especially in the wake of the twentieth-century Reformed aversion to natural theology, but Kuyper rests on solid historic Reformed precedent. Calvin, for example, writes, "That there exists in the human mind, and indeed by natural instinct, some sense of Deity, we hold to be beyond dispute, since God himself, to prevent any man from pretending ignorance, has endued all men with some idea of his Godhead."[19] Likewise, Kuyper cites the Belgic Confession's statement (art. II), namely, that we know God by two means, the book of nature and the book of Scripture.

To what end does God reveal this knowledge of himself in the creation? Kuyper explains, "By the light of the Scripture the sinner becomes able to give himself an account of the 'seed of religion' in his heart and of the 'divine things' visible in the cosmos, but where this light hides itself even upon the Areopagus they advance no farther than to the Unknown God."[20] As noted above, the Athenians knew God in some sense, but they also did not know him. But this does not mean that the knowledge of God that they possessed was entirely destitute of some inklings of truth, however small. Kuyper states the efficacy of general revelation and natural theological truth in the most general terms, but Bavinck gives a greater degree of specificity that brings us into the broader orbit of Paul's quotations of the pagan poets. Bavinck writes: "By nature and history, heart and conscience, blessings and judgments, law and gospel, he summons us to return to him. The call, in its broadest sense, is the preaching of God's claims upon his fallen creatures. . . . Religion, morality, law, art, science, family, society, the state—they all have their root and foundation in the call that comes from God to all people."[21]

All human activity in some sense reflects divine truth that God has embedded in the creation. Bavinck goes as far as to say that the testimony in the creation is not only a "repressive but also preparatory grace . . . that paves the way for the coming of Christ," though not in the sense that God has dispensed

17. Abraham Kuyper, *Principles of Sacred Theology*, trans. J. Henrick de Vries (Eerdmans, 1954), 373; Muller, "Kuyper and Bavinck," 12.

18. Kuyper, *Principles of Sacred Theology*, 374; Muller, "Kuyper and Bavinck," 14.

19. Calvin, *Institutes*, I.iii.1.

20. Kuyper, *Principles of Sacred Theology*, 378.

21. Bavinck, *Reformed Dogmatics*, IV:34.

universal prevenient but resistible grace in the creation as in the theology of Jacob Arminius (1560–1609).[22] Rather, grace presupposes nature, or in Paul's address at Mars Hill, Paul establishes the creation truth of God's existence to pave the way to appeal to Jesus, the incarnate God of salvation. Understanding the relationship between general and special revelation and natural and supernatural theology gives us the necessary framework to comprehend better Paul's arguments at Mars Hill.

Paul appeals to both general and special revelation and uses natural and supernatural theological truths in his address to the philosophers at Mars Hill. He does not, however, appeal to the natural theology of the Stoics in a naive or uncritical manner. Paul filters their natural theology through the corrective lenses of Scripture so that the philosophers no longer looked upon the world with blurry eyes. Noteworthy is that even though both quotations come from poems about Zeus, Paul never invokes this name. Yahweh, the one true God, is the Lord of heaven and earth. Moreover, when Paul uproots these statements from the pagan poets, he carefully replants them in the pure soil of special revelation when he explains that God created all people from one man, Adam, a claim that contradicts the notion that Zeus immediately created women. God neither haggles nor negotiates with other gods in his sovereign rule over the creation. God is also not like any of the gold or silver idols that littered Athens, statues "formed by the art and imagination of man" (Acts 17:29). However, as much as Paul appeals to natural theological arguments, he does not linger on the shores of general revelation. He moves to special revelation and discusses Christ, the final judgment, the need to repent of sin and unbelief, and the resurrection from the dead (Acts 17:30–31).

Even though Paul clearly employs both general and special revelation in his address at Mars Hill, the question persists: Why was Paul willing to quote pagan poets along with the teaching of Scripture? Appealing to God's creation is one thing, but why would he draw from the writings of sinners, works obviously contaminated with idolatrous and erroneous ideas? This question has not escaped scholars, some of whom have argued that Paul's speech is "alien to the New Testament" and is all too Stoic.[23] People sense the potentially problematic nature of going beyond natural revelation and using points drawn from Stoic natural theology. Yet, others in the historic Reformed tradition are not bothered by Paul's move. Paul's appeal was not an unfiltered use of raw Stoic natural theology, but as noted above, he refracted their knowledge

22. Bavinck, *Reformed Dogmatics*, IV:35. On universal prevenient grace in Arminius's theology, see J. V. Fesko, *Arminius and the Reformed Tradition: Grace and the Doctrine of Salvation* (Reformation Heritage Books, 2022), 13–30.

23. Martin Dibelius, *Studies in the Acts of the Apostles* (SCM Press, 1956), 63.

through Scripture. As Calvin explains, Paul quoted the pagan poets to shame the Athenians and to appeal to "no other fountain than nature and universal reason."[24] In other words, Paul was not appealing so much to the pagan poets but rather to the truth of God's existence that they knew and recorded in their poems, however clouded it was by error. Others have come to similar conclusions.

Joseph Addison Alexander (1809–1860), who was a biblical studies professor with Charles Hodge (1797–1878) at Princeton Theological Seminary, explains: "The use here made of heathen testimony is not an abuse, or even accommodation, of the language quoted, which although applied by Aratus and addressed by Cleanthes to a mythological divinity, could only be regarded, even by themselves, as true of the Supreme God, as distinguished from all others."[25] Paul appealed to the Stoic notion of Zeus but purified the idea through the filter of Scripture. Likewise, fellow Princetonian J. Gresham Machen (1881–1937) writes:

> One of the clearest instances of the broader use of the figure of fatherhood is found in the speech of Paul at Athens (Acts 17:28): "For we are also His offspring," Here it is plainly the relation in which God stands to all men, whether Christians or not, which is in mind. But the words form part of an hexameter line and are taken from a pagan poet; they are not represented as part of the gospel, but merely as belonging to the common meeting ground which Paul discovered in speaking to his pagan hearers.[26]

In Paul's hands, general and special revelation, natural and supernatural theology, work in tandem in the task of apologetics. Paul makes arguments from truth embedded in the creation and even in the literature of his pagan audience because, in the end, all truth belongs to God. But to what end did Paul make these apologetical arguments?

Apologetics and Worship

Remember that apologetics is one of the chief means by which Christians engage and tear down idols of unbelief. Recall that Paul's original motivation for preaching in Athens was the rampant idolatry that he saw—disordered love and the consequent false worship. Calvin explains: "Since it is certain that

24. John Calvin, *Acts 14–28*, Calvin's New Testament Commentaries, ed. David W. Torrance and Thomas F. Torrance, trans. John W. Fraser (Eerdmans, 1995), 120.

25. Joseph Addison Alexander, *The Acts of the Apostles*, vol. 2 (Charles Scribner, 1857), 157.

26. J. Gresham Machen, *Christianity and Liberalism* (Eerdmans, 1923), 61.

Paul is inveighing here against the common superstition of all the Gentiles, because they wished to worship God under corporeal figures, the general doctrine must be held that God is worshipped wrongly and irreverently, and His truth is turned into a lie as often as His majesty is represented by some visible form, as the same Paul teaches in the first chapter of Romans (v. 25)."[27] The only way Paul could turn the Athenians away from their idolatry was to turn them to the one true God, and he did so by teaching them truths from special revelation. Paul declaimed to the philosophers: "The God who made the world and everything in it, being Lord of heaven and earth, does not live in temples made by man, nor is he served by human hands, as though he needed anything, since he himself gives to all mankind life and breath and everything" (Acts 17:24–25). In this statement he draws upon Psalm 50:12–13, "If I were hungry, I would not tell you, for the world and its fullness are mine. Do I eat the flesh of bulls or drink the blood of goats?"[28] Zeus is not like Yahweh; he does not have aseity (self-existence)—he was born—there was a time when Zeus was not. According to some Greek myths, a goat named Amalthea raised Zeus.[29]

Greek myths portray Zeus using violence to get his way, and thus he would sling lightning bolts as his preferred weapon of choice. He was emotionally distraught when he learned the fate of Hector, who was killed by Achilles during the battle for Troy. Zeus demanded that Achilles release Hector's body so it could be honorably buried. In Greek mythology there is a real give and take, a tit for tat, relationship between the gods and mere mortals. This is something that even some unbelievers such as Roman orator Cicero (106–43 BC) found distasteful:

> They are actually represented as liable to passions and emotions—we hear of their being in love, sorrowful, angry; according to the myths they even engage in wars and battles, and that not only when as in Homer two armies are contending and the gods take sides and intervene on their behalf, but they actually fought wars of their own, for instance with the Titans and with the Giants. These stories and these beliefs are utterly foolish; they are stuffed with nonsense and absurdity of all sorts.[30]

In Greek mythology the gods were all too human, and so Paul contrasts Yahweh with Zeus to make the difference palpable between God and this so-called god. This is also why Paul goes after the physical idols, the statues,

27. Calvin, *Acts 14–28*, 122.
28. Pardigon, *Paul Against the Idols*, 159.
29. Hamilton, *Mythology*, 407.
30. Cicero, *De Natura Deorum et Academica*, trans. H. Rackham, Loeb Classical Library (Harvard University Press, 1951), II.xxviii.70–71 (190–93).

that he saw scattered throughout Athens. How can someone make an image with their own hands out of inert material and then bow down to it as if it were animate, even a god? So even though Paul found some common ground between Christianity and the Stoic notions of deity, this did not keep him both from purifying the knowledge that he did employ and at many other points directly contradicting it so that he could turn the philosophers to worship the one, true, living God. Paul employed apologetics for the sake of worship. He engaged the idols to destroy them.

Conclusion

Paul's encounter with the philosophers at Mars Hill shows us a biblical example of employing both books of creation and Scripture in the task of apologetics. Apologetics is not merely for the sake of winning arguments but for tearing down idols—for turning people away from their false gods and turning them to the one, true, living God—the Triune God of Scripture. Apologetics is all about ordering the disordered love of unbelievers. Far from taking a Scripture-only approach, Paul adjusted his methodology depending upon his audience. If he addressed Jews, then he appealed to their common ground of Old Testament Scripture. When he spoke to gentiles, he used the common meeting ground of the book of nature. There are times in defending the faith when the apologist can appeal to natural revelation in the effort to connect with unbelievers. Paul began with nature, but he also interlaced his arguments and eventually rested wholly upon special revelation as he announced salvation through Christ and the resurrection from the dead. In other words, while we can build bridges to dialogue with unbelievers, we build these bridges in order eventually to collide head-on with their unbelief. Given this twofold method of using Scripture and nature, it behooves us to read the Bible with an eye to the written page and an eye toward the creation—to gaze upon the grandeur of God's good cosmos. Used in concert with Scripture, the book of nature is powerful to tear down every argument that sets itself up against the truth of God, but it can also reassure our own hearts in times of doubt or fear that the God of Scripture is also the God of creation. But we must remember, apologetics exists because worship does not. Worship is ultimate, not apologetics, because the Triune God is ultimate, not humans. When the age is over and the countless millions of the saved fall on their faces before the throne of God, apologetics will be no more, and only worship will remain.[31] The love of God is the goal and aim of all apologetics.

31. John Piper, *Let the Nations Be Glad*, 3rd ed. (Baker Academic, 2010), 15.

4

Paul's Shipwreck

Confronting Unbelief

Thesis 4: Acts 27 shows that sometimes there is not a meeting of the minds as in Acts 17 but a head-on collision with unbelief.

Some of the Epicurean and Stoic philosophers also conversed with [Paul].

—Acts 17:18

Poggio Bracciolini (1380–1459) was a papal legate tasked with scouring monastic libraries throughout Europe to find rare books to add to the papal collection. As he rummaged through the libraries and inspected volume after volume, he encountered the last known copy of an ancient book by the Epicurean poet and philosopher Lucretius (99–55 BC), *On the Nature of Things*. We might not think that one book could change the world, but best-selling author and Harvard professor Stephen Greenblatt suggests otherwise. Greenblatt wrote his Pulitzer-prize winning book, *The Swerve*, where he documents the ripple effect that occurred in the wake of the discovery of *On the Nature of Things*.[1] Lucretius's ancient book argued that the world was made of atoms, but as they raced and swirled about, sometimes atoms swerved ever so slightly and collided into other atoms to produce unpredictable events and chaos. As innocuous as

1. Stephen Greenblatt, *The Swerve: How the World Became Modern* (Norton, 2011).

this theory might seem, Professor Greenblatt suggests this little book spread throughout Europe and influenced thinkers such as Voltaire (1694–1778), David Hume (1711–1776), Galileo (1564–1642), Thomas Jefferson (1743–1826), and even Albert Einstein (1879–1955). According to Greenblatt, Lucretius's wee book played a significant role in making the modern world that we know today. Yet, what has Lucretius's book to do with the apostle Paul's shipwreck in Acts 27, and how does the connection between Lucretius and Paul relate to apologetics?

Lucretius's book represents a major stream of pagan thought that was current in Paul's day, and Luke includes Paul's shipwreck to counter Epicurean false teaching. The historical account of Paul's shipwreck is a subtle apologetic refutation of Epicurean thought. Paul had something of a meeting of the minds with the Stoic philosophers when he quoted their own poets to them in his address at Mars Hill. Paul, of course, refracted their natural theological claims through the corrective lenses of special revelation. But at other times, things are different. *This chapter therefore argues the thesis that Acts 27 shows that sometimes there is not a meeting of the minds as in Acts 17 but a head-on collision with unbelief.* Luke's inclusion of Paul's shipwreck in the book of Acts is just such a collision. Luke includes three features in Paul's shipwreck that counter Epicurean claims: (1) our lives are in the sovereign all-encompassing providence of God; (2) we can pray to God knowing that he can and will intervene on our behalf; and (3) we worship a God who is able to perform miracles. These three points (providence, prayer, and miracles) strike against Epicurean claims to the contrary—that we are subject to the swerve, the random collision of atoms that produces chaos, that God is unconcerned with us, so prayer is pointless, and that there is no such thing as miracles. Studying the apologetic significance of Paul's shipwreck account both instructs us how to counter the claims of unbelief but also reminds us of the perennial relevance of Scripture's truth claims. Moreover, Acts 27 reinforces the idea that apologetics and worship go hand in hand, as Luke's inclusion of Paul's shipwreck once again shows unbelievers that they must turn away from their idols (in this case, the worship of random chance) and believe in and worship the one, true, living God—to order their disordered love.

This chapter demonstrates the apologetic significance of Acts 27 with an examination of Lucretius's main claims against providence, prayer, and miracles. It then surveys the events of Paul's shipwreck in Acts 27 to show how Luke counters the Epicurean notions of the swerve. Third, the chapter explores how Luke aims Acts 27 at the goal of worship—the whole chapter pulses with the love of God in Christ both for Paul and lost sinners. Fourth, and finally, the chapter briefly examines the significance of Luke's apologetic against the Epicurean rejections of providence, prayer, and miracles. Lucretius's influence upon the present-day culture demonstrates that the desire to disenchant the world long predates the Enlightenment and Reformation but goes back before the days of Christ. But far from disenchanting the world, Lucretius shows that humans have sought to harness divinity through knowledge—they have sought to enchant themselves with the mantle of deity. Acts 27 stands as a bulwark against this illegitimate quest for deity and reminds us once again that apologetics does not deal with unbelief but with idolatry.

Lucretius and the Swerve

We know from Paul's encounter with the philosophers at Mars Hill that Epicurean beliefs were a common presence in the first-century world, evidenced by the fact that Epicurean philosophers were present to hear Paul's Areopagus address (Acts 17:18). Lucretius's work *On the Nature of Things* was part of the corpus that defined Epicurean thought. Within this little tome, Lucretius outlines three chief claims where he denies providence, prayer, and miracles.

Providence

The belief that the gods providentially controlled events in the world was commonplace in antiquity, especially among Stoic philosophers. Cicero (106–43 BC), for example, argued, "The world is governed by divine providence"—that is, "The world is governed by the providence of the gods."[2] He further describes providence by writing that "the world and all its parts were set in order at the beginning and have been governed for all time by divine providence," which he proves through three points. First, the claim rests on the presupposition that the gods exist. Second, that the cosmos is under the sway of sentient nature, by which it reveals beauty. And third, the wonder and marvel that people sense from the celestial and terrestrial creation is evidence of divine providence.[3] Lucretius and the Epicureans, however, were unpersuaded by the Stoic claims of providence.

Lucretius believed that people trembled in fear at the thought of the ebb and flow of events in the world because they did not know what would happen next: "For just as children tremble and fear all things in blind darkness, so

2. Cicero, *De Natura Deorum Academica*, trans. H. Rackham, Loeb Classical Library (Harvard University Press, 1951), II.73–74 (194–95).

3. Cicero, *De Natura Deorum*, II.75 (196–97).

we in the light fear, at times, things that are no more to be feared than what children shiver at in the dark and imagine to be at hand. This terror of the mind, therefore, and this gloom must be dispelled, not by the sun's rays nor the bright shafts of day, but by the aspect and law of nature."[4] In other words, if people rightly understood the nature of things, the laws of nature, if they were philosophically astute, they would neither fear nor tremble at the turn of events in the world. Just as Cicero noted that the presupposition of providence was the existence of the gods, so Lucretius believed the antithesis—namely, one had to presuppose that the gods did not create the world. Lucretius writes: "The nature of the universe has by no means been made for us through divine power."[5] Instead of the divine providential control of nature, the world was subject to the random activity of atoms. Atoms invisibly move about and influence the course of events when they unpredictably "swerve a little from their course, just so much as you might call a change of motion."[6] Given the absence of providence and the presence of the swerve, "nature is to be free at once and rid of proud masters, herself doing all by herself of her own accord, without the help of the gods."[7] In fact, far from controlling events in the world, the gods were indifferent to the unfolding events of history: "Before me appear the gods in their majesty and their peaceful abodes, which no winds ever shake nor clouds besprinkle with rain, which no snow congealed by the bitter frost with its white fall, mars them; but the air ever cloudless encompasses them and laughs with its light spread abroad."[8] The gods rest undisturbed in their peaceful repose indifferent to the events of the world.

Prayer

If the gods are indifferent to the events of the world, then the Epicurean rejection of prayer naturally follows. If the gods did not create the world and do not providentially control it, then it is foolish to attribute events in the world to them.[9] Why, then, worship the gods? Why "show oneself with covered head, turning towards a stone and approaching every altar, none to fall prostrate upon the ground and to spread open the palms before shrines of the gods with the blood of beasts in showers and to link vow to vow; but

4. Lucretius, *On the Nature of Things*, trans. W. H. D. Rouse, Loeb Classical Library (Harvard University Press, 1975), II.55–60 (98–99).

5. Lucretius, *On the Nature of Things*, II.180 (108–9).

6. Lucretius, *On the Nature of Things*, II.220 (112–13).

7. Lucretius, *On the Nature of Things*, II.1095 (180–81).

8. Lucretius, *On the Nature of Things*, III.15–20 (188–91).

9. Lucretius, *On the Nature of Things*, V.1181–95 (470–71).

rather to be able to survey all things with tranquil mind."[10] If we understand the nature of the swerve, then we will never vainly try to turn to the gods to seek their assistance, appease their wrath, or receive their blessing. One passage in Lucretius's work is especially relevant given Luke's inclusion of Paul's shipwreck in Acts. Lucretius gives an example of how a person should react in adversity:

> When also the supreme violence of a furious wind upon the sea sweeps over the waters the chief admiral of a fleet along with his mighty legions and elephants, does he not crave the gods' peace with vows, does he not in his panic seek with prayers the peace of the winds and favoring breezes? But all in vain, since none the less he is often caught up in the furious hurricane and driven upon the shoals of death.[11]

When an admiral sailing upon a storm-tossed sea panics and seeks the assistance of the gods through prayer, he does so needlessly. If he truly understood the nature of things, he would instead serenely gaze into the face of death and know that he was facing the random chaos of the swerve. In such knowledge we can face our natural end of death with dignity rather than fear.

Miracles

If the gods neither created the world nor control the events in it, and prayer to them is useless, then the gods neither intervene in the world nor perform miracles. All too often people fear the gods and thus attribute events that transpire in the world to them, but the gods live in their tranquil repose unconcerned with human desires and fears.[12] "Men are unable to see the causes of these works at all, and think them to be done by divine power," writes Lucretius.[13] In other words, what people attribute to the gods and their apparent miraculous interventions is actually the atomic random swerve; people are ignorant of the truth and thus attribute to divine power what naturally occurs. Lucretius explains:

> This is to understand the true nature of the fiery thunderbolt, and to see by what power it plays its part; not by unrolling the scrolls of Tyrrhenian charms, vainly to search for signs of the hidden purpose of the gods, to learn whence

10. Lucretius, *On the Nature of Things*, V.1200–05 (470–73).
11. Lucretius, *On the Nature of Things*, V.1226–35 (472–75).
12. Lucretius, *On the Nature of Things*, VI.68–70 (496–99).
13. Lucretius, *On the Nature of Things*, VI.90–91 (498–99).

> the flying fire has come or into which of the two quarters it has turned hence, in what manner it has penetrated through walled places and after winning mastery how it has conveyed itself out, of what harm the stroke of a bold from heaven can do.[14]

Why hold on to a "Tyrrhenian charm" (a good luck amulet to ensure that you have a good journey or vainly seek to divine the intention of the gods)? Appealing to the gods is foolish when understanding nature is the preferred path to peace in the face of peril. Lucretius's rejection of providence, prayer, and miracles sets the stage for Luke's account of Paul's shipwreck.

Paul's Shipwreck

Luke's account of Paul's journey across the sea is not unique to the Bible, as accounts of sea journeys appear in ancient literature.[15] Think, for example, of Homer's *Odyssey*, where Odysseus suffers shipwreck and is befriended by the Phaeacians who help him along the way. But Odysseus was at the whim of the gods on Mount Olympus, unlike Paul, who was in the providential care of the one, true, living God. Luke begins the account of Paul's journey as the apostle warned the ship's owner about the dangers they faced (Acts 27:10). Paul was an experienced sea traveler, as he elsewhere recounts that he was shipwrecked three times and spent an entire night and day adrift on the sea (2 Cor 11:25–26). So, his concern was based in experience, not fear.[16] Once they set sail, Paul's ship quickly encountered unfriendly seas, and so the crew took measures to weather the storm by securing the ship's boat, jettisoning the cargo, and throwing the tackle overboard (Acts 27:16, 18, 19). But by the third day, Luke reported, "All hope of our being saved was at last abandoned" (Acts 27:20). The sinister sea looked as if it would swallow Paul's ship, which interestingly places us in the same place as Lucretius's admiral who resigned himself to the fate of the swerve rather than pray for the providential and miraculous intervention of the gods.

Providence

Luke reports that, when it seemed as if all hope was lost, Paul made a speech to his shipmates:

14. Lucretius, *On the Nature of Things*, VI.379–86 (520–21).
15. Darrell L. Bock, *Acts*, BECNT (Baker Academic, 2007), 726.
16. Bock, *Acts*, 726.

> Men, you should have listened to me and not have set sail from Crete and incurred this injury and loss. Yet now I urge you to take heart, for there will be no loss of life among you, but only of the ship. For this very night there stood before me an angel of God to whom I belong and whom I worship, and he said, "Do not be afraid, Paul; you must stand before Caesar. And behold, God has granted you all those who sail with you." So take heart, men, for I have faith in God that it will be exactly as I have been told. (Acts 27:21–25)

Speeches like Paul's in the face of certain doom were common in ancient literature. As Odysseus set out upon a storm-tossed sea, he proclaimed:

> Ah me, wretched that I am! What is to befall me at the last? I fear me that verily all that the goddess said was true, when she declared that on the sea, before ever I came to my native land, I should fill up my measure of woes; and lo, all this now is being brought to pass. In such wise does Zeus overcast the broad heaven with clouds, and has stirred up the sea, and the blasts of all manner of winds sweep upon me; now is my utter destruction sure.[17]

In this case, the two speeches have similar settings in the storm-tossed sea, but they hold out different ends—fear fills Odysseus's speech, whereas Paul's address brims with hope.[18] Fear versus hope marks the two speeches, but Luke's account is completely antithetical to Lucretius's beliefs, who argued the gods were indifferent to the world's events and human suffering. Luke shows that there are not gods but rather only one God, the God of Israel, and this one God was deeply concerned for Paul and his companions, so he sent an angel to inform them that all would be well. Moreover, unlike Lucretius, who believed that the world's events were driven by random swerving atoms, the one true God providentially cared for Paul and all aboard the stricken vessel. In God's providence and sovereign ordination of all things, Paul would eventually stand before Caesar, so God infallibly promised the apostle that he would see him through the dangers, toils, and snares of this storm.

Prayer

Lucretius believed prayer was useless because the gods were indifferent to human events and were not providentially governing the world. The God of Scripture, however, is the antithesis to these false beliefs, which is why Paul prays on two different occasions amid his peril upon the sea. When Paul's

17. Homer, *Odyssey*, vol. 1, trans. A. T. Murray, Loeb Classical Library (Harvard University Press, 1945), V.299–305 (190–93).

18. Bock, *Acts*, 739.

ship reached the fourteenth night (Acts 27:27), Paul and his companions "prayed for the day to come" (Acts 27:29). Luke's point is that God, unlike Lucretius's gods, is not indifferent to the sufferings of his people. In the face of the storm, Paul trusted in God's message to him from the angel, namely, "Not a hair is to perish from the head of any of you" (Acts 27:34). Paul also trusted in God's providential care and thus gave thanks for the food they ate. Paul elsewhere explains that God does care for his people, which is why he instructs us to pray and comforts us by telling us that he hears our prayers: "Likewise the Spirit helps us in our weakness. For we do not know what to pray for as we ought, but the Spirit himself intercedes for us with groanings too deep for words. And he who searches hearts knows what is the mind of the Spirit, because the Spirit intercedes for the saints according to the will of God" (Rom 8:26–27). Paul prayed because he knew God was providentially caring for him, would listen to his cries, and had the power to deliver him.

Miracles

We know the rest of the story of Paul's shipwreck: God safely delivered Paul and his fellow travelers. This is not to say that the journey was easy, as there were unquestionably harrowing moments; the deliverance was also not a natural event, as God miraculously delivered all who were on the ship as he promised. Paul's safe arrival is evidence enough that God performs miracles, which contradicts Lucretius's rejection of them. Paul was not an ignorant, uneducated peasant who could not tell the difference between natural and supernatural events. He looked upon the stormy sea and knew his end was assured death were it not for the supernatural message God delivered to him through the angel. That God sent word of their miraculous deliverance through an angel underscored the point that this was in no way a natural event—Paul's deliverance was not the result of the random and unpredictable collision of atoms. The swerve did not deliver Paul—God did.

Luke places an exclamation point on Paul's miraculous deliverance by recording the events that transpired when he arrived on dry land. As Paul was gathering firewood, a serpent darted out from a fire and bit Paul. The people thought it was venomous and Paul would die. The narrative records this when the people prematurely concluded, "No doubt this man is a murderer. Though he has escaped from the sea, Justice has not allowed him to live" (Acts 28:4).[19] An Epicurean witnessing these events might exclaim, "Look! The swerve! Atoms randomly collided and caused the viper to bite Paul despite his

19. Bock, *Acts*, 742–44.

supposedly 'miraculous' deliverance from his shipwreck." Yet, God promised to deliver Paul, and he kept his word, as Paul "shook off the creature into the fire and suffered no harm" (Acts 28:5). God miraculously delivered Paul from the serpent's bite. The people of Malta were amazed and even thought Paul was a god (Acts 28:6). Paul likely corrected this error as he did in Lystra when the people thought Paul was Hermes (Acts 14:8–15). Nevertheless, the point still stands: contrary to the Epicurean denial of miracles, God miraculously delivered Paul from death, both from the shipwreck and from the viper's venomous bite. Luke's account of Paul's shipwreck is an apologetic defense of the biblical doctrine of God: his providential control over the creation, the legitimacy of prayer, and the reality of divine miracles.

God's Love in Christ

Luke includes Paul's shipwreck to counter apologetically the Epicurean rejection of providence, prayer, and miracles, but we must situate this defense of providence within the broader framework of God's unfolding plan of salvation. Luke's aim is not merely to disprove erroneous Epicurean ideas but rather to keep the church focused upon the gospel of Christ. Like Paul, who wove together general and special revelation in his address at the Areopagus, Luke weaves the natural theology of providence together with the supernatural theology of the gospel. Some might object, however, because they believe that providence is a teaching of special, not general, revelation. One must recall, however, that Cicero taught a doctrine of providence, as did the Stoic philosopher Seneca (4 BC–AD 65) in his work *De Providentia*.[20] John Calvin (1509–1564) observed that the ancient philosophers taught a doctrine of providence but one that differed from the teaching of Scripture in a number of respects: the philosophers "have no apprehension of the special care of God, from which alone his paternal favor is known."[21] Like Paul at Mars Hill, Luke arguably makes an implicit connection with the Stoic doctrine of providence but corrects it through the lenses of Scripture. Recall that, within the larger context of Acts, the purpose of Paul's journey to Rome was to testify to Christ: "Take courage," Jesus tells Paul, "for as you have testified to the facts about me in Jerusalem, so you must testify also in Rome" (Acts 23:11). God's providential care for Paul served the greater purpose of the gospel of Christ.

20. Seneca, *De Providentia*, in *Moral Essays*, vol. 1, trans. John W. Basore, Loeb Classical Library (Harvard University Press, 1928), 3–47.

21. John Calvin, *Institutes of the Christian Religion*, trans. Henry Beveridge (Calvin Translation Society, 1845), I.xvi.1.

When he beautifully expounds the significance of God's providential purpose, Paul makes a christologically fine point to his doctrine when he writes: "And we know that for those who love God all things work together for good, for those who are called according to his purpose. For those whom he foreknew he also predestined to be conformed to the image of his Son, in order that he might be the firstborn among many brothers" (Rom 8:28–29). Given the goal of conformity to Christ and the propagation of the gospel, we too can look to God's providence knowing that he cares for us. As Jesus teaches,

> Consider the lilies of the field, how they grow: they neither toil nor spin, yet I tell you, even Solomon in all his glory was not arrayed like one of these. But if God so clothes the grass of the field, which today is alive and tomorrow is thrown into the oven, will he not much more clothe you, O you of little faith? Therefore do not be anxious, saying, "What shall we eat?" or "What shall we drink?" or "What shall we wear?" For the Gentiles seek after all these things, and your heavenly Father knows that you need them all. But seek first the kingdom of God and his righteousness, and all these things will be added to you. (Matt 6:28–33)

God providentially cares for his people, and in the words of the Westminster Confession of Faith, "foreordains whatsoever comes to pass" (3.1), and he does "uphold, direct, dispose, and govern all creatures, actions, and things, from the greatest even to the least, by his most wise and holy providence" (5.1). That he providentially oversees the creation means that we can pray to him amid our trials and that if he so chooses, God can miraculously intervene as he did in Paul's shipwreck. Again, in the words of the Westminster Confession, "God, in his ordinary providence, maketh use of means, yet is free to work without, above, and against them, at his pleasure" (5.3). But in his providence, God does not merely move pieces around the chessboard of the creation, indifferent to our suffering—pawns in God's greater plan. Rather, he ordains every event in our lives to glorify himself in the gospel of Christ and conform us more to Christ's holy image. In other words, God's providence is about Christ, his gospel, and our conformity unto his image. I will address this point in greater detail in a later chapter, but in all these things we must remember that the events in our lives pass through the nail-scarred hands of Jesus Christ.

Significance

If Professor Greenblatt is right about the influence of Lucretius's *On the Nature of Things*, this means that the roots of our present culture's idolatry lie partially in the ancient errors of Lucretius's little tome. Enlightenment historian Jonathan Israel observes that Poggio Bracciolini's discovery of Lucretius's work led to people employing it as a challenge to the status quo, a seed planted in the intellectual ferment of the Renaissance era that gradually developed into a larger system of anti-Christian thought.[22] Israel shows that Lucretius influenced Baruch Spinoza (1632–1677) to reject religious authority.[23] Lucretius was also an influence upon Nietzschean atheistic philosophies.[24] Friedrich Nietzsche (1844–1900) read Lucretius and saw its anti-Christ character: "One has but to read Lucretius to know *what* Epicurus made war upon—*not* paganism, but 'Christianity,' which is to say, the corruption of souls by means of the concepts of guilt, punishment and immortality."[25] Thomas Jefferson rejected revelation, miracles, the supernatural, and the intervention of any god in the creation. He gleaned some of his views from Lucretius's *On the Nature of the Gods*, of which he owned five copies. Jefferson believed that the genuine doctrines of Epicurus contained "everything rational in moral philosophy which Greece and Rome have left us."[26]

Lucretius's influence reaches even into twentieth-century physics, as one no less than Albert Einstein wrote the forward to a German edition of *On the Nature of Things*. Einstein observed:

> One sees here how an independent man equipped with lively senses and reasoning, endowed with scientific and speculative curiosity, a man who has not even the faintest notion of the results of today's science that we are taught in childhood, before we can consciously, much less critically, confront them, imagines the world. . . . He states as the primary objective of his work the liberation of humanity from the slavish fear, induced by religion and superstition, that he sees as nourished and exploited by priests for their own purposes.[27]

Einstein believed that Lucretius gave voice to modern concerns—to seek the cause of things apart from the shackles of religion. Some might cite Einstein's statement as evidence of the desire to disenchant the world, to place nature under humanity's thralldom. Yet, we must remember what lies at the heart

22. Jonathan I. Israel, *The Enlightenment That Failed: Ideas, Revolution, and Democratic Defeat* (Oxford University Press, 2020), 76.

23. Israel, *Enlightenment*, 80–91, 83–84.

24. Israel, *Enlightenment*, 88; Charles Taylor, *A Secular Age* (The Belknap Press, 2007), 599.

25. Friedrich Nietzsche, *The Anti-Christ*, trans. H. L. Mencken (Alfred A. Knopf, 1931), §58 (170–71); also see A. H. J. Knight, "Nietzsche and Epicurean Philosophy," *Philosophy* 8/32 (1933): 431–45.

26. As cited in Israel, *Enlightenment*, 96.

27. Albert Einstein, "Introduction to Lucretius, *De Rerum Natura*," in *The Collected Papers of Albert Einstein*, vol. 14 (Princeton University Press, 2015), 255–56.

of a sinful misuse of enchantment—namely, the desire to harness deity. When Satan first tempted Adam and Eve in the garden, he held out the prospects of becoming divine through the tree of *knowledge*: "For God knows that when you eat of it your eyes will be opened, and you will be like God, knowing good and evil" (Gen 3:5). Humanity has always believed that knowledge is the path to divinity and unlocking the secrets of enchantment.

For these reasons the Reformers saw Epicureanism as a great threat to Christianity. Long before Nietzsche detected the spirit of anti-Christ in Lucretius, Calvin and other Reformed theologians countered the errors in *On the Nature of Things*. Calvin characterized Lucretius as "licentious" and his work as "profane verses."[28] Commenting more broadly on Epicurean thought, Calvin places his finger on the pulse of the rejection of providence: "Here also they substitute nature in the place of God."[29] Lucretius does not disenchant the world as he thinks or as later philosophers like Nietzsche and scientists like Einstein believed. Rather, he turns the cosmos into *theos*; the material creation takes the place of God. Calvin runs with this diagnosis and presses the question: "Do all the treasures of heavenly wisdom concur with the government of a worm five feet in length?"[30] In other words, Lucretius makes grand claims and yet his own limited human perspective begs the question: How do you know such things? Does not God's revelation in the creation say something different? And in the case of Luke's inspired record of Paul's shipwreck, does not God's special revelation say something different?

Conclusion

Even if Bracciolini had never discovered Lucretius's *On the Nature of Things* and dispersed his notions throughout Europe, the same ideas would have originated and circulated from another source. We would know them by a different name, but they would still haunt the world. Ever since the garden and the fall of humanity, people have sought divinity through knowledge, and Lucretius is just one more person in a long line of sinners who try to unseat God from his throne in the heavens. Lucretius's rejection of providence, prayer, and miracles finds its antithesis in Luke's account of Paul's shipwreck and teaches us that God providentially cares for the creation but especially

28. Calvin, *Institutes*, I.v.5; cf. Nicolaas H. Gootjes, "Calvin on Epicurus and the Epicureans: Background to a Remark in Article 13 of the Belgic Confession," *Calvin Theological Journal* 40 (2005): 33–48.

29. Calvin, *Institutes*, I.v.4.

30. Calvin, *Institutes*, I.v.4.

his people. Luke shows us that the miserable and sinful worms that we are can nevertheless pray to the sovereign of the cosmos and rest assured that he will respond. And we know from Paul's miraculous deliverance from the shipwreck and venomous viper that God can intervene and often intervenes in the lives of his saints to protect them and see to their ultimate conformity unto the image of Christ. Beyond these observations, the abiding influence of Lucretius reminds us of two important truths for apologetics. First, as the preacher in Ecclesiastes has observed, "there is nothing new under the sun. Is there a thing of which it is said, 'See, this is new'? It has been already in the ages before us" (Eccl 1:9b–10). The quest to harness deity is as old as the creation itself. Second, Luke versus Lucretius reminds us that the Scriptures breathe the air of God's truth—truths that are never outdated or irrelevant. Yes, as with Paul's address at Mars Hill, sometimes we can cull truths from the creation and even the writings of unbelievers to create a bridge—to stand upon the common ground of creation—so we can share the good news of Christ. But Luke reminds us through Paul's shipwreck that sometimes we must be prepared for the head-on collision—the clash between Christ and anti-Christ—but we can rest assured that, in the end, God's love for sinners in Christ through the Spirit wins the battle.

5

Calvin and Cicero

The Books of Nature and Scripture in Calvin's Apologetics

> **Thesis 5:** Historic Reformed apologetics has followed the apostle Paul's approach to defending the faith, evident in the opening chapters of John Calvin's *Institutes of the Christian Religion*.

> In attestation of his wondrous wisdom, both the heavens and the earth present us with innumerable proofs which astronomy, medicine, and all the natural sciences, are designed to illustrate but proofs which force themselves on the notice of the most illiterate peasant, who cannot open his eyes without beholding them.
>
> —John Calvin, *Institutes*, I.v.2

Myths about the Reformation abound in popular theological literature, such as the claim that the Protestant Reformation was a complete break with the medieval past. According to John Frame, John Calvin's (1509–1564) epistemology (theory of knowledge) was a "sharp departure from the patterns of medieval and Renaissance philosophy," and Calvin makes "no accommodations to Greek philosophical views, or to intellectual autonomy."[1] Frame's claim echoes the earlier opinions of August Lang (1867–1945), who argued that Philip Melanchthon (1497–1560) introduced natural law into the Reformation, which is a compromise with fallen human

1. John Frame, *A History of Western Philosophy and Theology* (P&R, 2015), 174.

reason. Melanchthon's cordial relationship to natural law supposedly stands in stark contrast to Calvin's view, who was no friend of the idea and gave almost no attention to the topic; only later Calvinists introduced the topic for use in theology.[2] Lang was part of a cadre of twentieth-century historians and theologians who posited an antithesis between Calvin and the medieval past, on the one hand, and a subsequent bastardization of Calvin's theology by his followers, on the other hand. Karl Barth (1886–1968), for example, writes: "The possibility of a real knowledge by natural man of the true God, derived from creation, is, according to Calvin, a possibility in principle, but not in fact, not a possibility to be realized by us."[3] Barth argued that Thomas Aquinas (1225–1274) was the chief representative of natural theology, not Calvin; later Calvinists turned to the forbidden fruit of natural theology.

Similarly, Cornelius Van Til (1895–1987) tried to blanket his own apologetic program with the mantle of Calvin, who he believed had made a complete break with scholastic theology.[4] Van Til lobbied vigorously for the idea that Reformed theology needed to outgrow scholasticism's conceptions of natural theology and natural ethics, an implicit acknowledgment of Calvin versus the so-called Calvinists.[5] Calvin was not scholastic, whereas his followers were. But unlike Lang and Frame, Van Til admits that Calvin employed natural theology and pagan authorities in his theology, but it was only to render the unbeliever inexcusable before the divine bar.[6] What was implicit in Van Til's call for Reformed theology to outgrow scholasticism—namely, Calvin versus the Calvinists—is explicit elsewhere in his corpus: "But after Calvin the everlasting temptation besetting all Christians, especially sophisticated Christians, to make friends with those that are of Cain's lineage proved too much for many Lutheran and Reformed theologians and so Lutheran and Reformed Scholasticism was begotten and born."[7] Calvin's followers succumbed to the siren call of scholasticism and corrupted the Genevan's otherwise biblically pure theology. To Van Til, we can cap this twentieth-century line of argumentation with the assertions of Dutch philosopher Herman Dooyeweerd (1894–1977), who taught that Christians must begin

2. August Lang, "The Reformation and Natural Law," in *Calvin and the Reformation: Four Studies* (Fleming H. Revell Co., 1909), 56–98.

3. Karl Barth, *Natural Theology: Comprising Nature and Grace by Professor Dr. Emil Brunner and the Reply No! by Dr. Karl Barth* (Wipf & Stock, 2002), 94n88, also 100–105, 107.

4. Cornelius Van Til, *Defense of the Faith*, 3rd ed. (P&R, 1955), 210.

5. Cornelius Van Til, *Common Grace and the Gospel* (P&R, 1972), 93–94.

6. Cornelius Van Til, *Introduction to Systematic Theology* (P&R, 1974), 59.

7. Cornelius Van Til, *Herman Dooyeweerd and Reformed Apologetics*, 3 Parts (Westminster Theological Seminary, 1972), III:17.

with Calvin's starting place, not with human reason, but with God and his self-disclosure in Scripture.[8]

As common as the idea is, a closer reading of Calvin shows that he was not averse to natural law or natural theology. Calvin does not begin with the self-attesting Christ of Scripture or even the doctrine of Scripture; nor is his theology a complete break with the medieval past. Instead, Calvin's *Institutes* follows the structure of Paul's Epistle to Rome, and thus, like Paul, Calvin opens his *Institutes* with an appeal to general revelation and natural theology. Calvin structures the opening of *Institutes* in this manner and draws upon Cicero's (106–43 BC) *De Natura Deorum* ("On the Nature of the Gods") so that, like Paul at Mars Hills, he builds a bridge to the claims of unbelief by showing that all people know God through the creation, but that salvation only comes through Christ. Apologetically, like Paul, Calvin employs general and special revelation, natural and supernatural theology, so that they work in concert. Calvin uses both the books of nature and Scripture in the opening pages of his *Institutes*. *This chapter defends the thesis that historic Reformed apologetics has followed the apostle Paul's approach to defending the faith, evident in the opening chapters of John Calvin's* Institutes of the Christian Religion. To demonstrate this thesis, the chapter begins with a brief survey of Cicero's *On the Nature of the Gods*. Second, the chapter examines Calvin's use of Cicero. And, third, the chapter analyzes the significance of Calvin's use of Cicero. Far from capitulating to autonomous human reason or soiling his pristine biblically pure doctrine with the beliefs of sinners, Calvin employs the books of nature and Scripture in his theology, a move that is scripturally faithful and historically illustrative for those seeking to engage the idols of our world.

Cicero's *On the Nature of the Gods*

Marcus Tullius Cicero was a Roman orator and philosopher known for many works that fill some thirty volumes in the Loeb Classical Library series.[9] He studied Greek philosophy, including Plato's (ca. 428–348 BC) *Dialogues*, and introduced it to the Romans.[10] Cicero was a chief transmitter of Stoic ideas into

8. Herman Dooyeweerd, *In the Twilight of Western Thought*, Collected Works, Series B, vol. 16, ed. D. F. M. Strauss (Paideia Press, 2012), 116; *Reformation and Scholasticism in Philosophy*, 3 vols., Collected Works, Series A, vols. 5/1–3, ed. D. F. M. Strauss, trans. Ray Togtmann (Paideia Press, 2012), I:15.

9. For a biography of Cicero, see Anthony Everitt, *Cicero: The Life and Times of Rome's Greatest Politician* (Random House, 2002).

10. Plato, *Five Dialogues: Euthyphro, Apology, Crito, Meno, Phaedo*, 2nd ed., trans. G. M. A. Grube, ed. John M. Cooper (Hackett Publishing Co., 2002).

Roman culture. Our interest in Cicero, however, is limited to his work *On the Nature of the Gods*, written around 45 BC. The work is a dialogue between an Epicurean, Stoic, and Academic skeptic, which was Cicero's own personal point of view. Within this work, Cicero makes a number of claims about the gods and, in particular, he argues that the gods can be known through the creation; that is, people can use *a posteriori* arguments and work their way back from the effect (the creation) to the cause (the existence of the gods).[11]

Cicero records the ways in which humans can know the gods, both innately and externally in the larger world. We can know the gods from human nature: "The gods exist, because nature herself has imprinted a conception of them on the minds of all mankind."[12] Humans, writes Cicero, have an innate knowledge of the gods: "For what nation or what tribe of men is there but possesses untaught some 'preconception' [*prolepsis*] of the gods."[13] The innate knowledge of the gods begins in the mind but extends to the human body. Cicero explains: "Man has been cared for by divine providence will be more readily understood if we survey the whole structure of man [*tota hominis fabricatio*] and all the conformation and perfection of human nature."[14] Humans are a *microcosmos* ("miniature world") that fits within and parallels the *macrocosmos* ("large world"), wherein the gods leave evidence of their existence and providential care:

> At this point must I not marvel that there should be anyone who can persuade himself that there are certain solid and indivisible particles of matter born along by the force of gravity, and that the fortuitous collision of those particles produces this elaborate and beautiful world. I cannot understand why he would consider it possible for this to have occurred should not also think that, if a countless number of copies of the one-and-twenty letters of the alphabet, made of gold or what you will, were thrown together into some receptable and then shaken out on to the ground, it would be possible that they should produce the *Annals* of Ennius, all ready for the reader. I doubt whether chance could possibly succeed in producing even a single verse![15]

The creation, in its beauty and order, is like a wonderfully written book that cannot be the result of random events, as in the Epicurean beliefs of fate

11. Egil Grislis, "Calvin's Use of Cicero in the Institutes I:1–5—a Case Study in Theological Method," *Archiv für Reformationsgeschicte* 62/1 (1971): 5–37.

12. Cicero, *On the Nature of the Gods Academics*, trans. H. Rackham, Loeb Classical Library (Harvard University Press, 1951), I.xvi.43 (44–45).

13. Cicero, *On the Nature of the Gods*, I.xvi.43 (44–45).

14. Cicero, *On the Nature of the Gods*, II.liv.134 (250–51).

15. Cicero, *On the Nature of the Gods*, II.xxxvii.93 (212–13).

and the swerve.[16] A person cannot throw a series of letters in a bag, shake them up, dump them on the ground, and produce the histories of Ennius (239–169 BC), a Roman poet, historian, and playwright. If we cannot produce a work of literature in this manner, then neither can the order of the universe result from random chaotic events. Cosmos (lit. "order") does not arise out of chaos; only the gods take chaos and make cosmos. If the innate and external evidence for the existence of the gods is true, then we should worship them: "But the best and also purest, holiest and most pious way of worshipping the gods is ever to venerate them with purity, sincerity and innocence both of thought and of speech. For religion has been distinguished from superstition not only by philosophers but by our ancestors," writes Cicero.[17]

Calvin's Use of Cicero

As much as twentieth-century historians and theologians claim that Calvin begins with Scripture, the self-attesting Christ, or that he makes a total break with medieval and Renaissance thought, Calvin's own pen tells a different story. In his commentary on Romans, for example, Calvin invokes the Stoic idea of *prolepsis* ("preconception") in his exegesis of Romans 2:14, "For when Gentiles, who do not have the law, by nature do what the law requires, they are a law to themselves, even though they do not have the law." Calvin writes: "Since, therefore, all nations are disposed to make laws for themselves of their own accord, and without being instructed to do so, it is beyond all doubt that they have certain ideas of justice and rectitude, which the Greeks refer to as *prolepsis*, and which are implanted by nature in the hearts of men."[18] Calvin agreed with the Greek and Stoic notion of *prolepsis*, that is, that all human beings have an innate knowledge of God.[19] In this case, like Paul did at Mars Hill by drawing a connection between the Stoic poets and scriptural truth, Calvin makes a link between the works of the law inscribed on the heart and the Stoic idea of *prolepsis*. Calvin uses natural and supernatural revelation to make the point that all people know of God's law, either through Scripture or nature.

16. Cf. Lucretius, *On the Nature of Things*, trans. W. H. D. Rouse, ed. Martin F. Smith, Loeb Classical Library (Harvard University Press, 1992).

17. Cicero, *On the Nature of the Gods*, II.xxviii.71 (192–93).

18. John Calvin, *Romans and Thessalonians*, Calvin's New Testament Commentaries, ed. David W. Torrance and Thomas F. Torrance, trans. Ross Mackenzie (Eerdmans, 1995), 48.

19. On the concept of prolepsis, see J. V. Fesko, *Reforming Apologetics: Retrieving the Classic Reformed Approach to Defending the Faith* (Baker Academic, 2019), 27–48.

Beyond his Romans commentary, Calvin makes a similar observation in his *Institutes*: "That there exists in the human mind, and indeed by natural instinct, some sense of deity [*divinitatus sensum*], we hold to be beyond dispute, since God himself, to prevent any man from pretending ignorance, has endued all men with some idea of his godhead."[20] Calvin employs other terms that convey the same idea, including: "seed of religion" (*religionis semen*), "natural instinct" (*naturali instinctu*), "light of nature" (*natura luce*), and "signs of divinity" (*divinitas signa*).[21] Noteworthy, however, is that at the opening of Calvin's *Institutes*, he purposefully does not appeal to Scripture but only to general revelation and natural theology. More will be said below about the absence of Scripture in Calvin's argument. This does not mean that Calvin appeals to the Stoic idea of *prolepsis* or the natural theology of Cicero in an unreconstructed manner; like Paul, Calvin filters his natural theology through the corrective lenses of Scripture. Nevertheless, it is significant that Calvin makes direct appeal to Cicero: "But, as a heathen tells us, there is no nation so barbarous, no race so brutish, as not to be imbued with the conviction that there is a God."[22] In the 1550 edition of the *Institutes*, Calvin has a marginal reference to Cicero's *On the Nature of the Gods*, but he removes the reference in the 1559 edition but still leaves the statement.[23] Even though he eliminates the marginal note to Cicero, he explicitly mentions him in the 1559 edition two paragraphs later to counter Cicero's claim: "I do not say with Cicero, that errors wear out by age, and that religion increases and grows better day by day."[24] At this point Calvin positively yet critically draws upon Cicero's natural theology even while he more expansively employs the Roman orator's arguments concerning the human body and the creation.

Recall that Cicero argued that the human body was evidence of the existence of the gods, especially if we "survey the whole structure of man."[25] Calvin follows this line of thought when he writes: "The same is true in regard to the structure of the human frame [*humani corporis structura*]. To determine the connection of its parts, its symmetry and beauty, with the skill of a Galen (*Lib. De Usus Partium*), requires singular acuteness; and yet all men acknowledge that the human body bears on its face such proofs of ingenious contrivance as are sufficient to proclaim the admirable wisdom

20. John Calvin, *Institutes of the Christian Religion*, trans. Henry Beveridge (Calvin Translation Society, 1845), I.iii.1; *Institutio Religionis Christianae* (Robert Stephanus, 1559).

21. Calvin, *Institutes*, I.iv.1, 2; I.v.4.

22. Calvin, *Institutes*, I.iii.1; cf. Cicero, *On the Nature of the Gods*, I.xvi.43 (44–45), I.xxiii.62 (60–61).

23. John Calvin, *Institutio Totius Christianiae Religionis* (Jean Girard, 1550), I.i.4.

24. Calvin, *Institutes*, I.iii.3; cf. Cicero, *On the Nature of the Gods*, I.xxiii.

25. Cicero, *On the Nature of the Gods*, II.liv.134 (250–51).

of its Maker."[26] The structure of the human body is a walking proof for the existence of God, a point Calvin reinforces by invoking the ancient physician and philosopher Galen (129–216) and his *On the Uses of the Body*, a work available in a sixteenth-century edition.[27] Calvin adds a second layer to the significance of human anatomy by invoking Aristotle (384–22 BC) as an authority: "Hence certain of the philosophers have not improperly called man a *microcosm*, as being a rare specimen of divine power, wisdom, and goodness, and containing within himself wonders sufficient to occupy our minds, if we are willing to employ them."[28]

Aristotle argues in his *Physics* that things in motion are impelled by something else, whether animate or inanimate objects. He comments that all people witness this phenomenon, namely, when something outside of an inanimate object moves it; conversely, we observe that animate objects move themselves, even if they are at first motionless and at rest. Within this context, Aristotle writes: "If this can happen to a living thing, why not to the universe? And if in a lesser cosmos [*microcosmo*], why not in a greater, and if in *the* cosmos, why not in the limited?—if 'the unlimited' as a whole be susceptible of motion or rest."[29] Aristotle did not originate the idea of a *microcosmo*, as some date it to Democritus (ca. 460–370 BC).[30] The Greek philosophers believed that the human body was a micro world that bore similar characteristics to the macro world. If one can appeal to the larger world to demonstrate the existence of God, then the same holds true in appealing to the human body, a microcosmic creation. Calvin believed that Cicero's natural theological argument was basically sound and thus appeals to it as evidence of God's existence.

Calvin likewise points to the wider creation as evidence of God's existence. "In attestation of his wondrous wisdom, both the heavens and the earth present us with innumerable proofs which astronomy, medicine, and all the natural sciences, are designed to illustrate but proofs which force themselves on the notice of the most illiterate peasant, who cannot open his eyes without beholding them."[31] Calvin argues similarly to Cicero in this respect, but he also makes a telling admission that reveals the intentions of his arguments at this opening stage in his *Institutes*:

26. Calvin, *Institutes*, I.v.2.

27. Galen, *De Usu Partium Corporis Humani Libri XVII* (Christiani Wechelis, 1538); *Galen on the Usefulness of the Parts of the Body*, 2 vols. (Cornell University Press, 1968).

28. Calvin, *Institutes*, I.v.3.

29. Aristotle, *The Physics*, trans. Philip H. Wicksteed and Francis M. Cornford, vol. 2, Loeb Classical Library (Harvard University Press, 1934), VIII.ii (286–89).

30. George Perrigo Conger, *Theories of Macrocosms and Microcosms in the History of Philosophy* (Columbia University Press, 1922).

31. Calvin, *Institutes*, I.v.2.

> Here we might refer to those glowing descriptions of divine power, as illustrated by natural events, which occur throughout Scripture; but more especially in the book of Job, and the prophecies of Isaiah. These, however, I purposefully omit, because a better opportunity of introducing them will be found when I come to treat of the scriptural account of the creation. I only wish to observe here, that this method of investigating the divine perfections, by tracing the lineaments [*lineamenta sequantur*] of his countenance as shadowed forth in the firmament and on the earth, is common both to those within and to those without the pale of the church.[32]

Contrary to the claims that Calvin begins with the self-attesting Christ of Scripture or with the doctrine of Scripture, Calvin purposefully omits Scripture and delays its citation until later in his overall argument. But why does he omit Scripture? Because he wants to trace the knowledge of God's work in the heavens and earth "common both to those within and to those without the pale of the church." Calvin gives his rationale for not citing Scripture and invoking pagan authorities such as Cicero and Aristotle because he draws upon truth wherever he finds it to prove that all people, believer or not, know God as creator. Echoing Paul's arguments from Romans 1:19–20, Calvin explains what he means by "tracing the lineaments . . . shadowed forth . . . in the firmament and on the earth," when he writes: "From the power of God we are naturally led to consider his eternity, since that from which all other things derive their origin must necessarily be self-existent and eternal."[33] Like Paul at Mars Hill connecting to the Stoic philosophers and poets, Calvin draws upon the insights of Cicero and Aristotle.

The Significance of Calvin's Use of Cicero

Why was Calvin willing to appeal positively yet critically to Cicero's *On the Nature of the Gods*? How does Calvin's use of Cicero fit within his overall theology, and how does it factor into the discipline of apologetics? Calvin's Renaissance humanism and the structure of the 1559 *Institutes* provide answers to these questions. First, we must recall that Calvin was trained in Renaissance humanism, which was all about the recovery of the ancient texts of the Greeks and the Romans, among other works of antiquity.[34] In fact, Calvin's first work was a commentary on Seneca's (4 BC–AD 65) *De*

32. Calvin, *Institutes*, I.v.6; *Institutio*, I.v.5.
33. Calvin, *Institutes*, I.v.6.
34. Herman J. Selderhuis, ed., *The Calvin Handbook* (Eerdmans, 2009), 137–42.

Clementia.[35] Calvin's Renaissance humanism was not something that he later cast off as a Reformer but rather continued to employ throughout his career and even codified his commitment in the curriculum of the Academy of Geneva's statutes. The students were required to read and study Cicero's *Letters*, *On Friendship*, *On Old Age*, as well as other works of antiquity.[36] Reference to Cicero was not an outlier for Calvin; the Battles edition of the *Institutes* records fourteen references to him in the first five chapters alone.[37] Calvin's humanistic training brought Cicero to his attention and so he liberally but critically appealed to the Roman orator—but what was Calvin doing with Cicero?

Second, Calvin based the structure of his 1559 *Institutes* on Paul's Epistle to the Romans. When Calvin first penned the *Institutes* in 1536, he modeled it after the Apostles' Creed, but by the final edition he had rearranged it to trace Romans.[38] Just as Paul begins Romans with an appeal to the knowledge of God available in the creation (Rom 1:20), so Calvin likewise begins his *Institutes*. Calvin follows Paul in the truth that the creation renders sinful humans inexcusable before the divine bar—they cannot say they were ignorant of God's existence: "In vain, for us, therefore, does Creation exhibit so many bright lamps lighted up to show forth the glory of its Author. . . . The invisible Godhead is indeed represented by such displays, but . . . we have no eyes to perceive it until they are enlightened through faith by internal revelation from God."[39] Of the few passages of Scripture that Calvin does use in the opening five chapters of his *Institutes*, he quotes Romans 1:19, Acts 14:16–17, and Acts 17:27, among several other scattered references, to buttress his claim that the creation is evidence of God's existence.[40] As the introduction of this chapter showed, even though a number of twentieth-century historians and theologians have claimed that Calvin has no place for the natural in his

35. Cf. Seneca, *De Clementia*, ed. Susanna Braund (Oxford University Press, 2011); John Calvin, *Calvin's Commentary on Seneca's De Clementia*, ed. Ford Lewis Battles and André Malan Hugo (Brill, 1969).

36. John Calvin, *Leges Academiae Genevensis*, in *Ioannis Calvini Opera Quae Supersuent Omnia*, ed. Guilielmus Baum et al., vol. 10/1 (A. Schwetscke and Sons, 1871), cols. 78–79; cf. e.g., Cicero, *Letters to His Friends*, 3 vols., trans. W. Glynn Williams, Loeb Classical Library (Harvard University Press, 1953–1960); *De Senectute, De Amicitia, De Divinatione*, trans. William Armistead Falconer, Loeb Classical Library (Harvard University Press, 1964).

37. John Calvin, *Institutes of the Christian Religion*, 2 vols., trans. Ford Lewis Battles, ed. John T. McNeil, Library of Christian Classics (Westminster Press, 1960), I:42n7; 44nn3–5; 46n8; 48n4; 53n5; 55nn7, 12; 56n13; 57n18; 65n39; 66n39; 68n43.

38. Richard A. Muller, *The Unaccommodated Calvin: Studies in the Foundation of a Theological Tradition* (Oxford University Press, 2001), 21–38.

39. Calvin, *Institutes*, I.v.14.

40. Calvin, *Institutes*, I.v.1, 3, 14.

theology (Lang), or that natural theology is present only to render sinners inexcusable (Van Til), or that Calvin acknowledges only the possibility of natural theology in theory but dismisses it in practice (Barth), or that Calvin begins the *Institutes* with the doctrine of Scripture (Dooyeweerd), these claims fail to factor Calvin's opening argument and use of Cicero.

Calvin does not begin with Scripture, as Dooyeweerd believed, as Calvin does not formally treat Scripture until book II.[41] This is a fact obscured by the Battles edition of the *Institutes*, which inserts forty-three Scripture citations in the opening five chapters that do not appear in the 1559 Geneva Stephanus edition. Calvin does not actually cite Scripture until chapter 4, and even then, recall his explanation regarding why he purposefully omitted Scripture until further into his argument. This same structural pattern appears in the French Confession (1559), which Calvin co-authored with Theodore Beza (1519–1605):

> I. We believe and confess that there is but one God, who is one sole and simple essence, spiritual, eternal, invisible, immutable, infinite, incomprehensible, ineffable, omnipotent; who is all-wise, all-good, all-just, and all-merciful.
>
> II. As such this God reveals himself to men; firstly, in his works, in their creation, as well as in their preservation and control. Secondly, and more clearly, in his Word, which was in the beginning revealed through oracles, and which was afterward committed to writing in the books which we call the Holy Scriptures.

Calvin structurally reproduces in the French Confession what he does with the first five chapters of the *Institutes*: first the natural knowledge of God, followed by the supernatural knowledge of God—or first the book of nature, followed by the book of Scripture.

Contra Barth, Calvin does not merely theorize about the abstract possibility of natural theology only to abandon it in practice. What Calvin states is that the natural knowledge of God *alone* is insufficient and "in vain . . . show[s] forth the glory of its Author."[42] In other words, natural theology by itself is insufficient and only serves to render people inexcusable. So, on this count, Van Til is partially correct regarding the function of natural theology in Calvin's argument. But this does not mean that Calvin therefore pivots to and argues entirely from Scripture. Recall, again, Calvin's illustration of the corrective lenses of Scripture: "For as the aged, or those whose sight

41. Calvin, *Institutes*, II.vi.1; cf. I.vi.1. See also Stephen J. Grabill, *Rediscovering the Natural Law in Reformed Theological Ethics* (Eerdmans, 2006), 82–83.

42. Calvin, *Institutes*, I.v.14.

is defective, when any book, however fair, is set before them, though they perceive that there is something written, are scarcely able to make out two consecutive words, but, when aided by glasses, begin to read distinctly, so Scripture, gathering together the impressions of Deity, which, till then, lay confused in our minds, dissipates the darkness, and shows us the true God clearly."[43] What is Calvin doing with this illustration?

Abraham Kuyper's (1837–1920) analysis of Calvin's illustration is helpful and insightful. Kuyper observes: "Notice that Calvin does not call Scripture our *eyes*, but the glasses that come to the aid of our weak eyes."[44] Scripture (supernatural knowledge) is just as vital as our eyes (a means of natural knowledge). Kuyper objects to the tendency to say that the natural knowledge of God is unnecessary so long as we have Scripture:

> For this reason we must, before going any further, wipe out, root and branch, the erroneous view that the natural knowledge of God is not as indispensable for faith as the revelation in Christ. We must remove the false idea that the natural knowledge of God is even conceivable apart from faith. We must abandon the assumption that Revelation can ever compensate for what we would miss if the natural knowledge of God were absent. We must put a stop to the misconception that the natural knowledge of God ends where Revelation begins. All Scripture rests on the natural knowledge of God. . . . The natural knowledge of God, far from lying outside the area of faith, is an absurdity outside of faith. . . . It touches the conscience of the unbelieving world, awakens it from its unbelieving slumber, and looks in all living things for points of contact with the kingdom of God.[45]

Kuyper's historical point is that Calvin employs both the books of nature and Scripture in the opening chapters of his *Institutes*, and his broader theological point is that we need both for good theology. There is a caveat to note: natural revelation and theology are not a stepladder to supernatural revelation. Rather, to borrow the language of the Belgic Confession (art. II), we read both books in the divine library (nature and Scripture) in tandem. The necessity and utility of employing both books in theology and apologetics explains why Calvin was willing to cite Cicero and other pagan authorities.

Given Calvin's pattern of argument in the opening chapters of his *Institutes*, we can say that his use of natural revelation and theology goes beyond rendering the unbeliever inexcusable. Based on Calvin's use of Cicero, Egil

43. Calvin, *Institutes*, I.vi.1.

44. Abraham Kuyper, "The Natural Knowledge of God," trans. Harry Van Dyke, *Bavinck Review* 6 (2015): 73–112, here 84.

45. Kuyper, "Natural Knowledge," 85.

Grislis (1928–2020), professor of theology at the University of Manitoba in Winnipeg, Canada, proposed applying Calvin's threefold use of the law to his use of natural knowledge and theology to clarify Calvin's arguments.[46] Calvin follows Martin Luther (1483–1546) and Melanchthon and delineates three uses of the law: the pedagogical, civil, and normative.[47] The pedagogical use of the law confronts us with our sin because, "after attempting to do what is ordered, and so feeling our weakness under the law, [we] may learn to implore the help of grace."[48] The law in its pedagogical use drives sinners to Christ. The civil use brings "fearful denunciations and the consequent dread of punishment, to curb those who, unless forced, have no regard for rectitude and justice."[49] The civil use of the law holds people in check in their immorality. The third, and principal, use of the law "has respect to believers in whose hearts the Spirit of God already flourishes and reigns."[50] The law in its third use shows believers what conduct is pleasing to God and how to live the Christian life.

Grislis takes the threefold use of the law and explains that natural revelation in its pedagogical use convicts sinners of their idolatry, as their consciences accuse and excuse their conduct (Rom 2:15) and as they hear the creation herald God's existence, glory, and attributes (Ps 19:1–4; Rom 1:19–21). Natural revelation alone, however, does not save people from their sin, but only the Spirit of Christ through special revelation can bring them to repentance. In this case, natural revelation and purified natural theology work in tandem with supernatural revelation and theology through the convicting power of the Spirit. In its civil use, natural revelation and theology constrain the conduct of sinners as God reveals his natural law and creation's testimony restrains sinners' civil conduct. In its third (or normative use), natural revelation and theology read through the corrective lenses of Scripture and, illumined by the Holy Spirit, provides important guidance for the Christian life. Through natural theological observations, believers can learn more about who God is as they see his wisdom "fleshed out" before them in the creation. All in all, using the threefold use of the law schema helps us to see that natural revelation and theology are a key component of Calvin's opening chapters of his *Institutes* and his theology in general.

46. Grislis, "Calvin's Use of Cicero," 35.

47. Edward Engelbrecht, *Friends of the Law: Luther's Use of the Law for the Christian Life* (Concordia Publishing, 2011); Muller, *Unaccomodated Calvin*, 129.

48. Calvin, *Institutes*, II.vii.9.

49. Calvin, *Institutes*, II.vii.10.

50. Calvin, *Institutes*, II.vii.12.

Conclusion

Calvin is not a normative theologian of the Reformed tradition, but that the opening chapters of his *Institutes* traces Paul's opening chapter of Romans and his arguments at Mars Hill helps us to see how historic Reformed apologetics employs the books of nature and Scripture. Despite the tendency in the twentieth century to lean almost exclusively on Scripture in the task of apologetics, Calvin breathes fresh air into the discussion and allows the cool breeze of centuries past to blow through our minds and remind us of long-forgotten truths. When we see Calvin's citations of Cicero and other pagan writers from antiquity, we should not assume he has compromised with unbelief but rather recognize that he appeals to God's truth in the creation. To use only supernatural revelation (Scripture) is insufficient, as Kuyper warns; conversely, it is also the fool's errand to use only natural revelation. Rather, Calvin shows us how to use both books in the divine library, nature and Scripture. Calvin was not proposing a novel approach but was working with patterns he saw in Paul's Epistle to Rome as well as the apostle's encounter with the philosophers at Mars Hill. Like Paul, Calvin appealed to the truth that he found in Cicero, purified it of error, and plied it to the task of theology. Drawing upon Cicero, Calvin pointed both to the creation and to the human body, the macro- and microcosmic creations of God, as evidence of his existence, wisdom, and glory. If Calvin is any guide, we can appeal to both books in our apologetics point to the book of nature as we read it through the corrective lenses of Scripture. Like Paul and Calvin, we can go into the marketplaces, the halls of academia, and the green spaces in our communities and point to the book of nature and even quote some of the authors of our time to point to God's truth present in their works. We can appeal to the Stoic poets, Cicero, or the poets, musicians, and authors of our own day. But as we appeal to them, like Paul and Calvin, we filter through Scripture the error-tainted truths that we find so that unbelievers see them clearly. With such a methodology we defend the faith as we engage the idols of our day all in the service of evangelism and ultimately worship and love of our Triune God. We can help sinners rightly order their disordered love.

PART 2

BASIC REFORMED APOLOGETICS

6

God's Wisdom in Creation

The Foundation for the Teleological Argument

> **Thesis 6:** The book of Scripture shows how God has planted evidence of his being, wisdom, and power in the creation. Scripture warrants the teleological argument, or the argument from design.

The God who made the world and everything in it, being Lord of heaven and earth, . . . made from one man every nation of mankind to live on all the face of the earth, having determined allotted periods and the boundaries of their dwelling place, that they should seek God, and perhaps feel their way toward him and find him.

—Acts 17:24–27

For his invisible attributes, namely, his eternal power and divine nature, have been clearly perceived, ever since the creation of the world, in the things that have been made.

—Romans 1:20

Defending the faith from the creation was a common feature in theology for centuries as Christians pointed to the order, beauty, and design in the world as evidence for the existence of an all-wise, all-knowing, all-powerful creator. Eighteenth-century Anglican theologian Richard Blackmore (1654–1726) captures both the commonality and the beauty of the teleological argument when he writes:

> See, thro' this vast extended Theater
> Of Skill Divine what shining Marks appear:
> Creating Pow'r is all around exprest,
> The God discover'd, and his Care confest.
> Nature's high Birth her Heav'nly Beauties show;
> By ev'ry Feature we Parent know.[1]

But the argument from design, or the teleological argument, came under heavy criticism from the likes of Enlightenment philosopher David Hume (1711–1776). Hume admitted that we can observe patterns of correlation in the creation: "That a stone will fall, that fire will burn, that the earth has solidity, we have observed a thousand and a thousand times; and when any new instance of this nature is presented, we draw without hesitation the accustomed inference."[2] That is, we can discern a cause-and-effect relationship between fire and wood or that we require stable ground to facilitate travel, but people made an illegitimate leap when they argued from the existence of worlds to their designers: "But how this argument can have place where the objects, as in the present case, are single, individual, without parallel or specific resemblance, may be difficult to explain."[3] To argue from the existence of the world to the world's designer had to have a one-to-one comparison for legitimate conclusions. If we observe a house, then with the greatest certainty we can reason that it had an architect or builder because people commonly design and build homes—the cause and effect are of the same species. Hume avers: "But surely you will not affirm that the universe bears such a resemblance to a house that we can with the same certainty infer a similar cause, or that the analogy here is entire and perfect. The dissimilitude is so striking that the utmost you can here pretend to is a guess."[4] How can you go from a world to the world's designer?

Hume lived in the perceived light of science and technology and thought that the more people studied the world, they would discover how dissimilar the world and its supposed creator were. Hume explains:

> All the new discoveries in astronomy which prove the immense grandeur and magnificence of the works of nature are so many additional arguments for a Deity, according to the true system of theism; but, according to your hypothesis

1. Richard Blackmore, *Creation: A Philosophical Poem Demonstrating the Existence and Providence of God*, 5th ed. (S. Powell, 1727), 3.

2. David Hume, *Dialogues Concerning Natural Religion*, 2nd ed., ed. Richard H. Popkin (Hackett Publishing Co., 1998), 16.

3. Hume, *Dialogues*, 21.

4. Hume, *Dialogues*, 16.

> of experimental theism, they become so many objections, by removing the effect still farther from all resemblance to the effects of human art and contrivance. . . . The farther we push our researches of this kind, we are still led to infer the universal cause of all to be vastly different from mankind, or from any object of human experience and observation.[5]

As scientific discoveries uncovered the vastness of the cosmos, how more unlike a house is the universe? A builder constructing a house is one thing, but a deity "constructing" the "house" of the seemingly infinite cosmos is an entirely different proposition. How can we say that a flower is evidence of an infinite God? In addition to the apparent breakdown of the house and builder analogy, Hume pointed to what was in his mind a fatal flaw in the argument from design—namely, the existence of evil. Hume writes,

> The world . . . is very faulty and imperfect, compared to a superior standard; and was only the first rude essay of some infant deity who afterwards abandoned it, ashamed of his lame performance: It is the work only of some dependent, inferior deity, and is the object of derision to his superiors: It is the production of old age and dotage in some superannuated deity; and ever since his death has run on at adventures, from the first impulse and active force which it received from him.[6]

Is not the existence of evil, natural disasters, and entropy in the creation evidence of flaws and shortcomings in the creator?

At first glance, Hume's criticisms of the argument from design appear weighty if not downright fatal. Yet, an important question to ask is: What version of the argument from design did Hume engage? The short answer is, Hume engaged a rationalist version of the argument, one shorn from the authority of Scripture. Recall Abraham Kuyper's (1837–1920) diagnosis of the reason natural theology had fallen out of use in the late nineteenth century: rationalists scuttled Scripture because they thought natural theology was sufficient unto itself.[7] In rationalist theology, the common natural theological arguments for the existence of God became a prolegomena to theological systems that rested on reason rather than on revelation.[8] Premodern and early-modern versions of the argument are different, as they employ both books (nature

5. Hume, *Dialogue*, 34.

6. Hume, *Dialogue*, 37.

7. Abraham Kuyper, "The Natural Knowledge of God," trans. Harry Van Dyke, *Bavinck Review* 6 (2015): 73–112, here 84–88.

8. Richard A. Muller, "Kuyper and Bavinck on Natural Theology," *Bavinck Review* 10 (2019): 5–35, here 11n24.

and Scripture) in their arguments from design. We can contrast rationalistic versus revelational versions of the argument from design and retrieve it for use in apologetics. This chapter is the first step in retrieving the teleological argument for apologetics. The teleological argument has biblical weight and apologetic value if we appeal to both the books of nature and Scripture and show unbelievers that both books speak with one voice. *This chapter defends the thesis that the book of Scripture shows how God has planted evidence of his being, wisdom, and power in the creation. Scripture warrants the teleological argument, or the argument from design.* This chapter, therefore, lays the groundwork for the argument by first presenting a brief history of the argument. Second, it sets forth important scriptural foundations, especially from the wisdom literature, an often missing but key biblical witness that commends the argument from design. Far from being a relic of a bygone era, the argument from design helps image bearers see that the creation declares the glory of God and reveals his invisible being and attributes.

A Brief History

Thomas Aquinas (1225–1274) is likely the one theologian most associated with the argument from design, or the teleological argument. *Teleology* denotes the idea of *purpose*. In his well-known five arguments for the existence of God, Aquinas explains:

> The fifth way is taken from the governance of things. We see that things which lack knowledge, such as natural bodies, act for an end, and this is evident from their acting always, or nearly always, in the same way, so as to obtain the best result. Hence it is plain that they achieve their end not by chance, but by design. Now whatever lacks knowledge cannot but by design. Now whatever lacks knowledge cannot move towards an end, unless it be directed by some being endowed with knowledge and intelligence, as the arrow is directed by the archer. Therefore some intelligent being exists by whom all natural things are ordered to their end; and this being we call God.[9]

There are two noteworthy observations about Aquinas's argument. First, as much as Aquinas has been accused of putting forth a rationalist argument at the outset of his *Summa*, that is, a foundation of reason rather than revelation, this is not the case. First, Aquinas's five arguments for the existence of God are an extended explanation of the significance of Exodus 3:14: "God said to

9. Thomas Aquinas, *Summa Theologica* (Christian Classics, 1948), Ia q. 2 art. 3.

Moses, 'I AM WHO I AM.' And he said, 'Say this to the people of Israel: "I AM has sent me to you."'"[10] Second, as thorough as Aquinas's *Summa Theologica* is, readers must factor his *Summa* alongside of his biblical commentaries—in this case, especially his commentary on Paul's Epistle to the Romans.

In his commentary on Romans, Aquinas explains the meaning of Romans 1:20, "For his invisible attributes, namely, his eternal power and divine nature, have been clearly perceived, ever since the creation of the world, in the things that have been made. So they are without excuse." Aquinas writes: "For they did possess some true knowledge of God, because *what is known about God*, i.e., what can be known about God by men through reason, *is manifest in them*, i.e., is manifest to them from something in them, i.e. from an inner light. Therefore, it should be noted that some things about God are entirely unknown to man in this life, namely, what God is. Hence Paul found in Athens an altar inscribed 'To the unknown God' (Acts 17:23)."[11] Aquinas says that humans can know God through reason because Romans 1:20 teaches this truth, and he coordinates Paul's point with his encounter with the philosophers at Mars Hill in Acts 17. In other words, Aquinas bases the idea that humans can know God through reason on biblical revelation, not naked reason. Moreover, he also distinguishes between the things that can be known through reason versus those things that cannot, such as God's essence. Why does he distinguish between what can and cannot be known by reason?

Human knowledge begins with things that are connatural to him, such as sensible creatures—things that cannot represent the divine essence. Aquinas draws from Pseudo-Dionysius (ca. fifth or sixth century) to make this claim.[12] In other words, finite things cannot represent the infinite essence of God. But humans can know God from creatures in three different ways: causality, the way of excellence, and the way of negation. The way of causality rests on the principle of entropy—that is, things are subject to change and decay, which means there must be an unchangeable and unfailing principle. The way of excellence teaches that all things must have a common greater cause, though not in a univocal sense such as when a human produces a human. The way of negation explains that if God is the exceeding cause of all his effects, nothing in creatures can belong to him. That is, we use negative expressions to describe God. God is, for example, *incorporeal*; he does not have a body,

10. On the revelational character of Aquinas's conception of doctrine, see Erik Persson, *Sacra Doctrina: Reason and Revelation in Aquinas*, trans. Ross MacKenzie (Fortress, 1970), 17–90.

11. Thomas Aquinas, *Commentary on the Letter of Saint Paul to the Romans*, trans. F. R. Larcher, ed. J. Mortensen and E. Alarcón (The Aquinas Institute, 2012), §114.

12. Pseudo-Dionysius, *On the Divine Names*, VII.iv, in *The Complete Works*, trans. Colm Luibheid (Paulist Press, 1987), 47–132.

or he is *atemporal* because he dwells in an eternal state.[13] Once again, when Aquinas proposes these categories, he does not rest solely upon the powers of reason to draw these arguments but he also works from revelation.

Working from Paul's statement, "God has manifested it to them," he cites other passages of Scripture to confirm that God reveals truth about his being in the creation. God reveals knowledge of himself: "Who teaches us more than the beasts of the earth" (Job 35:11) and "Send out your light and your truth" (Ps 43:3). He summarizes these ideas with a statement from the Apocrypha, which does not possess canonical authority but nevertheless accurately synthesizes the biblical point: "'He poured her out,' namely wisdom, 'over all his works'" (Sir 1:9). Aquinas goes on, "Thus God manifested it to them either from within by endowing them with a light or from without by presenting visible creatures, in which, as in a book, the knowledge of God may be read."[14] What things can humans read in the book of nature through the God-given powers of reason? Based on Paul's statement, Aquinas lists three things: God's invisible attributes, his eternal power, and his divine nature. The first is that creation reveals God's invisible attributes, such as God's divine essence, which cannot be perceived by humans since no one has seen God (John 1:18; 1 Tim 1:17). But what does the creation reveal about God's essence? "But it is now manifested to us through certain likenesses found in creatures," writes Aquinas, "which participate in manifold ways that which is one in God. Accordingly, our intellect considers the one divine essence under the aspects of goodness, wisdom, power and so on, all of which are one in God."[15] In other words, things in the creation reveal something about God's wisdom and nature. The creation also reveals something about the eternal power of God because "all things proceed from him as from a principle: 'Great is our Lord, and abundant in power' (Psa. 147:5). This power the philosophers"—presumably the likes of Aristotle or the philosophers at Mars Hill—"knew to be eternal; hence it is called 'his eternal power.'"[16] Aquinas explains that the last thing that Paul lists is God's divine nature, which is "the ultimate end unto which all things tend. For the divine good is called the common good in which all things participate." Aquinas invokes the concept of participation because he likely has Paul's statement from his address at Mars Hill in mind, "In him we live and move and have our being" (Acts 17:28). All creatures participate in God because God is both the creator and sustainer of all things.[17]

13. Aquinas, *Romans*, §115.
14. Aquinas, *Romans*, §116.
15. Aquinas, *Romans*, §117.
16. Aquinas, *Romans*, §117.
17. Andrew Davison, *Participation in God: A Study in Christian Doctrine and Metaphysics* (Cambridge University Press, 2019).

Based on his exegesis of Romans 1:20, Aquinas summarizes Paul's point when he writes: "One must consider the medium through which they knew those things. This is designated when he says, *by the things that are made*. For just as an art is shown by an artist's works, so God's wisdom is shown by his creatures: 'From the greatness and beauty of created things comes a corresponding perception of their creator' (Wis 13:5)."[18] Aquinas bases the idea that we can know God through the creation on scriptural revelation, not merely the raw power of human reason as some erroneously accuse him.[19] And as much as people assume that the five arguments, and especially the teleological argument, originate with Aquinas, two clues reveal that the argument has roots in the early church. Aquinas cites Pseudo-Dionysius, who wrote sometime around the fifth or sixth century, and he also likens the creation unto a book that people can read to learn knowledge about God, an idea that goes back to Augustine (354–430). Augustine writes: "Some people read books in order to find God. Yet there is a great book, the very appearance of created things. Look above you; look below you! Note it; read it! God, whom you wish to find, never wrote that book with ink. Instead, He set before your eyes the things that He had made."[20] Augustine was not alone, as other church fathers also taught the argument from design.

Athanasius (d. 373) wrote his well-known defense of the doctrine of Christ, *On the Incarnation*, in the midst of the church's christological controversies. The work is a faithful and erudite treatise defending the full deity and humanity of Jesus, but key to his defense of Christ's deity is pointing to the creation to demonstrate what it means for Christ to be *God* incarnate. Athanasius runs through the different opinions regarding the origins of the world. Some say that the world came into being by chance, such as the Epicureans and their notions of the swerve, which leads them to deny the doctrine of providence. But if chaos brought the world into existence, there would be neither order nor differentiation in the creation. This, however, is not the state of the creation: "We see human bodies, here a foot, there a hand, and there a head. Such order indicates that they did not come into being spontaneously, but shows that a

18. Aquinas, *Romans*, §118.

19. E.g., K. Scott Oliphint, *Thomas Aquinas* (P&R, 2017); Jeffrey D. Johnson, *The Failure of Natural Theology: A Critical Appraisal of the Philosophical Theology of Thomas Aquinas* (Free Grace Press, 2021); cf. Richard A. Muller, "Reading Aquinas from a Reformed Perspective: A Review Essay," *Calvin Theological Journal* 53/2 (2018): 255–88; David VanDrunen, "Thomistic Natural Theology and Its Implications: A Review Article of Jeffrey Johnson's *The Failure of Natural Theology*," *Journal of the International Reformed Baptist Seminary* (2023): 109–26.

20. Augustine, *The Essential Augustine*, ed. Vernon J. Bourke (New American Library, 1964), 123. Bourke translates from sermon 126.6 in *Miscellanea Agostiniana*, E. G. Morin (Vatican, 1930).

cause preceded them, from which one can apprehend the God who ordered and created all things."[21] Athanasius looks at the effects (an orderly creation) and discerns a cause (an all-wise God who ordered the creation). Moreover, in line with Cicero's (106–43 BC) claims about the orderly microcosmic creation in the human body mirroring the macrocosmic creation, Athanasius likewise recognizes the parallel between the human and cosmic bodies.[22]

Another church father who makes similar arguments within the context of defending and explaining the doctrine of Christ is Gregory of Nazianzus (329–390). Gregory asks how the creation could have any other foundation unless God both gave creatures their being and providentially sustained them. Gregory answers, "No one seeing a beautifully elaborated lyre with its harmonious, orderly arrangement, and hearing the lyre's music will fail to form a notion of its craftsman-player, to recur to him in through though ignorant of him by sight."[23] How can one look upon the beauty, order, and purpose in the creation and think that it came about by chance? Gregory identifies one of the errors that people make when looking at the creation: they turn the creation itself into a god—a gross mistake. Instead, people must discover "God through the beauty and order of things seen, using sight as a guide to what transcends sight without losing God through the grandeur of what it sees."[24] There is a sense in which Gregory encourages readers of creation to look *through* rather than *at* the creation—to look through it to the transcendent God who stands behind it. If people look directly at the creation, they are liable to worship the creation rather than the creator.

Gregory recounts a conversation that he had with an unbeliever who asked the question, "What set these elements in motion and leads their ceaseless, unimpeded flow?" He says, "It was surely their designer, who implants in all things reason whereby the universe is conducted and carried along. And who is their designer? Surely he who made them and brought them into existence. . . . What can this 'something' be if not God? Thus God-derived reason, bound up, connected, with the whole of nature, man's most ancient law, has led us up from things of sight to God."[25] Like the philosophers at Mars Hill or Aristotle's unmoved mover, this unbeliever recognized that there was a designer behind the creation, and so Gregory pointed him to the one true God.

21. Athanasius, *On the Incarnation* (St. Vladimir's Seminary Press, 2011), §2 (50).

22. Cicero, *On the Nature of the Gods Academics*, trans. H. Rackham, Loeb Classical Library (Harvard University Press, 1951), II.liv.134 (250–51).

23. Gregory of Nazianzus, *On God and Christ: The Five Theological Orations and Two Letters to Cledonius* (St. Vladimir's Seminary Press, 2002), Oration XXVIII.6 (41).

24. Gregory, *On God and Christ*, Oration XXVIII.13 (47).

25. Gregory, *On God and Christ*, Oration XXVIII.16 (49).

But Gregory believed that the creation-God connection was apparent in other portions of the Scriptures. He casts his gaze away from the creation and looks to the Old Testament:

> What do you say? Shall we stop our preaching here at matter and objects of sight? Or, since Scripture recognizes the tabernacle of Moses as a symbol for the whole world (the world, I mean, of things "visible and invisible") shall we pass through the first veil transcending the sense, to bend our gaze on holy things, on ideal and heaven transcending reality. . . . So strongly do they bear the shape and imprint of God's beauty, that they become in their turn lights, able to give light to others by transmitting the stream that flows from the primal light of God.[26]

Gregory sees the tabernacle as an image of the visible and invisible creation, a point confirmed by contemporary scholarship.[27] Like Athanasius, Gregory invites us to look through the creation to the transcendent reality of God. The creation bears so much of God's beauty that it becomes a collection of lights that communicate the light of God's own eternal and immortal being.

This brief survey of Aquinas, Augustine, Athanasius, and Gregory reveals several important observations about the history of the argument from design. First, all four theologians affirm the principle that we can begin with the effect (the creation) and work our way back to the cause (God). This line of argument is neither strictly Thomistic nor Aristotelian, as Augustine, Athanasius, and Gregory antedate Thomas's argument from design and do not accent their presentations with Aristotelianism. Rather, these patristic and medieval theologians follow Paul's line of thought in Romans 1:19–20. All four theologians, especially Aquinas in his *Summa* and Romans commentary, read the book of nature through the corrective lenses of Scripture.

Second, all too often proponents and critics abstract the teleological argument from its wider context. Granted, for the sake of argument, one can present the argument from design in a stand-alone fashion. But such an abstraction is rhetorical rather than theological. A critic like Hume, however, only interacts with part of the overall argument—he only looks at the book of nature. Aquinas situates his argument within the context of both books, nature and Scripture. We can call this aspect of the argument the *revelational* context. Another aspect that we must factor is the *theological* context.

26. Gregory, *On God and Christ*, Oration XXVIII.31 (62–63).

27. See, e.g., G. K. Beale, *The Temple and the Church's Mission* (IVP Academic, 2004), 31–38, 46–47, 60–61; Gordon J. Wenham, "Sanctuary Symbolism in the Garden of Eden Story," in *I Studied Inscriptions from Before the Flood: Ancient Near Eastern, Literary, and Linguistic Approaches to Genesis 1–11*, ed. Richard S. Hess and David Toshio Tsumura, Sources for Biblical and Theological Study, vol. 4 (Eisenbrauns, 1994), 399–404.

Can critics who abstract Aquinas's argument from his *Summa* say that they are critiquing Thomas's argument when they ignore the greater context of his *Summa*? Aquinas presents the five ways to demonstrate God's existence within the greater context of the *Summa*, a context that leads to Christ and salvation. This line of argumentation is especially evident in Athanasius's and Gregory's statements of the argument; they both present the argument from design within the context of their defenses of the doctrine of Christ. Aquinas, Athanasius, and Gregory establish the nature and existence of God from both the books of nature and Scripture so that when they say that Jesus is *God* in the flesh, *God* has meaning derived from both books. Who is God? What has he done? And how is Jesus God? Thus, they establish God and creation first, and then redemption and God in the flesh second. Arguments from design can be abstracted for the sake of discussion, but they must rest within a revelational, theological (proper), and christological context so they bear the full weight of God's truth.

Third, Gregory makes the right connection between the earthly tabernacle and the creation. Just as the earthly tabernacle (and later temple) was an edifice bursting with symbolism and theological meaning, so too God fills the tabernacle of the cosmos with revelatory significance. God saturates the creation with his wisdom, truth, and glory. Gregory appeals to the tabernacle because he sees the argument from design in passages beyond Romans 1:19–20 and Psalm 19:1–4. This is not to say that arguing from Psalm 19 and Romans 1 is insufficient, but why ignore other portions of Scripture that only enrich and strengthen the argument from design? With these observations in mind, we can proceed to examine the scriptural building blocks for the teleological argument.

Scriptural Foundations

Two of the commonly cited passages of Scripture that apologists cite in support of the argument from design are Psalm 19:1–4 and Romans 1:19–20. These are vital texts that teach the importance of reading the book of nature. These passages capture the big-picture view, the wide-angle panoramic beauty, truth, and revelation that God has embedded in the creation. The Scripture's wisdom literature, however, is often ignored in arguments from design, perhaps because it does not communicate the significance of general revelation in a straightforward manner like the didactic letters of Paul do. Yet, the wisdom literature is crucial for a thicker teleological argument. The wisdom literature provides granular detail that Psalm 19:1–4 and Romans 1:19–20 assume but do not explain. In line with Psalm 19:1—"The heavens declare the glory of God, and the sky above proclaims his handwork"—Solomon explains that God has implanted his wisdom throughout the creation: "The Lord by wisdom founded the earth; by understanding he established the heavens; by his knowledge the deeps broke open, and the clouds drop down the dew" (Prov 3:19–20). Because God made the creation by his wisdom, the cosmos reflects his wisdom. If "day to day pours out speech, and night to night reveals knowledge" (Ps 19:2), then the creation is inherently didactic.[28]

Just as God's special revelation contains mysteries beyond the reach of human reason, such as the Trinity, the hypostatic union, or the nexus between divine sovereignty and human responsibility, mysteries beyond the powers of reason fill the creation: "Three things are too wonderful for me; four I do not understand: the way of an eagle in the sky, the way of a serpent on a rock, the way of a ship on the high seas, and the way of a man with a virgin" (Prov 30:18–19).[29] These four things in the creation capture truths that create wonder in the author's mind. Someone may be able scientifically to explain the principles of an eagle's flight in the sky, but to discover that an eagle can soar to ten thousand or even twenty thousand feet creates a sense of awe in the mind. Ships sailing on the seas have captivated the minds of many an author, from Herman Melville's (1819–1891) *The Whale* to Ernest Hemmingway's (1899–1961) *The Old Man and the Sea*. The sea is a place of awe and wonder not just because of its size or depth but because it reverberates with God's wisdom and beauty. Some of the knowledge that the creation teaches is wonder, human finitude, and divine wisdom. The creation teaches there are limits to human knowledge: "Surely I am too stupid to be a man. I have not the understanding of a man. I have not learned wisdom, nor have I knowledge of the Holy One. Who has ascended to heaven and come down? Who has gathered the wind in his fists? Who has wrapped up the waters in a garment? Who has established all the ends of the earth? What is his name, and what is his son's name? Surely you know!" (Prov 30:2–4).[30]

Proverbs reveals that there is a link between the cosmic and social realms; God has built a connection between the creation and cultures. The creation is not merely the stage upon which humans live and perform, but rather the creation is itself a performer: God "has set a tent for the sun, which comes out like a bridegroom leaving his chamber, and, like a strong man, runs its

28. William P. Brown, *Wisdom's Wonder: Character, Creation, and Crisis in the Bible's Wisdom Literature* (Eerdmans, 2014), 17; Leo G. Perdue, *Wisdom and Creation: The Theology of Wisdom Literature* (Abingdon Press, 1994), 82.

29. Brown, *Wisdom's Wonder*, 1.

30. Brown, *Wisdom's Wonder*, 63.

course with joy" (Ps 19:4–5).[31] This is why Proverbs repeatedly turns readers to the creation:

- "Go to the ant, O sluggard; consider her ways, and be wise. Without having any chief, officer, or ruler, she prepares her bread in summer and gathers her food in harvest" (Prov 6:6–8).
- "The north wind brings forth rain, and a backbiting tongue, angry looks" (Prov 25:23).
- "Like a muddied spring or a polluted fountain is a righteous man who gives way before the wicked" (Prov 25:26).
- "It is not good to eat much honey, nor is it glorious to seek one's own glory" (Prov 25:27).
- "Whoever meddles in a quarrel not his own is like one who takes a passing dog by the ears" (Prov 26:17).
- "Like a dog that returns to his vomit is a fool who repeats his folly" (Prov 26:11).
- "For pressing milk produces curds, pressing the nose produces blood, and pressing anger produces strife" (Prov 30:33).

Whether insects as small as an ant, wind, muddied springs, dogs, or milk, the creation is full of God's wisdom. Job even joins the chorus and tells his three critics to learn God's wisdom from the beasts: "But ask the beasts, and they will teach you; the birds of the heavens, and they will tell you; or the bushes of the earth, and they will teach you; and the fish of the sea will declare to you" (Job 12:7–8).[32]

Proverbs 8 gives greater detail regarding the relationship between God's wisdom and creation. Interestingly, the Septuagint inserts an explanatory transition between the Hebrew text of Proverbs 8:21–22 that clarifies the connections between wisdom's rewards in historic time (Prov 8:14–21) and wisdom's birth in primordial time (Prov 8:22–31): "If I declare to you the things that daily happen, I will remember also to recount the things of old."[33] The explanation of wisdom's origins begins in Proverbs 8:22, "The Lord brought me forth as the first of his works, before his deeds of old" (NIV). The metaphor קנני ("brought me forth") indicates that Solomon's wisdom

31. Brown, *Wisdom's Wonder*, 18.

32. Roland E. Murphy, "Wisdom and Creation," *Journal of Biblical Literature* 104/1 (1985): 3–11, here 6.

33. Bruce K. Waltke, *The Book of Proverbs: Chapters 1–15*, NICOT (Eerdmans, 2004), 406.

comes directly from God's being.[34] This means that God's wisdom pre-dates the creation: "Ages ago I was set up, at the first, before the beginning of the earth" (Prov 8:23). Wisdom thus comes from God, antedates all human wisdom, and consequently the creation is divine revelation. Solomon takes the reader on a panoramic tour of the creation to show that there is a cosmos, not chaos: he begins in the depths (v. 24a), mentions springs that lead to the surface (v. 24b), looks to the mountains that are rooted in the depths and yet jut into the sky (v. 25a), the hills (v. 25b), the land and its fields (v. 26), the sky and its horizon (v. 27). At the same time, we should recognize that Scripture does not describe these phenomena in modern scientific terms but in poetic and metaphorical imagery. The psalmist, for example, writes of the earth reeling and rocking, and the foundations of the earth quaking because of God's wrath (Ps 18:7), or that by God the mountains were ילדו (lit. "birthed") (Ps 90:2). The fact, however, that wisdom existed with God prior to the creation means it is close to him.[35]

God establishes all of the cosmic entities upon which humans rely; he fixes a cosmic order in the creation: "When he established the heavens, I was there; when he drew a circle on the face of the deep, when he made firm the skies above, when he established the fountains of the deep, when he assigned to the sea its limit, so that the waters might not transgress his command, when he marked out the foundations of the earth" (Prov 8:27–29). Solomon employs a merism that goes from the top, the heavens (v. 27a), to the bottom, the deep (v. 27b), to convey that from the heights to the depths, creation is full of God's wisdom. By wisdom God assigned the dwelling places of humans by setting limits and boundaries to the sea, which thus protects the land (v. 29). A common Old Testament idea is that the sea is hostile to human and animal life and yet God sovereignly rules over it (Job 28:10–11; Ps 148:5–6). In this vein, Solomon likens God's wise works of creation unto the labors of an artisan: "Then I was beside him, like a master workman, and I was daily his delight, rejoicing before him always, rejoicing in his inhabited world and delighting in the sons of Adam" (Prov 8:30–31, translation altered). Solomon's statement here brings the reader full circle to earlier statements in Proverbs: "The Lord by wisdom founded the earth; by understanding he established the heavens; by his knowledge the deeps broke open, and the clouds drop down the dew" (Prov 3:19–20). God formed the creation by his wisdom, and as

34. Waltke, *Proverbs 1–15*, 409; similarly, Matthew McAffee, "Creation and the Role of Wisdom in Proverbs 8: What Can We Learn?," *Southeastern Theological Review* 10/2 (2019): 31–57, here 33–35.

35. Waltke, *Proverbs 1–15*, 414.

such, the creation is chock-full of the marks of his wisdom.[36] In the words of John Calvin (1509–1564): "There is not one blade of grass and there is no color in this world that is not intended to make us rejoice."[37] One of God's goals of the creation is to fill Adam's children with praise. Just as we read the Scriptures and rejoice, so God intended for us to read the book of creation and have praise arise in our hearts.

But one of the most important points about Proverbs 8 and the wisdom literature as it pertains to the creation is that creation culminates in Christ.[38] There is a canonical pattern that moves from Solomon's "Lady Wisdom" as a metaphor, a personification of God's wisdom ingrained in the creation, to the incarnate wisdom of God, Jesus. The apostle Paul, for example, moves from general to special revelation, from creation to Christ: "He is the image of the invisible God, the firstborn of all creation. For by him all things were created, in heaven and on earth, visible and invisible, whether thrones or dominions or rulers or authorities—all things were created through him and for him. And he is before all things, and in him all things hold together" (Col 1:15–17). The Son's preparatory activity in creation finds its counterpart in his work of redemption—he reclaims the children of Adam and delights in them as they reflect his image. If the greatest manifestation of wisdom in the Old Testament was the Torah, the law of God, now the Messiah is the greatest expression of wisdom on the earth—the Torah points to Jesus.[39] The wisdom-Christ connection is significant for the creation. The creation reveals the wisdom of God, but redemption is the pinnacle of the Triune God's activity.

To fail, then, to move from creation to redemption stops short of Christ and the gospel and saving special revelation. In more specific terms, the *telos* of the teleological argument is Jesus Christ. We can employ it as a stand-alone argument for the sake of discussion, but at some point, we must show Christ. We find this creation to Christ pattern in Paul's address to the philosophers at Mars Hill. Paul, for example, appeals to the order of creation and God's providential superintendence of the world: "And he made from one man every nation of mankind to live on all the face of the earth, having determined allotted periods and the boundaries of their dwelling place" (Acts 17:26). But Paul eventually speaks of Christ and the resurrection: "The times of ignorance God overlooked,

36. Waltke, *Proverbs 1–15*, 417.

37. John Calvin, *Sermons on 1 Corinthians*, no. 10, quoted in William J. Bouwsma, *John Calvin: A Sixteenth-Century Portrait* (Oxford University Press, 1988), 134–35; Waltke, *Proverbs 1–15*, 422; see also Randall Zachman, "The Universe as the Living Image of God: Calvin's Doctrine of the Universe Reconsidered," *Concordia Theological Quarterly* 61/4 (1997): 299–313.

38. Derek Kidner, *Proverbs*, TOTC (IVP Academic, 2008), 74.

39. Cf. G. K. Beale and D. A. Carson, eds., *Commentary on the New Testament Use of the Old Testament* (Baker Academic, 2007), 855.

but now he commands all people everywhere to repent, because he has fixed a day on which he will judge the world in righteousness by a man whom he has appointed; and of this he has given assurance to all by raising him from the dead" (Acts 17:30–31). How long Paul rested on natural theological arguments before he drew upon special revelation we do not know. Luke most likely records a compressed version of Paul's address that probably unfolded over several hours, if Paul's sermons are any indication (Acts 20:7–9). Regardless of how long he presented natural theological arguments, this much is true: the teleological argument functions best in concert with special revelation and gets people to Christ.

Given everything that Scripture supplies for the argument from design, what of Hume's criticisms against it? What is the significance of a dual-sourced (nature and Scripture) argument from design for apologetics? Hume's criticisms carry weight if we are dealing with a rationalist version of the teleological argument. Separated from Scripture, Hume has a point. How do we know whether the sin we see in the world can be traced back to the god who made the creation? We can only get as far as the existence of a god, the "unknown god" of the Stoics and Epicureans (Acts 17:23). We can know that the God of creation should be worshiped and is eternal, all-powerful, and the creator (Rom 1:19–21), but we cannot get much further than that. We need the corrective lenses of Scripture to see God's wisdom clearly. In the words of Roland Murphy: "The Israelites did not hold creation / wisdom apart from their belief at a secondary level. In fact, they developed their own theology of wisdom / creation, and it should be accepted as a genuine heritage from the Bible. They did not advert to the 'tension' that modern theologians find between salvation and creation. They created a canon that embraces both."[40] Through the spectacles of Scripture we can see what Hume calls defects and imperfections and recognize they do not go back to the designer but to the sin introduced by the designed, by rebellious humans. More than this, we can appeal to nature and Scripture as Paul did at Mars Hill and point unbelievers to God's wisdom in the creation to something as small as the ant and as great as the seemingly unending cosmos. At its best, the teleological argument is a "dialogue with the created world," which explains who stands behind it as its creator.[41]

Conclusion

God never intended for his image bearers to close their eyes to the book of nature and only learn of his wisdom, power, and glory from the Scriptures.

40. Murphy, "Wisdom and Creation," 5.
41. Murphy, "Wisdom and Creation," 7.

Scripture is, of course, a *sine qua non* of our knowledge of the Triune God, Christ, and the gospel. But God has set the Scriptures within the larger book of nature, and we can read its testimony writ large in the cosmos. Even one such as Immanuel Kant (1724–1804) admitted the grandeur of the creation: "Two things fill the mind with ever new and increasing admiration and reverence, the more often and steadily one reflects on them: *the starry heaven above me and the moral law within me*. I do not need to search for them and merely conjecture them as though they were veiled in obscurity or in the transcendent religion beyond my horizon; I see them before me and connect them immediately with the consciousness of my existence." Kant looked upon the starry host and recognized that the vastness of the cosmos annihilated him—it relativized his importance as an animal creature. Kant meditated upon the presence of the moral law within him and saw that it testified to his worth as an intelligent, sentient creature.[42] These are important pieces of the overall framework for recognizing both human finitude and God's transcendence and at the same time human worth and God's immanence. They are part of setting the context for the gospel. When we press the claims of the argument for design upon unbelievers, it causes them to ask: Whence the cosmos and my sense of morality? We can point unbelievers to the God of Scripture as we read the book of nature. We can then open the book of Scripture to point them to Christ. In presenting the argument from design, we must read the books of nature and Scripture in concert.[43]

42. Immanuel Kant, *Critique of Practical Reason*, in *Practical Philosophy*, trans. and ed. Mary J. Gregor (Cambridge University Press, 1999), 269–70; cf. Paul Guyer, "Introduction: The Starry Heavens and the Moral Law," in *The Cambridge Companion to Kant*, ed. Paul Guyer (Cambridge University Press, 1992), 1–25.

43. Murphy, "Wisdom and Creation," 10.

7

The Macrocosmic Teleological Argument

Evidence for God's Existence from Creation

> **Thesis 7:** Since God has embedded knowledge of his being, wisdom, and power in the creation, Christians can appeal to teleological argument as they read the book of nature through the corrective lenses of Scripture.

> The God who made the world and everything in it, being Lord of heaven and earth, . . . gives to all mankind life and breath and everything.
>
> —Acts 17:24–25

Historically, the argument from design has probably been the most widely used to demonstrate the existence of God.[1] The prevalence of the teleological argument (TA) is especially true today since modern scientific discoveries show that the fundamental structure of the cosmos balances on a razor's edge. Given the vastness of the cosmos, the window for fostering life in the universe is amazingly microscopically small. This has led many leading scientific voices to conclude that life on earth is not by

1. Robin Collins, "The TA: An Exploration of the Fine-Tuning of the Universe," in *The Blackwell Companion to Natural Theology*, ed. William Lane Craig and J. P. Moreland (Wiley-Blackwell, 2012), 202–81, here 202.

chance but by design. In the light of the scientific discoveries, if the previous chapter examined the historical and scriptural foundations for the TA, then this chapter explores the TA in the light of some of these discoveries. The last chapter focused upon the book of Scripture, whereas this chapter focuses upon the book of nature. Both chapters work in concert to set forth a full-fledged account of the argument from design. *This chapter argues that since God has embedded knowledge of his being, wisdom, and power in the creation, Christians can appeal to the teleological argument as they read the book of nature through the corrective lenses of Scripture.*[2] However, we must first explain what the TA is not. The TA is like but ultimately different from intelligent design (ID) arguments recently associated with the work of William Dembski and Michael Behe.[3] ID arguments largely deal with biological organisms and argue from ignorance—that is, because we cannot explain how something works, that means it requires the intervention of an Intelligent Designer.[4] The TA is different than ID arguments because it employs the principle of *final causality*—there is a purpose for everything in the creation.[5] Moreover, the purpose (or *telos*) is not merely a natural end, such as a bird's coloring serving as camouflage to protect it from predators. Rather, we can distinguish between proximate natural *teloi* (ends) versus the ultimate *telos*, which is theological. The ultimate telos of the whole creation is to point to the existence and glory of the Triune God who created it all. ID arguments typically rest upon the idea of inexplicable complexity in biological organisms, whereas such a feature is unnecessary in created things, according to Thomas Aquinas (1225–1274).[6] Proponents of ID arguments might debate with evolutionary biologists whether a biological phenomenon comes about by design or natural processes, whereas the TA presupposes proximate and ultimate final causality, which bypasses the debate between natural selection and chance.[7] Moreover, ID arguments get us only to an Intelligent Designer, such as the god of Deism, but not necessarily to the God of Scripture. Whereas

2. Also John Polkinghorne, *Quarks, Chaos, and Christianity: Questions to Science and Religion*, rev. ed. (The Crossroad Publishing Company, 2005), 30.

3. James Dominic Rooney, "Evolutionary Biology and Classical TAs for God's Existence," *Heythrop Journal* 54 (2013): 617–30; William Newton, "A Case of Mistaken Identity: Aquinas's Fifth Way and Arguments of Intelligent Design," *New Blackfriars* (2014): 569–78; cf. e.g., Michael J. Behe, *Darwin's Black Box: The Biochemical Challenge to Evolution* (The Free Press, 1996); William Dembski, *Intelligent Design: The Bridge Between Science and Theology* (IVP Academic, 2002).

4. Newton, "Mistaken Identity," 571.

5. Edward Feser, *Scholastic Metaphysics: A Contemporary Introduction* (Editiones Scholasticae, 2014), 92–101.

6. Newton, "Mistaken Identity," 572.

7. Newton, "Mistaken Identity," 573.

Aquinas, for example, points us to the God of Scripture because his argument from design is an explanation of Exodus 3:14–15.[8] Recall from the previous chapter how Aquinas describes the TA:

> We see that things which lack intelligence, such as natural bodies, act for an end, and this is evident from their acting always, or nearly always, in the same way, so as to obtain the best result. Hence it is plain that not fortuitously, but designedly, do they achieve their end. Now whatever lacks intelligence cannot move towards an end, unless it be directed by some being endowed with knowledge and intelligence as the arrow is shot to its mark by the archer. Therefore some intelligent being exists by whom all natural things are directed to their end; and this being we call God.[9]

The inanimate creation reflects the design of the creator because the creation does not move by chance but is instead a reflection of the divine mind and thus evidence of his existence, wisdom, power, and glory. Correlatively, as the previous chapter demonstrated, Scripture joins the chorus of the creation, and they both sing with one voice—the God of Scripture is creator of the cosmos. This chapter therefore first surveys the TA as it comes from patristic, medieval, and early modern Reformed theologians. It then turns to illustrate the TA from some recent scientific examples from the book of nature. Second, the chapter considers two chief objections: Who designed God, and what about the existence of evil? Third, the chapter concludes with some scriptural observations about the TA.

The Argument from Design

Paley's Watchmaker

One of the most well-known versions of the TA appears in William Paley's (1743–1805) watchmaker analogy. Paley imagines walking through an uncultivated land and comes upon a stone. He asks himself how the stone came to be there. He supposes that if he did not know any better, he might believe that the stone had been there forever. A stone in a field seems like it fits—it is in a context where one might find many other stones. What, however, if Paley found a watch on the ground, and he asked the same question, "How did the watch get here?" Upon closer inspection, unlike the stone, the watch

8. Newton, "Mistaken Identity," 576; Thomas Aquinas, *Summa Theologica* (Christian Classics, 1948), Ia q. 2 art. 3, sed contra.

9. Aquinas, *Summa Theologica*, Ia q. 2 art. 3.

consists of many parts assembled for a specific purpose. The different parts create motion so that, as the different parts move, the watch keeps track of time. If the watch parts were assembled in any other way, or if they were of different sizes so they could not fit in the watch, then the watch would be incapable of motion and keeping time. Paley draws the inference that someone, therefore, at some point and at some place formed the watch for the purpose of keeping time; this person or persons both understood what was needed to create a machine capable of keeping time and thus designed it for this purpose.[10] No one can attribute the watch's configuration or existence to impersonal, accidental forces because of its complexity and proximate telos, telling time. The watch also has an ultimate telos of revealing the creativity, ingenuity, and intelligence of the watchmaker(s). Thus, there is an agent or agents who designed and made it. Paley applied this type of reasoning to the design in the creation and its relationship to its creator, God. Not everyone was persuaded by Paley's argument.

Charles Darwin (1809–1882) countered Paley's watchmaker analogy explicitly. Darwin writes: "The old argument of design in nature, as given by Paley, which formerly seemed to me so conclusive, fails, now that the law of natural selection had been discovered. We can no longer argue that, for instance, the beautiful hinge of a bivalve shell must have been made by an intelligent being, like the hinge of a door by man. There seems to be no more design in the variability of organic beings and in the action of natural selection, than in the course which the wind blows."[11] Darwin believed that given enough time, natural processes combined with random chance account for the complexity of natural things in the world.[12] Darwin's objection lives on in the present day in the claims of atheist scientists such as Richard Dawkins: "Although atheism might have been *logically* tenable before Darwin, Darwin made it possible to be an intellectually fulfilled atheist."[13] Yet, Darwin's and Dawkins's objections prove more than they likely admit. For Paley, *God* accounts for the design of the creation, whereas for Darwin and Dawkins, *nature* takes the place of God—nature is god. Remember, human beings are hardwired for worship;

10. William Paley, *Natural Theology, or Evidences of the Existence and Attributes of the Deity Collected from the Appearances of Nature* (Sheldon and Company, 1879), 5; John M. DePoe, "The Heavens Declaring the Glory of God: Contemporary TAs," *Review and Expositor* 111/3 (2014): 244–58, here 245–46.

11. Charles Darwin, *The Life and Letters of Charles Darwin: Including an Autobiographical Chapter*, vol. 1, ed. Francis Darwin (D. Appleton and Company, 1911), 278–79; DePoe, "Contemporary TAs," 246.

12. DePoe, "Contemporary Teleological Arguments," 246.

13. Richard Dawkins, *The Blind Watchmaker: Why the Evidence of Evolution Reveals a Universe Without Design* (Norton, 2015), 10; DePoe, "Contemporary TAs," 246.

thus, in the absence of God, atheists like Dawkins make nature take the place of God. Nature becomes its own creator in Dawkins's view. Upon closer examination of the evidence, however, these objections prove less weighty.

The Book of Nature

Since the earliest days of the church, theologians have appealed to the order present in creation as evidence of the existence of God.[14] In his *Apology*, a written defense of the Christian faith, Tertullian (160–240) explains: "The object of our worship is the One God, He who by his commanding word, His arranging wisdom, His mighty power, brought forth from nothing this entire mass of our world, with all its array of elements, bodies, spirits, for the glory of His majesty; whence also the Greeks have bestowed on it the name of κόσμος."[15] He goes on to explain, "You have the proof from the works of His hands, so numerous and so great, which both contain you and sustain you, which minister at once to your enjoyment, and strike you with awe."[16] That Tertullian appeals to the Greek philosophers and their observation that the world was not χαος (*chaos*) but rather κόσμος (*cosmos*), or order, is significant. In other words, even non-Christians recognized that there was order rather than disorder in the universe. He also appeals to another Greek philosophical idea: "We have already asserted that God made the world, and all which it contains, by His Word, and Reason, and Power. It is abundantly plain that your philosophers, too, regard the Logos—that is, the Word and Reason—as the Creator of the universe." Another noteworthy aspect of Tertullian's appeal to the order present in creation is that he first points to the order in the creation and then segues to the person of Christ.[17] In other words, the TA is part of the foundation of Christology, or, there is no redemption apart from creation.

As noted in the previous chapter, Athanasius (ca. 296–373) and Gregory of Nazianzus (329–390) both set their claims about the person of Christ upon the doctrine of creation and the order present in it. Athanasius writes of the order that marks human bodies: "Such order indicates that they did not come into being spontaneously, but shows that a cause preceded them, from which one can apprehend the God who ordered and created all things."[18] Likewise,

14. For what follows, see Matthew Levering, *Proofs of God: Classical Arguments from Tertullian to Barth* (Baker Academic, 2016), 29–39, 44, 67–68, 75–77.

15. Tertullian, *Apology*, XVII, in *ANF*, III:31.

16. Tertullian, *Apology*, XVII, in *ANF*, III:32.

17. Tertullian, *Apology*, XX, in *ANF*, III:34.

18. Athanasius, *On the Incarnation* (St. Vladimir's Seminary Press, 2011), §2 (50).

Gregory writes: "God through the beauty and order of things seen, using sight as a guide to what transcends sight without losing God through the grandeur of what it sees."[19] Gregory avers, "Anyone who refuses to progress this far in following instinctive proofs must be very wanting in judgment."[20] Like Tertullian, both Athanasius and Gregory see the creation as the entre to the doctrine of salvation. Either the sinner will look upon the creation and long "for God, the First Cause," or he "looks at things visible and makes of these a god."[21] Some scientists such as Dawkins do precisely this—they attribute the order in the creation to what amounts to a deified self-creating universe. Can we ascribe the order in the universe to random forces that are indifferent to what unfolds within its boundaries? What accounts for the κόσμος in the creation that enables scientists like Dawkins to explore and discover the repetitions that recede and run with rhythmic regularity? What would Gregory say to Dawkins? "Away with them, those who deny what is divine, and ascribe no cause to the good, ineffable composition of the universe, whether in creation or in the upkeep of all things."[22]

Other theologians who make similar arguments are Saint Augustine (354–430) and John of Damascus (ca. 675–749). Augustine included an appeal to the order of the cosmos in a catechism aimed at new converts. Augustine explained that a person can be familiar with the beauty of the landscape of the countryside to the point where it becomes commonplace to him until he introduces it to someone who has never seen it before. The person's excitement at the landscape's novelty and splendor renews his own appreciation of its beauty. He says that if this person is bound to the other in love, their excitement can make old things become new. If a beautifully manicured landscape can amaze us and strengthens the bond of love, though it is only the work of "men's hands," how much more can we lift up our minds "to the contemplation of the skill or design of the contriver, and thence have them soar upward to the admiration and praise of the all-creating God, in whom is the most fruitful end of love."[23] In John of Damascus's *The Orthodox Faith*, he opens his work with an appeal to the creation. Echoing Paul and Romans 1:20, he writes, "Creation itself in the way that it is maintained and

19. Gregory of Nazianzus, *On God and Christ: The Five Theological Orations and Two Letters to Cledonius* (St. Vladimir's Seminary Press, 2002), Oration XXVIII.xiii (47).

20. Gregory, *On God and Christ*, Oration XXVIII.vi (41).

21. Gregory, *On God and Christ*, Oration, XXVIII.xiii (47).

22. Gregory of Nazianzus, *On God and Man: The Theological Poetry of Gregory of Nazianzus*, trans. Peter Gilbert (St. Vladimir's Seminary Press, 2001), I.i.6 (76).

23. Augustine, *The First Catechetical Instruction*, trans. Joseph P. Christopher (The Newman Press, 1952), XII.xvii (41–42).

governed proclaims the grandeur of the divine nature."[24] John asks a series of rhetorical questions:

> What set these things in motion and keeps them in their ceaseless and unhindered course? Is there not an architect of these things, a principle inherent in all of them, by which the universe is moved and ordered? Who is the architect of these things? Is it not he who made them and brought them into being? For we cannot attribute such a power to a spontaneous process. Even if things have come into being by a spontaneous process, what has arranged it? Let us grant this too, if you wish. Then what maintains them and preserves them in accordance with the principles by which they first came to exist? Clearly something other than a spontaneous process. What else is this but God?[25]

Whether patristic (Tertullian, Athanasius, Gregory, Augustine) or early medieval (John of Damascus), these theologians appeal to the order of the creation as evidence of God's existence. Reformed theologians in the early modern period continue this trend.

Stephen Charnock (1628–1680) reached back to the Middle Ages and the arguments of Aquinas through the early modern commentary of Domingo Bàñez (1528–1604).[26] Aquinas argues that people can know God by both faith and natural reason, though because "human reason is very deficient in things concerning God . . . it was necessary for Divine matters to be delivered to them by way of faith."[27] Bàñez approvingly comments upon this conclusion by first reaching to Scripture and Romans 1, and second to the creation and the fact that the existence of creatures points back to the existence of a creator.[28] Charnock summarizes these points with the succinct statement: "So that [God's] existence is not only probably but demonstratively proved from the things of the world."[29] In addition to Bàñez and Aquinas, Charnock also positively appeals to John of Damascus.[30] Like the earlier patristic and medieval theologians, Charnock points to the production and harmony

24. John of Damascus, *On the Orthodox Faith*, trans. Norman Russell (St. Vladimir's Seminary Press, 2022), §1 (59).

25. John of Damascus, *Orthodox Faith*, §3 (64).

26. I am grateful for my friend and colleague, Jonathan Cruse, suggesting that I include Stephen Charnock.

27. Aquinas, *Summa Theologica*, IIaIIae q. 2 art 4.

28. Domingo Bàñez, *Scholastica Commentaria in Prima Partem Angelici Doctoris*, vol. 1 (Petrus Borremans, 1614), 78 col. 2.

29. Stephen Charnock, *The Existence and Attributes of God*, 2 vols., ed. Mark Jones (Crossway, 2022), I:67.

30. Charnock, *Existence and Attributes of God*, I:72; John of Damascus, *Orthodox Faith*, §3 (62–64).

throughout the creation that reveals God's wisdom: "As the cause is known by the effects, so the wisdom of the cause is known by the elegance of the work, the proportion of the parts to one another."[31] What types of harmony does Charnock have in mind? He explains that chance is incapable of fixing an order for general and particular ends, such that the creation down to its smallest details works in concert. He writes: "How conveniently is the sun placed, at a distance from the earth and the upper heavens to enlighten the stars above and enliven the earth below."[32] He asks the question, "Who can behold the sun rising in the morning, the moon shining in the night, increasing and decreasing in its due spaces, the stars in their regular motions night after night, for all ages, and yet deny a president over them?"[33]

What all these theologians argue is that there is an order in the universe that did not arise by chance or random factors. Rather, God designed everything, and even science confirms these claims. The scientific data is legion, so we can only examine a few examples, but these examples sufficiently illustrate the TA to show that Scripture and the book of nature speak with one voice. There are four basic forces in nature: strong nuclear force, weak nuclear force, electromagnetic force, and gravity. We can look at one of these forces to see how carefully balanced the universe is. The strong nuclear force defines how atomic nuclei bind together. The nucleus of an atom consists of positively charged protons and electrically neutral neutrons. The glue that binds these protons and neutrons together is called the *strong nuclear force*.

In the sun, hydrogen nuclei fuse to form helium and consequently release heat energy; the fraction of mass converted to heat is 0.007. If the strong force were weaker, with a conversion efficiency of only 0.006, helium fusion would not be possible, and the universe would have remained composed solely of hydrogen, incapable of supporting life. If the strong force were stronger and provided a conversion efficiency that was 0.008, then all the hydrogen in the universe would have quickly fused to helium, leaving no hydrogen for molecules such as water or the complex building blocks of life (DNA, proteins, and virtually all other biological molecules).[34] Furthermore, we can consider the electromagnetic and gravitational forces. Their relative strength can be expressed as the ratio of the electrostatic force between two protons to the

31. Charnock, *Existence and Attributes of God*, I:80.
32. Charnock, *Existence and Attributes of God*, I:82.
33. Charnock, *Existence and Attributes of God*, I:87.
34. Martin Rees, *Just Six Numbers: The Deep Forces That Shape the Universe* (Basic Books, 2000), 2; Alister E. McGrath, *A Fine-Tuned Universe: The Quest for God in Science and Theology* (Westminster John Knox, 2009), 119. My thanks to Bill Challener for helping me write this section to ensure its accuracy.

gravitational force between them, which is 10^{36}. The electromagnetic force binds electrons to atomic nuclei and enables all chemistry—the binding of atoms to one another to form molecules. The gravitational force becomes apparent only at macroscopic distances and is the dominant interaction force between matter at cosmological distances due to the nearly perfect cancellation at the macroscopic level of the electromagnetic force generated from equal numbers of positive and negative charges. What would happen if the gravitational force were larger and the force ratio was 10^{30} instead of 10^{36}? Atoms and molecules would behave as they do now, but objects would not need to be as large before gravity became comparable in strength to the other forces. The number of atoms required to make a star would be a billion times less in a universe with a force ratio of 10^{30}. Planets the size of the earth would have a gravitational force a billion times greater; the strength of gravity would stunt the possibility of life on them. In such an imaginary world, insects would need thick legs to support them, and animals could not get much larger. Gravity would crush creatures the size of humans.[35] Alternatively, planets with the same gravitational force as the earth would have a diameter of only a quarter mile and a surface area of only 0.2 square miles, insufficient to support the existence of intelligent beings.

The strong nuclear force and the electromagnetic force are just two of the six basic cosmological constants in the universe, though there are many other important constants. In addition to the four forces mentioned above, we may also add: the ratio of electromagnetic force constant to gravitational force constant, the ratio of electron to proton mass, the ratio of the number of protons to the number of electrons, the expansion rate of the universe, the entropy level of the universe, the mass density of the universe, the speed of light, the age of the universe, the initial uniformity of radiation, the fine structure constant, and the average distance between stars. These different parameters appear to be "just right" or "fine-tuned" to support intelligent life.[36] Scientists have said that the earth lies in a "Goldilocks zone," which means that all the right conditions exist that enable human life to exist.[37]

35. Rees, *Just Six Numbers*, 2, 30; McGrath, *Fine-Tuned Universe*, 119.

36. Doug Powell, *Holman QuickSource Guide to Christian Apologetics* (Holman Reference, 2006), 52–53; DePoe, "TAs," 246–47; William Lane Craig, "Design and the Anthropic Fine-Tuning of the Universe," in *God and Design: The TA and Modern Science*, ed. Neil A. Manson (Routledge, 2003), 155–77; Luke Barnes and Allen Hainline, "The Cosmic Coincidences of Fine Tuning," in *The Story of the Cosmos: How the Heavens Declare the Glory of God*, ed. Paul M. Gould and Daniel Ray (Harvest House Publishers, 2019), 183–202.

37. Paul Davies, *The Goldilocks Enigma: Why Is the Universe Just Right for Life?* (Allen Lane, 2006); Michael A. Corey, *The God Hypothesis: Discovering Design in Our "Just Right" Goldilocks Universe* (Rowman & Littlefield, 2001).

The fine-tuning of these astrophysical constants may be beyond the grasp of the average reader, but physicists have observed these "coincidences" necessary to support intelligent life for decades. But even the uninitiated have looked upon the cosmos and observed that life requires precision and has not come about through chance or from an inanimate creation. In the words of one poet,

> Now, who can this surprising Fact conceive,
> Who this Event Fortuitous believe,
> That the Brute Earth unguided should embrace
> The only Useful, only proper Place,
> Of all the Millions in the empty Space?[38]

The fine-tuning characteristics of the universe have not gone unnoticed by scientists. As noted above, theologians have appealed to them in the broadest of terms—the design, order, and regularity of the cosmos. Scientists have also observed the same patterns in the universe and have concluded that the universe bears the marks of design. Physicist Paul Davies, winner of the 1995 Templeton Prize and who carries no brief for traditional religious belief, has looked at the data and remarks:

> The very fact that the universe *is* creative, and that the laws have permitted complex structures to emerge and develop to the point of consciousness—in other words, that the universe has organized its own self-awareness—is for me powerful evidence that there is "something going on" behind it all. *The impression of design is overwhelming.*[39]

Theoretical physicist and cosmologist Stephen Hawking (1942–2018) has drawn similar conclusions as Davies when he writes of the cosmological constants:

> What can we make of these coincidences? Luck in the precise form and nature of fundamental physical law is a different kind of luck from the luck we find in environmental factors. It cannot be so easily explained, and has far deeper physical and philosophical implications. *Our universe and its laws appear to have a design that both is tailor-made to support us and, if we are to exist,*

38. Richard Blackmore, *Creation: A Philosophical Poem, Demonstrating the Existence and Providence of God* (S. Powell, 1727), 4.

39. Paul Davies, *The Cosmic Blueprint* (Unwin Ltd., 1989), 203, emphasis added; Hugh Ross, *The Creation and the Cosmos: How the Latest Scientific Discoveries Reveal God* (RTB Press, 2018), 177; Polkinghorne, *Quarks, Chaos, and Christianity*, 47.

> *leaves little room for alteration*. That is not easily explained, and raises the natural question of why it is that way.[40]

The scientific investigation of the cosmos is a vital labor as people read the book of nature and observe its design, harmony, and order. But such observations are not merely the wishful thinking of theologians.

NASA scientist and planetary physicist Robert Jastrow (1925–2008) has observed: "For the scientist who has lived by his faith in the power of reason, the story ends like a bad dream. He has scaled the mountains of ignorance; he is about to conquer the highest peak; as he pulls himself over the final rock, he is greeted by a band of theologians who have been sitting there for centuries."[41] Charnock sums up the overall force of the TA when he writes:

> As when a man comes into a palace, built according to the most exact rule of art and with an unexceptionable convenience for the inhabitants, he would acknowledge both the being and skill of the builder, so whoever shall observe the disposition of all the parts of the world—their connection, their comeliness, the variety of seasons, the swarms of different creatures, and the mutual offices they render to one another—cannot conclude less than that it was contrived by an infinite skill, effected by infinite power, and governed by infinite wisdom.[42]

Scientists such as those surveyed above and theologians agree that the order and even design of the cosmos is evidence for the existence of God, but not all are persuaded. Nobel Prize-winning theoretical physicist Steven Weinberg (1933–2021) has looked upon the order of the universe and has observed, "The more the universe seems comprehensible, the more it also seems pointless."[43] Weinberg presses in on this point: "The effort to understand the universe is one of the very few things that lifts human life a little above the level of farce, and gives it some of the grace of tragedy."[44] In other words, not all scientists are convinced that the order of the universe points to the existence of God.[45] This requires us to consider some objections.

40. Stephen Hawking and Leonard Mlodinow, *The Grand Design* (Bantam Books, 2012), 162.

41. Robert Jastrow, *God and the Astronomers* (Norton, 1978), 116; Ross, *Creation and the Cosmos*, 180.

42. Charnock, *Existence and Attributes of God*, I:91.

43. Steven Weinberg, *The First Three Minutes: A Modern View of the Origins of the Universe*, updated ed. (Basic Books, 1988), 154. I am grateful to Bill Challener and Earl Fyke, who passed on Weinberg's quote to me only days apart.

44. Weinberg, *The First Three Minutes*, 155.

45. For various responses to fine-tuning constants in the universe, see Geraint F. Lewis and Luke A. Barnes, *A Fortunate Universe: Life in a Finely Tuned Cosmos* (Cambridge University Press, 2016), 237–89.

Objections

Who Designed God?

When Christians present TAs and say that the design, proximate, and ultimate final causality of the creation point to the universe's creator, sometimes unbelievers press the question: Who designed God? If we seek a designer for the creation, then why not seek a designer for the designer?[46] Assuming that there is a designer for the designer, the TA supposedly collapses under its own weight. According to Dawkins, "the familiar question 'Who made God?'" is one that "most thinking people discover for themselves. A designer God cannot be used to explain organized complexity because any God capable of designing anything would have to be complex enough to demand the same kind of explanation in his own right. God presents an infinite regress from which he cannot help us to escape."[47] But Dawkins's objection fails and does not undermine the TA because, while it raises the question about God's origin and nature, it cannot easily dismiss the evidence.[48] Shorn from Scripture, Christians might have to admit that the TA leaves open the possibility that there is a deity greater than God, a rival power in the cosmos. There are, though, three further points of consideration in response to the question of who designed God.

First, there is a sense in which the question of who designed God is not unlike objections to the cosmological argument. Namely, every effect has a cause, which means that at the beginning of all things there must be an eternal uncaused God, which is God. Aquinas calls the cosmological argument "the argument from motion." He explains that all things in motion are put in motion by another, but that we cannot have an infinite regression of things moving from potentiality to actuality, from being inert to being in motion. There must be a first mover, a being that possesses pure actuality: "Therefore it is necessary to arrive at a first mover, put in motion by no other; and this everyone understands to be God."[49] Or in simpler terms, the buck must stop somewhere. Atheists have missed the fact that Aquinas says that God is the uncaused cause, that he is a being that possesses pure actuality, or that he is the first mover. Every effect must have an antecedent cause, but God is not an effect but is himself an uncaused cause. Likewise, everything in the creation is designed and created, yet God himself is neither created nor designed because he is self-existent.

46. For a philosophical treatment of this question, see Michael Augros, *Who Designed the Designer? A Rediscovered Path to God's Existence* (Ignatius Press, 2015).

47. Richard Dawkins, *The God Delusion* (Random House, 2006), 109.

48. DePoe, "Contemporary Teleological Arguments," 255–56.

49. Aquinas, *Summa Theologica*, Iae q. 2 art. 3.

Second, when we read the books of nature and Scripture in tandem, the Bible confirms the natural theological claim that God is an uncaused cause—that he is self-existent. Recall that Aquinas's five ways of demonstrating God's existence is an extended explanation of the significance of Exodus 3:14, "I AM WHO I AM." Aquinas does not take off on a philosophical flight of fancy and sophistry when he uses his five ways to explain the eternality and aseity of God, as he ultimately follows a path first cut by Scripture itself. New Testament scholarship rightly argues that Revelation 1:4 is an intra-canonical explanation of the divine name: "Grace to you and peace from him who is and who was and who is to come."[50] The apostle Paul also describes God as "immortal, invisible, the only God" (1 Tim 1:17; Rom 1:23).

Third, disconnected from Scripture, people might erroneously conclude that there could be competing deities in the cosmos and that there is another god besides the God of Christianity, a designer for the designer. Keep in mind that by virtue of their image-bearing status, all people intuitively know better: "For although they knew God, they did not honor him as God or give thanks to him, but they became futile in their thinking" (Rom 1:21). Nevertheless, the book of nature read in concert with the book of Scripture teaches us that there is only one true God. The apostle John takes us back to before the creation when nothing existed and tells us, "In the beginning was the Word, and the Word was with God, and the Word was God" (John 1:1). The Triune God of the Bible is the deity who stands behind the creation. Later in his gospel Christ tells us, "This is eternal life, that they know you, the only true God, and Jesus Christ whom you have sent" (John 17:3), which is another assertion of the Bible's God being the only true God. Asking the question of who designed the designer is understandable, but in the light of the books of nature and Scripture, unbelievers cannot persist in this question. They can object to the answer and say that the TA does not point to the existence of the one true God, but then it is incumbent upon them to offer better explanation for the fine-tuning features and statistical improbabilities of the creation's order. In truth, to attribute the universe's fine-tuning features to random chance and chaos requires greater faith than even the Bible asks of Christians.

Physicist Michael Guillen has pointed out the religious nature of science. Over the years overly confident scientists have predicted that scientific progress would drive religion and the supernatural into extinction, an echo of Max Weber's (1864–1920) claim that science has disenchanted the world.[51]

50. G. K. Beale and D. A. Carson, eds., *Commentary on the New Testament Use of the Old Testament* (Baker Academic, 2007), 1089.

51. Max Weber, *The Vocation Lectures*, trans. Rodney Livingstone, ed. David Owen and Tracy B. Strong (Hackett Publishing Co., 2004), 13.

Guillen counter argues that the concepts of physics, such as quantum mechanics, special relativity, and general relativity, border on the supernatural. The phenomena of quarks, the quantum vacuum, quantum entanglement, dark matter, dark energy, gravity waves, black holes, wormholes, and the like, "are no less other-worldly than any religion's God, gods, Supreme Being, or beings." Far from disenchanting the world, science "has increased by orders of magnitude our awareness of the universe's deep, jaw-dropping mysteries."[52] But rather than turn to the God who has created these mysteries, some scientists prefer to divinize the cosmos. They attribute order, design, and regularity to impersonal forces of the universe and place their faith in these forces. Furthermore, the sad fact is that when they divinize the cosmos and attribute the existence of the universe to chance, they strip it of meaning, ethics, and ultimate final causality. As astrophysicist Luke Barnes observes, we must here distinguish between science and naturalism. Science seeks to understand the world using concepts such as the laws of nature. Naturalism, on the other hand, claims that all that exists is the material universe and that everything has a natural cause—there is no divine being, no creator. Science is not the success of naturalism, and the claims of naturalists are not the conclusions of science.[53] As noted above, Weinberg is a naturalist and thus concludes that human existence is a tragedy. Contemporary English poet Steve Turner gives provocative expression to such tragedy when he writes that, if we owe our existence merely to chance, "disaster" and all manner of human chaos and cruelty are "but . . . man worshipping his maker."[54] If Weinberg is right, then humanity's existence is indeed a tragedy of epic proportions.

What About the Existence of Evil?

A second common objection relates to the evident evil, entropy, and chaos that we find in the world. Recall that Hume argued that the TA proved too much. That is, if design points to a creator, then does not the chaos and evil in the world say that the world's designer is evil? Following in Hume's footsteps, Dawkins writes that many human ailments, such as hernias, prolapsed uteruses, sinus infections, and the like directly result from the fact that we once ambulated on all fours but now walk upright. Our defects are simply

52. Michael Guillen, *Believing Is Seeing: A Physicist Explains How Science Shattered His Atheism and Revealed the Necessity of Faith* (Tyndale Refresh, 2021), 61.

53. Lewis and Barnes, *A Fortunate Universe*, 337.

54. Steve Turner, "Chance," in *Up to Date: Poems 1968–1982* (Hodder and Stoughton, 1982), 107.

the march of evolutionary progress over hundreds of millions of years. But he adds to his protest that humans can easily observe the cruelty and wastefulness of natural selection. Predators are beautifully designed to hunt their prey, while the prey are also beautifully designed to escape them. Such design seems like a zero-sum game; who does God favor, the hunter or the hunted?[55] The objection to the TA because of the existence of evil, chaos, and apparent defects in the world fails on at least three fronts.

First, assuming the validity of Dawkins's objection that the TA proves that the world is poorly designed does not mean that the world is not designed. A bad design does not negate the presence of design. Just because a car is poorly designed does not mean that the car is not designed. The universe may be the equivalent of a Ford Pinto, an AMC Pacer, a Zastava Yugo, or a Pontiac Aztec, but each of these infamously bad cars was designed by someone.

Second, to claim that something is poorly designed implies that the critic knows a better way to do it. Such an objection lacks humility given the extremely limited human perspective of the cosmos. Astrophysicists readily acknowledge that they can only observe five percent of the cosmos.[56] If 95 percent of the cosmos has gone unstudied, unobserved, and unexamined, how can someone who knows so little pass judgment on God's design? God's response to Job comes to mind:

> Who is this that darkens counsel by words without knowledge? Dress for action like a man; I will question you, and you make it known to me. Where were you when I laid the foundation of the earth? Tell me, if you have understanding. Who determined its measurements—surely you know! Or who stretched the line upon it? On what were its bases sunk, or who laid its cornerstone, when the morning stars sang together and all the sons of God shouted for joy? (Job 38:2–7)

Third, Scripture informs us that disease, frailty, natural disasters, and the like have entered the creation through sin: "Sin came into the world through one man, and death through sin, and so death spread to all men because all sinned" (Rom 5:12). God cursed the ground because of Adam's sin (Gen 3:17–18), and he subjected it to "futility" (Rom 8:20). So, the supposed defects are because of sin, not because there is a flaw in the design or in the designer. A later chapter examines the question regarding the existence of evil in greater detail. Nevertheless, critics might point to the existence of evil as an obstacle to the TA for the existence of God, but on naturalist assumptions, they have a

55. Dawkins, *God Delusion*, 134.
56. Lewis and Barnes, *A Fortunate Universe*, 141, 183.

bigger hill to climb. The Christian must explain why evil exists. The naturalist, on the other hand, must explain why evil *and* good exist.[57]

Conclusion

The Bible is our authoritative foundation for apologetics, but we must not forget to read and cite the book of nature. Read in concert, we hear the unified voice of both books testifying to the existence of the one, true God. When we consider the evidence and the weight of the fine-tuning required for the existence of life in the cosmos, the chances of random chance producing the conditions for life are staggeringly infinitesimal if not outright impossible—what some physicists have labeled a one in a trillion possibility.[58] Imagine a burglar correctly guessing the twelve-digit code to a safe on the first try.[59] This gives us an idea of how improbable the existence of human life in the cosmos is. Such observations should hopefully lead us to see our insignificance in the creation, our finitude, which led Gregory of Nyssa (ca. 335–395) to observe:

> When I behold each craggy hill, each valley, and each plain clothed with fresh-springing grass; the varied foliage with which the trees are adorned; at my feet the lilies to which nature has given a double dower, of sweet fragrance, and of beauty of color; and in the distance the sea, towards which the wandering cloud is sailing,—my mind is possessed with a sadness which is not devoid of enjoyment. When, in autumn, the fruits disappear, the leaves fall, and the branches of the trees stripped of their ornaments, hang lifeless, in viewing this perpetual and regularly recurring alternation the mind becomes absorbed in the contemplation, and rapt as it were in union with the many-voiced chorus of the wonderous forces of nature. Whoso gazes through these with the inward eye of the soul feels the littleness of man in the greatness of the universe.[60]

In the glorious light of nature, we sinners can then say with the psalmist, "When I look at your heavens, the work of your fingers, the moon and the stars, which you have set in place, what is man that you are mindful of him, and the son of man that you care for him?" (Ps 8:3–4).

57. Lewis and Barnes, *A Fortunate Universe*, 347. Note, the book's authors do not agree on the significance of fine-tuning constants, and this observation comes from Barnes, who believes fine-tuning points to the existence of God.

58. Polkinghorne, *Quarks, Chaos, and Christianity*, 38.

59. Lewis and Barnes, *A Fortunate Universe*, 241, 337–38.

60. Gregory of Nyssa, as quoted in Alexander von Humboldt, *Cosmos: A Sketch of a Physical Description of the Universe*, 2 vols., ed. E. C. Otté (George Bell & Sons, 1901), I:28–29.

As important as the scientific evidence for the TA is, we need not be intimidated that it lies beyond our grasp. If Jesus calls us to come unto him like little children (Matt 18:2–5), then it behooves us to read the book of nature in a similar fashion. Observing the beauty of the creation is not merely an emotional response but rather a window into the nature of reality—a glimpse into the mind of the creator.[61] We can behold the magnificence of the creation from the vast expanse of the cosmos to the smallest of creatures:

> What various wonders my Observers see
> In a small Insect, the sagacious Bee!
> Mark how the little untaught Builders square
> Their Rooms, and in the Dark their Lodgings reer!
> Nature's Mechanicks they unwearied strive,
> And fill with curious Labyrinths the Hive.
> See, what bright Strokes of Architecture shine
> Thro' the whole Frame, what Beauty, what Design.[62]

We can gaze upon the creation and see the handiwork of the creator. G. K. Chesterton (1874–1936) once pondered how children can revel in monotony. They can cry out to a parent, "Do it again," with the simplest of things until the parent is utterly exhausted: making a funny face, generating silly sounds, or tossing the child up in the air as she shouts with glee. Chesterton asks, is it possible for God to exult in monotony? "It is possible that God says every morning, 'Do it again' to the sun; and every evening, 'Do it again' to the moon. It may not be automatic necessity that makes daises alike; it may be that God makes every daisy separately, but has never got tired of making them. It may be that He has the eternal appetite of infancy; for we have sinned and grown old, and our Father is younger than we."[63]

The TA for the existence of God is not merely about putting scientific evidence in the balance and seeing whether it tips in favor of God. Instead, by the regenerative work of the Spirit and appealing to the book of nature, we can remove obstacles to belief and turn sinners to Christ. By contemplating the books of nature and Scripture, we can have God's divine library inspire us to worship: "O Lord, how manifold are your works! In wisdom have you made them all; the earth is full of your creatures" (Ps 104:24). A sanctified regenerated reason does not gaze upon the visible and material splendors of the cosmos alone but looks beyond them to their divine origin and contemplates

61. Polkinghorne, *Quarks, Chaos, and Christianity*, 24, 34, 78.
62. Blackmore, *Creation*, 156.
63. G. K. Chesterton, *Orthodoxy* (John Lane, 1909), 106–7.

their spiritual significance. Jesus himself did this very thing when he taught us to look to the lilies of the field and the ravens of the heavens to learn how God cares for his children (Luke 12:22–31). The books of creation and Scripture should never be separated in our minds. Every Christian should continuously cultivate in himself the habit of their hallowed association.[64] Like little children we can revel in the glory, beauty, and majesty of God's creation:

> See how sublime the uplifted Mountain rise,
> And with their pointed Heads invade the skies.
> How the high Cliffs their craggy Arms extend,
> Distinguish States, and sever'd Realms defend;
> How ambient Shores confine the restless Deep.
> And in their ancient Bounds the Billows keep;
> The hollow Vales their smiling Pride unfold;
> What rich Abundance do their Bosoms hold?
> Regard their lovely Verdure, ravish'd view
> The springing Flow'rs of various Scent and Hue.
> Not Eastern Monarchs, on their Nuptial Day
> In dazzling Gold and Purple shine so gay
> As the bright Natives of th'unlabor'd Field,
> Unverst in Spinning, and in Looms unskill'd.
> See how the rip'ning Fruits the Gardens crown,
> Imbibe the Sun, and make his Light their own.
> See the sweet Brooks in Silver Mazes creep,
> Enrich the Meadows, and supply the Deep;
> While from their weeping Urns the Fountains flow.
> And Vital Moisture, where they pass, bestow.
> Admire the narrow Stream, and spreading Lake.
> The proud aspiring Grove, and humble Brake.
> How do the Forests and the Woods delight?
> How the sweet Glades and Opening charm the Sight?
> Observe the pleasant Lawn and airy Plain,
> The fertile Furrows rich with various Grain;
> How useful all? How all conspire to grace
> Th' extended Earth, and beautifie her Face?[65]

Thus, the TA is beneficial both for defending the faith to others and also for feeding our own faith so that we can put our own fears and doubts to rest as we read the books of nature and Scripture in tandem. Contemplating the

64. Joseph Atkinson, "Moral Æsthetics; or the Goodness of God in the Ornaments of the Universe," *The Biblical Repertory and Princeton Review* 24/1 (1852): 38–52, here 50.

65. Blackmore, *Creation*, 15.

creation's design can instill love, praise, and worship in our hearts. And we can also point others to the sense of longing they have in their own hearts for God—we can turn them away from their idols so they too can behold the beauty, design, and order of the creation and worship God in love.

8

The Microcosmic Teleological Argument

Evidence for God's Existence in the Human Body

> **Thesis 8:** The teleological argument should include the microcosmos of the human body, which means that Christians should appeal to it in their apologetics.

And he made from one man every nation of mankind to live on all the face of the earth, having determined allotted periods and the boundaries of their dwelling place, that they should seek God, and perhaps feel their way toward him and find him.

—Acts 17:26–27

Male and female he created them.

—Genesis 1:27

I praise you, for I am fearfully and wonderfully made.

—Psalm 139:14a

William Shakespeare's *Hamlet* captures the world of ironies that we find in human beings: "What a piece of work is man! How noble in reason! how infinite in faculties! in form and moving, how express and admirable! in action how like an angel! in apprehension, how like a god! the beauty of the world! the paragon of animals! And yet, to me, what is this quintessence of dust?"[1] These words echo the psalmist, who asks, "What is man that you are mindful of him, and the son of man that you care for him? Yet you have made him a little lower than the heavenly beings and crowned him with glory and honor" (Ps 8:4–5). Human beings are mere dust, yet taken by God, raised, and crowned with glory. And by glory, we should understand that the psalmist refers to the fact that God has impressed his image upon humans.[2] This is why Paul says that "all have sinned and fall short of the glory of God" (Rom 3:23). That is, because we sin, we fall short of the righteous and holy image God first gave Adam. Paul appeals to this truth when he writes that man "is the image and glory of God" (1 Cor 11:7). Conversely, when God saves us in Christ, we behold the glory of God and "are being transformed into the same image from one degree of glory to another" (2 Cor 3:18). That humans possess the image of God rests within the larger framework of the creation. John Calvin (1509–1564) once observed: "In the whole architecture of his world God has given us clear evidence of his eternal wisdom, goodness, and power, and though he is invisible in himself he shows himself to us in some measure in his work. The world is therefore rightly called the mirror of his divinity."[3] In a sense, the creation bears God's image, which is why both humans and the creation reveal God's glory: "The heavens declare the glory of God" (Ps 19:1a).

In other words, everything that God creates bears traces of his attributes, from the least to the greatest of things: from things as small as the ant (Prov 6:6) to as great as stellar bodies (Ps 19:1–4). If the macro creation carries God's wisdom, and humans are a part of the creation, then they too carry God's wisdom and shine forth God's attributes. The macro- and microcosmic creations both testify to the wisdom, power, and existence of God. That God impresses his image upon both the macrocosmic and microcosmic creations, the cosmos and humans, means that both have apologetic value. The previous two chapters explored the teleological argument for God's existence from a macro perspective, yet in the contemporary period, how many extend this argument to the microcosmic creation of the human body? Calvin, recall, believed that human anatomy said as much about God's existence as

1. William Shakespeare, *Hamlet*, ed. Jeff Dolven (Barnes and Noble, 1994), act II, scene ii, 287–98.

2. Dane C. Ortlund, "What Does It Mean to Fall Short of the Glory of God? Romans 3:23 in Biblical-Theological Perspective," *Westminster Theological Journal* 80 (2018): 121–40.

3. John Calvin, *Hebrews and 1 & 2 Peter*, CNTC, ed. T. F. Torrance and David W. Torrance (Eerdmans, 1996), comm. Heb. 11:3 (160); Randall A. Zachman, "The Universe as the Living Image of God: Calvin's Doctrine of the Universe Reconsidered," *Concordia Theological Quarterly* 61/4 (1997): 299–312.

the cosmos: "Hence certain of the philosophers have not improperly called man a *microcosm* . . . as being a rare specimen of divine power, wisdom, and goodness, and containing within himself wonders sufficient to occupy our minds, if we are willing to employ them."[4] Calvin was reflecting upon and agreeing with an observation long ago made by Aristotle (384–322 BC): "Now if this can occur in an animal, why should not the same be true of the universe as a whole? If it can occur in a small world, it can also occur in a great one."[5] Calvin gleaned the idea from Aristotle and Cicero (106–43 BC). Other Reformed theologians like Francis Turretin (1623–1687), Johannes Heidegger (1633–1698), Peter Martyr Vermigli (1499–1562), Andreas Hyperius (1511–1564), Petrus Van Mastricht (1630–1706), and Guillaume Bucanus (d. 1603) followed suit.[6] Likewise, in the more recent past, the likes of Herman Bavinck (1854–1921) made the same argument regarding the significance of humans as image bearers:

> The essence of human nature is its being [created in] the image of God. The entire world is a revelation of God, a mirror of his attributes and perfections. Every creature in its own way and degree is the embodiment of a divine thought. But among creatures, only man is the image of God, God's highest and richest self-revelation and consequently the head and crown of the whole creation, the *imago Dei* and the epitome of nature, both *mikrotheos* and *mikrokosmos*.[7]

This means that in keeping with God's two books, nature and Scripture, the human body is as important as the wider creation as evidence for the existence of God. This idea is not peculiar to the Reformed tradition but has roots in patristic theology. Gregory of Nyssa (330–395) writes, "Man is a little world in himself and contains within himself all the elements which make up the universe."[8] The idea also appears in others such as Origen (ca. 185–253), Basil

4. John Calvin, *Institutes of the Christian Religion*, trans. Henry Beveridge (Eerdmans, 1957), I.v.3.

5. Aristotle, *The Physics*, trans. Philip H. Wicksteed and Francis M. Cornford, vol. 2, Loeb Classical Library (Harvard University Press, 1934), VIII.ii (286–89); cf. George Perrigo Conger, *Theories of Macrocosms and Microcosms in the History of Philosophy* (Columbia University Press, 1922).

6. Francis Turretin, *Institutes of Elenctic Theology*, trans. George Musgrave Giger, ed. James T. Dennison Jr. (P&R, 1992–1997), I.iii.7; III.i.12–13; Heinrich Heppe, *Reformed Dogmatics: Set Out and Illustrated from the Sources*, trans. G. T. Thompson (Allen & Unwin, 1950), 220–21.

7. Herman Bavinck, *Reformed Dogmatics*, 4 vols., ed. John Bolt, trans. John Vriend (Baker Academic, 2003–2007), II:530.

8. Gregory of Nyssa, *On the Soul and the Resurrection*, in *Nicene and Post-Nicene Fathers*, vol. 5, ed. Philip Schaff (Eerdmans, 1994), 433.

of Caesarea (330–ca. 378), Gregory of Nazianzus (329–390), and Maximus the Confessor (ca. 580–662).[9]

We need to understand what both books have to say about the body and consider its apologetic force. These truths are important in engaging unbelievers because, just as we point to the creation and the teleological argument, we can extend this argument to the teleology of the human body. There are macrocosmic and microcosmic teleological arguments. Pointing to the teleology of the human body is further evidence for God's existence, but in our present cultural moment, the body contains much-needed general revelation apologetic claims of the Christian faith. Many within the church are vulnerable to recent attacks upon Christian belief as it relates to sexuality and transgenderism. While we must bring Scripture to the discussions about God's existence, sexuality, and transgenderism, Christians needlessly impoverish their apologetics if they fail to appeal to the book of nature and the body. We can demonstrate that nature and Scripture speak with one voice, and we can equip the church with important knowledge, especially to protect our children and inform their parents, who often encounter false teaching as it relates to theological anthropology. *More specifically, this chapter defends the thesis that the teleological argument should include the microcosmos of the human body, which means that Christians should appeal to it in their apologetics.* This chapter, therefore, first explores the microcosmic teleology of the human body. Second, it sets forth the apologetic significance of the human body. Third, the chapter addresses the recent challenges brought by the religion—yes, *religion*—of transgenderism.

The Microcosmic Teleology of the Human Body

Beyond the general theological observations of Calvin and Bavinck, perhaps few have explored the human body with greater depth than William Paley (1743–1805) in his *Natural Theology*.[10] Paley goes into great detail about the structure, parts, and functions of plants and animals, insects, and the greater cosmos.[11] In the light of all of these bodies, he invokes his famous watchmaker analogy and argues: "Contrivance must have had a contriver; design, a

9. Origen, *Homilies on Genesis*, I.xi, in *Homilies on Genesis and Exodus*, The Fathers of the Church, trans. Ronald E. Heine (The Catholic University of America Press, 1982), 61; Lars Thunberg, *Microcosm and Mediator: The Theological Anthropology of Maximus the Confessor* (C. W. K. Gleerup Lund, 1965), 140–52.

10. William Paley, *Natural Theology: or, Evidences of the Existence and Attributes of the Deity Collected from the Appearances of Nature* (Sheldon & Company, 1879).

11. Paley, *Natural Theology*, 45–51, 180–92, 212–28.

designer; whether the machine immediately proceeded from another machine or not."[12] Paley, of course, also applies this principle of contrivance (creating with a purpose) to his examination of human anatomy: "I know no better method of introducing so large a subject, than that of comparing a single thing with a single thing; an eye, for example, with a telescope. As far as the examination of the instrument goes, there is precisely the same proof that the eye was made for vision, as there is that the telescope was made for assisting it. They are made upon the same principles; both being adjusted to the laws by which the transmission and refraction of rays and light are regulated."[13]

Paley includes diagrams of the eye and telescope to show how they are similarly constructed and then asks, "How is it possible, under circumstances of such close affinity, and under the operation of equal evidence, to exclude contrivance from the one, yet to acknowledge the proof of contrivance having been employed, as the plainest and clearest propositions, in the other?"[14] While Paley examines other examples from the creation (insects, astronomical phenomena, plants, and animals), in his judgment, human anatomy presents some of the most compelling evidence for the existence of God. Paley writes:

> Amongst the multitude of proofs, it is *one* that does the business. . . . For my part, I take my stand in human anatomy; and the examples of mechanism I should be apt to draw out from the copious catalogue which it supplies, are the pivot upon which the head turns the ligament within the socket of the hip-joint, the pully or trochlear muscles of the eye, the epiglottis, the bandages which tie down the tendons of the wrist and instep, the slit or perforated muscles at the hands and feet, the knitting of the intestines to the mesentery, the course of the chyle [fluid of fat and lymph droplets that drains from the lacteals of the small intestine into the lymphatic system during digestion] into the blood, and the constitution of the sexes as extended throughout the whole of the animal creation. To these instances the reader's memory will go back, as they are severally set forth in their places; there is not one of the number which I do not think decisive.[15]

Paley observes the intricacy, wonder, and evident design of the human body in its sundry parts and believes that, like the wider cosmos, it presents evidence of a designer, a maker—God. Paley admits that the invisible things of nature point to the existence of an intelligent mind concerned with production, order, and support—all teachings of natural theology. We, of course,

12. Paley, *Natural Theology*, 11.
13. Paley, *Natural Theology*, 13.
14. Paley, *Natural Theology*, 15.
15. Paley, *Natural Theology*, 292.

require special revelation to give us the particulars of who this God is given that human reason alone cannot explain everything of who God is. But at the same time, what Christian will turn away from any credible communication of divine knowledge, in this case, the truths communicated by the anatomy of the human body? No amount of natural theology diminishes the desire for the knowledge given by supernatural revelation or changes a person's disposition to receive it in any other manner than with humility and thankfulness.[16]

Paley has a point given what Scripture says about our image-bearing status and even human anatomy. The opening chapter of Scripture testifies that God made humans, male and female, and gave them his image (Gen 1:27). The psalmist gives praise to God for the intricacy and wonder of his body:

> For you formed my inward parts; you knitted me together in my mother's womb. I praise you, for I am fearfully and wonderfully made. Wonderful are your works; my soul knows it very well. My frame was not hidden from you, when I was being made in secret, intricately woven in the depths of the earth. Your eyes saw my unformed substance; in your book were written, every one of them, the days that were formed for me, when as yet there was none of them. (Ps 139:13–16)

Paley's natural theological observations concerning human anatomy invite us to read about the body in the book of nature—to have one eye on the book of Scripture and the other on the book of nature. Of course, given Paley's nineteenth-century context, we want to be cautious about employing his medical and scientific evidence and account for advances in these fields. Nevertheless, when we consider the microcosm of the human body, it presents us with a universe of wonder equal in beauty and design to the greater cosmos. In the words of Stephen Charnock (1628–1680), "All the sinews, veins, arteries, bones, like a piece of embroidery or tapestry, were wrought by God, as it were, with deliberation, like an artificer who draws out the model of what he is to do in writing and sets it before him when he begins his work. And indeed the fabric of man's body, as well as his soul, is an argument for a divinity."[17]

The human heart, for example, beats roughly once every second, 100,000 times a day, and as much as 3.5 billion times in a lifetime.[18] The heart pushes 70 gallons of blood per hour, 1,680 gallons of blood per day, and 45,990,000 gallons in a lifetime.[19] And, yet, one day it just stops. Why does it stop? We

16. Paley, *Natural Theology*, 295.

17. Stephen Charnock, *The Existence and Attributes of God*, 2 vols., ed. Mark Jones (Crossway, 2022), I:97.

18. Bill Bryson, *The Body: A Guide for Occupants* (Doubleday, 2019), 112.

19. Bryson, *The Body*, 113.

understand when the elderly die—they grow old, and their bodies degenerate to the point that they can no longer sustain life. But why do otherwise young, healthy individuals die in the prime of life apart from any known medical conditions? The simple yet profound and at times difficult answer is God's sovereign providence. As Job once observed, "You have decided the length of our lives. You know how many months we will live, and we are not given a minute longer" (Job 14:5 NLT).

The human body exhibits God's design in terms of sex—that is, that God has created humans male and female (Gen 1:27). In the nineteenth century scientists believed that diet, air temperature, and a woman's mood during the early stages of pregnancy determined a person's sex.[20] Scientific investigation proves that females have two X chromosomes and males have X and Y chromosomes, which confirms the biblical truth that God made humans male and female.[21] But the chromosomal differences between the sexes account for more than anatomical dissimilarities.[22] The differences between the sexes are not limited to those of height, weight, and genitalia. On average, women carry 50 percent more fat on their bodies than fit, healthy men. This fat gives women reserves that their bodies can employ for milk production during challenging dietary conditions while breast-feeding an infant. Women's bones wear out sooner, especially after menopause, and thus women typically suffer more bone breaks later in life in comparison to men. Women suffer from Alzheimer's twice as often as men, in part because they live longer, but also because they experience higher rates of autoimmune diseases. Women metabolize alcohol differently, which means that they become intoxicated more easily than men. Women carry bags differently than men; researchers believe it is because women typically have wider hips, which necessitates a less perpendicular carrying angle for their forearms so that their swinging arms do not constantly bang their legs. Women also generally carry bags with their palms facing forward, whereas men carry bags with their palms facing

20. Bryson, *The Body*, 276.

21. This is not to deny the existence of chromosomal abnormalities. Instead of the XX or XY chromosomal pairing, a person may only have one X chromosome or an extra chromosome, XXY. In such cases a person might have the male or female internal or external sex organs, though they may not go through full physical development at puberty. For example, a child with female sex organs may not start having menstrual periods. This condition is called disorders of sexual development, or DSD. This chapter does not address the issue of DSD, which is a rare occurrence. Incidents of DSD is approximately 1 in 4,500–5,500 in newborns (Mary García-Acero et al., "Disorders of Sexual Development: Current Status and Progress in the Diagnostic Approach," *Current Urology* 13/4 [2020]: 169–78, here 169). Unlike gender dysphoria that has no objective diagnostic markers, DSD involves objective, biological, diagnostic markers and thus is not in view.

22. For what follows, see Bryson, *The Body*, 282–83.

backward. Women have different heart-attack symptoms than men; women suffer abdominal pain and nausea, whereas men have pain in their chest and down their left arm. Men get Parkinson's disease more often than women. They also die by suicide more often, even though they suffer less than women from clinical depression. Men are more vulnerable to infection than women, which is true across most animal species, not just humans.

The difference between the sexes also impacts the administration of medication. Judith Mank of University College London told the BBC program *Inside Science* in 2017, "'People had been assuming that women are just 20 percent smaller than men, but otherwise are much the same.' We now know that there is much more to it than that."[23] The difference between the sexes can have significant consequences in drug trials because if the test patients are mostly men, it can skew data and be harmful to women because men and women respond differently to drugs. Phenylpropanolamine was an over-the-counter medicine for colds and coughs until doctors discovered that it increased the risk of hemorrhagic stroke in women but not in men. The sleeping drug Ambien officially cut their dose by half in 2013 when the manufacturer discovered that a large percentage of female users were suffering impairment when they tried to drive the morning after taking the medication according to the standard dose. In short, in a thousand small and large ways, men and women are very different beings.[24]

To these physiological features we can also add the faculties of the soul. As Charnock observes, "If we believe we have souls and understand the state of our own faculties, we must be assured that there was some invisible hand that bestowed those faculties and the riches of them upon us."[25] To put this in average terms, why do human beings, out of all the creatures on earth, possess a conscience, have notions of moral right versus wrong, admire beauty, and create inspiring works of art, music, and literature? How can swirling atomic collections of carbon create paintings like Leonardo da Vinci's (1452–1519) *Mona Lisa* (1503) or Vincent van Gogh's (1853–1890) *The Starry Night* (1889)? Does any other creature on the earth create music like Ludwig van Beethoven's (1770–1827) *Symphony No. 9* (1824), The Beatles's *White Album* (1968), or Sam Cooke's (1931–1964) "Twistin' the Night Away" (1960)? What creatures other than humans think through moral and ethical questions? What animals write beautiful poetry such as William Shakespeare's (1564–1616) *Sonnets* (1609), probing literature such as Fyodor Dostoevsky's (1821–1881) *Crime*

23. Bryson, *The Body*, 283.
24. Bryson, *The Body*, 282.
25. Charnock, *Existence and Attributes of God*, I:103.

and Punishment (1866), or autobiographical accounts of both suffering and triumph such as Frederick Douglass's (1818–1895) *Narrative of the Life of Frederick Douglass* (1845)? How can inanimate carbon become conscious unless God has created humans and breathed into them the breath of life and given them intellectual, moral, affective, voluntary faculties. In short, is this all not evidence that God has created human beings in his image?[26]

Apologetic Significance

If we take a stereoscopic view of humans through nature and Scripture, each book conveys important information about the God who made us in his image and the apologetic significance of a biblical anthropology.

Image Bearing

Beyond the wonders and marvels of human anatomy and how it displays the wisdom and creativity of God, as image bearers, humans are analogs of God. The Westminster Confession describes what it means to bear the image of God:

> After God had made all other creatures, he created man, male and female, with reasonable and immortal souls, endued with knowledge, righteousness, and true holiness, after his own image; having the law of God written in their hearts, and power to fulfill it: and yet under a possibility of transgressing, being left to the liberty of their own will, which was subject unto change. Beside this law written in their hearts, they received a command, not to eat of the tree of the knowledge of good and evil; which while they kept, they were happy in their communion with God, and had dominion over the creatures. (4.2)

Human beings bear the imprint of these attributes (knowledge, righteousness, and holiness) in our existence as well as in the common notions (the law written upon human hearts) that all human beings share (Rom 1:19–20; 2:14–15). Understanding the significance of bearing God's image plays an important role in what Calvin and other Reformed theologians have styled the twofold knowledge of God: the knowledge of God and of ourselves.[27] This means that,

26. See the arguments in Thomas Nagel, *Mind and Cosmos: Why the Materialist Neo-Darwinian Conception of Nature Is Almost Certainly False* (Oxford University Press, 2012). Note, Nagel is an atheist but nevertheless critiques neo-Darwinian materialist accounts for the origins of humans because they cannot account for consciousness.

27. Calvin, *Institutes*, I.i.1; see also Pierre Viret, *A Verie Familiare and Fruitful Exposition of the Christian Faith Contaeined in the Common Crede, Called the Apostles Crede* (n.d.), fol.

as when we consider the rest of the creation, when we study humanity we learn something about who God is. With an eye to Scripture, however, we can filter out that which is sinful and finite and recognize we are finite and fallen analogs of the infinite and sinless creator. With Scripture and nature, as we examine human beings, we can present information to people about who God is by appealing to love, creativity, and even storytelling (as we will examine in the next chapter) as human attributes that point to the existence of God.

Anthropology and Apologetics

The rise of the religion of transgenderism presents an urgent and pressing need that makes biblical anthropology a vital tool in apologetics in our current cultural moment.[28] Historic Christian orthodoxy has affirmed the unity of body and soul. Thomas Aquinas (1225–1274), for example, writes: "To be united to the body belongs to the soul by reason of itself, as it belongs to a light body by reason of itself to be raised up. And as a light body remains light when removed from its proper place, retaining its proper place; so the human soul retains proper existence when separated from the body, having an aptitude and a natural inclination to be united to the body."[29] The human soul retains its proper existence even when separated from the body at death because the soul awaits the resurrection for its reunification with the body; souls have a natural inclination to dwell in bodies. Humans consist of immaterial (soul) and material (body) aspects that God intended to harmoniously coexist in unity.[30] Humans are ensouled bodies, or conversely, they are bodied souls.[31] A concomitant truth of the body-soul unity is that God created humans with generally trustworthy bodily senses as our senses are how we interact with the world around us. As Bavinck observes, "Knowledge of the truth is possible only if we begin with the fact that subject and object, and knowing and being, correspond to each other."[32]

Bi; Richard A. Muller, "'*Duplex cognitio dei*' in the Theology of Early Reformed Orthodoxy," *Sixteenth Century Journal* 10/2 (1979): 51–62.

28. See similar comments by Helen Joyce, who calls transgenderism an ideology and "subjective belief system" (Helen Joyce, *Trans: When Ideology Meets Reality* [One World, 2021], 3–4).

29. Aquinas, *Summa Theologica*, Ia q. 76 art. 1 ad. 6.

30. Reformed theologians have historically argued that the faculty psychology, or parts of the soul, include the *intellect* and *will*, of which the former is associated with the mind (see Richard A. Muller, *Post-Reformation Reformed Dogmatics*, vol. 1, *Prolegomena to Theology*, 2nd ed. [Baker Academic, 2003], 355–59; *Dictionary of Latin and Greek Theological Terms: Drawn Principally from Protestant Scholastic Theology*, 2nd ed. [Baker Academic, 2017], s.v. *anima* [27–29]).

31. Aquinas, *Summa Theologica*, Ia q. 75 art. 4; also q. 76 art. 1.

32. Herman Bavinck, *Christian Worldview*, trans. and ed. Nathaniel Gray Sutanto et al. (Crossway, 2019), 38–39.

Bavinck's realism here does not ignore the noetic effects of sin, the effects of sin upon the mind. But he nevertheless presses the point that body and mind work in concert because this is the way that God has created us. God has connected human souls and minds to the external world around them through their bodies:

> The organs of our perception are thus connected to the elements, out of which the whole cosmos is composed, by virtue of a common origin, and so each of us knows the world in a particular way and from a particular side. In each of these resides a specific energy that corresponds to the distinct works that the objective world confers to the senses. Thus, all intellectual knowledge begins with sense perception. To acquire knowledge, Scripture refers man not to his own reason but to God's revelation in all his works. Lift up your eyes, and see the one who has created all things; [lift them up] to the teaching and the testimony; otherwise, they shall perish.[33]

Bavinck's realism (or for that matter, Scripture's realism) is the opposite of the Cartesian mind-body dualism and Kantian subjectivity that Enlightenment philosophers have pressed to devastating effect.

René Descartes (1596–1650) promoted two chief ideas in his philosophy and quest to establish a firm basis for human knowledge. First, he believed that freedom of the will was a necessary principle for human existence: "Now freewill is in itself the noblest thing we can have because it makes us in a certain manner equal to God and exempts us from being his subjects; and so its rightful use is the greatest of all the goods we possess, and further there is nothing that is more our own or the matters more to us. From all this it follows that nothing but free will can produce our greatest contentments."[34] Free will makes people "equal to God," which releases them from being God's subjects. Descartes sets his declaration of human independence within a framework of doubt made famous in his maxim *Cogito ergo sum*, "I think therefore I am." Descartes was unsure of his senses, as they could be misleading him; he set aside all other opinions because they too might be erroneous; he also rejected everything that he had previously known because he feared they could all be illusions. But one incontrovertible truth he could not deny is that he was thinking: "And noticing that this truth—*I think, therefore I am*—was so

33. Bavinck, *Christian Worldview*, 38–39.

34. René Descartes, "To Queen Christina, 20 November 1647," in *The Philosophical Writings of Descartes*, vol. 3, *Correspondence*, ed. John Cottingham et al. (Cambridge University Press, 1991), 324–26, here 326. See also Charles Taylor, *Sources of the Self: Making of the Modern Identity* (Harvard University Press, 1989), 147; Michael Waldstein, "Introduction," in John Paul II, *Man and Woman He Created Them: A Theology of the Body*, trans. Michael Waldstein (Pauline Books & Media, 2006), 1–124, here 41.

firm and so assured that all the most extravagant suppositions of the skeptics were incapable of shaking it, I judged that I could accept it without scruple as the first principle of the philosophy I was seeking."[35] Descartes combines the gasoline of free will untethered from the authority of revelation with the fire of denying the senses and locating a foundation of knowledge purely within the mind.

Immanuel Kant (1724–1804) only adds more combustible materials to this Cartesian bonfire when he pushes for the self-legislative nature of the human will. Kant promotes the "idea of the will of every rational being as a universally legislating will." "According to this principle," writes Kant, "all maxims are rejected that are not consistent with the will's own universal legislation. Thus the will is not just subject to the law, but subject in such a way that it must also be viewed as *self-legislating*."[36] So, ethically, people should only submit to the laws and ethics that they themselves deem right—they set their own moral standards. And if people shape their own moral standards, then it naturally agrees with Kant's principle that they also shape the world around them.

This is not to say that people take the real world and reshape it into something useful, like a carpenter reshaping planks of wood into a table, but rather the world has no objective character to it until humans give it shape and meaning. Kant argues that humanity in its full moral perfection is God's only-begotten Son, the "'*Word*' (the *Fiat!*) through which all other things are, and without whom nothing that is made would exist." Kant weaves scriptural language into his claim to give it gravitas, but his point is clear—humans shape reality, and in this way, humans become children of God.[37] With Kant's belief in human rational autonomy that shapes an individual's ethics and world combined with Descartes's rejection of the reliability of the senses, human subjectivity rivals and consumes all forms of objectivity. In this hyper-subjective context where human dignity rests exclusively in the human mind divorced from the body, the living human body is entirely without meaning and dignity on its own.[38] Enlightenment philosophers gave birth

35. René Descartes, *Discourse on Method*, IV.xxxii, in *Discourse on Method and Meditations on First Philosophy*, 4th ed., trans. Donald A. Cress (Hackett Publishing Co., 1998), 18.

36. Immanuel Kant, *Groundwork of the Metaphysics of Morals*, rev. ed., trans. and ed. Mary Gregor and Jens Timmermann (Cambridge University Press, 2012), 43; Waldstein, "Introduction," 50.

37. Immanuel Kant, *Religion Within the Boundaries of Mere Reason and Other Writings*, rev. ed., ed. Allen Wood and George di Giovanni (Cambridge University Press, 2018), 94; Waldstein, "Introduction," 55.

38. Leon R. Kass, *Toward a More Natural Science: Biology and Human Affairs* (The Free Press, 1985), 277; Waldstein, "Introduction," 62.

to what Charles Taylor has called the *buffered self*—that is, a person who is closed and insusceptible to the outside world. Taylor includes the idea that the buffered self is a key ingredient in the disenchantment thesis because people are no longer open to the idea of spirits and enchanted powers.[39] Yet, rather than disenchantment being a key ingredient in creating the buffered self, in some cases enchantment has migrated from the world to the self. In Kant's view, humans are gods who create their own enchanted world according to their own wills, but they are worlds divorced from both body and cosmos. This individualistic landscape has both sidelined the body and made the Enlightenment concept of worldviews irrelevant. People no longer subscribe to systems of thought, a coherent view of the world, but instead create their own worlds, worlds that have little place for their bodies. There is a head-on collision between the biblical and Cartesian-Kantian view of humans.

The Religion of Transgenderism

Where these Enlightenment ideas have come home to roost is in transgenderism, which is the belief that a person's biological sex does not always align with their self-conscious mental perception.[40] A biological male can believe that he is a woman trapped in a man's body. One of the common instructional tools is a diagram called the "Genderbread Person." In the children-friendly illustration, the "Genderbread Person" shows that the seat of gender identity is the brain, the seat of attraction is the heart, gender expression is the whole body, but biological sex is expressed only by the genitalia.[41] Transgenderism sets the mind on a collision course with the body, as mind and body may say different things. Descartes's denial of the senses and Kant's autonomous reality-shaping mind rises with a vengeance in transgenderism. Postmodern queer theory in this respect views experience as more valid than fact.[42] Within the scope of transgenderism there is a reported phenomenon that psychologists have termed "rapid onset gender dysphoria" (ROGD), where a person quickly becomes convinced that their gender identity does not match their sex. The most recent *Diagnostic and Statistical Manual of Mental Disorders* (DSM-5) places gender dysphoria at .005–.014 percent for natal males and .002–.003 percent for natal females based on information about those who

39. Charles Taylor, *A Secular Age* (The Belknap Press, 2007), 27.

40. For a detailed explanation of transgenderism, see Joyce, *Trans*, 53–70.

41. Abigail Shrier, *Irreversible Damage: The Transgender Craze Seducing Our Daughters* (Regnery Publishing, 2020), 9–10.

42. Shrier, *Irreversible Damage*, 186.

sought medical intervention approximately a decade ago. This means that there is an incidence of gender dysphoria of one in ten thousand people. In the past decade, statistics say that ROGD cases are up 1,000 percent in the United States and up 4,000 percent in Great Britain. Seventy-five percent of those seeking gender dysphoria treatment are adolescent girls.[43] How do people commonly and popularly define gender dysphoria? Some have said it is a feeling: "Feeling different, not really fitting in, and not feeling feminine or masculine enough, . . . ever feeling uncomfortable in your body."[44] One's diagnosis for ROGD rests entirely on a person's say-so.[45]

But we must remember that humans are hardwired for worship, and if we reject the one, true, living God and his revelation, whether in nature or in Scripture, we will always seek to fill the void with an idol. In this vein, the transgender movement is religious and unscientific; by *unscientific*, I mean it rejects the plain-sense meaning of the book of nature. Advocates of transgenderism reject what their God-given bodies say about their sex. Many of the parents who deal with adolescent girls struggling with ROGD report that the people who promote transgenderism come off as cult leaders or drug dealers.[46] Interviews with those interacting with advocates of transgenderism say they "peddle misinformation, and outright medical falsehoods" and "extol the glories of testosterone as if it were a protein shake, not a Schedule II controlled substance." "They enthuse over double mastectomies as if they were of no more significance than a hair cut."[47] None of the transgender advocates explain that there are no diagnostic or empirical benchmarks for deciding that a biological girl is really a boy.[48] Public schools once committed to catechizing children into the religion of secularism have now shifted to catechize children into the religion of transgenderism.[49] While many Christians find transgenderism alarming, they may at first wonder how it undermines the Christian faith. Why worry about whether a boy wears clothing designed for girls or a girl wants to be called by a boy's name so long as they believe in Jesus? As the transgender religion seeps further into the culture, school boards look to protect their latest idol, and so the California Board of Education, for example, has created the category of *spiritual abuse* to defend transgenderism.

43. Committee on Nomenclature and Statistics of the American Psychiatric Association, *Diagnostic and Statistical Manual of Mental Disorders*, 5th ed. (American Psychiatrist Association Publishing, 2022), 451–59, here 454; Schrier, *Irreversible Damage*, 27, 32.

44. Shrier, *Irreversible Damage*, 45.

45. Shrier, *Irreversible Damage*, 45.

46. Shrier, *Irreversible Damage*, 54.

47. Shrier, *Irreversible Damage*, 55.

48. Shrier, *Irreversible Damage*, 64.

49. Shrier, *Irreversible Damage*, 60–61.

If parents or a church use spiritual beliefs to force others to adhere to rigid gender roles, then they are guilty of spiritual abuse.[50] Those who abuse their children naturally become the target of government intervention and have their children removed from their care. How can a child learn the gospel and Christian faith if they have been removed from their Christian home and placed in a context where they are catechized in an entirely different religion?

In this type of cultural setting, the book of nature takes on a whole new importance, though Scripture of course is an irreplaceable tool in the apologist's tool chest. Scripture clearly informs us that because of the fall, humans exchange the truth of God for a lie, and that their rejection of God's revelation manifests itself in unnatural relations: "For their women exchanged natural relations [φυσικὴν χρῆσιν] for those that are contrary to nature [παρὰ φύσιν]; and the men likewise gave up natural relations with women and were consumed with passion for one another, men committing shameless acts with men and receiving in themselves the due penalty for their error" (Rom 1:26–27). Note that Paul says that women (we can also include men, Rom 1:27) exchanged "natural" relations for those that are "contrary to nature." In Paul's usage, "nature" denotes the way something is by reason of its intrinsic state (Rom 2:14; 11:21, 24; Gal 2:15; 4:8; Eph 2:3); a rock by nature is hard, for example. In their fallen state, sinners exchange (μετήλλαξαν) what God has given by creation for things that go against his natural created order.[51] In other words, Scripture clearly teaches that God created humans male and female (Gen 1:26), and the existence of two sexes is clearly the natural order of things.

When we look to the book of nature, there are other relevant truths that confirm the book of Scripture. Deny the natural revelation that God has created humans male and female, and there are consequences when surgeries and drugs do not deliver the desired outcome, when the mind alone cannot bend reality to fit its will. If there are no diagnostic markers, measurable identifiers, or objective tests to confirm gender dysphoria, the only thing left is a feeling.[52] The religion of transgenderism has cast off Descartes's principle of knowledge: it is no longer "I think, therefore, I am," but "I feel, therefore I am." But what happens when one's feelings change?[53] Unsurprisingly, in 88 percent of cases of ROGD, parents who did nothing found that their children outgrew it.[54] Moreover, what does it say when over 90 percent of ROGD patients are

50. Shrier, *Irreversible Damage*, 76.

51. Douglas J. Moo, *The Letter to the Romans*, 2nd ed., NICNT (Eerdmans, 2018), 125–26.

52. Shrier, *Irreversible Damage*, 135.

53. I borrow this line from the title of Mark Goldblatt's *I Feel, Therefore I Am: The Triumph of Woke Subjectivism* (Bombardier Books, 2022).

54. Shrier, *Irreversible Damage*, 124.

white females?[55] ROGD looks more like religious hysteria akin to the Salem witch trials than a genuine medical phenomenon.[56]

The book of nature still has more data to consider, such as the anatomical differences between men and women. As noted above, the differences between the sexes have to do with more than genitalia. At the skeletal level, there are profound differences between men and women. Men have thicker and more sloped foreheads, and the mastoid region behind the ears is more pronounced in men. Men generally have squarer jaws, their pelvises are narrower, and the legs attach at the hip in a more parallel fashion, at less of an angle than a woman's. This means that men stand differently than women. Even after death these skeletal differences are noticeable; when archeologists find skeletal remains, they can determine whether the person was a male or female.[57] Differences regularly surface in the most mundane parts of life, such as the ways in which boys and girls play.[58] In the simplest of terms, from the youngest of ages, girls tend toward dolls and boys gravitate toward blocks.[59] There are obviously exceptions to the general observation, but the illustration reveals that boys and girls are different.

For those young women who transition, puberty blockers can irreversibly alter their development, stunt the growth of their brains, and sterilize them. For those women who take testosterone, they must take doses anywhere between ten and forty times the natural levels to produce the desired effects.[60] In high doses, testosterone can cause cancer in women and irreversible vaginal atrophy requiring a hysterectomy. The commonly performed double mastectomy for women who want to become men is irreversible and only serves an aesthetic, not a medical, purpose. Many women seeking to transition to try to become men also have phalloplasty performed, which is a highly painful and often unsuccessful surgery.[61] In an Orwellian fashion, these medical procedures are called "gender *affirming* surgeries" and not

55. Shrier, *Irreversible Damage*, 154; Joyce, *Trans*, 7.

56. See Emerson W. Baker, *A Storm of Witchcraft: The Salem Trials and the American Experience* (Oxford University Press, 2015). Also note that Joyce attributes the spread of transgenderism to the internet, which puts the American psyche on display to the world and makes people want to emulate American ways. Such desire to emulate a phenomenon colored those accused of being witches (Joyce, *Trans*, 110).

57. Shrier, *Irreversible Damage*, 162.

58. Jonathan Gottschall, *The Storytelling Animal: How Stories Make Us Human* (Mariner Books, 2012), 36–42.

59. Vivian Gussin Paley, *Boys and Girls: Superheroes in the Doll Corner* (University of Chicago Press, 2014).

60. Shrier, *Irreversible Damage*, 169.

61. Shrier, *Irreversible Damage*, 168, 170–71, 176–78, 182, 188; Joyce, *Trans*, 41.

what they really are: mutilations.[62] We should not be surprised by these facts given the religious character of transgenderism, as self-mutilation is not an uncommon practice among pagan religions. When Elijah faced off against the prophets of Baal at Mount Carmel, they "cried aloud and cut themselves after their custom with swords and lances, until the blood gushed out upon them" (1 Kings 18:28).

Once again, we must not underestimate the religious character of transgenderism, evident in the description of one former transgender believer. One author interviewed a young woman and recorded her observations:

> The gender ideology world she inhabited was a "cult," she insists because "when you're inside, you believe non-reality and you disbelieve reality. It literally got to a point where if I was in a queer space," she said, "I would look at someone, and I couldn't tell if they were male or female until they told me because I had trained myself to think that way. I would look at somebody and be like, 'I don't even know what their sex or gender is because I haven't asked them their pronouns yet.' I was so brainwashed."[63]

Transgenderism is dangerous because it rejects God's revelation. Try to bend God's natural or special revelation and there are spiritual and even physical consequences. Begin to deny natural revelation and it is much easier to reject special revelation. Why listen to the word of God when you refuse to acknowledge the reality of your own body?

Conclusion

The teleological argument for the existence of God is a powerful witness to the existence of God, but Christians need to follow the lead of the likes of Calvin, who extended the argument to the human body. At both the macrocosmic and the microcosmic levels, creation heralds God's wisdom and glory. We are "fearfully and wonderfully made" (Ps 139:14). Those words are not merely effusive praise but indicative of the revelatory character of the human body. As embodied creatures, our bodies are both organized and self-organizing entities, centers of consciousness, thought, desire, and the origin of deliberative action. We are not only self-maintaining and self-healing creatures, individuated, defined, and discrete; not only upright, proportioned, and invested with dignity; not only clever and smart, but capable of face-to-face

62. Shrier, *Irreversible Damage*, 182; see also Joyce, *Trans*, 71–111.
63. Shrier, *Irreversible Damage*, 188.

communication with other humans through gestures, verbal articulations, and even poetic speech.[64]

To borrow a line from Psalm 19, image bearer unto image bearer pours out speech, and human unto human reveals knowledge. One of the most powerful examples of this truth comes from Whittaker Chambers (1901–1961), who was an American citizen who joined the Communist Party after reading Vladimir Lenin's (1870–1924) *Soviets at Work*. He believed the dysfunction in his childhood family was the very chaos from which Communism promised to deliver him. Chambers believed he "found his church" in Communism, and he was zealous for it, as he became a Soviet spy.[65] But an unexpected, seemingly mundane observation set him on an entirely different path. He dates his break from his commitment to the Soviet Union and its atheism to one morning when he was sitting at his kitchen table with his daughter:

> My daughter was in her high chair. I was watching her eat. She was the most miraculous thing that had ever happened in my life. I liked to watch her even when she smeared porridge on her face or dropped it meditatively on the floor. My eye came to rest on the delicate convolutions of her ear—those intricate, perfect ears. The thought passed through my mind: "No, those ears were not created by any chance coming together of atoms in nature (the Communist view). They could have been created only by immense design." The thought was involuntary and unwanted. I crowded it out of my mind. If I had completed it, I should have had to say: Design presupposes God. I did not then know that, at that moment, the finger of God was first laid upon my forehead.[66]

Watching a child eat and marveling at her ear caused Chambers to defect from his Soviet masters and turn to the Christian faith.

The human body preaches the wisdom and creativity of God, and in our present cultural moment, the reality and truth of the body is ever more relevant as religious movements like transgenderism try to sweep away objective natural and supernatural revelation beneath a sea of human subjectivity. This chapter has touched on only some of the truths related to human anatomy, and thus it behooves Christians to learn more about the biology of the body so they can be prepared to answer for the hope that lies within them. Christians need to study the natural theological significance of the body so they can see that the books of nature and Scripture speak with one voice related to the

64. Kass, *Toward a More Natural Science*, 200.

65. Sam Tanenhaus, *Whittaker Chambers: A Biography* (Random House, 1998), 46.

66. Whittaker Chambers, *Witness: A True Story of Soviet Spies in America and the Trial That Captivated the Nation* (Regnery History, 1997), xlv.

human person and condition. Parents and churches need to study the book of nature so they can protect their covenant children from the false religion of transgenderism. Schooled in the books of nature and Scripture, Christians can be confident in the power of God's revelation and effectively defend the claims of the Christian faith in a world given over to idolatry.

9

Apologetics and Literature

Evidence for God's Existence in the Human Heart

Thesis 9: As Paul appealed to the pagan literature of his day, Christians can likewise employ literature written by unbelievers as they defend the faith.

> "In him we live and move and have our being"; as even some of your own poets have said, "For we are indeed his offspring."
>
> —Acts 17:28

"Image bearer unto image bearer pours out speech, and human unto human reveals knowledge, and there is no language in which their voice is not heard." These are words that do not appear in Scripture, but the truth of this statement certainly does. The psalmist wrote of the creation trumpeting the knowledge of God (Ps 19), but as we saw in the last chapter, we can say this about both the macro- and microcosmic creations. Human beings, embodied bearers of the image of God, are little *cosmoi*—little universes that reflect and are connected to the larger universe. Just as God has embedded his wisdom in the creation, so he has written his law upon the hearts of all people (Rom 2:15). Or to put this in terms that John Calvin (1509–1564) employs, "God has not only implanted in men's minds a seed of religion, but He also, lest anyone be excluded from happiness, so reveals Himself in the order of the universe and so clearly discloses Himself every day that men cannot open their eyes without being compelled to see Him."[1] God has implanted in every human being the *semen religionis*, "the seed of religion." Likewise, Abraham Kuyper (1837–1920) has rightly argued that "God speaks into man's conscience."[2] One of the places where we find a transcript of the seed of religion, a record of God speaking into the consciences of all peoples, is in literature, whether written by a Christian or not.

The Old Testament records the exile of Israel as many were carried off to Babylon, and among the throng were Daniel, Hananiah, Mishael, and Azariah. The book of Daniel tells us they were "youths without blemish, of good appearance and skillful in all wisdom, endowed with knowledge, and understanding learning, and competent to stand in the king's palace, and to teach them the literature and language of the Chaldeans" (Dan 1:4). God providentially gave these young men "learning and skill in all literature and wisdom" (Dan1:17). God had these Israelite young men study the literature of pagan Babylon. As verse 4 makes clear, God had "endowed [them] with knowledge, understanding learning" (Dan 1:4). As they studied, God gave them the ability to discern what was true and reject what was false so that they would more effectively serve in this gentile court. Like Moses before them, who was "instructed in all the wisdom of the Egyptians" (Acts 7:22), they were knowledgeable of pagan literature.[3] They were not alone, as the apostle Paul was able to engage the philosophers at Mars Hill and was sufficiently educated to quote the literature of his audience, the Stoic poets (Acts 17:22–23, 28). When Paul quoted the line, "In him we live and move and have our being," he was quoting the poet Aratus (ca. 315–240 BC) and his poem *Phaenomena*; when he quoted the line, "For we are indeed his offspring," he was quoting a *Hymn to Zeus* by Cleanthes (331–232 BC). To what extent can contemporary Christians say the same thing? How familiar are we with the literature of our own day?

With the corrective lenses of Scripture before our eyes to clarify our vision, can we read the literature of unbelievers in order to connect with them? Mind you, I refer not to philosophical literature, although that can certainly be useful. Thomas Aquinas (1225–1274) employed Aristotle, in part, to dialogue with Muslim Aristotelian philosophers.[4] And Cornelius Van Til (1895–1987) used the language and concepts of Idealism to make a connection with

1. John Calvin, *Institutes of the Christian Religion*, trans. Henry Beveridge (Calvin Translation Society, 1845), I.v.1.

2. Abraham Kuyper, "The Natural Knowledge of God," trans. Harry Van Dyke, *The Bavinck Review* 6 (2015): 73–112, here 73.

3. E. J. Young, *A Prophecy of Daniel: A Commentary* (Eerdmans, 1949), 48–49; Jerome, *Jerome's Commentary on Daniel*, trans. Gleason L. Archer Jr. (Baker Book House, 1958), 22.

4. Thomas Aquinas, *Summa Contra Gentiles*, 5 vols., trans. Anton C. Pegis (University of Notre Dame Press, 1975), I.ii.3.

Kantians.[5] Nevertheless, by "literature," I mean pedestrian fiction. Are we reading the things that our neighbors are reading? Are we reading books that our communities are reading? Are we sufficiently versed in the popular fictional narratives of our culture? Can we take this literature and, like Paul, say, "As some of your own authors have written . . ."? In short, if Paul employed pagan literature in his apologetics, then it behooves us to do the same.

However, we want to move beyond imitation and have an informed, exegetical, and theological foundation for our use of all literature in our apologetics. *This chapter defends the thesis that as Paul appealed to the pagan literature of his day, Christians can likewise employ literature written by unbelievers as they defend the faith.* Note, while this chapter focuses upon literature, we can expand this strategy to include other culturally relevant forms of expression: art, cinema, television, music, and the like. Because God's creation is replete with his wisdom and truth, both in the macro- and microcosmic worlds, humans cannot help but capture this truth in their works of literature. As authors create their work, the only raw materials they possess is God's truth, so even though fallen and corrupted by sin, even unbelievers capture God's truth in their stories. They write of good, evil, redemption, the fall, truth, and deception, among a host of other virtues such as prudence, temperance, justice, courage, faith, hope, love, chastity, diligence, patience, kindness, and humility.[6] Although he writes of the power of art, painter Pablo Picasso (1881–1973) explains this point this way: "We all know that Art is not truth. Art is a lie that makes us realize the truth, at least the truth that is given us to understand."[7] In other words, we know that art is like fiction but that it nevertheless captures truth that we might not otherwise perceive. In pursuit of the necessity of appealing to literature, the chapter first examines why humans are storytelling people.[8] Second, it explains the inherently theological

5. Cornelius Van Til, "Introduction," in Benjamin B. Warfield, *The Inspiration and Authority of the Bible* (P&R, 1948), 36, also 24; *Christian Apologetics* (P&R, 1976), 38–58, 61; *Introduction to Systematic Theology* (P&R, 1974), 26, 28, 29; *Defense of the Faith*, 3rd ed. (P&R, 1967), 169, 212; *Common Grace and the Gospel* (P&R, 1972), 151; *The Doctrine of Scripture*, In Defense of the Faith, vol. 1 (The Den Dulk Christian Foundation, 1967), 130; *Essays on Christian Education* (P&R, 1979), 83, 187, 192–93. Cf. Nathaniel Gray Sutanto, "From Antithesis to Synthesis: A Neo-Calvinistic Theological Strategy in Herman Bavinck and Cornelius Van Til," *Journal of Reformed Theology* 9 (2015): 348–74, here 360–62.

6. These are the virtues that Karen Swallow Prior covers in her book *On Reading Well: Finding the Good Through Great Books* (Brazos Press, 2018).

7. Pablo Picasso, "To Statements by Picasso," *Picasso on Art: A Selection of Views*, ed. Dore Ashton (The Viking Press, 1972), 3–6, here 3.

8. Jonathan Gottschall, *The Storytelling Animal: How Stories Make Us Human* (Mariner Books, 2012); similarly, James K. A. Smith, *Imagining the Kingdom: How Worship Works* (Baker Academic, 2013), 108.

nature of literature, Christian and non-Christian alike. Third, and finally, the chapter shows the apologetic significance of literature.

Why Are We a Storytelling People?

Two literary giants, J. R. R. Tolkien and philosopher and novelist Umberto Eco, drill down into the foundations of why people tell stories. Tolkien addresses the fantasy genre, and Eco explores fiction. Both give important insights that place human storytelling in our nature as divine image bearers and sub-creators.

J. R. R. Tolkien and Fantasy

J. R. R. Tolkien (1892–1973) has made insightful observations on the nature of fantasy literature in his famous lecture "On Fairy Stories."[9] Despite the Enlightenment's efforts to disenchant the world, people nevertheless persist in their unrepentant quest for enchantment through fictional stories: "The realm of fairy-story is wide and deep and high and filled with many things: all manner of beasts and birds are found there; shoreless seas and stars uncounted; beauty that is an enchantment, and an ever-present peril; both joy and sorrow as sharp as swords."[10] But these enchanted stories are not merely the product of a vivid imagination; there is something much deeper at work: "But if a waking writer tells you that his tale is only a thing imagined in his sleep, he cheats deliberately the primary desire at the heart of the Faërie: the realization, independent of the conceiving mind, of imagined wonder."[11] Fairy stories are ancient in their origins, and mythology is not a disease that hampers intelligent, thoughtful people, though mythology can become diseased.[12]

Rather, creating stories lies at the heart of what it means to be human. Tolkien explains: "When we take green from grass, blue from heaven, and red from blood, we have already an enchanter's power—upon one plane; and the desire to wield that power in the world external to our minds awakes."[13] There is an energy within the human heart that desires to create worlds and stories. In theological terms, we cannot elude the fact that we bear the image of God. Or in simpler terms, like father, like son. That is, just as our Father

9. J. R. R. Tolkien, "On Fairy Stories," in *The Monsters and the Critics and Other Essays: The Essays of J. R. R. Tolkien* (Harper Collins, 1983), 109–61.

10. Tolkien, "On Fairy Stories," 108.

11. Tolkien, "On Fairy Stories," 116.

12. Tolkien, "On Fairy Stories," 121.

13. Tolkien, "On Fairy Stories," 122.

is creator, so we, his sons and daughters and image bearers, are creators. Our creative nature comes from our Creator, and thus in this way mythology and religion overlap: "Something really 'higher' is occasionally glimpsed in mythology: Divinity, the right to power (as distinct from its possession), the due of worship . . . . mythology and religion (in the strict sense of that word) are two distinct things that have become inextricably entangled."[14]

Fantasy, therefore, is a natural human activity. Fantasy neither destroys nor insults reason, and it neither blunts nor obscures the perception of scientific truth. On the contrary, the greater one's immersion in fantasy clarifies and sharpens his faculty of reason. Why? Fantasy rests on a solid understanding of the nature of the world, a realistic assessment and comprehension of reality—seeing the world as it is. People, of course, can carry fantasy to excess or it can be poorly executed; they can use fantasy to evil ends and even delude the minds whence it came. "But of what human thing in this fallen world is that not true?" asks Tolkien. Writers have conceived of elves, gods, and worshiped them, but they have made false gods out of other materials, notions, banners, and monies. Theorists have even made idols out of their social and economic ideas to the point of offering human sacrifices. *Abusus non tollit usum*, "abuse does not destroy use." "Fantasy," writes Tolkien, "remains a human right: we make in our measure in our derivative mode, because we are made: and not only made, but made in the image and likeness of a Maker."[15] We are sub-creators under the aegis of the Creator.

Humans create worlds in which they play the role of a creator and thus take the fundamental truths of this real world and arrange them in such a fashion to create metanarratives, morality, ideas of justice, good, and evil. All these ideas come from somewhere—not simply from the imagination of the author but from an imagination informed by the image of God and the created world around them. Authors, Christian or not, read the book of nature and use the information they find in their own fantasy worlds. Authors take these truths and embed them in their own tales: "Fairy-stories deal largely, or (the better ones) mainly, with simple or fundamental things, untouched by Fantasy, but these simplicities are made all the more luminous by their setting."[16] When we reflect upon these fundamental truths of this real world in fairy stories, we can often isolate, highlight, and see these truths with greater clarity as we focus our conscience upon them with the spotlight of fantasy. In our fairy stories we can escape from many of the truths of the world, such as hunger,

14. Tolkien, "On Fairy Stories," 124.
15. Tolkien, "On Fairy Stories," 144–45.
16. Tolkien, "On Fairy Stories," 147.

thirst, poverty, pain, sorrow, or injustice.[17] But Tolkien observes that the keenest desire is the great escape from death.[18]

Fictional stories possess a teleological drive for righting wrongs and for redemption. Tolkien captures this notion in a term he coined, "eucatastrophe." He explains that tragedy is the true form of drama, but the opposite is true of the fairy story. Eucatastrophe is the great reversal, the joy of the happy ending, the good catastrophe—the sudden miraculous turn that stands in the face of universal final defeat and is thus *evangelium*. The eucatastrophe is "a fleeting glimpse of joy, joy beyond the walls of the world, poignant as grief."[19] But in the eucatastrophic ending in the fictional tale we see a brief glimpse of an even greater answer, a far-off gleam or echo of *evangelium* in the real world.[20] The birth of Christ is the eucatastrophe of humanity's history, and the resurrection is the eucatastrophe of the story of the incarnation.[21]

Umberto Eco and Fiction

Italian philosopher and novelist Umberto Eco (1932–2016) has made similar observations about fiction, which is a broader category than Tolkien's fairy stories. Eco explains that a narrative text may lack a plot, but it cannot possibly exist without story or discourse.[22] All texts tell a story. Moreover, like Tolkien's idea of authors as sub-creators, Eco argues that "fictional worlds are parasites of the real world."[23] Authors must study and learn things about the actual world in order to create accurate backgrounds for their fictional worlds. While fictional worlds are parasites on the real world, they are in effect *microcosmoi*, "small worlds," that bracket most of our competence of the actual world to allow us to concentrate on a finite, miniature world, one like ours but ontologically inferior.[24]

Like the author of the fairy story, when authors write fiction, they capture truth—God's truth embedded in the creation. Children play with puppets, toy horses, or kites and learn about the physical laws of the universe with actions that they will one day really perform. Similarly, to read fiction means to play a game by which we give sense to the vastness

17. Tolkien, "On Fairy Stories," 151.
18. Tolkien, "On Fairy Stories," 153.
19. Tolkien, "On Fairy Stories," 153.
20. Tolkien, "On Fairy Stories," 155.
21. Tolkien, "On Fairy Stories," 156.
22. Umberto Eco, *Six Walks in the Fictional Woods* (Harvard University Press, 1994), 35.
23. Eco, *Six Walks*, 83.
24. Eco, *Six Walks*, 85.

of things that have happened in the past, are presently occurring, and will occur in the future in the actual world. By reading narrative, we escape the anxieties that have us in their grip when we try to say something true about the world. This is the comforting function of narrative—this is the reason people have told stories, continue to tell stories, and will tell stories until the end of time. People tell stories because they want to find shape, form, and meaning in the turmoil of human existence.[25] Once again, the Creator-creature relationship is at work here: as God brought order to the chaos of Genesis 1:1, so humans take the apparent chaos they see in the world, and they bring cosmos to it. Humans sub-create orderly worlds in their fictional tales.

Eco explains that fictional narratives assist us in our metaphysical narrow-mindedness. We live in the great labyrinth of the real world, which is much larger and more complex than the fictional world of Little Red Riding Hood. The world is filled with paths that we have not mapped out, and we are thus incapable of describing its total structure. In the hopes that there are rules to the game, humans throughout the ages have speculated whether the labyrinth has an author.[26] But there is another reason why fiction makes us more metaphysically comfortable in the real world. Cryptanalysts and code breakers rely on a cardinal rule—namely, every secret message can be deciphered provided that one knows that it is a message. The problem is that, since the beginning of history, people have wondered whether there is a message and, if so, whether the message makes sense. In fictional universes, we know beyond a shadow of a doubt that they do have a message and that an author stands behind them as a creator as well as within them to provide a set of rules for reading.[27] For all of these reasons, Eco concludes that humans will never stop writing or reading fictional stories because stories are the way that we seek to find meaning in our existence. People search their whole lives to discover a story of their origins, so we know why we were born and why we have lived. Sometimes people look for a cosmic story, the story of the galaxy, or for our own personal story. And sometimes our personal story coincides with the story of the universe.[28] Nevertheless, fictional stories are laden with God's truth and are thus a rich resource for connecting with the unbelievers around us. Literature gives us truths about life.[29]

25. Eco, *Six Walks*, 87.
26. Eco, *Six Walks*, 115.
27. Eco, *Six Walks*, 116.
28. Eco, *Six Walks*, 139.
29. C. S. Lewis, *An Experiment in Criticism* (Cambridge University Press, 2013), 130.

The Inherently Theological Nature of All Literature

The observations of Tolkien and Eco regarding the nature of fairy stories and fiction necessitates a deeper dive into the theological character of all literature. Saint Augustine (354–430) provides a gateway to this closer look at literature through his personal reflections on the path of his conversion to Christianity. Augustine recounts that he read the now non-extant work of Cicero (106–43 BC) *Hortensius*, which immediately changed him. The pagan book altered his prayers and caused him to turn to God: "It gave me different values and priorities. Suddenly every vain hope became empty to me, and I longed for the immortality of wisdom with an incredible ardor in my heart. I began to rise up to return to you. . . . My God, how I burned, how I burned with longing to leave earthly things and fly back to you. . . . 'Love of wisdom' is the meaning of the Greek word *philosophia*. This book kindled my love for it."[30] To be clear, Cicero did not bring about Augustine's conversion; ultimately, Scripture and the Spirit of God converted him. Augustine makes this clear when he observes, "One thing alone put a brake on my intense enthusiasm—that the name of Christ was not contained in the book."[31] But this does not diminish the fact that Cicero's work contained truth, and God used this book to clear debris from the road to Augustine's heart—to create a clear path for the gospel.

Tolkien, Eco, and Augustine all testify to the fact, then, that all literature (Christian or not) is theological given the truth of God captured therein, however fragmentary and at times clouded by sin. Southern Gothic novelist Flannery O'Connor (1925–1964) complained that fiction offended her when it inverted truth by calling what was wrong right, or making what was right wrong. "Fiction," she writes, "is the concrete expression of mystery—mystery that is lived." And while she believed that it was nearly impossible to write about supernatural grace in fiction, she maintained that writing about natural grace was a different matter: "As to natural Grace, we have to take that the way it comes—through nature. In any case, it operates surrounded by evil."[32] In other words, when authors write about the world, they write about the world that God created. When they write of a sunset, this is the same celestial body that God has fastened to the heavens and that has run its course like a strong man, like a bridegroom leaving his chamber (Ps 19:5–6). This is the same sun that proclaims the handiwork of God (Ps 19:1) and the same sun that evinces

30. Augustine, *Confessions*, trans. Henry Chadwick (Oxford University Press, 1991), III.iv (7).
31. Augustine, *Confessions*, III.iv (7).
32. Flannery O'Conner, *Spiritual Writings*, ed. Robert Ellsberg (Orbis Books, 2003), 130.

God's providential control of the cosmos. When authors write of evil or especially of the "redemption" of a character, they acknowledge humanity's sinfulness and the need for salvation. Moreover, whether they admit it or not, they are image bearers and have God's law written on their hearts (Rom 2:14–15), and whether they worship God rightly or not, they "hold the truth in unrighteousness" (Rom 1:18 KJV). This means that literature can give us a connection to the world around us through eyes that might see things differently than we do. It might give us a connection to our neighbors, because while they might not have read the Bible or be familiar with its contents, like Paul we can quote "some of their own poets" and make a connection to them. We can appeal to the truth that they do know.

The Apologetic Significance of Literature

In what ways can literature assist Christians in the defense of the faith? There are innumerable books in the Western canon, but there are several examples that illustrate the point under three overarching themes: understanding evil and sin, learning empathy, and recognizing the goodness of embodied existence.

Understanding Evil and Sin

Herman Melville's (1819–1891) *The Whale*, also known as *Moby Dick*, has lodged itself in the collective memory of Western culture. Even though Melville was not a Christian, he was theologically informed, having read, among others, the writings of Friedreich Schleiermacher (1768–1834).[33] Nevertheless, literary scholars have explained that the tale of Captain Ahab relentlessly pursuing the whale across the seas is, in part, about humanity's hatred for God.[34] Melville features the titular character Ishmael and his ruminations on the significance of the whiteness of the whale. Whiteness is often associated with royalty and holiness, but there is an "elusive something in the innermost idea of this hue, which strikes more of panic to the soul than that redness which affrights in blood."[35] Ishmael associates whiteness with "God's great,

33. Frank Troy, *Herman Melville's Genius: The Author of Moby-Dick on How to Think About Religion and Other Ideologies* (Cave Canem Press, 2012), 27–28, 31, 88–90.

34. T. Walter Herbert Jr., "Calvinist Earthquake: *Moby-Dick* and Religious Tradition," in *New Essays on Moby-Dick, or The Whale*, ed. Richard H. Brodhead (Cambridge University Press, 1986), 109–40, esp. 126–27.

35. Herman Melville, *Moby Dick*, in *Redburn, White-Jacket, and Moby Dick, or The Whale* (The Library of America, 1983), 771–1413, here 993–94.

unflattering laureate, Nature."[36] Whiteness can inspire awe but also terror, which is why it powerfully appeals to the soul, as it is a "symbol of spiritual things." In particular, "it is the veil of the Christian's Deity; and yet should be as it is, the intensifying agent in things the most appalling to mankind." Ishmael concludes his dissertation by speaking of all the things that whiteness conveys, especially the great vastness of the cosmos, and says, "And of all these things the Albino whale was the symbol. Wonder ye then at the fiery hunt?"[37]

Ahab's quest to kill the whale is not so much about destroying the creature that took his leg but rather attacking the idea that the whale symbolizes—namely, God. In the climactic conflict, Ahab "piled upon the whale's white hump the sum of all the general rage and hate felt by his whole race from Adam down."[38] Given the whale's status as a simulacrum for God, Ahab's final words uttered against the whale take on greater significance: "Towards thee I roll, thou all-destroying but unconquering whale; to the last I grapple with thee; from hell's heart I stab at thee; for hate's sake I spit my last breath at thee. Sink all coffins and all hearses to one common pool! and since neither can be mine, let me then tow to pieces, while still chasing thee, though tied to thee, thou damned whale! Thus, I give up the spear!"[39] In the end, the all-destroying whale sank his ship and took Ahab to his watery grave. Melville gives us a glimpse into the human self-destructive hatred of God, a perspective that Scripture does not reveal. Yes, the apostle Paul describes the sinful human from without, as one who hates God, whose throat is an open grave, a mouth full of curses and bitterness, and no fear of God before his eyes (Rom 3:12–18). But Melville gives us a glimpse from *inside* the sinful human heart.

We find a similar revealing portrait of the rationalization of sin in Fyodor Dostoevsky's (1821–1881) main protagonist Raskolnikov in his novel *Crime and Punishment*. In the novel, Raskolnikov thinks about killing an evil pawnbroker, Alyona Ivanovna. He sees her as a "stupid, senseless, worthless, spiteful, ailing, horrid old woman . . . who will die in a day or two in any case." If he kills her, Raskolnikov imagines what he can do with her money:

> A hundred thousand good deeds could be done and helped, on that old woman's money which will be buried in a monastery! Hundreds, thousands perhaps, might be set on the right path; dozens of families saved from destitution, from ruin, from vice, from the Lock hospitals—and all with her money. Kill her, take her money and with the help of it devote oneself to the service of humanity

36. Melville, *Moby Dick*, 995.
37. Melville, *Moby Dick*, 1001.
38. Melville, *Moby Dick*, 989.
39. Melville, *Moby Dick*, 1406.

> and the good of all. What do you think, would not one tiny crime be wiped out by thousands of good deeds? For one life thousands would be saved from corruption and decay. One death, and a hundred lives in exchange—it's simple arithmetic.[40]

Infrequently can we enter the mind of another who is contemplating great sin and listen to the debate between sin and one's inner sense of morality. And yet, here in Raskolnikov's dialogue we find precisely that: he places sin and morality in the balance and rationalizes committing one sin so that, in his mind, he can carry out many greater goods.

Whether in Ahab's final words or Raskolnikov's rationalization, these fictional passages brim with natural theological truths that give us insights into the fallen human condition. They help us see our own fallen state and corrupted reason prior to our conversion as well as help us guard against such thoughts in our own hearts. How many times have we tried to rationalize our own sin? Stepping out of our own lives and into the life of another, even if a fictional character, gives us a better vantage point on truth. We often learn better looking in from the outside rather than looking around within ourselves. In the words of C. S. Lewis (1898–1963), "One of the chief operations of art is to remove our gaze from that mirrored face, to deliver us from that solitude."[41] Such a vantage point on life is an asset to the apologist who wants to study human nature and connect with non-Christians. But there are other benefits to reading literature for apologetics, especially as it pertains to learning empathy.

Learning Empathy

Literacy expert Maryanne Wolf recounts how a young Roman Catholic man read the diary of Anne Frank (1929–1945), a Jewish young woman who famously lived in hiding until the Gestapo found her and sent her to die in a concentration camp.[42] The young man described the life-changing epiphany he had upon entering the life of this young Jewish girl, with all of her hopes, dreams, and enthusiasm for life, which she maintained despite the violent hatred of the Jews that ultimately saw to the demise of her and her family.[43]

40. Fyodor Dostoyevsky, *Crime and Punishment*, trans. Constance Garnett (Barnes and Noble, 1994), 53.

41. Lewis, *Experiment*, 85, also 101–2.

42. Anne Frank, *The Diary of a Young Girl: The Definitive Edition*, ed. Otto M. Frank and Mirjam Presler, trans. Susan Massotty (Bantam Books, 1997).

43. Maryanne Wolf, *Reader, Come Home: The Reading Brain in a Digital World* (Harper, 2018), 48.

The larger point in Wolf's observation is that, in an increasingly digital age, reading on screens diminishes our capacity to read in general. Digital readers risk losing their capacity to read and along with it their ability to empathize with others. Wolf draws upon the research of MIT scholar Sherry Turkle, whose research has shown that there has been a 40 percent decrease in empathy among young people over the past two decades, with the most precipitous decline occurring in the past ten years. Turkle attributes the loss of empathy to young peoples' immersion in the digital realm where they lose track of real-time, face-to-face relationships. Technology puts humans at a distance from real-life, flesh-and-blood people.[44] While Wolfe's wider point is salutary, we should not lose sight of the connection between learning empathy and reading books.[45] Why is this the case?

We can liken literature to a flight simulator—a computer simulation that allows pilots to practice their potentially dangerous craft without consequences. If they crash, they simply reset the simulator and start over. Psychologists have called stories the flight simulators of human social life.[46] In stories we explore the actions, thoughts, and lives of others. Reading the works of others, whether historical, autobiographical, or fictional, requires that we empty ourselves of our own thoughts so we can fill our minds with the author's thoughts—so we can listen to the voice of another.[47] Reading is a most intimate act as we enter into the thoughts of another and allow their thoughts to enter our own minds, unless, of course, we only offer a halfhearted ear to the author.[48] At its best, reading charitably is an act of love, one shaped by the cross of Christ as we listen to another, but at the biological level there are important things occurring. Neuroscientists have studied the human brain as it consumes fiction and have concluded that when we experience fiction, our neurons are firing much as they would if we were actually faced with the situation that we read on the pages of a book.[49] Cognitive psychologist Steven Pinker has shown how reading stories equips readers with a mental file of dilemmas that we might face one day, which stimulates us to think about solutions to those problems.[50] All of these facts add up to giving Christians an important tool for the apologist's toolbox.

44. Wolff, *Reader, Come Home*, 50.

45. Lewis, *Experiment*, 54.

46. Gottschall, *Storytelling Animal*, 58.

47. Alan Jacobs, *A Theology of Reading: The Hermeneutics of Love* (Westview Press, 2001), 104.

48. Lewis, *Experiment*, 47.

49. Gottschall, *Storytelling Animal*, 63.

50. Steven Pinker, *How the Mind Works* (Norton, 1997), 521–66; Gottschall, *Storytelling Animal*, 64.

The apostle Paul used Stoic literature to connect to the philosophers at Mars Hill; he was able to get inside their minds, dissect, and excise the truth therein. He made a connection that he could not immediately make by appealing to the Old Testament as he did with the Jews in the synagogues of Thessalonica (Acts 17:1–3). Paul could see how the philosophers thought, pinpoint errors, exploit them, and then introduce special revelation and the gospel. However, beyond Paul's use of the Stoic poets, if literature acts as a simulator, one that helps us to think through issues and even at an intellectual level mentally experience what we read, we can apologetically do more with literature.[51] We can use literature to get into the lives of unbelievers so that we do not merely see them as targets to be carpet bombed with biblical truth. We should not excuse sin, but if we better understand why people act and how they think, humanly speaking, we have a greater chance of connecting with them. John Steinbeck's (1902–1968) *Grapes of Wrath*, for example, chronicles the cross-country journey of the down-on-their luck Joad family as they try to escape the 1930s Oklahoma dustbowl. There seems to be little redeeming qualities about these characters, as they are crass and uncouth. Yet along the journey the impoverished family stops in a small diner on Route 66 and seeks to buy a loaf of bread. The waitress, Mae, does not like the migrant workers who come to the diner to eat because they cannot usually afford to pay for the food. She prefers the truck drivers who flirt with her and pay for their meals.

When the family stops in the diner, they ask if they can purchase a loaf of bread, but Mae puts them off because the diner does not sell loaves of bread—they sell only sandwiches. But the family cannot afford to buy sandwiches; they have just enough money to pay for the bread. The short-order cook prods Mae to sell the family the bread. Eventually, she begrudgingly relents, but not before she spies the children gazing at candy in the display case at the register. The father asks how much the candy costs, and Mae tells him that they are one cent each (they really cost a nickel). So, he purchases the bread (for ten cents when it was actually fifteen cents) and two pieces of candy, and they leave to get back on the road. Two truckers witness the whole exchange, and as they depart, they pay their check and leave a large tip to cover the discounted bread and candy.[52]

This seemingly ordinary account may seem irrelevant to Christian apologetics, but there is much here to learn and experience. When will the average person investigate the life of a poor migrant worker? When will they stand

51. Prior, *On Reading Well*, 21, 28; Lewis, *Experiment*, 37.

52. John Steinbeck, *The Grapes of Wrath*, in *The Grapes of Wrath and Other Writings, 1936–41* (The Library of America, 1996), 207–692, here 378–81.

behind a register and be asked to sell a loaf of bread for less than what it costs? When will they sit at the counter and watch an exchange between a poor migrant worker and a waitress, and be moved to leave a large tip to cover the cost of food for the poor migrant family, an act of unsolicited kindness? Reading this fictional account can teach us more about being human, but more importantly, it can teach us about loving our neighbors as ourselves, a vitally needed virtue in apologetics. If we seek to evangelize the people of our community, to what extent do we try to know who they are, how they think, and what they believe—not so that we can win arguments, but so we can see them as fellow image bearers lost in sin and thus more effectively connect with and love them? In the words of English professor Jonathan Gottschall, "The constant firing of our neurons in response to fictional stimuli strengthens and refines the neural pathways that lead to skillful navigation of life's problems. . . . Human life, especially social life, is intensely complicated and the stakes are high. Fiction allows our brains to practice reacting to the kinds of challenges that are, and always were, most crucial to our success as a species."[53] Literature has the same immense practical utility for apologetics.

The Goodness of Embodied Existence

These days our culture seems hell-bent in its frontal assault on our embodied existence, whether in the transgender efforts to deny what general revelation reveals about humans being either male or female or through the ever-evolving technology of virtual reality that beckons us to divorce our existence and humanity from the very real world in which we live. Christians know of both the goodness of the creation and of our embodied existence (Gen 1:31), but even popular fiction has captured these truths. Ernest Cline's *Ready Player One*, a number one New York Times bestseller that was turned into a Hollywood movie directed by Steven Spielberg, explores the relationship between virtual reality and reality. At key junctures in the story, characters wrestle with the illusory nature of virtual reality. In the story two of the chief characters, Wade Watts (who uses the handle Parzival) and Art3mis (who refuses to reveal her real-world name to anyone in the virtual world) verbally spar back and forth when Wade reveals his love for Art3mis even though he has never seen her in the real world; he has fallen in love with her avatar. What does Art3mis say in response to Wade's profession of love? "'You don't live in the real world, Z. From what you've told me, I don't think you ever have. You're like me. You live inside the illusion.' She motioned to our virtual

53. Gottschall, *Storytelling Animal*, 67.

surroundings. 'You can't possibly know what real love is.'"[54] Cline suggests that real love cannot thrive in a virtual, immaterial, digital world because it requires real-world, embodied, human-to-human interaction.

Cline captures the fact that, while people feel safe in the virtual world because they can control all the variables, such "safety" is illusory. At one point in the story, Wade withdraws to the "safety" of his virtual world: "It was the one place in the entire simulation where I was truly safe."[55] And yet, one of the themes that Cline weaves through the book is that we cannot control everything in our lives: "No one in the world ever gets what they want and that is beautiful."[56] At the end of the novel, when Wade wins the contest to secure control of the virtual world that James Halliday created for users around the world (something akin to winning the biggest lottery ever known to history, at least within this fictional story), Wade encounters Halliday's avatar, who explains why he created the virtual world, the OASIS: "I created the OASIS because I never felt at home in the real world. I didn't know how to connect with the people there. I was afraid, for all of my life. Right up until I knew it was ending. That was when I realized, as terrifying and painful as reality can be, it's also the only place where you can find true happiness. Because reality is *real*."[57] The technology of virtual reality calls to us and utters the same twisted truth that Satan first spoke to Eve: "Your eyes shall be opened, and ye shall be as gods" (Gen 3:5 KJV). And yet, Cline's fictional story captures the truth that, no matter how appealing virtual reality is, it falls short because it is not real. We are embodied creatures that need interaction with other embodied creatures, and even when things do not go right and we do not get what we want, this is a beautiful thing. The road to happiness does not lie, therefore, in fulfilling our every desire, but in not getting what we want.

Cline recognizes natural theological truths that we find attested to in both natural and special revelation: that God has created us with bodies, and that matter and the real world is an inherently good place. Cline gives expression to what Lewis called "*Sehnsucht*," or the sense of deep yearning and longing for something missing for which we cannot even articulate.[58] Lewis explains that we have a desire "for our own far off country," for a greater homeland:

> The books or music in which we thought the beauty was located will betray us if we trust to them; it was not in them, it only came through them, and

54. Ernest Cline, *Ready Player One* (Balantine Books, 2011), 186.
55. Cline, *Ready Player One*, 200–201.
56. Cline, *Ready Player One*, 199.
57. Cline, *Ready Player One*, 364.
58. C. S. Lewis, *Surprised by Joy: The Shape of My Early Life* (HarperOne, 1955), 6.

> what came through them was longing. These things—the beauty, the memory of our own past—are good images of what we really desire; but if they are mistaken for the thing itself they turn into dumb idols, breaking the hearts of their worshippers. For they are not the thing itself; they are only the scent of a flower we have not found, the echo of a tune we have not heard, news from a country we have never visited.[59]

Our longing for real, embodied existence and community beckons us to something greater. Again, the words of Augustine: "You stir man to take pleasure in praising you, because you have made us for yourself, and our heart is restless until it rests in you."[60] Like Paul pointing to the Stoic "unknown god" (Acts 17:23) and making him known in Christ, we can point to these longings for embodiment, community, and connection and show unbelievers that they can find them in Christ, the church, and the embodied eternal existence in the new heavens and earth. We can appeal to books like Cline's *Ready Player One* and its themes of the goodness of embodied existence and show how this longing finds its ultimate answer in Christ.

Conclusion

At Mars Hill, Paul appealed to the creation, the innate knowledge of God, including what the philosophers had recorded in their written works, and special revelation. We need to learn from and emulate Paul's apologetic strategy. Christians are willing to appeal to Scripture, and most are willing to use the book of nature to corroborate the claims of God's word. The God of Scripture is also the God of nature. But there is sometimes a reluctance to refer to the writings of unbelievers, especially their fiction. What insights does an unbeliever have if they are devoid of the knowledge and wisdom of Christ? Why not stand firm on the authority of God's word and pass by pagan literature? People see the use of the literature of unbelievers as a dubious wager; maybe non-Christians will stumble upon the truth and Christians can appeal to it—a blind squirrel can find a nut every now and then. Yet as English professor Alan Jacobs observes, "Charitable readers do not calculate the likelihood of reward for their loving attention, but their commitment to hope in a kind of calculation, a wager on the graciousness of God and on the *imago dei* present in the writers of books."[61] In other words, in our appeal to any and all

59. C. S. Lewis, *The Weight of Glory and Other Addresses* (HarperOne,1980), 30–31.
60. Augustine, *Confessions*, trans. Henry Chadwick (Oxford University Press, 1991), I.i.
61. Jacobs, *Theology of Reading*, 148.

literature, we do not so much wager as rest in God's natural revelation and the scriptural teaching that image bearers know God and "hold the truth," even if they do so in unrighteousness (Rom 1:18 KJV). Our confident and yet discerning appeal, then, to all types of literature (Christian or not) is not so much a wager but a reliance upon God's truth wherever we find it—truth that we can ply in the defense of the Christian faith, truth that we can use to connect with our friends, neighbors, and family as we seek to share the gospel of Christ.[62]

62. Lewis, *Experiment*, 86.

10

The Resurrection

Evidence for the Gospel in Scripture and History

> **Thesis 10:** The resurrection of Christ rests in both the books of nature and Scripture; as Paul appealed to the resurrection, so Christians can appeal to this doctrine in defending the faith.

> [God] has fixed a day on which he will judge the world in righteousness by a man whom he has appointed; and of this he has given assurance to all by raising him from the dead.
>
> —Acts 17:31

God the Father never uttered the words, "Arise, my Son, arise!" but he did nevertheless speak volumes when he raised Jesus from the dead (e.g., Acts 2:24, 32; 3:15, 26; 4:10; 5:30; 10:40; 13:30, 33–34, 37). As J. R. R. Tolkien (1892–1973) once observed, the resurrection of Christ is the great eucatastrophe, the great reversal, the Triune God's victory over Satan, sin, and death.[1] While there are any number of points in the Christian faith that, if removed, would cause the collapse of the gospel, the apostle Paul explicitly identifies the resurrection as a *sine qua non* of the Christian faith: "For if the dead are not raised, not even Christ has been raised. And if Christ has not been raised, your faith is futile and you are still in your sins. Then those also

1. J. R. R. Tolkien, "On Fairy Stories," in *The Monsters and the Critics and Other Essays: The Essays of J. R. R. Tolkien* (Harper Collins, 1983), 109–61, here 156.

who have fallen asleep in Christ have perished. If in Christ we have hope in this life only, we are of all people most to be pitied" (1 Cor 15:16–19). Naturally, Christians throughout the ages have consequently appealed to and defended the resurrection of Christ as a crucial linchpin of the Christian faith. However, some, such as Van Tillian apologist Greg Bahnsen (1948–1995), argued that the only way to defend the resurrection was exclusively from Scripture:

> Scripture itself should be enough to dissuade a person from depending upon evidential arguments for Christ's resurrection. . . . The only tool an apologete needs is the word of God, for the sinner will either presuppose its truth and find Christianity to be coherent and convincing (given his spiritual condition and past experience) or he will reject it and never be able to come to a knowledge of the truth.[2]

Is Scripture enough to convince a person of the truth of the resurrection? Yes, without a doubt. Nevertheless, why would we turn away from history and ignore the evidence for the resurrection? As Herman Bavinck (1854–1921) once observed, nature and history are the external means by which God unveils revelation.[3]

Geerhardus Vos (1862–1949) criticized efforts to sideline history in the effort to emphasize the mystical aspect of faith, a parallel notion to relying exclusively on Scripture in one's apologetics. Vos argued, "How much better that we should all strive to raise our drooping faith and to reënrich our depleted experience up to the standard of those blessed periods in the life of the Church, when the belief in Bible history and the religion of the heart went hand in hand and kept equal pace." Neither antithetical to Scripture nor a capitulation to autonomous reason, Vos explains, "People were ready to lay down their lives for facts and doctrines, because facts and doctrines formed the daily spiritual nourishment of their souls." Vos prayed for the day when true piety would not merely tolerate facts and doctrines, but draw its strength and inspiration in life and service as its only comfort and hope in the hour of death.[4] What is good for the goose is good for the gander, so if using the

2. Greg Bahnsen, "The Impropriety of Evidentially Arguing for the Resurrection," *Synapse* 2 (1972). I obtained this essay from https://answersingenesis.org/apologetics/the-impropriety-of-evidentially-arguing-for-the-resurrection/ on October 31, 2024. This essay is also available at https://www.cmfnow.com/articles/apologetics (accessed October 31, 2024).

3. Herman Bavinck, *Reformed Dogmatics*, vol. 1, *Prolegomena*, trans. John Vriend, ed. John Bolt (Baker Academic, 2003), 341.

4. Geerhardus Vos, "Christian Faith and the Truthfulness of Bible History," *Princeton Theological Review* 4/3 (1906): 289–305, here 304–5; see similar comments in Bavinck, *Reformed Dogmatics*, I:345.

facts of biblical history and doctrines are beneficial to one's piety, then they are certainly helpful for apologetics. Vos is not the first to make this type of observation, as the author of the Apostles' Creed long ago recognized the need to ground the claims of Scripture in history.

The Creed famously states, "I believe in Jesus Christ, his only Son, our Lord, who was conceived by the Holy Spirit and born of the virgin Mary." Not satisfied with rehearsing this biblical truth, the author also anchors Christ's ministry in history by including reference to a historical figure: "He suffered under Pontius Pilate." Jesus is a real, historical person who was crucified under Pilate in the midst of real history. The Bible is not a collection of myths or general philosophical truths but exists in the grit, dirt, and sweat of historical events.[5] Faith, therefore, does not transcend but also includes history. And if God the Father raised Jesus within history, then it is not only beneficial but morally incumbent upon Christians to examine, study, and know this truth.[6] Or, in the words of J. Gresham Machen (1881–1937), "We are pleading, in other words, for a truly comprehensive apologetic—an apologetic which does not neglect the theistic proofs or the historical evidence of the New Testament account of Jesus, but which also does not neglect the facts of the inner life of man. The force of such an apologetic is, we think, cumulative; such an apologetic is strong in its details; but it is even stronger because the details are embraced in a harmonious whole."[7]

This chapter plies the "harmonious whole" by defending the thesis that *the resurrection of Christ rests in both the books of nature and Scripture. As Paul at Mars Hill appealed to the resurrection, so Christians can appeal to this doctrine in defending the faith.* Note, when I say the resurrection rests in both the books of nature and Scripture, by "nature" I mean to say that the historical evidence for the resurrection is not inspired special revelation. Technically speaking, history is evidence but not precisely general revelation. At the same time, we should remember Bavinck's observation: "The Bible's view of nature and history is religious and hence also supernatural."[8] In light of the scriptural and historical evidence, the chapter first explores the historical evidence for Christ's existence, crucifixion, and resurrection. Lest one hastily conclude that the chapter first rests on history rather than the authority of Scripture,

5. Francis Martin and William M. Wright IV, *The Gospel of John*, Catholic Commentary on Sacred Scripture (Baker Academic, 2015), 302.

6. N. T. Wright, *Surprised by Scripture: Engaging Contemporary Issues* (HarperOne, 2015), 61.

7. J. Gresham Machen, "Religion, Science and Philosophy," *Princeton Theological Review* 24/1 (1926): 38–66, here 64–65.

8. Bavinck, *Reformed Dogmatics*, I:307–8.

we should recall that the *ordo docendi* ("order of teaching") does not always trace the *ordo essendi* ("the order of things as they are in themselves"). In other words, to begin with history for the sake of discussion is not a capitulation to autonomous human reason but rather approaches the resurrection of Christ as many people encountered it in the ancient world—as a historical event. Second, the chapter turns to Scripture to examine the resurrection from the Old and New Testaments. Too many believe that the resurrection appears unexpectedly in the pages of the New Testament, when in fact the Old Testament looked toward and prophesied it. The New Testament records the long-awaited and promised resurrection of Christ. Third, the chapter considers objections to the resurrection to demonstrate that, in the end, fall short. The chapter concludes with summary observations about the importance of believing in and defending the resurrection of Christ.

The Historical Evidence for Christ and the Resurrection

Critics of Christianity are often unaware of the historical evidence for the existence of Christ, his ministry, crucifixion, and resurrection from the dead. And yet, there is a considerable body of evidence that corroborates the claims of Scripture. This section examines the historical records of Flavius Josephus, Tacitus, Suetonius, and Pliny the Younger.[9]

Flavius Josephus

Flavius Josephus (37–100) was a Jewish historian and Pharisee who initially opposed the Roman Empire and then later defected. He wrote several works chronicling Jewish history.[10] There are two passages in his *Antiquities* that are relevant to establishing the historicity of Christ's ministry.

In the first, Josephus gives the history of the Jews' interaction with Pontius Pilate, which immediately corroborates scriptural claims regarding Pilate's existence. The gospel writers neither invented him, nor is he merely a literary character. In his account, Josephus writes:

> Now there was about this time Jesus, a wise man, if it be lawful to call him a man; for he was a doer of wonderful works, a teacher of such men as receive

9. For a more detailed examination of these and other relevant historical evidence, see Gary R. Habermas, *On the Resurrection*, vol. 1, *Evidences* (B&H Academic, 2024), 155–226.

10. Flavius Josephus, *The Works of Flavius Josephus: Comprising the Antiquities of the Jews; A History of the Jewish Wars; and Life of Flavius Josephus*, trans. William Whiston (The S. S. Scranton Co., 1905).

> the truth with pleasure. He drew over to him both many of the Jews and many of the Gentiles. *He was [the] Christ*. And when Pilate, at the suggestion of the principal men amongst us, had condemned him to the cross, those that loved him at the first did not forsake him; *for he appeared to them alive again the third day; as the divine prophets had foretold these and ten thousand other wonderful things concerning him*. And the tribe of Christians, so named from him, are not extinct at this day.[11]

We have a passage from a non-Christian source that mentions Jesus, his miracles, Pilate, Jesus's crucifixion, as well as his resurrection. However, scholars debate some of this passage's details, especially as it pertains to the resurrection.

Some have argued that later Christian copyists added the italicized words concerning Christ's resurrection to Josephus's original text, as no Jew and Pharisee would acknowledge that Jesus was the Messiah. On this basis alone, some scholars have rejected the passage entirely.[12] But even then, other scholars, such as Joseph Klausner (1874–1958), an Israeli historian and non-Christian, believed that the entire passage was not spurious.[13] Klausner concludes that no Christian would refer to Jesus merely as a "wise man," or as one who performed "wonderful works," or that his disciples were simply "those that loved him." Thus, in Klausner's judgment, Josephus's passage should instead read as follows:

> Now there was about this time Jesus, a wise man, if it be lawful to call him a man; for he was a doer of wonderful works, a teacher of such men as receive the truth with pleasure. He drew over to him both many of the Jews and many of the Gentiles. And when Pilate, at the suggestion of the principal men amongst us, had condemned him to the cross, those that loved him at the first did not forsake him; And the tribe of Christians, so named from him, are not extinct at this day.[14]

Klausner supposes that these remarks are befitting a man who was both a Jew and Pharisee who would neither want to upset the Jewish people nor the Romans regarding Christian claims about Jesus. And so, he says that these remarks say nothing favorable about Jesus or Christians, and they are just a "few general and superficial remarks, written with great care and containing nothing of

11. Josephus, *Antiquities*, XVIII.iii, in *Works*, 548, emphasis added.
12. Joseph Klausner, *Jesus of Nazareth: His Life, Times, and Teaching*, trans. Herbert Danby (The Macmillan Company, 1925), 56.
13. Klausner, *Jesus of Nazareth*, 57.
14. Klausner, *Jesus of Nazareth*, 57–58.

much positive value to the Christians, nor much about their Messiah."[15] For the sake of argument, we can sidestep the debate regarding the authenticity of the italicized portions of Josephus's text that refer to Jesus as the Messiah and his resurrection.[16] Without the disputed text, Josephus's words hardly qualify as "superficial." The fact that scholars acknowledge that there is a genuine historical nucleus to this text is significant.[17] The statement recognizes that there was a real, flesh-and-blood human being named Jesus who performed miraculous works, had many Jewish and gentile followers, and was crucified by Pilate on a cross. This is significant extrabiblical testimony regarding the existence, ministry, and crucifixion of Christ that can neither be ignored nor set aside.

In a second passage from Josephus, the Jewish historian makes reference to James, the brother of Jesus: "Festus was now dead, and Albinus was but upon the road; so he assembled the Sanhedrin of judges, and brought before them the brother of Jesus, who was called Christ, whose name was James."[18] Unlike the above-disputed passage, Klausner admits there is no need to assume that this is a later Christian interpolation of Josephus's text, especially because no Christian would say that Jesus "was called Christ." Klausner concludes that this passage is "wholly genuine," and from the two passages combined, "It must be confessed that from neither do we learn much about Jesus; yet even from these fragmentary statements we at least receive confirmation of his and his brother James' existence, of his career as a wonder-worker and teacher, and of his terrible death—his crucifixion at the hands of Pilate with, at least the consent of the principal Jews."[19]

Tacitus, Suetonius, and Pliny the Younger

A second witness comes from the ancient Roman historian Tacitus (ca. 56–120), who refers to Jesus in his book *Annals*.[20] Tacitus rehearses the history

15. Klausner, *Jesus of Nazareth*, 58.

16. On the history of the reception of this disputed text, see Alice Whealey, *Josephus on Jesus: The Testimonium Flavianum Controversy from Late Antiquity to Modern Times* (Peter Lang, 2003); also see T. C. Schmidt, *Josephus and Jesus: New Evidence for the One Called Christ* (Oxford University Press, 2025).

17. James D. G. Dunn, *Jesus Remembered: Christianity in the Making*, vol. 1 (Eerdmans, 2003), 141–43.

18. Josephus, *Antiquities*, XX.ix, in *Works*, 613; see also Gary R. Habermas and Michael R. Licona, *The Case for the Resurrection of Jesus* (Kregel, 2004), 67.

19. Klausner, *Jesus of Nazareth*, 59–60. See also Richard Bauckham, "For What Offense Was James Put to Death?," in *James the Just and Christian Origins*, ed. Bruce Chilton and Craig Evans (Brill, 1999), 199–232, here 199–203; Habermas, *On the Resurrection*, 179–80.

20. Simon Hornblower and Anthony Spawforth, eds., *The Oxford Classical Dictionary: The Ultimate Reference Work on the Classical World*, 3rd ed. (Oxford University Press, 1996), s.v. Tacitus (pp. 1469–71).

of Nero's (37–68) burning of Rome and how he attempted to deflect accusations that he himself set the city ablaze:

> But neither human aid, nor imperial bounty, nor atoning-offerings to the Gods, could remove the sinister suspicion that the fire had been brought about by Nero's order. To put an end therefore to this rumor, he shifted the charge on to others, and inflicted the most cruel tortures upon a body of men detested for their abominations and popularly known by the name of Christians. This name came from one Christus, who was put to death in the reign of Tiberius by the Procurator Pontius Pilate; but though checked for the time, the detestable superstition broke out again, not in Judea only, where the mischief began, but even in Rome, where every horrible and shameful iniquity, from every quarter of the world, pours in and finds a welcome.[21]

Tacitus reports that Nero shifted the blame and eventually persecuted Christians for their alleged crime of setting Rome on fire.[22] This is a significant text for several reasons. First, Tacitus wrote his *Annals* around AD 115–117, which places him within close historical proximity to the timeframe for the life of Christ. Second, he mentions Tiberius, who was emperor between AD 14 and 37, and Pilate, who was prefect of Judea between AD 26 and 36, two known historical figures that confirm that "Christus," or Jesus, existed in the 30s and was executed. Third, he mentions the existence of Jesus's followers, or Christians.[23] Once again we have a second non-Christian witness that testifies to the existence and crucifixion of Jesus.[24]

A third witness comes from Suetonius (ca. 69–122), who was a Roman historian who wrote on the lives of the Caesars. Suetonius writes. "Since the Jews constantly made disturbances at the instigation of Chrestus, he [emperor Claudius] expelled them from Rome."[25] Suetonius was a contemporary of Tacitus, and he confirms ideas that the latter records—namely, the presence of a messianic movement during the time of Claudius (41–54), who preceded Nero. This means that soon after the crucifixion of Jesus, a movement of followers grew such that he had to expel them from Rome, which agrees with what we find in Acts 18:1–2: "After this Paul left Athens and went to Corinth. And he found a Jew named Aquila, a native of Pontus, recently

21. Tacitus, *The Annals of Tacitus: Books XI-XVI*, ed. George Gilbert Ramsay (London: John Murray, 1909), XV.xliv (pp. 28–81).

22. Tacitus, *Annals*, XV.xliv (281).

23. Klausner, *Jesus of Nazareth*, 60; Habermas and Licona, *The Case for the Resurrection*, 49.

24. Habermas, *On the Resurrection*, 167–72.

25. Suetonius, *Lives of the Caesars*, in *Suetonius II*, trans. John Carew Rolfe, Loeb Classical Library (Harvard University Press, 1979), V.xxv (53).

come from Italy with his wife Priscilla, because Claudius had commanded all the Jews to leave Rome."[26] Some scholars demure, however, because they question whether this reference to "Chrestus" is to Christ or perhaps a Christian teacher. Yet, Klausner admits that even if it is a reference to a Christian teacher rather than to Jesus, the fact that only twenty years after his death there was a significant movement of people following him is not only proof of his existence but also of his influence; plus, this is evidence that there was a Christian community as far away as Rome as early as the 40s, only some ten years after the crucifixion. "This," Klausner writes, "is an important fact from every point of view."[27]

A fourth witness comes from Pliny the Younger (ca. 61–113), who was the Roman governor of Bithynia and Pontus, which lies in modern-day Turkey. Pliny wrote a letter to Emperor Trajan (ca. 112) asking his counsel for how to deal with Christians in his province. He was frustrated because he had not personally encountered them before and was unsure what to do with those who repented of their wrongdoings. He would threaten them with execution because, at a minimum, their unwillingness to repent and hold fast to their faith in Christ constituted contumacy against Roman authority. He released those, however, who were willing to recant, offer incense to the emperor, and curse Christ. For those who persisted in their faith, Pliny records:

> They affirmed, however, the whole of their guilt or their error, was, that they were in the habit of meeting on a certain fixed day before it was light, when they sang in alternate verses of a hymn to Christ, as to a god, and bound themselves by a solemn oath, not to any wicked deeds, but never to commit any fraud, theft, or adultery, never to falsify their word, nor deny a trust when they should be called upon to deliver it up; after which it was their custom to separate, and then reassemble to partake of food—but food of an ordinary and innocent kind.[28]

This is important testimony because Pliny recognizes that the Christians worshiped Christ as "a god," which means that they acknowledged that Jesus was God in the flesh. Granted, this evidence is not as relevant for the ministry of Christ and his resurrection; furthermore, it is written in the early second century.[29] Nevertheless, it is a piece of extrabiblical evidence that testifies to the existence of Christians who worshiped Jesus as God.

26. Klausner, *Jesus of Nazareth*, 60–61.

27. Klausner, *Jesus of Nazareth*, 61; also see Habermas, *On the Resurrection*, 180–81.

28. Pliny the Younger, *Pliny: Letters*, vol. 2, ed. W. M. L. Hutchinson, Loeb Classical Library (The Macmillan Co., 1915), X.xcvi (400–405).

29. Klausner, *Jesus of Nazareth*, 61–62; also see Habermas, *On the Resurrection*, 184–86.

Josephus, Tacitus, Suetonius, and Pliny are not the only extrabiblical sources that acknowledge the historicity of Jesus, as there are a sprinkling of other witnesses that mention Jesus, but they date from the middle of the second to third centuries and thus lack a historical proximity to the earthly ministry of Jesus.[30] Nevertheless, the gathered historical evidence from these four extrabiblical witnesses is significant because they attest to the existence, ministry, and crucifixion of Jesus. Extrabiblical sources confirm that Jesus existed and was crucified. But these same sources also record the fact that, on the heels of Christ's crucifixion, a large number of Jews and gentiles began following his teaching and were willing to die for him. Why would people across the Mediterranean world follow a dead, crucified criminal, let alone sing hymns to him as if he were "a god"? People follow dead leaders all the time, but why would they worship him as God unless something dramatic occurred, such as his resurrection from the dead? One last consideration regarding these extrabiblical historical witnesses is their nature. These four men carry no brief for the Christian faith; they have no reason, therefore, to confirm the biblical witness. So, this evidence from the book of nature, from extrabiblical historical witnesses, is a first step in defending the authenticity and historicity of the resurrection. A second step comes in considering the biblical evidence.

Old Testament

Beginning with the Old Testament might seem like a nonstarter, as some believe the resurrection does not appear in its pages. No doctrine, however, rests merely on the New Testament but on the whole of Scripture. Thus, any defense of the resurrection of Christ must begin from the Old Testament to demonstrate that it looks forward to this event.[31] There are several New Testament passages that confirm this interpretive strategy.[32] When Jesus walked on the road to Emmaus with his disciples, he opened their eyes that they might recognize him, and then he told them: "Thus it is written, that the Christ should suffer and on the third day rise from the dead" (Luke 24:46). When Luke uses the phrase γέγραπται ("it is written"), he refers to the Old Testament. In other words, Jesus taught about his resurrection from the Old

30. Habermas and Licona, *The Case for the Resurrection*, 49.

31. Matthew Levering, *Did Jesus Rise from the Dead? Historical and Theological Reflections* (Oxford University Press, 2019), 93.

32. For what follows, see Brant Pitre, *The Case for Jesus: The Biblical and Historical Evidence for Christ* (Image, 2016), 184.

Testament. The apostle John makes a similar observation when he recounts the resurrection of Christ. When the disciples ran to the tomb and discovered it was empty, John comments, "For as yet they did not understand the Scripture, that he must rise from the dead" (John 20:9). The apostle Paul likewise echoes this point in his own defense of the resurrection when he writes: "For I delivered to you as of first importance what I also received: that Christ died for our sins in accordance with the Scriptures, that he was buried, that he was raised on the third day in accordance with the Scriptures" (1 Cor 15:3–4). By "the Scriptures" Paul means the Old Testament, and thus Christ's resurrection occurred κατὰ τὰς γραφὰς (lit. "according to the writings"). For New Testament writers, therefore, one of the most significant pieces of evidence is that Christ's resurrection was a fulfillment of Scripture.[33]

Thomas Aquinas (1225–1274) makes this point when he draws attention to Acts 1:3, "He presented himself alive to them after his suffering by many proofs." Aquinas writes: "Christ is said to have demonstrated His Resurrection by proofs, inasmuch as by most evident signs He showed that He was truly risen. Hence where our version has 'by many proofs,' the Greek text, instead of proof has *tekmerion*, i.e., 'an evident sign affording positive proof.'"[34] What proof did Jesus offer? Aquinas says he employed a double testimony: the angels' testimony and the testimony of the Scriptures, the Old Testament.[35] On the road to Emmaus Jesus taught from the whole Old Testament canon, including the Law, Prophets, and Psalms (Luke 24:44–46; 16:31).[36] But the question remains, in what sense did Christ's resurrection fulfill Old Testament Scripture? Christians often scratch their heads looking for passages that explicitly teach this. How, then, do we proceed?

Starting with the Old Testament is important because it establishes a theistic foundation for the doctrine of Christ, and it provides the framework for the history of redemption in which Christ's resurrection makes sense.[37] We need to see, first, who God is so we can understand that he can raise Jesus from the dead. And second, Christ's resurrection is one of the anticipated outcomes of God's plan for redemption. As an interesting sidenote, when Aquinas discusses the resurrection of Christ in his commentary on John

33. Pitre, *The Case for Jesus*, 185.

34. Thomas Aquinas, *Summa Theologica* (Christian Classics, 1948), III q. 55 art. 5, sed contra.

35. Aquinas, *Summa Theologica*, III q. 55 art. 6, sed contra; Levering, *Did Jesus Rise from the Dead?*, 92.

36. G. K. Beale and D. A. Carson, eds., *Commentary on New Testament Use of the Old Testament* (Baker Academic, 2007), 401; Levering, *Did Jesus Rise from the Dead?*, 92.

37. Levering, *Did Jesus Rise from the Dead?*, 103.

20–21, he includes 128 citations from the Old Testament.[38] He cites Genesis (10x), Psalms (46x), Isaiah (16x), Proverbs (15x), and Job (3x).[39] In what way are these passages relevant? They establish that God is the omnipotent creator, and if he could not create life, then he would be incapable of raising anyone from the dead.[40] God's wisdom in Proverbs shows that God has rewarded Christ for his wisdom, humility, purity of heart, and obedience.[41] Job reveals that this Old Testament saint yearned for life even after his death: "If a man dies, shall he live again? All the days of my service I would wait, till my renewal should come" (Job 14:14).[42] The Old Testament therefore establishes the larger theological framework for the resurrection.

The New Testament itself, however, focuses upon several passages that reveal the Old Testament foundations for the resurrection. During Christ's Last Supper discourse, Jesus said to his disciples: "For I tell you that this Scripture must be fulfilled in me: 'And he was numbered with the transgressors.' For what is written about me has its fulfillment" (Luke 22:37).[43] Here Jesus quotes Isaiah 53:12. Jesus clearly pinpoints his own crucifixion as the fulfillment of Isaiah's fourth Servant Song, but within this context the verse immediately before it speaks of the servant's resurrection: "Out of the anguish of his soul he shall see and be satisfied; by his knowledge shall the righteous one, my servant, make many to be accounted righteous, and he shall bear their iniquities" (Isa 53:11). When Isaiah writes that "out of the anguish of his soul he shall see," the prophet explains that the servant will die and rise again. The Septuagint makes this clear when it translates Isaiah 53:11 as follows, "The Lord also is pleased to take away from the travail of his soul, to shew him light [δεῖξαι αὐτῷ φῶς]."

To "see light" is a metaphor for life.[44] The psalmist, for example, writes: "For with you is the fountain of life; in your light do we see light" (Ps 36:9), and "His soul will go to the generation of his fathers, who will never again see light" (Ps 49:19). Job similarly says, "Or why was I not as a hidden stillborn child, as infants who never see the light?" (Job 3:16). The apostle Paul

38. Levering, *Did Jesus Rise from the Dead?*, 91, 103.

39. Levering, *Did Jesus Rise from the Dead?*, 104–11; Thomas Aquinas, *Commentary on the Gospel of John, Chapters 13–21*, trans. Fabian Larcher et al. (The Catholic University of America Press, 2010), 252–81.

40. Levering, *Did Jesus Rise from the Dead?*, 104, 107.

41. Levering, *Did Jesus Rise from the Dead?*, 109.

42. Levering, *Did Jesus Rise from the Dead?*, 111.

43. Beale and Carson, *Commentary*, 401.

44. Hans-Joachim Kraus, *Psalms 1–59* (Fortress, 1993), 399–400, 483–84, 527; David J. A. Clines, *Job 1–20*, WBC 17 (Word Books, 1989), 95; *Job 21–37*, WBC 18a (Thomas Nelson, 2006), 740.

confirms this connection when he makes a brief but pithy statement using Isaianic language: "Jesus our Lord, who was delivered up for our trespasses [παρεδόθη διὰ τὰ παραπτώματα]" (Rom 4:24–25), which echoes Isaiah 53:12's διὰ τὰς ἁμαρτίας αὐτῶν παρεδόθη ("delivered because of their sins"). Paul immediately follows this with reference to the resurrection, "Who was delivered up for our trespasses and *raised for our justification*" (Rom 4:25, emphasis added).[45]

Another New Testament passage that appeals to several Old Testament passages on the resurrection is Paul's sermon in Acts 13. Paul explains that God raised Jesus from the dead and then he appeared to his disciples (Acts 13:30–32). But then Paul specifically says that Christ's resurrection was a fulfillment of God's promises in the Old Testament:

> And we bring you the good news that what God promised to the fathers, this he has fulfilled to us their children by raising Jesus, as also *it is written in the second Psalm, 'You are my Son, today I have begotten you.'* [Ps 2:7] And as for the fact that he raised him from the dead, no more to return to corruption, he has spoken in this way, *'I will give you the holy and sure blessings of David.'* [Isa 55:3] Therefore he says also in another psalm, *'You will not let your Holy One see corruption.'* [Ps 16:10] For David, after he had served the purpose of God in his own generation, fell asleep and was laid with his fathers and saw corruption, but he whom God raised up did not see corruption. (Acts 13:32–37, emphasis added)

In this one statement Paul refers to Psalm 2:7 (v. 33), Isaiah 55:3 (v. 34), and Psalm 16:10 (v. 35). In each of these quotations Paul explains that they refer to the resurrection of Christ. Here Paul combines these three Old Testament texts that stress the promise to the fathers (Ps 2:7; cf. 2 Sam 7:14; Ps 89), the fulfillment for their children (Isa 55:3), and the resurrection of Jesus (Ps 16:10). God promised David, one of the fathers of Israel, that his son would sit on Israel's throne (Ps 2:7); Isaiah 55:3 communicates a promise to "you"; and Psalm 16:10 offers a promise of the incorruptibility of the Holy One.[46]

The prophet Daniel gives another multilayered reference to the resurrection that has branches that spread into the prophets Isaiah and Hosea.[47] Daniel writes: "And many of those who sleep in the dust of the earth shall awake,

45. Otfried Hofius, "The Fourth Servant Son in the New Testament Letters," in *The Suffering Servant: Isaiah 53 in Jewish and Christian Sources*, ed. Bernd Janowski and Peter Stuhlmacher (Eerdmans, 2004),163–88, here 180–81.

46. Beale and Carson, *Commentary*, 584–85.

47. Levering, *Did Jesus Rise from the Dead?*, 98–99; N. T. Wright, *The Resurrection of the Son of God* (Fortress, 2003), 110–13.

some to everlasting life, and some to shame and everlasting contempt. And those who are wise shall shine like the brightness of the sky above; and those who turn many to righteousness, like the stars forever and ever" (Dan 12:2–3). Isaiah 26:19 lies behind Daniel's statements about the future resurrection: "Your dead shall live; their bodies shall rise. You who dwell in the dust, awake and sing for joy! For your dew is a dew of light, and the earth will give birth to the dead."[48] Isaiah foretold of the resurrection, and the prophet Hosea later echoed him when he wrote, "I shall ransom them from the power of Sheol; I shall redeem them from Death. O Death, where are your plagues? O Sheol, where is your sting? Compassion is hidden from my eyes" (Hos 13:14). This web of texts is relevant from the standpoint of the New Testament because the apostle Paul quotes Hosea 13:14 in his taunt against death: "'O death, where is your victory? O death, where is your sting?' The sting of death is sin, and the power of sin is the law. But thanks be to God, who gives us the victory through our Lord Jesus Christ" (1 Cor 15:55–57). Paul's resurrection hope had a foundation in the Old Testament prophets, in Daniel, Isaiah, and Hosea.

One of the most powerful and direct Old Testament passages that foreshadows and promises the resurrection of Christ is when the prophet Jonah was swallowed by a large fish. Jonah is an important Old Testament book because Jesus specifically cites this event in connection with his resurrection: "Then some of the scribes and Pharisees answered him, saying, 'Teacher, we wish to see a sign from you.' But he answered them, 'An evil and adulterous generation seeks for a sign, but no sign will be given to it except the sign of the prophet Jonah. For just as Jonah was three days and three nights in the belly of the great fish, so will the Son of Man be three days and three nights in the heart of the earth'" (Matt 12:38–40; Luke 11:29–30). People often assume that Jonah was alive in the belly of the fish for three days and nights, but the text does not say this.[49] The text says Jonah cried out from "the belly of Sheol" and "the pit," which are standard Old Testament terms for the realm of the dead (Jonah 2:2, 6; Ps 139:7–8; Job 17:13–16; 33:22–30).[50] Jonah says

48. Levering, *Did Jesus Rise from the Dead?*, 100; Wright, *Resurrection of the Son of God*, 126.

49. E.g., Douglas Stuart, *Hosea–Jonah*, WBC (Word Books, 1987), 472, 474; Joyce Baldwin, *Jonah*, in *The Minor Prophets*, ed. Thomas Edward McComiskey (Baker, 1993), 566; Josephus, *Antiquities*, IX.x, in *The Works of Flavius Josephus*, trans. William Whiston (The S. S. Scranton Co., 1905), 298; Simon Chow, *The Sign of Jonah Reconsidered: A Study of Its Meaning In the Gospel Traditions* (Almquist & Wiksell Intl., 1995), 33; *Annotations upon all the Books of the Old and New Testament* (Evan Tyler, 1657), comm. Jonah 1:17.

50. Pitre, *Case for Jesus*, 187; Chow, *The Sign of Jonah*, 31, 36–37, 43; *pace* Stuart and Baldwin, who argue Jonah's language of Sheol is metaphorical (Stuart, *Hosea–Jonah*, 475–76; Baldwin, *Jonah*, 570).

that his נפש ("life," ESV) was "fainting away," which indicates that he was dying and his prayer was the last gasps of a dying man (Jonah 2:7). Thus, when the fish vomited Jonah onto the land, it coughed up a corpse.

What are God's first words to Jonah? "'Arise [קום], go to Nineveh, that great city, and call out against it the message that I tell you.' So Jonah arose and went to Nineveh, according to the word of the Lord" (Jonah 3:2–3a). This is the same word that Jesus spoke to Jairus's daughter when he raised her from the dead: "Taking her by the hand he said to her, 'Talitha cumi,' which means, 'Little girl, I say to you, arise'" (Mark 5:41).[51] Jesus spoke in Aramaic, but the verbs are the same, "arise" (קום). The history of Jonah is not one of the miraculous preservation of the prophet in the belly of a fish but rather the miracle of death and resurrection.[52] For this reason Jesus invoked Jonah's death and resurrection as the only sign he would give to the wicked generation. Just as Jonah died and was raised, which was followed by the repentance of the Ninevites (gentiles), so Jesus's own death and resurrection would be followed by the repentance of great numbers of gentiles in response to his preaching.[53] The entire Old Testament, therefore, forms the intelligible backdrop for the resurrection of Christ.[54] Far from unexpected, the Old Testament promised Christ's resurrection, and the New Testament records its fulfillment.

One of the clearest pictures of resurrection in the Old Testament comes from the prophet Ezekiel and his vision of dry bones. Ezekiel sees a vision of a valley of dry bones, a symbolic portrait of Israel lying in the graveyard of exile. God instructs the prophet to speak to the dry bones: "Behold, I will cause breath to enter you, and you shall live. And I will lay sinews upon you, and will cause flesh to come upon you, and cover you with skin, and put breath in you, and you shall live, and you shall know that I am the Lord" (Ezek 37:5–6). Within its immediate historical context, the resurrection imagery is clear and refers to Israel's return from exile, a restoration of the people to the promised land. The imagery finds its origins in an intra-canonical echo of God's creation of Adam as he breathed life into his lifeless body (Gen 2:7) but undoubtedly projects and injects the hope of life after death through resurrection. The hope of this passage presents the prospects of deliverance from the curse of death for humanity's rebellion against God. But within the overall unfolding narrative of Scripture, as God raised Adam, his son (Luke 3:38),

51. R. T. France, *The Gospel of Mark*, NIGTC (Eerdmans, 2002), 240; William Lane, *The Gospel According to Mark*, NICNT (Eerdmans, 1974), 197–98.

52. Pitre, *The Case for Jesus*, 188.

53. Pitre, *The Case for Jesus*, 189.

54. Levering, *Did Jesus Rise from the Dead?*, 113.

from the dust unto life, and as he would raise Israel, his firstborn son (Exod 4:23), unto life after suffering the curse of death, so these events typologically foreshadow the resurrection of God's only begotten Son. There is thus the hope of life after death for those united to God's Son.[55] In fact, Ezekiel 37:1–14 underlies several key passages in the Gospel of John, but especially the resurrection of Lazarus (John 11). First, Mary and Martha's despair parallels the prophet's angst as they waited three days for Jesus to arrive (John 11:5). Second, God asked the prophet whether the dry bones could live, and Ezekiel responded, "O Lord God, you know" (Ezek 37:4). Martha's statement to Christ echoes the prophet's response: "Lord, if you had been there, my brother would not have died. But even now I know that whatever you ask from God, God will give you" (John 11:21–22). When Jesus told Martha, "I am the resurrection and the life. Whoever believes in me, though he die, yet shall he live, and everyone who lives and believes in me shall never die. Do you believe this?" (John 11:25–26), her response is timid like Ezekiel's response to God: "Yes, Lord; I believe that you are the Christ, the Son of God, who is coming into the world" (John 11:27). Third, just as God called the valley of dry bones to life through the prophet, "O dry bones, hear the word of the Lord" (Ezek 37:4), so Jesus called Lazarus to life: "Lazarus, come out" (John 11:43).[56] More broadly, the resurrection of Lazarus at the same time points backward to several resurrection passages in the Old Testament and forward to the resurrection of Christ. The resurrection of Lazarus recalls Elijah's raising of the widow's son (1 Kgs 17:17–24), Elisha's resurrection of the son of the Shunamite woman (2 Kgs 4:32–37), and Elisha's postmortem raising of a dead man (2 Kgs 13:21).[57]

New Testament

When we survey the New Testament evidence, we must place its witness within the context of three observations. First, philosophers such as Thomas Reid (1710–1796) have noted that virtually all the information we learn in the world comes to us through the testimony of others.[58] Before we are capable of scrutinizing testimony or the nature of authority, we receive information about many things for which we have no corroborating evidence. God has

55. Daniel I. Block, *The Book of Ezekiel, Chapters 25–48*, NICOT (Eerdmans, 1998), 367–423.

56. Brian Neil Peterson, *John's Use of Ezekiel: Understanding the Unique Perspective of the Fourth Gospel* (Fortress, 2015), 151.

57. Beale and Carson, *Commentary*, 467.

58. Levering, *Did Jesus Rise from the Dead?*, 80–81.

created us in such a manner to rely on this evidence before we can provide a reason for doing so. How many children accept on testimony that their parents are who they say they are? How many patients accept on testimony that the person in the white medical coat is in fact a trained physician? Reid observes, "If children were so framed, as to pay no regard to testimony or to authority, they must, in the literal sense, 'perish for lack of knowledge.' It is more necessary that they should be fed before they can feed themselves, than that they should be instructed in many things before they can discover them by their own judgment."[59]

Second, historical critical biblical scholars have subjected the Scriptures to what has been called "higher criticism," which in its more benign form simply means to study the literary methods and sources in the Bible. But higher criticism often harbors unbelief in the biblical studies guild.[60] Historian Donald Kagan (1932–2021) describes the attitude of higher criticism as, "I won't believe anything unless it is proven to me." Instead of this attitude of doubt, Kagan opts for what he calls "higher naïveté." He says that he believes anything written in ancient Greek or Latin unless he cannot. What prevents him from believing ancient claims? If they are openly contradictory, say something impossible, or if two texts contradict each other, then both cannot be correct. In such cases Kagan sets aside the ancient evidence.[61] Kagan was not the first to use the phrase, as historian Peter Gay (1923–2015) first made the case for "speculating" from historical material so long as such speculation grew naturally from the primary sources at hand, from the concerns of the historical period under examination, and not from the concerns of the historian. And so, he called for higher naïveté.[62] In other words, we should approach the New Testament witness with a receptivity, like we would the testimony of any other human being. If there is enough credible testimony to demonstrate that human beings have walked on the moon, then in our higher naïveté, not ignorant gullibility, we should accept such testimony as true. We can say the same thing about the New Testament's witness to the resurrection of Christ.

Third, and finally, while Scripture comprises a historical record, we must not forget that it is divine revelation. This chapter says more about this in

59. Thomas Reid, *Essays on the Intellectual Powers of Man* (John Bartlett, 1852), 395; Mats Wahlberg, *Revelation as Testimony: A Philosophical-Theological Study* (Eerdmans, 2014), 129–30.

60. Michael C. Legaspi, *The Death of Scripture and the Rise of Biblical Studies* (Oxford University Press, 2011).

61. Kagan makes these remarks in "Introduction to Ancient Greek History," at https://oyc.yale.edu/classics/clcv-205/lecture-3, accessed June 29, 2023.

62. Peter Gay, "Rhetoric and Politics in the French Revolution," *The American Historical Review* 66/3 (1961): 664–76, here 676.

its conclusion. With these three ideas—the New Testament as the testimony of another, an attitude of higher naïveté, and recognizing the Scriptures as divine and authoritative revelation—we can proceed to consider the New Testament's witness concerning the resurrection under the following topics: the empty tomb, post-resurrection appearances, and bodily resurrection.

The Empty Tomb

We can begin our survey of the New Testament evidence by considering Jesus's empty tomb.[63] New Testament scholars recognize that Mark's Gospel was written prior to AD 70, and his gospel records the burial of Jesus: "And when he learned from the centurion that he was dead, he granted the corpse to Joseph. And Joseph bought a linen shroud, and taking him down, wrapped him in the linen shroud and laid him in a tomb that had been cut out of the rock. And he rolled a stone against the entrance of the tomb. Mary Magdalene and Mary the mother of Joses saw where he was laid" (Mark 15:45–47).[64] There does not appear to be any reason to doubt the authenticity or historicity of this event. The apostle Paul received this information when he visited with the disciples in Jerusalem around AD 36: "For I delivered to you as of first importance what I also received: that Christ died for our sins in accordance with the Scriptures, that he was buried, that he was raised on the third day in accordance with the Scriptures" (1 Cor 15:3–4; Gal 1:18).[65] Paul's testimony goes back to within five years of Christ's crucifixion. So, we have a line of evidence that testifies both to the burial and resurrection of Christ.

There are other credible accounts of the empty tomb from the Gospel of Matthew and the book of Acts.[66] Matthew records the following:

> While they were going, behold, some of the guard went into the city and told the chief priests all that had taken place. And when they had assembled with the elders and taken counsel, they gave a sufficient sum of money to the soldiers and said, "Tell people, 'His disciples came by night and stole him away while we were asleep.' And if this comes to the governor's ears, we will satisfy him and keep you out of trouble." So they took the money and did as they were directed. And this story has been spread among the Jews to this day. (Matt 28:11–15)

63. For an in-depth examination of the evidence, see Habermas, *On the Resurrection*, 597–634.

64. William Lane Craig, *Did Jesus Rise from the Dead?* (Impact 360 Institute, 2019), 17.

65. Craig, *Did Jesus Rise from the Dead?*, 17.

66. Craig, *Did Jesus Rise from the Dead?*, 23.

The soldiers who were guarding Christ's tomb testified to the religious leaders that the tomb was empty, Jesus's body was gone, and the religious leaders believed them.[67] The leaders instructed the soldiers to concoct a story to explain the empty tomb. Why, if Jesus was still dead in the tomb, would there be reason to try to cover up the fact that the tomb was empty? Luke records Peter's sermon at Pentecost, which corroborates Matthew's account: "Brothers, I may say to you with confidence about the patriarch David that he both died and was buried, and his tomb is with us to this day. Being therefore a prophet, and knowing that God had sworn with an oath to him that he would set one of his descendants on his throne, he foresaw and spoke about the resurrection of the Christ, that he was not abandoned to Hades, nor did his flesh see corruption" (Acts 2:29–32). Peter confirms the empty tomb and substantiates the fact by explaining it is the fulfillment of Old Testament prophecy.

Further historical evidence concerning the empty tomb comes with the first eyewitnesses, namely, the women. All four Gospels record that women were the first to see the empty tomb and report this fact to the disciples (Matt 28:1–10; Mark 16:1–8; Luke 24:1–12; John 20:1–18).[68] However, if the authors of the Gospels were trying to fabricate a cover story to fool readers into thinking that Jesus had been raised from the dead, they made a strategic blunder by saying that women were the first witnesses. In the ancient world women were barred from being witnesses in a court of law. Josephus explains why this was so: "But let not the testimony of women be admitted, on account of the levity and boldness of their sex."[69] Why, then, record that women were the first witnesses—when they could instead say that men were the first to find the empty tomb—unless the Gospel writers were documenting actual historical facts?[70] They did not invent the story of the empty tomb but recorded the facts as they occurred. And while the statistics are not a foundation for claims about the empty tomb, apologist William Lane Craig has surveyed two thousand publications on the resurrection in English, French, and German since 1975, and 75 percent of them accept the historicity of the empty tomb.[71] These statistics do not establish the historicity of the empty tomb, but they do reveal that it is not unreasonable to believe that the Gospels

67. Craig, *Did Jesus Rise from the Dead?*, 29.

68. Craig, *Did Jesus Rise from the Dead?*, 26.

69. Josephus, *Antiquities*, IV.viii.15.

70. Habermas, *On the Resurrection*, 607.

71. Craig, *Did Jesus Rise from the Dead?*, 30. See also Gary R. Habermas, "Resurrection Research from 1975 to the Present: What Are Critical Scholars Saying?," *Journal for the Study of the Historical Jesus* 3/2 (2005): 135–53; "The Case for Christ's Resurrection," in *To Everyone an Answer: A Case for the Christian Worldview*, ed. Francis J. Beckwith et al. (IVP Academic, 2004), 179–98; "The Minimal Facts Approach to the Resurrection of Jesus: The Role of Methodology

record accurate historical information. There is no credible counterevidence that offers a better explanation.

Post-Resurrection Appearances

The New Testament recounts that after his resurrection from the dead, Jesus appeared a number of times to his disciples (Matt 28:9–10, 16–20; Luke 24:13–32, 34, 36–43; Luke 24:45–53; John 20:11–18, 19–29; 21:1–25; Acts 1:3–12; 9:1–6; 18:9–10; 23:11). But Paul's testimony offers a helpful summary of these post-resurrection appearances:

> For I delivered to you as of first importance what I also received: that Christ died for our sins in accordance with the Scriptures, that he was buried, that he was raised on the third day in accordance with the Scriptures, and that he appeared to Cephas, then to the twelve. Then he appeared to more than five hundred brothers at one time, most of whom are still alive, though some have fallen asleep. Then he appeared to James, then to all the apostles. Last of all, as to one untimely born, he appeared also to me. (1 Cor 15:3–8)

In this one statement, Paul provides a list of the people to whom Christ appeared after his resurrection: Peter (Cephas), the twelve disciples, and five hundred people all at once, James, and lastly, Paul himself. One of the main thrusts of Paul's comment is, "Go question the witnesses if you like."[72] Especially noteworthy among the list of witnesses is James, one of Jesus's siblings. Recall that Jesus's family initially thought he was mad: "Then [Jesus] went home, and the crowd gathered again, so that they could not even eat. And when his family heard it, they went out to seize him, for they were saying, 'He is out of his mind'" (Mark 3:20–21). What happened to change James's mind? The New Testament quietly observes that something dramatic occurred to change the mind of his family: "All these with one accord were devoting themselves to prayer, together with the women and Mary the mother of Jesus, and his brothers" (Acts 1:14), and "Then after three years I [Paul] went up to Jerusalem to visit Cephas and remained with him fifteen days. But I saw none of the other apostles except James the Lord's brother" (Gal 1:18–19). Recall from the testimony of Josephus (above) that the Sanhedrin stoned James to death for his faith in Christ in AD 60.[73] There were a significant number of people who were eyewitnesses to the resurrected Christ, including James,

---

as a Crucial Component in Establishing Historicity," *Southeastern Theological Review* 3/1 (2012): 15–26.

72. Craig, *Did Jesus Rise from the Dead?*, 35.

73. Craig, *Did Jesus Rise from the Dead?*, 38; Josephus, *Antiquities*, XX.ix, in *Works*, 613.

Jesus's own brother, who was initially skeptical about his messianic claims and was then convinced—sufficiently persuaded to the extent that he was willing to die for his faith in his brother.

Christ's Bodily Resurrection

If Christ's tomb was empty, then this means that his body was absent, but in what sense? The apostle Paul explains that Christ's body was transformed and glorified. About the resurrection transformation, Paul writes: "It is sown a natural body; it is raised a spiritual body. If there is a natural body, there is also a spiritual body" (1 Cor 15:44). People might initially think that Paul writes of a ghostly, immaterial body because he mentions a "spiritual body." But when Paul contrasts the σῶμα ψυχικόν ("natural body") with the σῶμα πνευματικόν ("spiritual body") he does not differentiate a physical from a non-physical body; rather, he contrasts a physical body dominated either by the flesh or by the Holy Spirit.[74] Christ, therefore, was neither a disembodied ghost nor spirit, which is evident from the record of his post-resurrection appearances. When Jesus appeared amid his disciples, he bid Thomas, "Put your finger here, and see my hands; and put out your hand, and place it in my side. Do not disbelieve, but believe" (John 20:27). Yes, Jesus miraculously appeared in the room when the doors were locked, but this does not deny the fact that Jesus stood before Thomas in bodily, physical form. In another post-resurrection appearance Jesus ate food in the presence of his disciples: "Jesus said to them, 'Come and have breakfast.' Now none of the disciples dared ask him, 'Who are you?' They knew it was the Lord. Jesus came and took the bread and gave it to them, and so with the fish. This was now the third time that Jesus was revealed to the disciples after he was raised from the dead. When they had finished breakfast" (John 21:12–15a).

The collective New Testament evidence clearly reveals that, in the words of the Apostles' Creed, Jesus "suffered under Pontius Pilate, was crucified, died, and was buried; he descended into hell. The third day he rose again from the dead. He ascended to heaven." There is no credible reason to object to the historical authenticity of these claims. The collective New Testament witness is coherent and does not contradict itself. We can exercise higher naïveté and take these claims at face value. Over the centuries, however, there have been doubters who have offered alternative explanations of the New Testament evidence. So, we now turn to the objections to the resurrection of Christ.

74. Geerhardus Vos, "The Eschatological Aspect of the Spirit," in *Biblical and Theological Studies by the Members of the Faculty of Princeton Theological Seminary* (Charles Scribner's Sons, 1912), 211–59.

Answering Objections

The chief objections to the New Testament's witness to the resurrection of Christ are that the disciples conspired to cover up his death, that Jesus did not actually die on the cross but passed out and was later revived, that someone misplaced Jesus's body, and that people experienced a hallucination of seeing the "resurrected" Jesus. We can briefly consider each of these objections.

Conspiracy

Recall that Matthew was eager to dispel the notion of a conspiracy. Matthew records that the religious leaders bribed the soldiers and told them to devise the story that the disciples stole Christ's body (Matt 28:11–15). Others have argued that the disciples invented the resurrection claim because they were familiar with other resurrection myths from the ancient world. The Greek god Hercules died and was carried to heaven after his body was placed on a funeral pyre.[75] This is not a bodily resurrection but an assumption to heaven. Some sources have Empedocles (ca. 494–434 BC) being removed from earth or simply disappearing. Diogenes Laërtius (AD 180–240), a biographer of the Greek philosophers, writes:

> Some of his friends had been invited to the sacrifice, including Pausanias. Then, after the feast, the remainder of the company dispersed and retired to rest, some under the trees in the adjoining field, others wherever they chose, while Empedocles himself remained on the spot where he had reclined at table. At daybreak all got up, and he was the only one missing. A search was made, and they questioned the servants, who said they did not know where he was. Thereupon someone said that in the middle of the night he heard an exceedingly loud voice calling Empedocles. Then he got up and beheld a light in the heavens and a glitter of lamps, but nothing else. His hearers were amazed at what had occurred, and Pausanias came down and set people to search for him. But later he bade them to take no further trouble, for things beyond expectation had happened to him, and it was their duty to sacrifice to him since he was now a god.[76]

Again, there is little, if any, resemblance to the biblical narratives of Christ's resurrection. Empedocles was not dead and then raised to life but was alive and then disappeared under strange circumstances. Moreover, assuming the accuracy of this narrative, people supposed that Empedocles became a god

75. Edith Hamilton, *Mythology* (Little, Brown and Company, 1969), 236; Craig, *Did Jesus Rise from the Dead?*, 62.

76. Diogenes Laertius, *Lives of Eminent Philosophers*, Diogenes Laertius, vol. 2, trans. R. D. Hicks, Loeb Classical Library (G. P. Putnam's Sons, 1925), VIII.67 (383).

through his assumption, but Jesus already claimed to be God before his resurrection (e.g., John 8:48–59).

In Egyptian mythology, Osiris, the god of the deceased, fertility, and the afterlife, is a seasonal symbol of the crop cycle—the crops die in the dry season and they come back to life in the rainy season.[77] One scholar explains, "The resurrection of Osiris is closely connected with the germination of wheat; the grain which is put into the ground is the dead Osiris, and the grain which has germinated is the Osiris who has once again renewed his life."[78] Osiris is an explanatory myth ungrounded in history, unlike Jesus, for whom there are both biblical and extrabiblical historical records regarding his life, death, and resurrection. Moreover, Christ's resurrection was "according to the Scriptures" (Luke 24:45–46; John 20:28–29; 1 Cor 15:3–4), which means that the disciples did not create a conspiracy but were instead documenting the fulfillment of Old Testament prophecy.

Swoon Theory

Some have argued that Jesus only appeared to die, was removed from the cross, placed in the tomb, and when sufficiently rested, he revived. He was never dead but merely swooned (or passed out) on the cross. This theory ignores the stone placed over the tomb and the posted guard (Matt 27:66; Mark 15:46; 16:3; Luke 23:53; 24:2; John 20:1). Nevertheless, Gospel details preclude the swoon theory. When the Romans crucified criminals, they wanted to ensure they were truly dead, so soldiers stabbed them with a spear.[79] This is a fact that John records: "But one of the soldiers pierced his side with a spear, and at once there came out blood and water" (John 19:34). Over the years medical doctors have examined the historical evidence in the New Testament, especially this verse (John 19:34), and have concluded that Jesus was truly dead. They believe that because both blood and water came out of Jesus's side, the spear likely pierced his pericardial sack. Another possibility is that the water was a pleural effusion, which combined with blood was a hemothorax. A hemothorax is a collection of blood in the space between the wall of the chest and the lungs.[80] In addition to his crucifixion, we must not

77. Craig, *Did Jesus Rise from the Dead?*, 62.

78. E. A. Wallis Budge, *Osiris and the Egyptian Resurrection*, 2 vols. (G. P. Putnam's Sons, 1911), II:32.

79. Craig, *Did Jesus Rise from the Dead?*, 68.

80. Frederick T. Zugibe, *The Crucifixion of Jesus: A Forensic Inquiry*, 2nd ed. (M. Evans and Company, 2005), 137–66. For a more exhaustive examination of the medical evidence for Jesus's death, see Habermas, *On the Resurrection*, 302–29.

forget Christ's torture and beating as contributing factors to his death (Matt 27:27–31; Mark 15:16–20; Luke 23:11; John 19:1–25).

Displaced Body

Israeli historian Joseph Klausner claimed that Joseph of Arimathea temporarily placed Jesus's body in the tomb and then later moved him to a common graveyard reserved for criminals. The disciples were unaware of this move and therefore erroneously believed that Jesus was resurrected.[81] Klausner writes:

> We must assume that the owner of the tomb, Joseph of Arimathea, thought it unfitting that one who had been crucified should remain in his own ancestral tomb. Matthew alone tells us that the tomb was new, hewn out of the rock specially for Jesus the Messiah (just as the ass's colt on which Jesus rode was one on which none other had ever sat). Joseph of Arimathea, therefore, secretly removed the body at the close of the Sabbath and buried it in an unknown grave; and since he was, according to the Gospels, "one of the disciples of Jesus," or "one who was looking for the kingdom of God," there was some measure of truth in the report spread by the Jews, though it was, in the main, only the malicious invention of the enemies unable to explain the "miracle."[82]

Klausner was a Jew who acknowledged the empty tomb (an important admission) but then posits an unlikely theory that Joseph moved the body, never mind the significant list of eyewitness testimony of more than five hundred people that personally saw the bodily resurrected Christ or the religious leaders who paid the tomb guards to lie as a cover story to explain away the empty tomb.

Hallucination

German New Testament scholar David Friedrich Strauss (1808–1874) first proposed the idea that the resurrection appearances of Christ were only hallucinations. People did not actually see Jesus but only imagined that they did.[83] Strauss, however, was no fair-minded historian but prejudicially decided that supernatural events were impossible: "The proposition: a dead man has returned to life, is composed of two such contradictory elements, that whenever it is attempted to maintain the one, the other threatens to disappear. If

81. Craig, *Did Jesus Rise from the Dead?*, 71.

82. Klausner, *Jesus of Nazareth*, 357.

83. See Gary Habermas, "Explaining Away Jesus' Resurrection: The Recent Revival of Hallucination Theories," in *Christian Research Institute* 23/4 (2001), http://www.garyhabermas.com/articles/crj_explainingaway/crj_explainingaway.htm.

he has really returned to life, it is natural to conclude that he was not wholly dead; if he was really dead, it is difficult to believe that he has really become living."[84] Strauss believed it was unreasonable that a dead man could be raised back to life, so this sent him hunting for other options. How else, then, could the disciples erroneously conclude that Jesus rose from the dead?

Strauss played on the fact that Jesus left a deep impression upon his disciples that he was indeed the Messiah:

> In order to form a correct judgment on this subject, we must transport ourselves yet more completely into the situation and frame of mind into which the disciples of Jesus were thrown by his death. During several years' intercourse with them he had constantly impressed them more and more decidedly with the belief that he was the Messiah; but his death, which they were unable to reconcile with their messianic ideas, had for the moment annihilated this belief. Now when, after the first shock was past, the earlier impression began to revive: there spontaneously arose in them the psychological necessity of solving the contradiction between the ultimate fate of Jesus and their earlier opinion of him—of adopting into their idea of the Messiah the characteristics of suffering and death.[85]

The disciples truly believed Jesus was the Messiah and so his death by crucifixion was a traumatic shock that sent them reeling. Once they regained their composure, they had to ransack the Old Testament to find proof that Jesus was supposed to suffer and die. But what drove the disciples to conclude that Jesus arose from the dead? In short, Strauss suggests that the disciples suffered from what we would now call post-traumatic stress disorder (PTSD):

> Lastly, how conceivable is it that in individuals, especially women, these impressions were heightened, in a purely subjective manner, into actual vision; that on others, even on whole assemblies, something or other of an objective nature, visible or audible, sometimes perhaps the sight an unknown person, created the impression of a revelation or appearance of Jesus: a height of pious enthusiasm which is wont to appear elsewhere in religious societies peculiarly oppressed and persecuted.[86]

The disciples either *thought* they saw Jesus, or if they saw someone who vaguely resembled Jesus, they mistakenly concluded that they actually saw

84. David Friedrich Strauss, *The Life of Jesus Critically Examined*, 4th ed., trans. George Eliot (Swan Sonnenschein & Co., 1902), 735–36.

85. Strauss, *Life of Jesus*, 742.

86. Strauss, *Life of Jesus*, 741.

him. Notable is that Strauss attributes their mental condition to *hysteria*. Hysteria was a common nineteenth-century psychological disorder attributed to women.[87] What about the fact that there were over five hundred witnesses to Christ's resurrection?

Strauss was aware of these five hundred witnesses, but he stipulated that they only *believed* they saw the resurrected Jesus. This did not mean, however, that they actually saw him: "To the Apostle Paul, namely, the idea that Jesus had risen and appeared to many persons was delivered as the belief of the sect which he persecuted; he had only to receive it into his conviction and to vivify it in his imagination until it became a part of his own experience."[88] The apostle Paul was aware of this claim and so, out of a sense of guilt for the Christians he once persecuted, he adopted this mistaken belief and passed it on as fact. So under the duress of PTSD, suffering from a guilty conscience, and wanting to make these hallucinations his own, Paul passed these notions on to the churches, and tradition took over: "When once the idea of a resurrection of Jesus had been formed in this manner, the great event could not be allowed to have happened so simply, but must be surrounded and embellished with all the pomp which the Jewish imagination flourished. The chief ornaments which stood at command for this purpose, were angels."[89] How likely is Strauss's explanation of mass hysteria, or mass hallucination?

While there have been cases of mass hysteria before, such as the Salem witch trials or the Communist political hunts of the 1950s, they commonly exhibit certain traits that do not occur in the New Testament claims about Christ's resurrection. First, how have the cases of mass hysteria turned out? The Salem witch trials and the Communist political hunts both lost steam and vanished. Second, people might express great interest in finding Bigfoot, the elusive yet never caught gargantuan creature that supposedly walks the forests of the Pacific Northwest, but when there is a lack of credible evidence to sustain the movement, it dies a natural death. Third, mass hysteria events that focus on a charismatic leader do not typically survive the leader's death. And fourth, every mass delusion disappears once the cause is removed.[90] Additionally, something Strauss does not factor is the first-century meaning of seeing a deceased person. To see a vision of a deceased person was evidence

87. See, e.g., Sigmund Freud, *The Interpretation of Dreams*, in *The Basic Writings of Sigmund Freud*, trans. A. A. Brill (The Modern Library, 1995), 149–517, here 445–46; also Josef Breur and Sigmund Freud, *Studies on Hysteria*, trans. James Strachey (Basic Books, 1895).

88. Strauss, *Life of Jesus*, 741.

89. Strauss, *Life of Jesus*, 744.

90. John J. Johnson, *Currents in Twenty-First Century Christian Apologetics: Challenges Confronting the Faith* (Wipf & Stock, 2008), 108–9; see also Habermas and Licona, *The Case for the Resurrection*, 104–19.

of their death, not resurrection.[91] Recall, for example, when the apostle Peter was miraculously released from prison by an angel, he went to the house of Mary, the mother of John, where many were gathered to pray. He knocked at the door, and a young girl named Rhoda answered. She heard Peter's voice and ran to tell the others in the house, but people insisted that she did not actually see Peter but his angel (Acts 12:12–16). The people in the house believed Peter's appearance was ghostly—evidence of his death, not his resurrection. Yet, people did not characterize Christ's resurrection in this manner. That more than five hundred people would have the same hallucination defies a common mass hysteria hypothesis. These people could all see him, touch him, watch him eat food, as well as cling to him. Jesus was present in bodily form. Moreover, the chief problem with Strauss's theory is that he stacks the deck; from the outset, he prejudicially excludes the possibility of the resurrection. How can one enter a rational discussion if the topic is prejudged as impossible despite the extrabiblical and biblical evidence?

Conclusion

Overall, when we weigh all the evidence, the most plausible answer is that Jesus arose from the dead. As New Testament scholar N. T. Wright concludes: "Far and away the best historical explanation is that Jesus of Nazareth, having been thoroughly dead and buried, really was raised to life on the third day with a new *kind* of physical body."[92] There is significant extrabiblical historical evidence that attests to Christ's existence, ministry, miracles, crucifixion, empty tomb, and that his followers worshiped him as God. The biblical witness is clear with the Old Testament prophesying and anticipating the resurrection of Christ and the New Testament confirming the fulfillment of these Old Testament expectations. Even some of the critics acknowledge certain facts, such as the empty tomb, but then seek to dismiss the evidence with other explanations, such as the displaced body, swoon, or mass hysteria theories. Yet, these counter-theories fall short. By reading the books of nature and Scripture, there is a compelling case for the historicity and authenticity of Christ's resurrection from the dead. In the face of unbelief and especially with the rise of Islam, understanding the evidence and biblical teaching on this topic is vital to defending the faith.

According to the Quran, Jesus did not rise from the dead. The Quran states: "And for their saying, 'Indeed, we have killed the Messiah, Jesus, the

91. Craig, *Did Jesus Rise from the Dead?*, 76.
92. Wright, *Surprised by Scripture*, 57.

son of Mary, the messenger of Allah.' And they did not kill him, nor did they crucify him; but another was made to resemble him to them. And indeed, those who differ over it are in doubt about it. They have no knowledge of it except the following of assumption. And they did not kill him, for certain" (Q 4:157). While there are varying interpretations of this passage, the most common is that Jesus was not crucified but that someone else took his place.[93] The substitute died, and Jesus remained alive. Such a claim, of course, directly contradicts the clear witness of Scripture. Engagement with this Islamic claim goes back more than a thousand years to John of Damascus (ca. 675–749) and his work *On Heresies*.[94] In the Quran, Jesus simply ascends to heaven.[95] About this statement from the Quran, John of Damascus writes: "There are many other extraordinary and quite ridiculous things in this book [the Quran] which he [Mohammed] boasts was sent down to him from God."[96] We have a collision between the claims of Mohammed and the claims of Scripture and the facts of history. There are no historically verifiable facts to corroborate the claims of the Quran concerning its denials of the death and resurrection of Jesus. Knowing the historical and biblical evidence equips Christians to confront Muslim denial of the resurrection head-on. Either Scripture or the Quran is right concerning the death and resurrection of Christ—both cannot be true. Moreover, in light of Paul's teaching, if Jesus was not crucified, then he did not die; if he did not die, then he was not raised from the dead; if he was not raised from the dead, no one is raised from the dead. Hence, "If in Christ we have hope in this life only, we are of all people most to be pitied" (1 Cor 15:19).

But in this presentation of the historical and biblical evidence concerning the resurrection of Christ, we must remember that only a heart regenerated by the Holy Spirit will acknowledge, comprehend, trust, and love the truth of the resurrection. In the words of the Westminster Confession of Faith, there is much in Scripture that "doth abundantly evidence itself to the Word of God, yet notwithstanding, our full persuasion and assurance of the infallible truth and divine authority therefore, is from the inward work of the Holy Spirit bearing witness by and with the Word in our hearts" (1.5). Apologetic arguments do not convert sinners. Only the sovereign work of the Spirit opens

93. *Sahih International Translation*, as cited in Greg Lanier, "'It Was Made to Appear Like That to Them': Islam's Denial of Jesus' Crucifixion," *Reformed Faith & Practice* 1 (2016): 39–55, here 44.

94. John of Damascus, *On Heresies*, no. 101, in *Writings*, The Fathers of the Church, vol. 37, ed. Frederic H. Chase Jr. (The Catholic University of America Press, 1958), 154.

95. Levering, *Did Jesus Rise from the Dead?*, 135–36.

96. John of Damascus, *On Heresies*, no. 101 (p. 154).

hearts and enables sinners to trust in Christ for salvation. At the same time, understanding and presenting the historical evidence along with the witness of Scripture can accomplish two things. First, we can clear intellectual obstacles and debris from the road to the heart and mind so the message of the gospel can travel unhindered. And second, we can reassure and bolster our own faith in the face of doubts. The gospel is rooted in real history. As the apostle John testifies, "That which we have seen and heard we proclaim also to you, so that you too may have fellowship with us; and indeed our fellowship is with the Father and with his Son Jesus Christ" (1 John 1:3). When asked why we believe in the message of the gospel, we will not merely reply with the words of the old hymn, "Ask me how I know he lives, he lives within my heart." Rather, we can say with bold confidence from a foundation of a God-given faith and the testimony of history and Scripture: "I believe in God, the Father almighty, creator of heaven and earth. I believe in Jesus Christ, his only Son, our Lord, who was conceived by the Holy Spirit and born of the virgin Mary. He suffered under Pontius Pilate, was crucified, died, and was buried; he descended to hell. The third day he rose again from the dead." Or in the words of sixteenth-century poet John Donne (1572–1631):

> Death be not proud, though some have called thee
> Mighty and dreadful, for thou art not so.
> For, those, whom thou think'st dost overthrow,
> Die not, poor death, nor yet canst thou kill me;
> From rest and sleep, which but thy pictures be,
> Much pleasure, then from thee, much more must flow,
> And soonest our best men with thee do go,
> Rest of their bones, and souls delivery.
> Thou art slave to Fate, chance, kings, and desperate men,
> And dost with poison, war, and sickness dwell,
> And poppy, or charms can make us sleep as well,
> And better then thy stroke, why swell'st thou then?
> One short sleep past, we wake eternally,
> And death shall be no more, death, thou shalt die.[97]

97. John Donne, *Poems and Prose* (Alfred A. Knopf, 1995), 167.

11

Evil and Suffering

The Cross of Christ as the Answer to Human Sin

Thesis 11: As Paul appealed to the book of nature by invoking the doctrine of providence, Christians can appeal to this doctrine as they explain why evil exists and how the book of Scripture points us to the cross of Christ as God's answer to evil.

> God who made the world and everything in it, being Lord of heaven and earth, does not live in temples made by man, nor is he served by human hands, as though he needed anything, since he himself gives to all mankind life and breath and everything. And he made from one man every nation of mankind to live on all the face of the earth, having determined allotted periods and the boundaries of their dwelling place, that they should seek God, and perhaps feel their way toward him and find him.
>
> —Acts 17:24–27

Theodicy is a theological topic that addresses the thorny question of how God can be good given the presence of evil and suffering in the world. Dorothy Sayers (1893–1957) captures the challenging nature of theodicy when she poses the question, "If God made everything, did He make the Devil?" This is the type of question that a child can ask, and there is no easy, quick answer. But the older we get, the question becomes more pressing, and we cannot tell a grown adult to go away and play. "The world has grown hoary," Sayers writes, "and the questions are still unanswered."[1] What we must realize is that the Bible answers this question, though it does not necessarily answer it in the manner that we anticipate. If we ask question A, and expect answer B, the Bible instead gives us C as a response. Like the disciples' question to Jesus about the man born blind, "Who sinned, this man or his parents?" (John 9:2), the disciples expected one of two responses rather than the response that Jesus gave: "It was not that this man sinned, or his parents, but that the works of God might be displayed in him" (John 9:3). The disciples expected Jesus to answer A or B, but Jesus answered C. When we ask, therefore, how can a good God allow suffering in the world, the Bible answers by turning our gaze to the cross of Christ, a response that is filled with love, presence, and comfort in the face of our sufferings. In the end, God's loving, redemptive, saving presence in Christ is the response to theodicy.

This chapter argues the thesis that as Paul appealed to the book of nature by invoking the doctrine of providence, Christians can appeal to this doctrine as they explain why evil exists and how the book of Scripture points us to the cross of Christ as God's answer to evil. The chapter fleshes out the cruciform response to theodicy by first surveying historic objections to the goodness of God. Second, the chapter considers a theology of theodicy, especially the relationship between divine sovereignty and human responsibility. Third, the chapter addresses the relationship between apologetics and theodicy. Christians need to know how the cross of Christ answers the question of theodicy, not merely for the sake of apologetics, but also for answering their own questions of doubt and confusion as they walk through the valley of the shadow of death. But the cross of Christ is not a disjointed answer that we append to the earlier arguments from design. Rather, just as Paul moved from creation to Christ in his Mars Hill address, we will see how creation in a fallen world sets the stage for Christians to introduce Christ. In this respect, the book of Job makes this same move: God takes Job on a tour of the creation to show him that there is indeed divine order. The teleology of the creation rests in God's presence with Job—God is Immanuel with Job. God's presence with Job shows us that his supreme presence with his people in the cross of Christ is the capstone to the teleological argument for the existence of God.

Historic Objections

Over the centuries there have been numerous objections to and criticisms of the Christian faith regarding the perceived incompatibility between the

1. Dorothy Sayers, *The Mind of the Maker* (Harper Collins, 1987), 93ff.

existence of a good and merciful God and the presence of suffering and evil in the world. This section examines objections through the works of two well-known writers who wrestled with the question of theodicy: Voltaire and Fyodor Dostoevsky.

Voltaire

In his novella *Candide*, French eighteenth-century philosopher Voltaire (1694–1778) tells the story of a young man, Candide, who dwelled in an Edenic paradise where he was instructed by his Leibnizian professor, Pangloss. The novella chronicles Candide's disillusionment as he observes and experiences tragedy in the world. Among the events that Voltaire includes in his book is the 1755 Lisbon earthquake. On Saturday, November 1, 1755, an earthquake in the Atlantic Ocean roughly 120 miles west-southwest of Lisbon, Portugal, struck and produced a tsunami that wreaked massive destruction. Estimates place deaths at thirty thousand to fifty thousand people. In his book Voltaire ridicules both philosophers and theologians for their inability to explain such massive devastation. The chief foil in Voltaire's *Candide* is Gottfried Wilhelm Leibniz (1646–1716), who made the claim that, despite the suffering we see, we live in the best of all possible worlds. This is the best possible world that God could have made.[2] In his novel, Pangloss is dedicated to Leibniz's philosophy: "Pangloss taught metaphysico-theologico-cosmo-codology. He could prove wonderfully that there was no effect without cause and that, in this best of all possible worlds, His Lordship the Baron's castle was the most beautiful of castles and Madam the best of all possible baronesses."[3] But how could such a claim be true in the wake of the Great Lisbon earthquake when so many people lost their lives?

In Voltaire's famous "Poem on the Lisbon Earthquake" the philosopher asks:

> Women and children heaped up mountain high,
> Limbs crushed which under ponderous marble lie;
> Wretches unnumbered in the pangs of death,
> Who mangled, torn, and panting for their breath,
> Buried beneath their sinking roofs expire,
> And end their wretched lives in torments dire.
> Say, when you hear their piteous, half-formed cries,

2. G. W. Leibniz, *Theodicy: Essays on the Goodness of God the Freedom of Man and the Origin of Evil*, ed. Austin Farrer, trans. F. M. Uggard (Open Court, 1985); Maria Rosa Antognazza, *Leibniz: A Very Short Introduction* (Oxford University Press, 2016), 62–73.

3. Voltaire, *Candide and Other Stories* (Alfred A. Knopf, 1992), 2.

Or from their ashes see the smoke arise,
Say, will you then eternal laws maintain,
Which God to cruelties like these constrain?
Whilst you these facts replete with horror view,
Will you maintain death to their crimes was due?
And can you then impute a sinful deed
To babes who on their mothers' bosoms bleed?
Was then more vice in fallen Lisbon found,
Than Paris, where voluptuous joys abound?[4]

These questions animate Voltaire's novella, which he embodies in the misfortunes that Candide suffers. Candide lives in a castle and pursues a love interest, Cunégonde, whom he kisses and is consequently expelled. Prussians capture him and press him into military service where they flog and thrust him into battle. Candide escapes to Holland where he finds his old professor, Pangloss, who is suffering from syphilis. Pangloss tells him that the castle where he lived was destroyed by the Prussians, and Cunégonde was raped, and she and her whole family were killed. Pangloss is cured of his syphilis but nevertheless loses an eye and ear. Both men board a ship, which sinks in a storm, but they survive to arrive in Lisbon in time for the great earthquake that kills tens of thousands. Amid all of these tragedies, Pangloss nevertheless maintains that this is still the best of all possible worlds. Pangloss and Candide encounter a member of the Portuguese Inquisition who asks about their views on theodicy, and they are both arrested. Candide is flogged, and Pangloss is hanged for his heresy. At this point, Candide finds Cunégonde—she is alive, but she has been rescued by a Jewish merchant and sold into slavery. Candide kills her owners, and the two flee to the Americas.

The novella concludes with Pangloss reappearing, as he survived his hanging. Despite the horrors of his life, Pangloss still maintained his Leibnizian optimism: "'I still feel now as I did at the outset,' replied Pangloss. 'I am a philosopher after all. It wouldn't do for me to go back on what I said before, what with Leibniz not being able to be wrong, and pre-established harmony being the finest thing in the world.'"[5] The book ends with Pangloss and Candide resolving to make the best of things in the face of tragedy:

"I also know," said Candide, "that we must cultivate our garden."

"You're right," said Pangloss; "for when man was placed in the garden of Eden, he was placed there *ut operaetur eum*—that he might work—which proves that man was not born to rest."

4. Voltaire, "The Lisbon Earthquake," in *The Works of Voltaire*, vol. 36 (E. R. DuMont, 1901), 8–9.

5. Voltaire, *Candide*, 87.

"Let's get down to work and stop all this philosophizing," said Martin. "It's the only way to make life bearable."

. . .

"All events form a chain in the best of all possible worlds. For in the end, if you had not been given a good kick up the backside and chased out of a beautiful castle for loving Miss Cunégonde, and if you hadn't been subjected to the Inquisition, and if you hadn't wandered about America on foot, and if you hadn't dealt the Baron a good blow with your sword, and if you hadn't lost all your sheep from that fine country of Eldorado, you wouldn't be here now eating candied citron and pistachio nuts."

"That is well put," replied Candide, "but we must cultivate our garden."[6]

Voltaire's novella is reputed to be one of the greatest books in the Western literary canon but also represents a popular and well-known criticism against Christian theodicy. This is not to say that Leibniz's "best of all possible worlds" is a distinctly biblical theodicy, but it does bear a resemblance to the apostle Paul's statement, "And we know that for those who love God all things work together for good, for those who are called according to his purpose" (Rom 8:28). And thus, given the apparent similarity between the two ideas, regardless of what significant dissimilarities exist between the two very different ideas, people register Voltaire's novella as a devastating critique against biblical theodicy and organized religion.[7]

Fyodor Dostoyevsky

Russian novelist Fyodor Dostoyevsky (1821–1881) recounts the story of the Karamazov brothers in his well-known novel *The Brothers Karamazov*. In the novel three brothers, Dmitri, Ivan, and Alyosha, determine to differentiate themselves from their profligate father, Fyodor. Dmitri joins the army, Ivan becomes a journalist, and Alyosha enters a monastery. In one of the dialogues between Ivan and Alyosha, Ivan debates his brother about God's existence and the question of evil. Ivan says that he cannot accept how a supposedly just God can permit the suffering of children, creatures who are too young to have sinned and thus deserve punishment. To love a God who allows such things would be akin to a tortured man choosing to love his torturer. Ivan then tells Alyosha a story. In the darkest days of serfdom in Russia, there was a general who was powerful and wealthy. His service to his country in war convinced him

6. Voltaire, *Candide*, 92–93.

7. Michel S. Lecavalier, "Religious Criticism in Voltaire's *Candide*" (MA Thesis, McMaster University, 1970).

that he had earned the power to decide questions of life and death. He owned hundreds of dogs and nearly a hundred handlers; one day a house-serf, a young boy, threw a rock while he was playing and injured the paw of one of the dogs, which happened to be the general's favorite.[8] The general was incensed and had the boy and his mother incarcerated. The next day the general ordered the boy stripped naked, told him to run, and then he loosed his dogs on him; they tore the boy to pieces. Ivan confronted his brother and asked him what should be done. Alyosha responded that the general should be shot.[9]

Ivan then cornered his brother and asked why children have to suffer. If people must endure suffering in order to buy their eternal harmony, why are children included? Ivan understood solidarity in sin, solidarity in retribution, but what share do children have with the solidarity in sin since they are too young to have sinned? Ivan was aware that some might say that the child would eventually grow up, sin, and thus warrant inclusion in the grand cosmic scheme of suffering for sin, but what about the boy who died at the age of eight at the vicious fangs of dogs? Ivan then sighed,

> Oh, Alyosha, I'm not blaspheming! I do understand how the universe will tremble when all in heaven and under the earth merge in one voice of praise, and all that lives and has lived cries out: "Just are thou, O Lord, for thy ways are revealed!" Oh, yes, when the mother and the torturer whose hounds tore her son to pieces embrace each other, and all three cry out with tears: "Just art thou, O Lord," then of course the crown of knowledge will have come and everything will be explained. But there is the hitch: that is what I cannot accept. And while I am on earth, I hasten to take my own measures. You see, Alyosha, it may well be that if I live until that moment, or rise again in order to see it, I myself will perhaps cry out with all the rest, looking at the mother embracing her child's tormentor. "Just art thou, O Lord!" but I do not want to cry out with them. While there's still time, I hasten to defend myself against it, and therefore I absolutely renounce all higher harmony. . . . Let her [the mother] forgive him [the tormentor] herself, if she wants to, let her forgive the tormentor her immeasurable maternal suffering; but she has no right to forgive the suffering of her child who was torn to pieces, she dare not forgive the tormentor, even if the child himself were to forgive him![10]

Ivan was unpersuaded that even the return of Christ and the supposed righting of all wrongs could alleviate the injustice of the death of innocent children.

8. Fyodor Dostoevsky, *The Brothers Karamazov*, trans. Richard Pevear and Larissa Volokhonsky (Alfred A. Knopf, 1992), 242.

9. Dostoevsky, *The Brothers Karamazov*, 243.

10. Dostoevsky, *The Brothers Karamazov*, 244–45.

Even if fictional, *Candide* and *The Brothers Karamazov* capture common objections to the Christian faith. These fictional forays into the question of theodicy are reflections of real human suffering. The Great Lisbon earthquake was a real, devastating tragedy. In our own time we know all too well of similar suffering. In the terrorist attacks of 9/11, 2,977 people died in the World Trade Center collapse and Pentagon.[11] In 2004, a tsunami struck Thailand with devastating force, killing 227,899 people and leaving in its wake 13 billion dollars of damage.[12] Or, in 2011, a tsunami off the coast of Japan killed nearly 20,000 people and created 360 billion dollars' worth of damage.[13] We can take a step back and survey the carnage of the twentieth century and note that in armed conflict alone, not counting disease, famine, and the like, 108 million people have died. Yet even though such statistics are of great enormity, we need not look for large-scale suffering but can be equally vexed when death and suffering strike us at a personal level. The unexpected loss of a child, spouse, family member, or friend is devastating and leaves us reeling—we ask questions about God's goodness and wisdom. Does not all this suffering invalidate the claims of the Christian faith and refute both the existence and, if he exists, the benevolence of God? Philosopher David Hume (1711–1776) famously put the question this way:

1. If God is unable to prevent evil, then he is not all-powerful.
2. If God is not willing to prevent evil, then he is not all-good.
3. If God is both willing and able to prevent evil, then why does evil exist?[14]

This is indeed a challenging question and perhaps one of the most pressing given that all people face death and tragedy.

A Theology of Theodicy

The first step in answering the question of theodicy is to lay a theological foundation by answering Hume's trilemma: God is all-powerful and all-good, and

11. Katherine Huiskes, "Timeline: The September 11 Terrorist Attacks," Miller Center, https://millercenter.org/remembering-september-11/september-11-terrorist-attacks.

12. "JetStream Max: 2004 Indian Ocean Tsunami," https://www.noaa.gov/jetstream/2004tsu_max.

13. Mari Saito, "Ten Years On, Grief Never Subsides for Some Survivors of Japan's Tsunami," *Reuters,* March 10, 2021, https://www.reuters.com/investigates/special-report/japan-tsunami-survivors/.

14. David Hume, *Dialogues Concerning Natural Religion*, 2nd ed., ed. Richard H. Popkin (Hackett Publishing Co., 1980), 63.

the existence of evil brings neither his omnipotence nor his benevolence into question. To answer Hume's trilemma, we must understand three chief ideas that equip us to explain the existence of evil: (1) divine and human agency, (2) divine concurrence, and (3) the origins of evil. With these three ideas in hand, we can then briefly address why evil exists in the world. These ideas come from classic Reformed theology and equip us to address the question of the existence of evil and how it relates to apologetics. The short answer is, God is completely sovereign over the creation, and human beings are free creatures who are entirely responsible for their sinful actions. Evil arises from humans, not from God, and yet God is sovereign over freely chosen human actions. However, before we proceed, we should note one important caveat: just because we can theologically explain God's relationship to the existence of evil does not mean there are no unanswered questions. Neither does understanding the theology of theodicy minimize or eliminate the pain that people suffer in the face of evil. But understanding the theology of theodicy helps us to see two things. First, we understand that God is not the author of evil, though he is sovereign over it. And second, in the light of the theology of theodicy, we can see a clear path to the cross of Christ.

Divine and Human Agency

When we examine the relationship between divine and human agency, we can examine it through the lens of the doctrine of providence—that is, God's sovereign superintendence of every event in the world.[15] There are many statements in Scripture that attest to the idea that God has created all things and that he sovereignly determines all things. The prophet Isaiah, for example, writes: "I am God, and there is no other; I am God, and there is none like me, declaring the end from the beginning and from ancient times things not yet done, saying, 'My counsel shall stand, and I will accomplish all my purpose'" (Isa 46:9–10). God declares through the prophet that he alone is sovereign and the whole sweep of history, from its beginning to things in the present, all the way to the end, is under his sovereign rule. He does not wait for events to transpire but instead fulfills his purposes and will.[16] The psalmist echoes this idea when he writes: "For I know that the Lord is great, and that our Lord is above all gods. Whatever the Lord pleases, he does, in heaven and on earth, in the seas and all deeps. He it is who makes the clouds rise at the end of the

15. James Dolezal, "Agency, Concurrence, and Evil: A Study in Divine Providence," *Journal of IRBS Theological Seminary* (2019): 61–89, here 63.

16. Alec Motyer, *Isaiah: An Introduction and Commentary*, TOTC (InterVarsity Press, 1999), 295–96.

earth, who makes lightnings for the rain and brings forth the wind from his storehouses" (Ps 135:5–6; cf. Exod 18:11; Ps 115:3; Jer 10:13).[17] The New Testament puts a fine point on these ideas when Paul reveals that the Son of God was "before all things, and in him all things hold together" (Col 1:17). Paul unfolded this same truth to the philosophers at Mars Hill when he told them that God "himself gives to all mankind life and breath and everything" (Acts 17:25). The apostle John gives a brief yet potent summary of God's sovereignty over the creation when he writes: "For you created all things, and by your will they existed and were created" (Rev 4:11). The Scriptures are abundantly clear: God is sovereign over all things. In the words of Hume's trilemma, God is unquestionably all-powerful, or omnipotent.

On the flip side, the Scriptures equally affirm the idea of human responsibility and freedom. The apostle Paul writes to the Corinthians, "No temptation has overtaken you that is not common to man. God is faithful, and he will not let you be tempted beyond your ability, but with the temptation he will also provide the way of escape, that you may be able to endure it" (1 Cor 10:13). Paul similarly exhorted the Galatians, "For you were called to freedom, brothers. Only do not use your freedom as an opportunity for the flesh, but through love serve one another" (Gal 5:13). In these statements Paul presents Christians as ones who can resist temptation and that their Christ-bought freedom should not be used for sin but for love. Paul's words echo the teaching of Jesus, who taught the crowds: "If anyone would come after me, let him deny himself and take up his cross and follow me" (Mark 8:34). Jesus represents the life of discipleship as one of denying one's self and voluntarily taking up the cross. In these three different statements, the New Testament teaches that believers are free to obey or sin because God has released them from the bondage of sin through the sovereign regenerating work of the Spirit and the gift of faith. But even with unbelievers, the Scriptures show that God does not coerce them into sinning. When Joseph's brothers sinned against him by selling him into slavery and lying to Jacob about his death, Joseph told his brothers, "As for you, *you meant evil against me*, but God meant it for good" (Gen 50:20, emphasis added). Joseph's brothers had entirely different intentions than God's. The apostle Peter made a similar statement in his Pentecost sermon when he indicted the crowds for their sin: "This Jesus, delivered up according to the definite plan and foreknowledge of God, *you crucified and killed by the hands of lawless men*" (Acts 2:23, emphasis added). God and the people who killed Jesus had entirely different purposes and motives. God ordained Christ's crucifixion by his "definite plan and foreknowledge," yet

17. Derek Kidner, *Psalms 73–150: A Commentary*, TOTC (InterVarsity Press, 1973), 455–56.

this is not in the least bit exculpatory for the people who crucified Christ by their "lawless" act. The Scriptures are clear: God is sovereign, yet humans are entirely free and responsible for their sinful actions.

How can we account for the relationship between divine sovereignty and human responsibility? We can dismiss two historically common ways of answering this question: deism and pantheism. In deism, God creates and initiates the existence of the world and humans but then withdraws to the observer's perch, where he watches the events of history unfold. In this scheme, he only creates but does not providentially superintend the world. God is creator but not sovereign over history; humans control history. Against deism, if God is not concurrently active as the primary cause of all events, then there is some sort of cosmic dualism present in the creation. That is, God is not the sole primary cause in the cosmos; rather, humans are also the primary causes of their own actions rather than secondary causes. There are competing godlike entities in the universe that can only execute their wills by allying with other powers or conquering them. In the cosmos there is God and there are many other gods who control their own destinies apart from the will of God. Deism runs against the grain of Scripture because it clearly states that God ordains all events, as with Joseph's descent into slavery as well as Christ's crucifixion. Pantheism, on the other hand, is equally problematic because it maintains that all things are in some sense God. God is the universal agent for all things and is thus the sole actor in the cosmos. Contra pantheism, there are no genuine creaturely causes because God is the sole immediate cause of all actions, whether good or evil. Deism sacrifices God's sovereignty for the sake of human freedom, and pantheism obliterates human freedom for the sake of God's sovereignty. Both are equally problematic and unbiblical in light of the clear biblical teaching that divine sovereignty and human responsibility are entirely compatible. To answer the question of how they are compatible requires an examination of the doctrine of divine concurrence.

Divine Concurrence

The reason that God is sovereign over all actions is because he both decrees whatsoever comes to pass and he also undergirds the existence of all things. As the Westminster Confession states: "God, from all eternity, did, by the most wise and holy counsel of his own will, freely, and unchangeably ordain whatsoever comes to pass: yet so, as thereby neither is God the author of sin, nor is violence offered to the will of the creatures; nor is the liberty or contingency of second causes taken away, but rather established" (3.1). God ordains all things in such a way that he neither forces people to sin nor is he sin's author. Elihu makes this clear when he says, "If he should set his heart to it and gather to himself his Spirit and his breath, all flesh would perish together, and man would return to dust" (Job 34:14–15, translation mine).[18] God sustains all life, apart from which nothing could exist or act. The New Testament likewise affirms this point when the author of Hebrews writes of the Son: "He is the radiance of the glory of God and the exact imprint of his nature, and he upholds the universe by the word of his power" (Heb 1:3). That the Son φέρων ("upholds") the universe leaves no room for the watchmaker god of deism, who creates the world and then leaves it to run on its own mechanism.[19] As Thomas Aquinas (1225–1274) explains, anything that cannot stand by itself requires that something else support it. No finite creature can support itself; in technical terms, no finite creature possesses aseity, or self-existence. Thus, God must sustain a creature's existence. Aquinas explains this in terms of primary (God) and secondary causality (the creature): "He upholds all things in their existence and in their activity: because when the divine influence is removed, all the activities of secondary causes are removed, because He is the first cause; and the first cause does more than the second."[20] God must sustain all that exists by the work of the Son and Spirit. Historically, theologians have explained God's sustenance of the creation through the doctrine of divine concurrence.

The Reformed doctrine of concurrence runs from the seventeenth century from high orthodox theologians back through the Middle Ages all the way to Augustine (354–430). In his commentary on Genesis, Augustine explains that God as creator causes all things to exist because he has created them. Apart from his sustenance, the entire cosmos would collapse. Unlike a mason who builds a house, completes his work, walks away, and the house remains standing, the creation is not like this house. The world cannot go on standing apart from God's providential sustenance.[21] Augustine does not have deism in view, but his point contradicts the idea that God only creates as in the deist scheme. Aquinas picks up on this Augustinian line of argument, evident in his exegesis of Hebrews 1:3 as well as in his apologetics manual, his *Summa Contra Gentiles*. God both creates and conserves what he creates: "Has He not

18. Francis I. Andersen, *Job: An Introduction and Commentary*, TOTC (InterVarsity Press, 1976), 253.

19. Donald Guthrie, *Hebrews: An Introduction and Commentary*, TNTC (InterVarsity Press, 1983), 71.

20. Thomas Aquinas, *Commentary on the Letter of St. Paul to the Hebrews*, trans. F. R. Larcher, ed. J. Mortensen and E. Alarcón (The Aquinas Institute for the Study of Sacred Doctrine, 2012), §31 (16).

21. Augustine, *On Genesis*, vol. I/13, The Works of Saint Augustine: A Translation for the 21st Century (New City Press, 2002), IV.xii (253).

merely granted operative powers to them when they were originally created, but He always causes these powers in things. Hence, if this divine influence were to cease, every operation would cease. Therefore, every operation of a thing is traced back to Him as to its cause."[22] Imagine a hand holding a ball—apart from the hand holding the ball, the ball would fall to the floor. So it is with the creation: apart from the hand of God's providence sustaining, conserving, and concurring in all human action, humans would fall to the floor of nonexistence. In the words of the Westminster Confession, "God the great Creator of all things doth uphold, direct, dispose, and govern all creatures, actions, and things" (5.1).

Seventeenth-century Dutch Reformed theologian Wilhelmus à Brakel (1635–1711) explains divine concurrence in the following manner:

> *Cooperation* (*concursus*), that is, *the concurrence of the power of God with the motions of His creatures*. All creatures have received an independent and unique existence from God so as to move in a manner unique to themselves. They set themselves in motion, as man for instance walks, speaks, and works—all of which he does of himself. Since every creature exists, however, by the energizing and preserving power of God, comes about by the influence of God's cooperative power, without which it would not be able to move. As is its manner of existence, so likewise is its manner of motion; both existence and motion are dependent upon God.[23]

Creatures set themselves in motion, but they can only do so through the primary motion of God's cooperative power. Divine concurrence is not deism because God upholds both the existence and actions of the creature, but neither is it pantheism because the actions of the creature are distinct from the actions of God. As Francis Turretin (1623–1687) explains: "The first cause is the prime mover in every action so that the second cause cannot move unless it is moved, nor act unless acted upon by the first."[24] The Westminster Confession explains that God's concurrence comes in three forms: God "ordereth them to fall out, according to the nature of second causes, either necessarily, freely, or contingently" (5.2).

In his providential preservation of the creation, God orders things to fall out according to the nature of secondary causes. He orders things to occur

22. Thomas Aquinas, *Summa Contra Gentiles*, trans. Vernon J. Bourke (Notre Dame Press, 1956), bk. III/1, ch. 67.3 (221); also Dolezal, "Agency, Concurrence, and Evil," 66–67.

23. Wilhelmus à Brakel, *The Christian's Reasonable Service*, 4 vols., trans. Bartel Elshout (Soli Deo Gloria, 1992), I:336; also Dolezal, "Agency, Concurrence, and Evil," 67–68.

24. Francis Turretin, *Institutes of Elenctic Theology*, trans. George Musgrave Giger, ed. James T. Dennison Jr. (P&R, 1992–1997), VI.v.7.

necessarily, such as with the laws of physics or the laws of nature: "While the earth remains, seedtime and harvest, cold and heat, summer and winter, day and night, shall not cease" (Gen 8:22). Paper burns in fire, water boils at 212 degrees Fahrenheit, sunlight causes things to grow, day follows night—all these things occur *necessarily*. With human agents, God orders their actions to occur *freely*—they are not compelled to act. Recall the words of the Confession: "Nor is violence offered to the will of creatures" (3.1). God does not force people to act, let alone sin. However, the Confession also notes that God orders things to occur freely and *contingently*. That is, things can be otherwise. When a human agent freely chooses to eat a bowl of cereal for breakfast, she could have chosen otherwise—she could have chosen to eat eggs instead.[25] Note, however, that the contingency exists in the realm of secondary causes, not with God. As the Confession notes, "In relation to the foreknowledge and decree of God, the first Cause, all things come to pass immutably, and infallibly; yet, by the same providence, he ordereth them to fall out, according to the nature of second causes, either necessarily, freely, or contingently" (5.2). Zacharias Ursinus (1534–1583), author of the Heidelberg Catechism (1563), summarizes this point: "Hence in regard to God it is necessary, but in regard to the creature it is contingent in the same effect. Therefore it is not absurd that the same effect should be said to be necessary and contingent in respect to different causes, that is, in respect to an unchangeable first cause acting necessarily, and in respect to a changeable second cause acting contingently."[26]

Over the years some have objected to the idea that God concurs with human actions, because then those actions cannot be truly free. Augustine refuted this objection as it was expressed by Cicero (106–43 BC), who argued that either God could have foreknowledge of an event or an agent could act freely, but both cannot be true at the same time and in the same relationship. Augustine countered, however, "The religious mind chooses both, confesses both, and maintains both by the faith of piety."[27] Augustine maintained that

25. See, e.g., John Owen, *A Display of Arminianism*, in *The Works of John Owen*, vol. 10 (Banner of Truth, 1993), 2–139, here 24; Thomas Aquinas, *Summa Theologica* (Christian Classics, 1948), Ia q. 23 art. 4; Girolamo Zanchi, *De Natura Dei, seu De Divinis Attributis* (Wilhelm Harnis, 1598) V.i.4, esp. thesis II (582–91, esp. 584–91).

26. Zacharias Ursinus, *The Commentary of Dr. Zacharias Ursinus on the Heidelberg Catechism*, trans. G. W. Williard (P&R, n.d.), 161–62. For secondary literature on this point, see Richard A. Muller, *Divine Will and Human Choice: Freedom, Contingency, and Necessity in Early Modern Reformed Thought* (Baker Academic, 2017); *Grace and Freedom: William Perkins and the Early Modern Reformed Understanding of Free Choice and Divine Grace* (Oxford University Press, 2020); "Neither Libertarian nor Compatibilist: A Response to Paul Helm," *Journal of Reformed Theology* 13 (2019): 267–86.

27. Augustine, *City of God*, trans. Marcus Dods (Modern Library, 1993), V.ix.

when a person suffered contrary to his own will, he should not attribute it to the will of people, or angels, but ultimately to God. But whatever another human being willed against us was both in the foreknowledge of God and yet a free human act.[28] How do we maintain the compatibility between divine sovereignty and human responsibility?

God is the primary cause, and the human agent is the secondary cause of an action, but here we should factor the difference between *subordinate* and *coordinate* causation.[29] A *coordinate cause* is when an agent works by itself independently from its co-working cause. If humans were a coordinate cause of their actions, it would mean that God and the human agent are two primary causes of an event. A *subordinate cause* is when the secondary cause depends upon the primary cause. À Brakel explains the principle of subordinate causality by showing that in any human action, God is not collaterally involved in the action such as when two horses pull a wagon. Under these circumstances, the human would act independently of the will of God rather than through divine concursus. It would also mean that God would merely join the human in his action, each exercising causal power independently. Instead, God's initiative precedes the creature's motion, placing the human in a specific situation, place, and time. Thus, having initiated and determined the human's motion and position, God continues to involve himself in the creature's action to accomplish what he has determined. This type of divine concursus does not only refer to God's omnipotent and omnipresent power whereby he preserves the creature, but also refers to a special, physical, natural, and immediate operation by which he precedes the creature in every action, directing the action and preserving the person while in action. God permeates all secondary causes and their actions to their conclusive effect.[30] Again, this manner of explaining concursus goes back to Augustine and the likes of Aquinas, who gave the idea clarity and precision: "Therefore, God causes each action inasmuch as he bestows the power to act, preserves it, and applies it to action, and inasmuch as every other power acts by his power."[31] But this undoubtedly raises the question: If God acts as the primary cause immediately upon human agents as secondary causes, is he not by irresistible logic the author of evil? In Hume's trilemma, is he therefore not all-good?

28. Augustine, *City of God*, V.x.

29. Dolezal, "Agency, Concurrence, and Evil," 72.

30. À Brakel, *Christian's Reasonable Service*, I:337; Dolezal, "Agency, Concurrency, and Evil," 72–73.

31. Thomas Aquinas, *The Power of God*, trans. Richard J. Regan (Oxford University Press, 2012), q. 3 art. 7.

The Origins of Evil

God is not the author of evil even though he sovereignly ordains whatsoever comes to pass. To understand this claim we must account for the difference between primary and secondary causality and the different intentions and goals of the two agents, God and the human. As noted above, one of the clearest scriptural testimonies on this point comes from the Joseph narrative in Genesis, when Joseph's brothers came to him to seek forgiveness for selling him into slavery. Joseph responded: "As for you, you meant evil against me, but God meant it for good, to bring it about that many people should be kept alive, as they are today" (Gen 50:20). The narrative clearly attributes different motives to the actions of the divine and human agents: God intended good, whereas Joseph's brothers intended evil. John Calvin (1509–1564) explains the significance of the antithetical motivations. God did not sit idly by in the heavens and let Joseph's brothers carry out their plan and then, only after the fact, try to pick up the pieces and do something good with the situation. On the contrary, God ordained the whole event: Joseph's brothers wickedly sold him into slavery by the secret providence of God. "Yet," writes Calvin, "it was not a work common to both." God ordained the event for the sake of delivering the nascent people of Israel all the while Joseph's brothers acted in sin. But Calvin stipulates and distinguishes between God's providence vis-à-vis righteousness versus sin. If people undertake any act of righteousness, God inwardly moves people by his Spirit; but if Satan and ungodly people rage, God acts in such a manner so that their sin rests entirely upon them: "For they are not induced to sin, as the faithful are to act aright, by the impulse of the Spirit, but they are the authors of their own evil, and follow Satan as their leader."[32]

A second example comes from Job, where multiple agents act with different intentions and goals. In this narrative we find God, Satan, and the Chaldean raiders. God ordained everything that happened to Job. Satan persecuted Job. The Chaldean raiders slew his shepherds and stole his flocks and herds. Yet even though there are intermediate causes in Satan and the Chaldean raiders, to whom does Job attribute the events that have befallen him? "The Lord gave, and the Lord has taken away; blessed be the name of the Lord" (Job 1:21). Calvin asks how we can attribute the same event to God, Satan, and humans unless we excuse Satan because God ordained it all, or make God the author of the crime. Calvin detangles the knotty question by pinpointing the motives of each agent: "The Lord designs to exercise the patience

32. John Calvin, *Genesis*, Calvin Translation Society, trans. John King (Baker Books, 1993), 487–87.

of his servant by adversity; Satan's plan is to drive him to despair; while the Chaldeans are bent on making unlawful gain by plunder. Such diversity of purpose makes a wide distinction in the act." Not only do motives matter, but so does the mode of executing those motives: "The Lord permits Satan to afflict his servant; and the Chaldeans, who had been chosen as the ministers to execute the deed, he hands over to the impulses of Satan, who, pricking on the already depraved Chaldeans with his poisoned darts, instigates them to commit the crime. They rush furiously on to the unrighteous deed, and become its guilty perpetrators." Calvin concludes, "We thus see that there is no inconsistency in attributing the same act to God, to Satan, and to man, while, from the difference in the end and mode of action, the spotless righteousness of God shines forth at the same time that the iniquity of Satan and of man is manifested in all its deformity."[33]

Reformed theologians have sought to bring greater clarity to these ideas by explaining a few of the finer points. First, Turretin notes, "Predetermination does not destroy, but conserves the liberty of the will."[34] In other words, creatures do not have an independent existence but require God to decree, create, and undergird their existence and free actions. Apart from God undergirding their existence and actions, there would neither be a human nor any action for the human to perform. Second, when God acts by concurrence with human actions, "These actions belong to God only efficiently, but to creatures they belong not only efficiently, but also formally and subjectively (as from them the creatures are better denominated than God himself)."[35] In other words, if a person lights a fire, he is the efficient cause of the fire existing. But the fire, not the human, is hot. In parallel fashion, God is the efficient cause of decreeing a sinful human action, but the sin comes from the human, not God. Calvin illustrates this point with the sun's rays as they fall on a dead body. As the sun's rays strike the body, the rays cause the body to smell and decompose, but no one in their right mind would say that the sun's rays smell; they rightly attribute the stench to the decomposing body.[36] The sin is the subjective action, therefore, of the human, not God. Third, Turretin explains that though God's premotion extends to evil actions, this neither makes God guilty nor the author of the sin. God's actions only pertain to their material substance, not to their morality. Like Calvin's sun and corpse illustration, Turretin says that a harp player is the cause of the harp's sound,

33. John Calvin, *Institutes of the Christian Religion*, trans. Henry Beveridge (Calvin Translation Society, 1845), II.iv.2.

34. Turretin, *Institutes*, VI.v.11.

35. Turretin, *Institutes*, VI.v.14.

36. Calvin, *Institutes*, I.xvii.5.

but the actual noise comes from the strings. Likewise, when a rider mounts a lame horse to ride it, the rider is the cause of the horse's movement but not the horse's hampered gate.[37]

These explanations are not unique to Turretin or Reformed theology as they once again have roots in the catholic tradition and are also common to early modern Roman Catholics. Turretin approvingly cites both Aquinas and Tomaso de Vio Cajetan (1468–1534) in support of his arguments. Aquinas writes: "God in an action connected with deformity, does what belongs to the action, does not do what belongs to the deformity; for although in any effect there are many things inseparably connected, it does not behoove that whatever may be the cause of it as to one, should also be the cause as to the other."[38] Cajetan similarly explains: "It is not the same to concur with such an act according to what it has from the agent as such, and according to what it has from the agent as deficient, just as it is not the same to be an agent and to be deficient."[39]

Some might balk at these explanations and accuse them of speculation and sophistry and question their necessity. How can they be conducive to piety or apologetics? The explanations are both necessary and salutary to Christians for their own understanding of Scripture, reassurance of God's goodness, and defending the faith. They are necessary because in addition to Genesis 50:20 and Acts 2:23, where Scripture reveals God's sovereignty and human responsibility, there are other passages of Scripture that speak much more bluntly.[40] When God judged Ahab for his sin and ordained that King Ahab should go to war that he might die in battle, the book of Kings pulls back the veil and allows us to peer into the inner workings of the courts of heaven where we hear the following exchange:

> And Micaiah said, "Therefore hear the word of the Lord: I saw the Lord sitting on his throne, and all the host of heaven standing beside him on his right hand and on his left; and the Lord said, 'Who will entice Ahab, that he may go up and fall at Ramoth-gilead?' And one said one thing, and another said another. Then a spirit came forward and stood before the Lord, saying, 'I will entice him.' And the Lord said to him, 'By what means?' And he said, 'I will go out, and will be a lying spirit in the mouth of all his prophets.' And he said,

37. Turretin, *Institutes*, VI.v.16.

38. Thomas Aquinas, *Scriptum super Sententiis Magistri Petri Lombardi*, ed. Roberto Busa (1856), II d. 37 q. 2 art. 2 ad 5.

39. *Commentaria in Summam Theologicam Divi Thomae, I–II QQ. LXXI–CXIV* [1948], as cited in Turretin, *Institutes*, VI.v.16; cf. Aquinas, *Summa Theologica*, I–IIae q. 79 art. 1.

40. Dolezal, "Agency, Concurrence, and Evil," 76; also D. A. Carson, *Divine Sovereignty and Human Responsibility: Biblical Perspectives in Tension* (Baker, 1994).

> 'You are to entice him, and you shall succeed; go out and do so.' Now therefore behold, the LORD has put a lying spirit in the mouth of all these your prophets; the LORD has declared disaster for you." (1 Kgs 22:19–23)[41]

Like God's dealings with Satan in Job's trials, God puts spirits to work to place lies in the mouths of Ahab's loyal prophets. First Kings reveals that Ahab failed to distinguish between true and false prophecy (Deut 18:15–22), but the author also gives us an unvarnished account of how God accomplishes his will.

Elsewhere the Scriptures are equally blunt: "I form light and create darkness; I make well-being and create calamity; I am the LORD, who does all these things" (Isa 45:7). Jeremiah laments, "Is it not from the mouth of the Most High that good and bad come?" (Lam 3:38). Why do people stumble over the gospel of Christ and refuse to believe? "They stumble because they disobey the word, as they were destined to do" (1 Pet 2:8). Why do people give themselves over to the power of the beast in the book of Revelation? "God has put it into their hearts to carry out his purpose by being of one mind and handing over their royal power to the beast, until the words of God are fulfilled" (Rev 17:17). Given this scriptural data, the Reformed and whole catholic tradition has labored to affirm God's sovereignty over all things alongside of human responsibility. Again, we do well to remind ourselves of the simple yet deep currents of truth that run through Westminster Confession: "God, from all eternity, did, by the most wise and holy counsel of his own will, freely, and unchangeably ordain whatsoever comes to pass: yet so, as thereby neither is God the author of sin, nor is violence offered to the will of the creatures; nor is the liberty or contingency of second causes taken away, but rather established" (3.1).

Why Does Evil Exist?

With an understanding of theodicy in hand, including divine and human agency, divine concurrence, and the origin of evil, we can turn to ask the important question, why is there evil in the world? We can say, against Hume's trilemma, that God is all-good and all-powerful, and yet God is able to but does not prevent evil in the world. Why? To answer this question we first must ask, why is there evil in the world? In short, we can say that God is the ultimate cause of evil but not its proximate cause. In simpler terms, God is not the author of sin; humans are the authors of sin. When God first created humans, he made them good but mutable (Gen 1:28–31). In the words of the Westminster Confession, "God hath endued the will of man with that natural

41. Mordechai Cogan, *1 Kings*, Anchor Bible (Doubleday, 1964), 496–98.

liberty, that it is neither forced, nor, by any absolute necessity of nature, determined to good or evil" (9.1). And "in his state of innocency, [Adam] had freedom, and power to will and to do that which was good and well pleasing to God; but yet, mutably, so that he might fall from it" (9.2). Adam and Eve freely chose to disobey God by eating fruit from the forbidden tree of knowledge (Gen 2:16–17; 3:1–7). By Adam's sin, sin, evil, and death entered the world. As the apostle Paul explains: "Therefore, just as sin came into the world through one man, and death through sin, and so death spread to all men because all sinned" (Rom 5:12). In short, Augustine pithily observes: "The free choice of the will is the reason why we do wrong and suffer [God's] just judgment."[42] Evil exists in the world because humans opened the door to let it in, and they opened the door by their free and voluntary choice. Yes, this was a voluntary choice ordained by God, but God ordained it in such a way that there was no violence offered to Adam's will. Sin exists in the world because of the free choice of Adam, but this is only one part of the overall answer to the question about theodicy.

Apologetics and Theodicy

Understanding the theology of theodicy and explaining the relationship between divine sovereignty and human responsibility and the origins of evil is one thing. We need to understand what Scripture teaches, how the catholic tradition has explained the various passages that speak to the doctrine of concursus, and most importantly, unabashedly and unflinchingly affirm that God is not the author of sin. But knowing the theology behind theodicy is one thing, and defending the faith is another. We need to understand the theology behind theodicy for three chief reasons. First, to ensure that we do not fall into the errors of deism, pantheism, or conclude that God is the author of sin, which is blasphemy. As James reflected upon human suffering (Jas 1:2–4, 12), he reminds us: "Every good gift and every perfect gift is from above, coming down from the Father of lights, with whom there is no variation or shadow due to change" (Jas 1:17). Second, we need to understand that the church has seriously meditated upon this question both exegetically and theologically—our faith is not a blind faith. Third, we can instruct, console, and buttress our own faith when we doubt God's goodness. But we should distinguish between rational, biblical, and theological arguments versus what sinners need most—namely, Christ. If we fail to come to Christ

42. Augustine, *Confessions*, trans. Henry Chadwick (Oxford University Press, 1992), VII.ii (5).

in our efforts to address questions related to theodicy, we fall short of the goal of apologetics.

The most powerful answer to theodicy finds expression in the cross of Christ. At the end of Turretin's explanation of the relationship between divine and human agency and sin, he draws a connection between the Joseph and Christ narratives: "God was unwilling that the brethren of Joseph should sell him and that the Jews should crucify Christ, since they were most heinous crimes against the law. Yet he is said to have willed, yea, even to have done these things (Gen. 45:7; Acts 4:28)."[43] The same divine providence that ordained Joseph's descent into slavery, which saved his family, is the same merciful providence that ordained Jesus's crucifixion so that the people of God would be saved from eternal damnation. The amazing irony in all of this is that God created humans free, and they squandered that freedom on self, sin, and sedition. The infinitely free and self-existent Son of God became a man and voluntarily gave up his freedom to redeem those who had squandered theirs. In the beautiful words of Paul's Christ hymn: "Though he was in the form of God, did not count equality with God a thing to be grasped, but emptied himself, by taking the form of a servant, being born in the likeness of men. And being found in human form, he humbled himself by becoming obedient to the point of death, even death on a cross" (Phil 2:6–8).

We can return to Dostoevsky's *Brothers Karamazov* and Ivan's seemingly devastating indictment against the Christian faith: "Can you admit the idea that the people for whom you are building would agree to accept their happiness on the unjustified blood of a tortured child, and having accepted it, to remain forever happy?" Alyosha responds,

> "No, I cannot admit it. Brother," Alyosha said suddenly, his eyes beginning to flash, "you asked just now if there is in the whole world a being who could and would have the right to forgive. But there is such a being, and he can forgive everything, forgive all *and for all*, because he himself gave his innocent blood for all and for everything. You've forgotten about him, but it is on him that the structure is being built, and it is to him that they will cry out: 'Just art thou, O Lord, for they ways have been revealed!'"[44]

Alyosha points Ivan to the cross of Christ as the answer to theodicy.

When we defend the faith and do any form of theology, we must remember Martin Luther's (1483–1546) wise counsel from his famous Heidelberg Disputation: "He deserves to be called a theologian, however, who comprehends

43. Turretin, *Institutes*, VI.v.19.
44. Dostoyevsky, *The Brothers Karamazov*, 246.

the visible and manifest things of God seen through suffering and the cross."[45] We always must look to the cross of Christ as the supreme revelation of God and the lens through which we see all of God's dealings with humanity. All the theological distinctions and explanations that lie behind theodicy are necessary and vital, but apart from the cross of Christ they become empty because they fail to reach the goal of Christ, the whole point of life, theology, and especially apologetics. We can invoke distinctions like primary and secondary causality, but "it is not sufficient for anyone, and it does him no good to recognize God in his glory and majesty, unless he recognizes him in the humility and shame of the cross. . . . For this reason true theology and recognition of God are in the crucified Christ."[46] In short, "God can be found only in suffering and the cross."[47]

When we discuss theodicy within the context of apologetics, we must come to the foot of the cross. We will either seek God elsewhere, or we will make the cross the lens through which we think and discuss the Triune God. We can only speak of God's glory, wisdom, righteousness, and strength in its fullest sense if we look to the crucified Christ.[48] In terms of theodicy, Acts 2:23 speaks volumes: "This Jesus, delivered up according to the definite plan and foreknowledge of God, you crucified and killed by the hands of lawless men." Primary and secondary causality are at work here. The Father delivered up Jesus according to his "definite plan and foreknowledge," and yet he still holds the Jews and Roman officials guilty because they did this heinous act by lawless hands. Once again, God is sovereign, and humans are responsible. This verse also reveals a stunning truth: God in the flesh, the God-man, subjected himself to his own providential decree—the Son of God suffers on the cross. The Son God has entered our frail and fallen condition, yet without sin, and has suffered in our place. As Thomas Weinandy observes, "If the Son of God experienced suffering in his divine nature, then it would be God suffering as God *in a man*. But the Incarnation, which demands that the Son of God actually exists as a man and not just dwells in a man, equally demands that the Son of God suffers *as a man* and not just suffers divinely in a man."[49] God, the second person of the Trinity, *as man* suffered on the cross.[50]

45. Martin Luther, "Heidelberg Disputation," in *The Basic Theological Writings*, 2nd ed., ed. Timothy F. Lull (Fortress, 2005), 49.

46. Luther, "Heidelberg Disputation," 57.

47. Luther, "Heidelberg Disputation," 58.

48. Alister E. McGrath, *Luther's Theology of the Cross* (Blackwell, 1993), 1.

49. Thomas Weinandy, *Does God Suffer?* (University of Notre Dame Press, 2000), 204–5.

50. Kevin Vanhoozer, *Remythologizing Theology: Divine Action, Passion, and Authorship* (Cambridge University Press, 2010), 424.

God is in no way indifferent, let alone remote, from human evil and suffering. In the words of Sayers, "That God should play the tyrant over man is a dismal story of unrelieved oppression; that man should play the tyrant over man is the usual dreary record of human futility; but that man should play the tyrant over God and find him a better man than himself is an astonishing drama indeed."[51] The cross of Christ is the larger context and goal for theodicy. God gave Adam a free will, and he chose to squander it and consequently unleashed sin, death, and evil into the world. The God-man, the last Adam, takes his free will and uses it to conquer sin, death, and evil. Adam betrayed God in a garden where he had every one of his needs met, and yet the last Adam in the garden of Gethsemane prayed simple yet powerfully profound words when he said, "Father, if you are willing, remove this cup from me. Nevertheless, not my will, but yours, be done" (Luke 22:42). Even in the depths of his suffering and torment, Christ still held fast to his Father when he cried out, "*My* God, *my* God, why have you forsaken me?" (Matt 27:46, emphasis added). Amid his suffering, Christ nevertheless perseveres because of his love for his Father and his love for fallen sinners. Christ is the answer to theodicy. As the introduction noted, Christ may not be the answer that we want, but he is nonetheless the answer that we need.

The cross of Christ is the answer to theodicy; it gives us a big-picture response but does not provide specific answers as to why certain evils occur in the world. Why does one person live and another person die? Why is one house destroyed and another escapes a terrible storm unscathed? Why is one evil nation victorious over another in war? The cross does not answer granular questions about individual events in God's overall providential superintendence of the world. But this does not mean that the cross therefore leaves us empty, lacking peace or comfort. Strictly speaking, the book of Job is not a theodicy, but it does answer the question as to why the righteous seemingly suffer for no reason. Job is instructive and constructive for theodicy and apologetics because "it is occupied with a profound and difficult theme, the mystery of divine providence in the sufferings of good men. This is not treated in the abstract, in simple prose or in a plain didactic method. But an actual case is set vividly before the reader, in which the difficulty appears in its most aggravated form."[52] Job is a righteous man who nevertheless suffers, and in this way, he paints both a shadowy portrait of Christ and gives us insight into the nature of the Christian life in the face of questions about theodicy. Job

51. Dorothy Sayers, *Letters to a Diminished Church: Passionate Arguments for the Relevance of Christian Doctrine* (Thomas Nelson, 2004), 6–7.

52. William Henry Green, *Conflict and Triumph: The Argument of the Book of Job Unfolded* (Banner of Truth Trust, 1999), 3.

was a forerunner of Christ, and just as Christ said, “Not my will, but thine, be done” (Luke 22:42 KJV), in the depths of his suffering Job said, “Though he slay me, I will hope in him” (Job 13:15a). Job was a type of Christ, but he also shows Christians how to live the way of the cross in the midst of their own sufferings.[53] In the words of William Henry Green (1825–1900), erstwhile professor of Old Testament at Princeton Theological Seminary,

> The human aspect of Christ’s work, so far as it is foreshown in the book of Job, is chiefly set forth by Job himself, in his own person, as the type of the man of sorrows, forsaken and persecuted by his friends, and abandoned apparently by God, and yet for whom the cross was the passage way to the crown, and suffering to a glorious reward, and the fruit of the travail of whose souls abounded to the blessing of others, as Job’s intercession brought healing to his three friends, and he has been a helper to the distressed from his own day to this.[54]

What, then, does Job help us see as we look into the face of evil? There are two points that he teaches us about suffering.

First, despite the apparent chaos of the world and the impression that God is absent, when God confronted Job, he showed him that there is order in the world and that he stands behind it: “Then the LORD answered Job out of the whirlwind and said: ‘Who is this that darkens counsel by words without knowledge? Dress for action like a man; I will question you, and you make it known to me. Where were you when I laid the foundation of the earth? Tell me, if you have understanding’” (Job 38:1–4). God takes Job on a tour of the creation to change his perception of the world and alter his sense of who Job is in the light of this truth. Rather than partaking of wisdom from a “tree of knowledge” in a secluded pristine garden, God feeds Job his wisdom from the book of nature.[55] God teaches Job that, even if at times it might seem that chaos reigns, that in truth, God is in control. In a powerful way, theodicy and the teleological argument meet here in God’s response to Job. But just as the apostle Paul segued from creation to special revelation and the gospel of Christ, so too God goes from the creation to his all-comforting presence.

Second, God’s personal presence is the answer to Job’s many questions about his sufferings. This may not be the answer Job wants, but it is the answer that he needs. Our first impression of God’s response to Job, however, is only likely one of terror as the text seemingly suggests that God rebukes

53. Green, *Conflict and Triumph*, 44.

54. Green, *Conflict and Triumph*, 104.

55. William P. Brown, *Wisdom’s Wonder: Character, Creation, and Crisis in the Bible’s Wisdom Literature* (Eerdmans, 2014), 125.

him: "Who is this that darkens counsel by words without knowledge? Dress for action like a man; I will question you, and you make it known to me" (Job 38:2–3). But the fact that God tells Job to "dress for action like a man," means that God has mercifully condescended to Job's level to address him as a man.[56] God condescends to Job from the heavens and speaks to him out of the whirlwind to be present with Job. God is *Immanuel* to comfort him with his presence. The fact that God's name, *Yahweh*, occurs only once between chapters 3 and 37, and that chapter 38 begins with the divine name, alerts us to the fact that God has drawn near—God is in covenant with Job. God's condescension to the suffering saint is a shadowy image of the pinnacle of God's presence with his people—namely, the incarnation of the Son of God.

When we think of Christ's incarnation, we must not look at the saccharine portrait of Christ, but instead meditate upon the gritty, earthly, biblical portrayal. The shortest verse of the Scriptures captures this picture with two simple words in the English text: "Jesus wept" (John 11:35). The context of this simple yet profound statement is the death of Jesus's friend Lazarus. And in this case, Jesus wept both in sorrow as well as in anger. In the words of B. B. Warfield (1851–1921), "Anger always has pain at its root, and is a reaction of the soul against what gives it discomfort."[57] Lazarus's death angered Jesus: "When Jesus saw her [Mary's] weeping and saw the other people wailing with her, a deep anger welled up within him, and he was deeply troubled" (John 11:33 NLT; see also 11:38). Why was Jesus angered? Why did he weep? The spectacle of Mary's distress enraged Jesus because it powerfully pressed upon his consciousness the violent tyranny of death, and so he burned with rage against humanity's oppressor. Here death is the object of his wrath, and behind him the one who holds the power of death.[58] Jesus wept, and in his weeping, he forever united himself with those who mourn. Jesus comforts those who weep and mourn and wraps his arms around them: "Blessed are those who mourn, for they shall be comforted" (Matt 5:4). Jesus stands with those who mourn, for his name is Immanuel, God with us. Jesus wept.[59]

Thus, God does not answer Job's many questions in the way that he expected, but God's presence exceeded his expectations and was the response Job needed most. God provided his loving and comforting presence. In C. S.

56. Kelly Kapic, *Embodied Hope: A Theological Meditation on Pain and Suffering* (IVP Academic, 2017), 67–72.

57. B. B. Warfield, "The Emotional Life of Our Lord," in *Biblical and Theological Studies* (Charles Scribner's Sons, 1912), 37–90, here 52.

58. Warfield, "Emotional Life of Our Lord," 61.

59. Ann Weems, *Psalms of Lament* (Westminster John Knox Press, 1995), xxi; Kapic, *Embodied Hope*, 73.

Lewis's (1898–1963) novel *Till We Have Faces*, he retells the story of Cupid and Psyche. The novel's main character, Orual, is convinced that the gods have been unjust in allowing her to suffer various tragedies throughout her life. When she finally stands in their presence to present her case, she realizes things have changed: "I ended my first book with the words, *no answer*. I know now, Lord, why you utter no answer. You are yourself the answer. Before your face questions die away. What other answer would suffice? Only Words, worship. To be let out to battle against other words. Long did I hate you, long did I fear you. I might . . . ."[60] Orual's words drift off to make the point that they are irrelevant in the face of the gods. This is not to minimize her suffering but rather to highlight that the very presence of the gods far surpasses any pressing question that she had. Lewis, I believe, borrows this ending from the ending of the book of Job, and Job's final words confirm this idea.

The suffering saint's final words have been traditionally translated as, "I despise myself, and repent in dust and ashes" (Job 42:6). Yet, there are good reasons to reexamine this common translation. A closer look sharpens the clarity of the ending of Job. In the first half of Job 42:6, "therefore I despise myself," the underlying Hebrew term translated as "despise" is מאס (*ma'as*), which occurs seven times in the book of Job (see Job 5:17; 8:20; 9:21; 10:3; 19:18; 30:1; 31:13) with the meaning of "despise" or "loathe." Yet, in Job 42:6 the verb lacks an object, which means the verb can mean "become weak" or "waste away." The second clause in Job 42:6, "and repent in dust and ashes," uses the Hebrew verb נחם (*nacham*), which exhibits a wide range of meaning from "being sorry" to "being comforted." *Nacham* occurs seven other times in Job (see Job 2:11; 7:13; 15:11, 16.2, 21.34, 29:25; 42:11) with a sense of "being comforted."[61] In the light of these observations, a sharper translation of Job 42:6 is, "I waste away, yet I am comforted upon dust and ashes."[62] What does this mean for the ending of Job and for the larger question of theodicy? "Upon the ash heap and before the grand sweep of the cosmos, in the throe of sublime wonder, Job has found comfort for his state of desolation."[63] The answer to Job's many questions about evil and suffering is God's loving and comforting presence, Immanuel, which is a response that leads us to the foot of the cross. The cross of Christ is God's ultimate answer to theodicy. It may not be the answer we expect, but it is the answer we desperately need.

60. C. S. Lewis, *Till We Have Faces: A Myth Retold* (HarperOne, 2017), 351.

61. Brown, *Wisdom's Wonder*, 126–27.

62. Thomas Krüger, "Did Job Repent?," in *Das Buch Hiob unde seine Interpretationen: Beiträge sum Hiob-Symposium auf dem Monte Verità vom 14–19 August 2005*, ed. Thomas Krüger et al. (Theologischer Verlag Zürich, 2007), 271–29.

63. Brown, *Wisdom's Wonder*, 127.

Conclusion

The book of Job gives Christians an answer to the question of theodicy that begins with the creation and leads us to Christ. In technical terms, the teleological argument beckons us to the incarnation of Christ and his sufferings on the cross. So often people come at the question of theodicy from the perspective of evil. Why is there evil in the world? But they seldom stop and ask the opposing question, namely, why is there good in the world? In the powerful pondering of Eastern Orthodox theologian Kalistos Ware (1934–2022): "There is *the world around us*. What do we see? Much disorder and apparent waste, much tragic despair and seemingly useless suffering. And is that all? Surely not. If there is a 'problem of evil,' there is also a 'problem of good.' Wherever we look, we see not only confusion but beauty. In snowflake, leaf or insect, we discover structured patterns of a delicacy and balance that nothing manufactured by human skill can equal."[64] Why is there good in the world? Ware quotes the observations of Vladimir Monomakh (1053–1125), the grand prince of medieval Rus, who beckons us to behold the creation: "See how the sky, the sun and moon and stars, the darkness and light, and the earth that is laid upon the waters, are ordered, O Lord, by thy providence! See how the different animals, and the birds and fishes, are adorned through thy loving care, O Lord! This wonder, also, we admire."[65] The question of evil is only one half of the issue because we must also contend with the question of good.

In the face of evil, Dostoevsky gives the antithesis to Ivan's gut-wrenching questions about evil in Father Zosimus's call to look to the creation and contemplate God's power in it: "Love all God's creation both the whole of it and every grain of sand. Love every leaf, every ray of God's light. Love animals, love plants, love each thing. If you love each thing, you will perceive the mystery of God in things. Once you have perceived it, you will begin tirelessly to perceive more and more of it every day."[66] As we contemplate the order of the creation, and hear and see its rhythms—as night follows day, the sun always rises, the waves of the ocean unendingly lap upon the shore, and as the stars shine brightly in the dark night—the tapestry of God's creation should remind us of God's presence with Job and point us to the ultimate presence of Christ: "For we do not have a high priest who is unable to sympathize with our weaknesses, but one who in every respect has been tempted as we are, yet without sin" (Heb 4:15). And as we meditate upon and treasure God's great

64. Kalistos Ware, *The Orthodox Way* (St. Vladimir's Seminary Press, 1993), 23.
65. Vladimir Monomakh of Kiev, as quoted in Ware, *The Orthodox Way*, 19–20.
66. Dostoevsky, *Brothers Karamazov*, 319.

love in Christ, we should remember that God's love in his Son is the ultimate response to theodicy: "A loving humility is a terrible power, the most powerful of all, nothing compares with it."[67] And even if unbelievers are unpersuaded when you point them to Christ, "if you cannot speak with the embittered, serve them silently and in humility, never losing hope."[68]

67. Dostoevsky, *Brothers Karamazov*, 319.
68. Dostoevsky, *Brothers Karamazov*, 321.

12

Love

The Goal of All Apologetics

> **Thesis 12:** A love for the Triune God and for sinners must be the driving force for apologetics and is the greatest apologetic tool in an age when rationalism has given way to irrationalism.

Now while Paul was waiting for them at Athens, his spirit was provoked within him as he saw that the city was full of idols. So he reasoned in the synagogue with the Jews and the devout persons, and in the marketplace every day with those who happened to be there.

—Acts 17:16–17

Love is patient and kind; love does not envy or boast; it is not arrogant or rude. It does not insist on its own way; it is not irritable or resentful; it does not rejoice at wrongdoing, but rejoices with the truth. Love bears all things, believes all things, hopes all things, endures all things. Love never ends.

—1 Corinthians 13:4–8

Rationality is something the church could always count on in centuries past when it sought to present and defend the gospel of Christ. The apostle Paul reasoned in the synagogues in and around Athens (Acts 17:2, 17), and he made a rational presentation to Festus (Acts 24–25). When Festus thought that Paul's great learning had driven him insane, Paul responded: "I am not out of my mind, most excellent Festus, but I am speaking true and rational words" (Acts

26:24–25). Thomas Aquinas (1224–1275) wrote his *Summa Contra Gentiles* as an effort to engage in reasoned rational arguments to defend the Christian faith against Muslim Aristotelian philosophers. And in the twentieth century, C. S. Lewis (1898–1963) famously proposed his trilemma argument against those who tried to claim that Jesus was merely a good moral teacher. Lewis argued that Jesus could not be just a good teacher because he did not leave that option open to us. He claimed to be the Son of God, which means either he was mad, on the level of someone who believed he was a poached egg; or he was a devil, because who else but a demon would say he was the Son of God if in fact he was not; or he is Lord and God. So we cannot come to him with any patronizing nonsense about him being just a great moral teacher.[1] But what if for various reasons large swaths of the culture have intentionally or unintentionally fallen into an irrational mindset? As G. K. Chesterton (1874–1936) once observed, "If you argue with a madman, it is extremely probable that you will get the worst of it; for in many ways his mind moves all the quicker for not being delayed by the things that go with good judgment."[2]

In the face of the world's present moment of madness, Solomon's wisdom warns us of arguing with a lunatic: "Answer not a fool according to his folly, lest you be like him yourself" (Prov 26:4). At the same time, we know we must present and defend the gospel in a world gone mad. Has the world outfoxed the church by building an impenetrable fortress built out of bricks of irrationality? How do we defend the gospel in a world that resembles M. C. Escher's (1898–1972) famous lithograph *Relativity* (1953), which has staircases going in different directions: up, down, upside down, horizontal, vertical; no one staircase follows the path of gravity, and people are suspended upside down as they walk on staircases? Or Salvador Dali's (1904–1989) *The Persistence of Memory* (1931), where clocks melt upon the landscape, suggesting the very warping of time and distortion of reality? Seemingly gone are the days of Pieter Claesz's (ca. 1597–1660) *Skull and Writing Quill* (1628) or *Beer and Food*, both of which capture a simple, realistic, and perceptible setting of objectively observable ordinary objects. While it may seem as if the church has no recourse in the face of the world's madness, the truth of the matter is that we have a powerful weapon in our arsenal that often goes ignored—namely, love. Love is when one chooses to will the good of another.[3] The apostle Paul beautifully describes love in his letter to the Corinthians: "Love is patient and kind; love does not envy or boast; it is not arrogant or rude. It

1. C. S. Lewis, *Mere Christianity* (HarperOne, 2001), 52.

2. G. K. Chesterton, *Orthodoxy* (John Lane Company, 1909), 32.

3. Thomas Aquinas, *Summa Contra Gentiles*, trans. Anton C. Pegis (University of Notre Dame Press, 1975), III.xl.6.

does not insist on its own way; it is not irritable or resentful; it does not rejoice at wrongdoing, but rejoices with the truth. Love bears all things, believes all things, hopes all things, endures all things. Love never ends" (1 Cor 13:4–8).

This chapter defends the thesis that a love for the Triune God and for sinners must be the driving force for apologetics and is the greatest apologetic tool in an age when rationalism has given way to irrationalism. When we have neither the opportunity nor the context to present rational arguments, we can still love the world around us. We love people to show them the love of Christ and establish a foundation of trust upon which we can present the gospel. Just as the teleological argument leads us to the cross of Christ, our apologetical arguments must rest in a Christian heart of love where unbelievers have an immediate firsthand encounter with Christ's love in the heart of the apologist. This chapter, therefore, first examines the sources of the irrational age in which we live. Second, the chapter explores love and apologetics. The chapter concludes with observations about the need for love in our apologetics.

Origins of Our Irrational Age

Our irrational age has its roots in the Enlightenment philosophy of Immanuel Kant and Friedrich Nietzsche, among others. They set the stage for more recent developments in the neo-Marxist Frankfurt School that has promoted critical theory, a school of thought that has embraced irrationality as a weapon. Beyond more philosophically oriented portions of our culture, due to the rise of the internet, rational discourse has taken a hit with the creation of the meme. These different influences have all contributed to the madness of the age in which we live.

Kant and Nietzsche

Immanuel Kant (1724–1804) famously argued in his essay "What Is Enlightenment?" that moral autonomy is the most important value for individuals. Freedom to act and believe lies at the heart of enlightenment. Rather than submit to the army officer who says, "Do not argue but drill!" or the tax official who insists, "Do not argue but pay!" or the minister who proclaims, "Do not argue but believe!" individuals must ignore all authority and use their own reason to make their own decisions.[4] Friedrich Nietzsche (1844–1900) added

4. Immanuel Kant, "An Answer to the Question: What Is Enlightenment?," in *Practical Philosophy*, The Cambridge Edition of the Works of Immanuel Kant, ed. Allen W. Wood, trans. Mary J. Gregor (Cambridge University Press, 1999), 18.

to Kant's ideas of freedom when he announced that there is no objective truth except for the truth that the individual creates:

> Will to truth is a making firm, a making true and durable, an abolition of the false character of things, a reinterpretation of it into beings. "Truth" is therefore not something there, that might be found or discovered—but something that must be created and that gives a name to a process, or rather to a will to overcome that has in itself no end—introducing truth, as a *processus in infinitum*, an active determining—not a becoming conscious of something, that is in itself firm and determined. It is a word for the "will to power."[5]

The human will is what ultimately structures reality. Nietzsche inverts the common understanding that the objective world presses its existence upon our consciences and instead argues that our consciences press objective meaning upon the external world:

> That we are always unconscious of the real activity of the outer world—The fragment of outer world of which we are conscious is born after an effect from the outside has impressed itself upon us, and is subsequently projected as its "cause"—In the phenomenalism of the "inner world" we invert the chronological order of cause and effect. The fundamental fact of "inner experience" is that the cause is imagined after the effect has taken place—The same applies to the succession of thoughts: —we seek the reason for a thought before we are conscious of it and the reason enters consciousness first, and then its consequence.[6]

By inverting the relationship between the objective world and the subjective experience of it, Nietzsche produces two important outcomes.

First, if the human is autonomous and submits to no authority, not even the authority of the objective reality of the external world and its status as God's natural revelation, then there is no place for God. The autonomous individual becomes god and takes the place of God. Nietzsche famously wrote of the death of God when he put these words in the mouth of his madman: "The madman jumped into their midst and pierced them with his eyes. 'Wither is God?' he cried; 'I will tell you. *We have killed him*—you and I. All of us are his murderers."[7] If humans assert their absolute autonomy, then there is no transcendent creator or law-giver, which also means that there is, second,

5. Friedrich Nietzsche, *The Will to Power*, trans. Walter Kaufmann and R. J. Hollingdale, ed. Walter Kaufmann (Vintage Books, 1967), 298.

6. Nietzsche, *Will to Power*, 265.

7. Friedrich Nietzsche, *The Gay Science*, trans. Walter Kaufman (Vintage Books, 1974), 181–82.

no objective truth—no good or evil—but only whatever ethical norms the autonomous individual creates: "True philosophers reach for the future with a creative hand and everything that is and was becomes a means, a tool, a hammer for them. Their 'knowing' is *creating*, their creating is legislating, their will to truth is—*will to power*."[8] Kant and Nietzsche set the stage for the subjective irrationalism of the so-called postmodern (or more properly, hypermodern) age, the context in which critical theory has arisen.

Critical Theory

Within our hypermodern context, critical theory has been born from a small cadre of thinkers otherwise known as the Frankfurt School, which includes philosophers such as Herbert Marcuse (1898–1979), Jürgen Habermas (1929–), and Max Horkheimer (1895–1973).[9] Critical theory was conceived within the crucible of Marxism.[10] Critical theory is a way of looking at culture and literature that seeks to confront and deconstruct ideologies that create and govern it.

There are five main characteristics to critical theory:

1. skepticism of tradition and all claims concerning absolute truth[11]
2. promotion of a general theory of society that is fueled by the desire for liberation from corrupt authority[12]
3. concern with social action[13]
4. rejection of the idea that human subjectivity can be categorized or defined[14]
5. modern, enlightenment philosophical foundations[15]

Critical theory has spread into legal studies, ideologies about race, and gender.[16] The next two sections consequently explore critical race theory and

8. Friedrich Nietzsche, *Beyond Good and Evil: Prelude to a Philosophy of the Future*, ed. Rolf-Peter Horstmann and Judith Norman, trans. Judith Norman (Cambridge University Press, 2003), §211 (106).

9. Stephen Eric Bronner, *Critical Theory: A Very Short Introduction*, 2nd ed. (Oxford University Press, 2017), 3. See also Neil Shenvi and Pat Sawyer, *Critical Dilemma: The Rise of Critical Theories and Social Justice Ideology—Implications for Church and Society* (Harvest House Publishers, 2023), 61–140.

10. Bronner, *Critical Theory*, 2, 17.

11. Bronner, *Critical Theory*, 1.

12. Bronner, *Critical Theory*, 21.

13. Bronner, *Critical Theory*, 21.

14. Bronner, *Critical Theory*, 29.

15. Bronner, *Critical Theory*, 30.

16. Bronner, *Critical Theory*, 100–101.

critical gender studies to see how Enlightenment rationalism has embraced irrationalism.

Critical Race Theory

Kimberlé Crenshaw is one of the pioneers of critical race theory (CRT) and intersectionality, which she admits has roots in postmodern philosophy. Intersectionality examines the interrelated nature of social categories such as race, social class, and gender as they apply to people and groups. How do these different categories intersect? A Black lesbian woman finds meaning and identity in these three different intersecting categories, for example. Crenshaw explains the roots of intersectionality: "I consider intersectionality to be a provisional concept linking contemporary politics with postmodern theory."[17] Crenshaw has argued that postmodern philosophy provides oppressed people with tools to challenge existing power structures that those in authority employ against minorities: "While the descriptive project of postmodernism of questioning the ways in which meaning is socially constructed is generally sound, this critique sometimes misreads the meaning of social construction and distorts its political relevance. . . . A large and continuing project for subordinated people—and indeed, one of the projects for which postmodern theories have been very helpful—is thinking about the way power has clustered around certain categories and is exercised against others."[18] Given the commitment to the ideals of postmodernism, it should be no surprise that CRT advocates reject traditional reasoning and rationality: "Sociologists, theologians, and health care specialists use critical theory and its ideas. Philosophers incorporate critical race ideas in analyzing issues such as viewpoint discrimination and whether Western philosophy is inherently white in its orientation, values, and methods of reasoning."[19] The ideas of postmodern philosophers such as Jean-François Lyotard (1924–1998) have been employed to advance CRT in the wider culture.

In league with CRT, intersectionality scholars specifically target the need for a radical shift in epistemology, especially against traditional ways of thinking:

17. Kimberlé Crenshaw, "Mapping the Margins: Intersectionality, Identity Politics, and Violence Against Women of Color," *Stanford Law Review* 43/6 (1991): 1241–99, here 1244n9; also Shevni and Sawyer, *Critical Dilemma*, 141–74.

18. Crenshaw, "Mapping the Margins," 1296.

19. Richard Delgado and Jean Stefancic, *Critical Race Theory: An Introduction*, 3rd ed. (New York University Press, 2017), 7–8; Helen Pluckrose and James Lindsay, *Cynical Theories: How Activist Scholarship Made Everything About Race, Gender, and Identity—and Why This Harms Everybody* (Pitchstone Publishing, 2020), 121.

> The appropriation of intersectionality by lay practitioners and scholars outside of critical theory approaches continues to incorrectly conceptualize and execute intersectional analyses based on their prior ontological and epistemological frameworks, . . . which increases the risk of intersectionality's cooptation as a tool for reform at the margins, rather than its being a framework with the potential to radically reform our structures of government and public policies, as well as to make other changes.[20]

In other words, intersectionality scholars believe that if they continue to use traditional ways of thinking, their movement will always remain on the periphery and fail to institute system-wide changes in the culture. Thus, "Last but not least, this epistemology is not reliant on an Aristotelian levels of analysis approach, where each level of analysis offers something objectively relevant to understanding the organism or phenomenon in question."[21] Intersectionality also has intellectual roots in postmodernist philosophers such as Jacques Derrida (1930–2004), Paul-Michel Foucault (1926–1984), and Gilles Deleuze (1925–1995) and their understanding of social power dynamics.[22]

The cauldron of contemporary culture brims with autonomy, a rejection of objectivity, a declaration of the death of God, the elevation and exaltation of subjectivity, a dismissal of absolute truth, and a desire to rethink and restructure rationality, which leads CRT advocates to derationalize discourse: "The West has constructed the idea that rationality and science are good in order to perpetuate its own power and marginalize nonrational, nonscientific forms of knowledge production from elsewhere. *Therefore, we must now devalue white, Western ways of knowing for belonging to white Westerners and promote Eastern ones (in order to equalize the power imbalance).*"[23] With a move away from rationality, CRT advocates move to the asserted superiority of "lived experience."[24] In other words, CRT elevates the personal experience of oppressed people—nothing can trump their personal narrative. Any analytical methods, evidence, or arguments that contradict CRT, intersectionality, or social justice claims are automatically and prejudicially regarded as invalid.[25] In fact, CRT scholar José Medina has advocated the idea of "hermeneutical privacy," which is the "right not to be understandable

20. Ange-Marie Hancock, *Intersectionality: An Intellectual History* (Oxford University Press, 2016), 13.
21. Hancock, *Intersectionality*, 119.
22. Hancock, *Intersectionality*, 164.
23. Pluckrose and Lindsay, *Cynical Theories*, 76.
24. Pluckrose and Lindsay, *Cynical Theories*, 83.
25. Pluckrose and Lindsay, *Cynical Theories*, 187.

at all."[26] Rationality is the mark of whiteness and oppression, whereas irrationality and the supremacy of a person's own story is the only truth that matters, regardless of what facts or evidence say.

Critical Gender Studies

Critical theory has spread to gender studies and brings with it the same commitments to irrationality out of the desire to prevent anyone from unseating a person's subjective sense of who they are. If others can categorize another person's gender or sexuality—if there are gender norms—then such categories become constraints against expressions of personal freedom.[27] Thus, queer theory deliberately weaponizes irrationality, as Annamarie Jagose, a queer theory advocate, explains: "It is not simply that queer has yet to solidify and take on a more consistent profile, but rather that its definitional indeterminacy, its elasticity, is one of its constituent characteristics."[28] Deploying irrationality against religious and societal norms makes sense, but some have even objected to the sciences because they too play an oppressive role.[29] Michel Foucault targets the sciences because he believes they are subordinated to societal norms of morality: "Claiming to speak the truth, it stirred up people's fears; to the least oscillations of sexuality, it ascribed an imaginary dynasty of evils destined to be passed on for generations; it declared the furtive customs of the timid, and the most solitary of petty manias dangerous for the whole of society; strange pleasures, it warned, would eventually result in nothing short of death: that of individuals, generations, the species itself."[30] Sexuality and gender are not biologically but socially determined, according to Foucault.[31] Picking up on the postmodern idea of blurring boundaries, queer theory intentionally focuses upon distorting language in its effort to defy categorizing gender.[32] What underlies elements of critical gender studies is Marxism, which is epistemologically problematic because it employs

26. Pluckrose and Lindsay, *Cynical Theories*, 190; José Medina, "Varieties of Hermeneutical Injustice," in *The Routledge Handbook of Epistemic Injustice*, ed. Ian James Kidd et al. (Routledge, 2017), 41–52.

27. Pluckrose and Lindsay, *Cynical Theories*, 95; also Shevni and Sawyer, *Critical Dilemma*, 175–204.

28. Annamarie Jagose, *Queer Theory: An Introduction* (New York University Press, 1997), 1; Pluckrose and Lindsay, *Cynical Theories*, 95.

29. Pluckrose and Lindsay, *Cynical Theories*, 97.

30. Michel Foucault, *The History of Sexuality*, vol. 1, *An Introduction*, trans. Robert Hurley (Vintage Books, 1990), 53–54.

31. Pluckrose and Lindsay, *Cynical Theories*, 99.

32. Pluckrose and Lindsay, *Cynical Theories*, 108; Shevni and Sawyer, *Critical Dilemma*, 179–80.

Hegelianism in the construction of its ideology. Hegelianism advances by way of combining antithetical ideas to form a new concept: thesis + antithesis = synthesis.[33] In other words, combining contradictory ideas is part of its ethos. Can we arrive at the truth if we combine the ideas of Christ and the antichrist so we arrive at some sort of truth synthesis?

Internet Discourse

Another factor contributing to the irrationality of our age is how technological developments have poured gasoline on the ideological fire of critical theory. The advent of the internet and social media has brought about the rise of the meme. Very few internet users are willing to justify their political, philosophical, theological, or ideological positions by means of reasoned arguments. Instead, they launch memes to engage in discourse, memes that have the power to alter people's perceptions of ideas without the use of any critical processes of reflection. It seems as if the days of reasoned debate and discourse have been swallowed whole by an exchange of tropes we know from storybooks, of crones, wizards, and naked emperors. With the rise of the meme as a definitive and conversation-ending response to reasoned argument, hundreds of years of reading literacy and educational advancements have been lost beneath a sea of images.[34]

The Enlightenment has turned the culture inside out so that belief in an objective world has vanished beneath the tidal wave of subjectivity, which has bred a culture of suspicion and distrust of rationality. Social and cultural exegete Tara Isabella Burton has observed: "A black man cannot fully apprehend the lived experience of a white woman; a straight cisgender woman can never understand what it is to be a queer nonbinary person. 'Rationality' is often treated with suspicion—it is, for many activists, a pretense for the powerful status quo to legitimize itself, a chance for straight, white, male, colonialist bias to exhibit itself in action."[35] In this context of distrust and suspicion, how can Christians engage in rational dialogue with unbelievers, with those committed to a suspicion of rationality? Combine irrationality with autonomy, and the result is an apparently impenetrable fortress of solitude. Burton discerns that hypermoderns reject appeals to "knowledge" and "truth" because these sideline their personal experiences. People shy away

33. Douglas Murray, *The Madness of Crowds: Gender, Race and Identity* (Bloomsbury Continuum, 2019), 58.

34. Justin E. H. Smith, *Irrationality: A History of the Dark Side of Reason* (Princeton University Press, 2019), 17.

35. Tara Isabella Burton, *Strange Rites: New Religions for a Godless World* (Public Affairs, 2020), 184.

from debates that feature point-by-point rational arguments because such debates force personal experiences into a framework of "academic exercises," which is depersonalizing.[36] Christians should not be shocked, as the rise of irrationality is simply the next natural stage in the (d)evolution of Enlightenment rationalism. Chesterton long ago pithily diagnosed the natural course of Nietzschean rationalism: "Nietzsche will stand very well as the type of the whole of this failure of abstract violence. The softening of the brain which ultimately overtook him was not a physical accident. If Nietzsche had not ended in imbecility, Nietzscheism would end in imbecility. Thinking in isolation with pride ends in being an idiot. Every man who will not have softening of the heart must at last have softening of the brain."[37] Chesterton gets to the heart of the matter, and his analysis can help us avert irrationalism from rising in our own minds, but how do we engage a world gone mad?

Love and Apologetics

Large parts of the culture may have sidelined rationality, but this does not mean that Christians have been defeated. Love is the Christian's best response to the culture's irrationality, but lest we have a misguided notion of love, we must first begin with God so that we understand its nature and power. The next step is recognizing how the love of our Triune God flows into redeemed sinners. With this foundation of God's love, we can then turn to think about love and apologetics.

God and Love

One of the simplest and yet most profound statements in Scripture comes from the apostle John: "God is love" (1 John 4:7–8). "God is love"—three simple words in the English text, and yet deep currents of theology run beneath their surface. As we probe the depths of Scripture regarding God and love, we find out more about God's nature as we encounter descriptions of the intra-Trinitarian relations in terms of their processions and missions, or the *opera ad intra* and *opera ad extra*. The "Father loves the Son and has given all things into his hand" (John 3:35). The "Father loves the Son and shows him all that he himself is doing" (John 5:20). Jesus knew that the Father loved him and wanted the world to see the glory the Father had given him because he loved him before the foundation of the world (John 17:24). Likewise, the

36. Burton, *Strange Rites*, 185.
37. Chesterton, *Orthodoxy*, 75.

Son loves the Father and was obedient to his commands so that the world would know that he loves his Father (John 14:31). The apostle Paul tellingly describes the Holy Spirit as the love of God: "God's love has been poured into our hearts through the Holy Spirit who has been given to us" (Rom 5:5). Love, therefore, among Father, Son, and Holy Spirit is manifest in that they each will good to the other. The Father glorifies the Son (John 8:54), the Son glorifies the Father through his obedience (John 14:31), and the Holy Spirit glorifies the Father and Son by teaching the church all Christ has revealed (John 14:26). The revealed love of the Triune God has its roots in the eternal existence of God. Father, Son, and Holy Spirit exist in a state of eternal love for one another, and this love overflows into their work of creation.

The Triune God creates neither out of a sense of need or absence but rather from an overabundance of love. Part of the nature of God's love is its voluntary character—it is spontaneous and self-originating, as creatures come into existence by God's will, nothing more. But God's creative will is not capricious but has a goal in the creature's good, and the goal is that the creature would know God's love as a gift. As John Webster (1955–2016) explains, "Love *gives* life, and love gives *life*. In willing to create, God wills the realization of life which is not his own: 'Love is also a lover of life.'"[38] God's love overflows to the creation and to his image bearers, but humans rejected God's love when they disobeyed his command not to eat from the tree of knowledge. Even then, when God had every right to judge and condemn, he responded with mercy and love.

God's Love to Sinners

John Owen (1616–1683) traces the lines of God's love from eternity into history by drawing attention to the fountain of God's love in his election of sinners: "In love he predestined us for adoption to himself as sons through Jesus Christ, according to the purpose of his will" (Eph 1:4–5). From this foundation of election God pours out his Spirit upon fallen but elect sinners through Christ (Titus 3:6). Owen looks back to Psalm 133 and the typological imagery of the anointing of Aaron the high priest as it foreshadows the outpouring of the Spirit first upon the head, Jesus Christ, and then to every part of the body, the church:

> Love is first poured out on Christ; and from him, it drops as the dew of Hermon upon the souls of his saints. . . . Though the love of the Father's purpose and

38. John Webster, "'Love Is Also a Lover of Life': *Creatio ex Nihilo* and Creaturely Goodness," *Modern Theology* 29/2 (2013): 156–71, here 168.

> good pleasure have its rise and foundation in his mere grace and will, yet the design of its accomplishment is only in Christ. All the fruits of it are first given to him; and it is in him only that they are dispensed to us. So that though the saints may, nay, do, see an infinite ocean of love unto them in the bosom of the Father, yet they are not to look for one drop from him but what comes through Christ.[39]

The love of the Triune God flows to redeemed sinners by Christ through the Spirit, which enables them to love others: "In this the love of God was made manifest among us, that God sent his only Son into the world, so that we might live through him. In this is love, not that we have loved God but that he loved us and sent his Son to be the propitiation for our sins. Beloved, if God so loved us, we also ought to love one another" (1 John 4:9–11).

As the body of Christ, we incarnate God's love to those around us. We are the hands and feet of Christ. In the wake of Christ's ascension, he poured out the Holy Spirit upon the church, and so Christ has no body now but the church. He has no feet in the world but the feet of the church. Christ has no eyes on the earth except for the eyes of the church, through which he looks upon the world in compassion. He has no hands in the world but the hands of the church, through which he extends a cup of cold water to those who are thirsty. The church is the body of Christ and are his hands, feet, and eyes by which we extend his love to sinners.[40] Jesus adds another layer to the significance of the church's earthly ministry when he teaches that when the church loves sinners, they are ministering to Christ himself: "For I was hungry and you gave me food, I was thirsty and you gave me drink, I was a stranger and you welcomed me, I was naked and you clothed me, I was sick and you visited me, I was in prison and you came to me" (Matt 25:35–36). When does the church get the opportunity to minister to Christ himself? Jesus responds, "Truly, I say to you, as you did it to one of the least of these my brothers, you did it to me" (Matt 25:40). This means that the face of anyone we meet on the street might be Christ. As the body of Christ, the church is a revelation of Jesus. In the words of poet Gerard Manley Hopkins (1844–1889),

> For Christ plays in ten thousand places,
> Lovely limbs, and love in eyes not his
> To the Father through the features of men's faces.[41]

39. John Owen, *Communion with God*, in *The Works of John Owen*, 24 vols., ed. William H. Goold (Banner of Truth, 1966), II:27.

40. Dorothy M. Stewart, ed., *Christian Prayers: Over 1,500 Prayers Arranged by Theme* (Westminster John Knox Press, 2020), 320.

41. Gerard Manley Hopkins, "As Kingfishers Catch Fire," in *Hopkins: Poems and Prose* (Alfred A. Knopf, 1995), 18.

Christ gives the church the privilege of revealing his face as we love others, but we also have the joy of beholding Christ's face in others as we spread God's love to the world.

The Scriptures clearly reveal that a stream of love flows out of the heavens from the throne of God into the hearts of the redeemed and into some of the most unexpected places. Christ overturned common assumptions about love by teaching that Christians love even their enemies. Jesus grounds the Christian's love for his enemy in the doctrine of God: "You therefore must be perfect, as your heavenly Father is perfect" (Matt 5:48). Just as "Christ died for the ungodly" (Rom 5:6), so too Christians love the ungodly, their enemies: "Love your enemies and pray for those who persecute you, so that you may be sons of your Father who is in heaven" (Matt 5:44–45). Christ ties loving one's enemy to being a son of God, which rests in the framework of image-bearing. Sons bear the image and likeness of their fathers, and so the love of God in Christ forms and shapes sinners into the image and likeness of Christ so that they too share God's love with other sinners. Christ does not restrict love exclusively to the church but expands its reach even to those who persecute the church.

The apostle Paul gives similar instruction explicitly rooted in the Old Testament and in Jesus's teaching when he counsels the Romans: "Bless those who persecute you; bless and do not curse them" (Rom 12:14; cf. Matt 5:43–48; Luke 6:29–30).[42] Paul instructs the Romans not to think more highly of themselves than they should, in other words, not to allow arrogance to swell in their hearts so that they would look down upon others, especially upon their enemies. "To the contrary," writes Paul, "'if your enemy is hungry, feed him; if he is thirsty, give him something to drink; for by so doing you will heap burning coals on his head.' Do not be overcome by evil, but overcome evil with good" (Rom 12:20–21). Like Jesus, Paul teaches the Romans to embody the love of Christ, even to their enemies, those who persecute them. Interestingly, he quotes Proverbs 25:21–22, which is from a section of Proverbs drawn from the Thirty Sayings of the Egyptian sage, Amenemope.[43] Solomon quotes the pagan sage because he recognizes God's truth and thus puts it to use.

In its original context, the proverb supposes that you have a neighbor that hates you: "Let your foot be seldom in your neighbor's house, lest he have his fill of you and hate you" (Prov 25:17).[44] But the proverb assumes there will come a point when your hate-filled neighbor will have a time of

42. Douglas J. Moo, *The Letter to the Romans*, 2nd ed., NICNT (Eerdmans, 2018), 805.

43. Bruce K. Waltke, "The Book of Proverbs and Ancient Wisdom Literature," *Bibliotheca Sacra* 136 (1979): 211–38.

44. Bruce K. Waltke, *Proverbs 15–31*, NICOT (Eerdmans, 2005), 330.

desperate need. Rather than exact revenge when he is at his lowest, Solomon counsels: "If your enemy is hungry, give him bread to eat, and if he is thirsty, give him water to drink, for you will heap burning coals on his head, and the LORD will reward you" (Prov 25:21–22). The point of this proverb and thus the reason for Paul's quotation of it is that we seek to show love to our enemies. There is no greater encouragement to love others than to be the first to love—to break open the storehouses of divine love and liberally pour them out upon undeserving sinners.[45] Our demonstrations of love have one of two effects: either our love melts the hardhearted heart of our enemy and paves the way for the reception of the gospel, or our love becomes an act of judgment. "Coals of fire" can either be God's blessing or judgment—purgative fires of cleansing or flames of wrath (cf. Lev 16:12; 2 Sam 22:9, 13; Ps 18:8, 12).[46]

Within the larger framework of his Epistle to Rome, Paul draws a line from the redemptive love of the Triune God given to sinners that runs through their hearts and into the lives of other sinners: "God shows his love for us in that while we were still sinners, Christ died for us" (Rom 5:8). Either our enemies will be ashamed and humbled by our acts of kindness, or our love will heap condemnation upon them.[47] Our love can either cleanse, like the coals from the altar that cleansed Isaiah's lips (Isa 6:6), or it can become burning coals of judgment. We, of course, do not show love to our enemies to see them condemned but rather act out of a genuine love for them. The apostle Paul both taught these truths and also lived them out, evident in his prayerful lament: "I have great sorrow and unceasing anguish in my heart. For I could pray that I myself were accursed and cut off [ἀνάθεμα] from Christ for the sake of my brothers, my kinsmen according to the flesh" (Rom 9:2–3, translation mine). Paul was willing to be cursed for the sake of his fellow Jews (cf. Josh 6:17 LXX).[48] Like Moses before him, however, out of a Christ-shaped love for his fellow Jews, he stood in the breach—he was willing to have his name removed from the book of life if it meant they would be saved (Exod 32:30–32).[49] This is an amazing display of love considering that the Jews nearly whipped him to death on five different occasions, beat him three times, and stoned and

45. Thomas Aquinas, *Commentary on the Letter of Saint Paul to the Romans*, trans. F. R. Larcher, ed. J. Mortense and E. Alarcón (The Aquinas Institute for the Study of Sacred Doctrine, 2012), c. 12 l. 3, §1014 (345–46).

46. Moo, *Romans*, 806.

47. G. K. Beale and D. A. Carson, eds., *Commentary on the New Testament Use of the Old Testament* (Baker Academic, 2007), 681; Derek Kidner, *Proverbs*, TOTC (IVP Academic, 2008), 153.

48. Aquinas, *Romans*, c. 9 l. 1, §739 (247).

49. Moo, *Romans*, 579.

left him for dead (2 Cor 11:24–25). In the words of John Chrysostom (ca. 347–407), "Love so ruled his mind that to please Christ he would not only sacrifice being with Christ, which he deemed more desirable than anything else, but also the kingdom of heaven, which would be the reward of his labor for Christ."[50] Christ's prayer, "Father, forgive them, for they know not what they do" (Luke 23:34), as he hung in torment upon the cross became manifest in Paul's love for his fellow countrymen.

Love and Apologetics

We find cruciform love in Paul's instruction and his personal testimony regarding his fellow countrymen, as well as in his apologetic efforts in Athens. When Paul was waiting for the other disciples in Athens, "his spirit was provoked [παροξύνω] within him as he saw that the city was full of idols" (Acts 17:16). The term παροξύνω ("provoked") denotes a strong and abiding anger. Paul elsewhere explains that love is the exact opposite, as love "does not insist on its own way; it is not irritable [παροξύνεται] or resentful" (1 Cor 13:5).[51] We can say that Paul was filled with righteous anger based on his teaching elsewhere as well as his ensuing conduct (Eph 4:26–27). Before Paul's conversion, his anger drove him to violence as he ravaged the church, breathing threats and murder against Christians (Acts 8:3; 9:1–2), but now in the grip of Christ's love he instead *reasoned* with the citizens of Athens: "So he reasoned in the synagogue with the Jews and the devout persons, and in the marketplace every day with those who happened to be there."[52] Bridled by the Spirit of Christ, he expressed his anger with self-controlled and loving reasoning.[53] His love for God and neighbor drove him into the synagogue and marketplace "every day" that he might reason "with those who happened to be there" (Acts 17:17). Though Paul wrote these words to the Corinthians, they likely colored his actions in Athens: "For I wrote to you out of much affliction and anguish of heart and with many tears, not to cause you pain but to let you know the abundant love that I have for you" (2 Cor 2:4). When people turned away from Christ, Paul watched them depart through a veil of tears (Phil 3:18). Love shaped Paul's apologetic efforts because Christ both animated and motivated his efforts.

50. As cited in Aquinas, *Romans*, c. 9. l. 1, §740 (248).

51. Darrel L. Bock, *Acts*, BECNT (Baker Academic, 2007), 561.

52. Guy Prentiss Waters, *Acts: EP Study Commentary* (Evangelical Press, 2014), 415; C. K. Barrett, *Acts*, vol. 2, ICC (T&T Clark, 1998), 827.

53. James Addison Alexander, *The Acts of the Apostles Explained*, vol. 2 (Charles Scribner, 1857), 145.

Paul was as bold as a lion as he stood on Mars Hill and engaged the idols and superstitions of the Athenians, though he was also likely moved to tears on account of their rejection of Christ. We see the same pattern in Christ, who shed many a tear of sympathy and compassion. He wept at the grave of Lazarus and mourned the fate of Jerusalem. When he beheld the city, he wept over it: "O Jerusalem, Jerusalem, the city that kills the prophets and stones those who are sent to it! How often would I have gathered your children together as a hen gathers her brood under her wings, and you were not willing" (Luke 13:34). "And when he drew near and saw the city, he wept [ἔκλαυσεν] over it" (Luke 19:41). Jesus's tears are like those of the Old Testament prophets (Gen 50:1; Num 11:4; Judg 11:37–38; 2 Kgs 8:11; Jer 9:1; 14:17).[54] The term κλαίω ("weep") refers to sobbing or wailing. Jesus conducted his ministry in love, which is why Paul carried out his own ministry as well as his apologetic defense of the gospel in love. What, then, shapes and motivates our apologetics?

Does the love of God in Christ motivate and fill our apologetics? Paul casts a wide all-encompassing blanket of faith in Christ over every activity that we do: "For whatever does not proceed from faith is sin" (Rom 14:23). Our faith in Christ is a foundation for our apologetic efforts as we defend the gospel, which is the message of God's reconciling love for sinners (2 Cor 5:20). This means apologetics begins with a love for our Triune God and the gospel of Christ. But we must also love our neighbors as ourselves, which then shapes our apologetic efforts. How often, though, do we get caught up in winning arguments and vindicating the Christian faith or our own reputations? Social media is not exhaustive of life, but it is a microcosm that shows how often online discourse can circle the drain of immorality. Online incivility quantifies and objectifies how people allow debate to degenerate into a den of iniquity. One recent study documents how incivility mars 20 percent of online comments.[55] To cite one specific example: in a study of 3,508 online comments, 109 (3.1 percent) contained profanity, 478 (13.6 percent) contained insulting language, and 83 (2.4 percent) contained racist, sexist, and xenophobic language.[56] Those who were attacked online responded in kind and typically met insult for insult.[57] As most of us know, comment streams are havens for crudity, prejudice, and cruelty that perhaps no longer shocks the senses because the

54. Darrell L. Bock, *Luke 9:51–24:53*, BECNT(Baker Academic, 1996), 1560.

55. Gina Masullo Chen, *Nasty Talk: Online Incivility and Public Debate* (Palgrave Macmillan, 2017), 116.

56. Chen, *Nasty Talk*, 117.

57. Chen, *Nasty Talk*, 64.

medium has conformed us to its method.[58] How much of the world's vitriol carries over to the real-world conduct of Christians? Do we truly love the people we engage? Are we willing to give of ourselves sacrificially? Are we willing to step in the breach like Moses and Paul? Do we weep over the lost as Christ wept for Jerusalem?

These questions do not merely highlight the need for a disposition of love within our hearts, a love for God and for our neighbor. Within the discipline of apologetics, love is vital because it must animate our efforts and because it might be the only thing that can break through the madness and irrationality of our age. Love might be the only thing that will make unbelievers willing to listen to what we have to say because we have earned their trust and confirmed our message by concrete deeds of love. Once again, Martin Luther's (1483–1546) Heidelberg Disputation gives us sage counsel:

> The love of God which lives in a person loves sinners, evil persons, fools, and weaklings, in order to make them righteous, good, wise, and strong. Rather than seeking its own good, the love of God flows forth and bestows good. Therefore sinners are attractive because they are loved; they are not loved because they are attractive. For this reason human love avoids sinners and evil persons. Thus Christ says: "For I came not to call the righteous, but sinners" [Matt 9:13]. This is the love of the cross, born of the cross, which turns in the direction where it does not find good which it may enjoy, but where it may confer good upon the bad and needy person.[59]

Human love is self-seeking and thus avoids evil people. But God's love in Christ seeks sinners to transform them. The same transforming, redemptive, cruciform love must inform our apologetics.

When we conduct our apologetics in love, we bring the revelation of the majesty of absolute love to the unconverted sinner.[60] God reveals his absolute love to sinners, invites them, and elevates them to inconceivable heights of intimacy.[61] When fallen humans encounter God's love in Christ, they experience what true love is, but they also learn what selfish sinners they are and that they do not possess true love.[62] Only when we look to the crucified Messiah by faith alone by God's grace alone do we recognize the abyss of selfishness

58. Chen, *Nasty Talk*, 63.

59. Martin Luther, "Heidelberg Disputation," thesis 28, in *Martin Luther's Basic Theological Writings*, 3rd ed., ed. Timothy F. Lull and William R. Russell (Fortress, 2012), 25.

60. Hans Urs von Balthasar, *Love Alone Is Credible*, trans. D. C. Schindler (Ignatius Press, 2004), 56.

61. Balthasar, *Love Alone Is Credible*, 57.

62. Balthasar, *Love Alone Is Credible*, 61.

that we call "love."[63] We therefore carry this love into the world, not merely in words, but in deeds: "Little children, let us not love in word or talk but in deed and in truth" (1 John 3:18). Love in apologetics must become incarnate in real world deeds. Too many Christians fall into the internet's gnostic trap where they think that disembodied hashtag activism accomplishes something concrete. So much of hashtag activism is merely self-promotion, vanity, and narcissism veiled as concern, action, and love, which has nothing to do with true love or the theology of the cross.[64] Virtue signaling is not true love.

Rosaria Butterfield powerfully shows how love and apologetics meets real life in her own conversion narrative. She recounts how she was an unbeliever mired in homosexuality and feminism, highly educated, and a professor of English literature.[65] What melted through her cold fortress of unbelief? Christian love shown through simple hospitality. A pastor and his family regularly opened their home to her, fed her, and showed her kindness, care, and concern, and she was able concretely to see that Christianity is more than words. There is a sense in which presenting an apologetic argument in every detail and then walking away is easy—we return to the comfort of our homes away from the unbelieving world. This is especially true of our online engagements: we fire off posts and digital missives and then walk away from our screens without ever coming into direct face-to-face incarnate contact with unbelievers. Butterfield pushes against these trends and encourages Christians: "Our post-Christian neighbors need to hear and see and taste and feel authentic Christianity, hospitality spreading from every Christian home that includes neighbors in prayer, food, friendship, childcare, dog walking, and all the daily matters upon which friendships are built."[66] This may mean that we make ourselves uncomfortable as we show hospitality to those who look, act, and believe very differently than we do. Their irrationality and attempted defiance against God's general revelation will be patently and painfully evident, but this does not mean we cannot extend to them a cup of cold water. On the heels of receiving that cup of cold water, they may be willing to listen to a rational defense of the gospel. Regardless, love and apologetics go hand in hand, and we must beware lest we forget God's love in Christ and fall into the trap of rationalism ourselves—where we mistakenly believe that apologetics

63. Balthasar, *Love Alone Is Credible*, 66.

64. Justin Tosi and Brandon Warmke, *Grandstanding: The Use and Abuse of Moral Talk* (Oxford University Press, 2020).

65. Rosaria Champagne Butterfield, *The Secret Thoughts of an Unlikely Convert*, 2nd ed. (Crown & Covenant Publications, 2014).

66. Rosaria Butterfield, *The Gospel Comes with a House Key: Practicing Radically Ordinary Hospitality in Our Post-Christian World* (Crossway, 2018), 95.

is merely the presentation of arguments, facts, and evidence. Apologetics divorced from love is a noisy gong or clanging cymbal but certainly not the cruciform truth of God.

Conclusion

Apologetics in our irrational age presents significant challenges for Christians. How do you argue with a madman without losing your own sanity? Yet, all is not lost if we cannot demonstrate the rationality and veracity of the Christian faith. If the world will not listen to our defense of the gospel and prejudicially dismisses it, we still have the opportunity to love unbelievers. As the apostle John tells us, "Little children, let us not love in word or talk but in deed and in truth" (1 John 3:18). The greatest apologetic tool might be the cup of cold water we give to a person dying of thirst. The best argument for the Christian faith might be sacrificially serving our unbelieving neighbor expecting nothing in return. Our prayer should be that Christ would use our minds, hands, feet—in short, our whole beings—to serve and love our neighbors as ourselves. In our quest to defend the faith, we must never forget that apologetics is not ultimately about winning arguments but about showing people the truth of the love of God in Christ in word and deed.

Conclusion

In our efforts always to be ready to give an answer for the hope that lies within, we Christians must rest our apologetic efforts upon the authority and power of Scripture, as Paul reminds us, "For the weapons of our warfare are not of the flesh but have divine power to destroy strongholds" (2 Cor 10:4). "For the word of God," writes the author of Hebrews, "is living and active, sharper than any two-edged sword, piercing to the division of soul and of spirit, of joints and of marrow, and discerning the thoughts and intentions of the heart" (Heb 4:12). As important and foundational as Scripture is, the Bible draws our eyes and faith to behold the creation and beckons us to call unbelievers to reckon with the truths that it proclaims about God. Together, the books of nature and Scripture comprise a formidable arsenal with which Christians can arm themselves to evangelize the lost. Through Scripture we can see that God has hardwired the human heart to worship him and that fallen image bearers try to erase the image of God and make themselves God. In the insightful words of Friedrich Nietzsche, "He who does not find greatness in God finds it nowhere. He must either deny it or create it."[1] Humans will either worship the one, true God or an idol of their own making. Thus, apologetics seeks to engage the idols of the human heart and thus re-order disordered human love. We can reorient wayward, fallen humans toward the Triune God by pointing them to the revelation of God in the cosmos, in the human heart, and even in the human body. As the psalmist observes the wisdom and knowledge of God and the creation and then seamlessly moves to God's law, so we can guide wayward humans through the creation and then

1. As quoted in Michael Tanner, *Nietzsche: A Very Short Introduction* (Oxford University Press, 1996), 42.

bring them to the pages of holy writ where they can come face-to-face, so to speak, with God's special revelation in Christ, both in the grit and grime of history as well as in the pages of holy writ. Such a course does not trailblaze an unknown path cutting our way through the thicket of unbelief with a machete of human reason but rather revisits the old and worn paths of the Reformed tradition, such as Calvin's appeal to Cicero in the opening pages of his *Institutes* before he cited Scripture. As we engage the idols with the books of nature and Scripture, we ideally do so out of a love for our Triune God and our fellow, fallen image bearers. In a world gone mad where people try to build fortresses out of blocks of irrationality and confusion, we not only shine the light of truth to dispel falsehood and the darkness of sin, but by God's grace that light also brings the heat and warmth of love. In this way, unbelievers can see that our defense of the truth is not merely about winning arguments but about showing them the sacrificial love that God has graciously given us in the cross of Christ. We are beggars showing other beggars where they can find a sumptuous feast.

We can summarize these truths and the overall import of this book in three theses:

1. Apologetics seeks to dethrone idols within the human heart by turning people away from their false gods to the one, true, living Triune God chiefly revealed in Christ.
2. Apologists employ the books of nature and Scripture, general and special revelation, in their defense of the faith.
3. Love of the Triune God and of our fellow human beings motivates apologetics so that we glorify God and herald his beauty, truth, and salvation for fallen sinners.

As we seek to defend our faith, our prayer must be that God would both arm us with his truth and fill us with the mercy and compassion of Christ. We must also pray that we would never rest in our arguments or the evidence for Christianity but recognize that only a sovereign regenerating work of the Spirit gives unbelievers the gift of faith that enables them to believe in Christ. As we point people to Christ, present rational arguments to demonstrate the truth of Scripture, by God's power and Spirit we can engage and tear down idols so that people will worship the one, true, living God through Jesus Christ in the power of the Holy Spirit. In the light of Christ's gospel, we will then be able to see the twilight of the idols. Only when we confront unbelievers with their idolatry will they see that their restless hearts will find rest only in

Christ. In the light of this truth and the idols of our lives, may the words of this prayer be in our hearts:

> Heavenly Father, you have made us for yourself, and our hearts are restless until they rest in you: Look with compassion upon the heartfelt desires of your servants, and purify our disordered affections, that we may behold your eternal glory in the face of Christ Jesus; who lives and reigns with you and the Holy Spirit, one God, for ever and ever. Amen.[2]

2. "The Third Sunday in Lent," in *The Book of Common Prayer and Administration of the Sacraments with Other Rites and Ceremonies of the Church According to the Use of the Anglican Church in North America: Together with The New Coverdale Psalter* (Anglican Liturgy Press, 2019), 606. My thanks to Todd Hains for suggesting this prayer's inclusion.

Bibliography

à Brakel, Wilhelmus. *The Christian's Reasonable Service*. 4 vols. Translated by Bartel Elshout. Soli Deo Gloria, 1992.

Alexander, Joseph Addison. *The Acts of the Apostles*. Vol. 2. Charles Scribner, 1857.

Andersen, Francis I. *Job: An Introduction and Commentary*. Tyndale Old Testament Commentary. Inter-Varsity Press, 1976.

Annotations upon All the Books of the Old and New Testament. Evan Tyler, 1657.

Anselm. *The Major Works*. Edited by Brian Davies and G. R. Evans. Oxford University Press, 2008.

Antognazza, Maria Rosa. *Leibniz: A Very Short Introduction*. Oxford University Press, 2016.

Aquinas, Thomas. *Commentary on the Gospel of John, Chapters 13–21*. Translated by Fabian Larcher et al. The Catholic University of America Press, 2010.

———. *Commentary on the Letter of St. Paul to the Hebrews*. Translated by F. R. Larcher. Edited by J. Mortensen and E. Alarcón. The Aquinas Institute for the Study of Sacred Doctrine, 2012.

———. *Commentary on the Letter of St. Paul to the Romans*. Translated by F. R. Larcher. Edited by J. Mortensen and E. Alarcón. The Aquinas Institute, 2012.

———. *The Power of God*. Translated by Richard J. Regan. Oxford University Press, 2012.

———. *Scriptum Super Sententiis Magistri Petri Lombardi*. Edited by Roberto Busa. Parma: 1856.

———. *Summa Contra Gentiles*. Translated by Anton C. Pegis. University of Notre Dame Press, 1975.

———. *Summa Contra Gentiles*. Translated by Vernon J. Bourke. Notre Dame Press, 1956.

———. *Summa Theologica*. Christian Classics, 1948.

Aratus. *Phaenomena*. Edited by Douglas Kidd. Cambridge University Press, 1997.

Aristotle. *Nicomachean Ethics*. Translated by H. Rackham. Loeb Classical Library. G. P. Putnam's Sons, 1926.

———. *The Physics*. Loeb Classical Library. Translated by Philip H. Wicksteed and Francis M. Cornford. Vol. 2. Harvard University Press, 1934.

Arnold, Clinton. *Power and Magic: The Concept of Power in Ephesians*. Wipf & Stock, 1989.

Arnold, Matthew. *Dover Beach and Other Poems*. Dover Publications, Inc., 1994.

Athanasius. *On the Incarnation*. St. Vladimir's Seminary Press, 2011.

Atkinson, Joseph. "Moral Æsthetics; or the Goodness of God in the Ornaments of the Universe." *The Biblical Repertory and Princeton Review* 24 (1852): 38–52.

Augros, Michael. *Who Designed the Designer? A Rediscovered Path to God's Existence*. Ignatius Press, 2015.

Augustine. *City of God*. Translated by Marcus Dods. Random House, 1993.

———. *The City of God*. 2 vols. New City Press, 2012.

———. *Confessions*. Translated by Henry Chadwick. Oxford University Press, 1991.

———. *The Essential Augustine*. Edited by Vernon J. Bourke. New American Library, 1964.

———. *The First Catechetical Instruction*. Translated by Joseph P. Christopher. The Newman Press, 1952.

———. *Miscellanea Agostiniana*. Edited by G. Morin. Vatican, 1930.

———. *Of the Works of Monks*. In *The Fathers of the Church*, vol. 16, edited by Roy J. Deferrari. The Catholic University of America Press, 1952.

———. *The Works of Saint Augustine: A Translation for the 21st Century*. New City Press, 2002.

Bahnsen, Greg. "The Impropriety of Evidentially Arguing for the Resurrection." *Synapse* 2 (1972). https://answersingenesis.org/apologetics/the-impropriety-of-evidentially-arguing-for-the-resurrection/.

Baker, Emerson W. *A Storm of Witchcraft: The Salem Trials and the American Experience*. Oxford University Press, 2015.

Baldwin, Joyce. "Jonah." In *The Minor Prophets*, edited by Thomas Edward McComiskey. Baker, 1993.

Balthasar, Hans Urs von. *Love Alone Is Credible*. Translated by D. C. Schindler. Ignatius Press, 2004.

Bàñez, Domingo. *Scholastica Commentaria in Prima Partem Angelici Doctoris*. Vol. 1. Petrus Borremans, 1614.

Barker, William. *Erasmus of Rotterdam: The Spirit of a Scholar*. Reaktion Books, 2021.

Barnes, Luke, and Allen Hainline. "The Cosmic Coincidences of Fine Tuning." In *The Story of the Cosmos: How the Heavens Declare the Glory of God*, edited by Paul M. Gould and Daniel Ray. Harvest House Publishers, 2019.

Barnes, Robin B. *Astrology and Reformation*. Oxford University Press, 2016.

Barrett, C. K. *Acts*. Vol. 1. ICC. T&T Clark, 2006.

———. *Acts*. Vol. 2. ICC. T&T Clark, 1998.

Barth, Karl. *Church Dogmatics*. 14 vols. Translated and edited by G. W. Bromiley et al. T&T Clark, 1936–1968.

———. *The Epistle to the Ephesians*. Edited by David Nelson. Translated by Ross Wright. Baker Academic, 2017.

———. *The Knowledge of God and the Service of God According to the Teaching of the Reformation: Recalling the Scottish Confession of 1560; The Gifford Lectures Delivered in the University of Aberdeen in 1937 and 1938*. Translated by J. L. M. Haire and Ian Henderson. Hodder and Stoughton, 1960.

———. *Natural Theology: Comprising Nature and Grace by Professor Dr. Emil Brunner and the Reply 'No!' by Dr. Karl Barth*. Wipf & Stock, 2002.

Bauckham, Richard. "For What Offense Was James Put to Death?" In *James the Just and Christian Origins*, edited by Bruce Chilton and Craig Evans. Brill, 1999.

Bavinck, Herman. *Christian Worldview*. Translated and edited by Nathaniel Gray Sutanto, James Eglinton, and Cory C. Brock. Crossway Publishing, 2019.

———. *Christianity and Science*. Translated and edited by Cory Brock, N. Gray Sutanto, and James Eglinton. Crossway, 2023.

———. *Reformed Dogmatics*. 4 vols. Translated by John Vriend. Edited by John Bolt. Baker Academic, 2003–2008.

———. *Saved By Grace: The Holy Spirit's Work in Calling and Regeneration*. Translated by Nelson Kloosterman. Reformation Heritage Books, 2008.

Beale, G. K. *The Book of Revelation*. NIGNTC. Eerdmans, 1999.

———. *The Temple and the Church's Mission*. IVP Academic, 2004.

Beale, G. K., and D. A. Carson, eds. *Commentary on the New Testament Use of the Old Testament*. Baker Academic, 2007.

Beck, Julie. "The Church of CrossFit." *The Atlantic*, June 24, 2017. https://www.theatlantic.com/health/archive/2017/06/the-church-of-crossfit/531501/.

Beckwith, Francis J. *Never Doubt Thomas: The Catholic Aquinas as Evangelical and Protestant*. Baylor University Press, 2019.

Behe, Michael J. *Darwin's Black Box: The Biochemical Challenge to Evolution*. The Free Press, 1996.

Berger, Peter L. *The Many Altars of Modernity: Toward a Paradigm for Religion in a Pluralist Age*. De Grutyer, 2014.

Berry, Wendell. "The Body and the Earth." In *The Art of the Commonplace: The Agrarian Essays of Wendell Berry*, edited by Norman Wirzba. Counterpoint, 2002.

Blackmore, Richard. *Creation: A Philosophical Poem Demonstrating the Existence and Providence of God*. 5th ed. S. Powell, 1727.

Block, Daniel I. *The Book of Ezekiel: Chapters 1–24*. NICOT. Eerdmans, 1997.

———. *The Book of Ezekiel: Chapters 25–48*. NICOT. Eerdmans, 1998.

Bock, Darrell L. *Acts*. BECNT. Baker Academic, 2007.

———. *Luke 9:51–24:53*. BECNT. Baker Academic, 1996.

Bouwsma, William J. *John Calvin: A Sixteenth-Century Portrait*. Oxford University Press, 1988.

Bray, Gerald L. *The Pastoral Epistles*. ITC. T&T Clark, 2019.

Breur, Josef, and Sigmund Freud. *Studies on Hysteria*. Translated by James Strachey. Basic Books, 1895.

Bronner, Stephen Eric. *Critical Theory: A Very Short Introduction*. 2nd ed. Oxford University Press, 2017.

Brown, William P. *Wisdom's Wonder: Character, Creation, and Crisis in the Bible's Wisdom Literature*. Eerdmans, 2014.

Bryson, Bill. *The Body: A Guide for Occupants*. Doubleday, 2019.

Budge, E. A. Wallis. *Osiris and the Egyptian Resurrection*. 2 vols. G. P. Putnam's Sons, 1911.

Bullivant, Stephen. *Nonverts: The Making of Ex-Christian America*. Oxford University Press, 2022.

Burke, Edmund. *Reflections on the Revolutions in France and Other Writings*. Edited by Jesse Norman. Alfred A. Knopf, 2015.

Burton, Tara Isabella. *Self-Made: Creating Our Identities from Da Vinci to the Kardashians*. Public Affairs, 2023.

———. *Strange Rites: New Religions for a Godless World*. Hachette Book Group, 2020.

Butterfield, Rosaria Champagne. *The Gospel Comes with a House Key: Practicing Radically Ordinary Hospitality in Our Post-Christian World*. Crossway, 2018.

———. *The Secret Thoughts of an Unlikely Convert*. 2nd ed. Crown & Covenant Publications, 2014.

Calvin, John. *Calvin's Commentary on Seneca's De Clementia*. Edited by Ford Lewis Battles and André Malan Hugo. Brill, 1969.

———. *Calvin's New Testament Commentaries*. Edited by David W. Torrance and Thomas F. Torrance. Translated by John W. Fraser. Eerdmans, 1995.

———. *Genesis*. Calvin Translation Society. Translated by John King. Baker Books, 1993.

———. *Hebrews and 1 & 2 Peter*. CNTC. Edited by T. F. Torrance and David W. Torrance. Eerdmans, 1996.

———. *Institutes of the Christian Religion*. Translated by Ford Lewis Battles. Edited by John T. McNeil. Westminster Press, 1960.

———. *Institutes of the Christian Religion*. Translated by Henry Beveridge. Calvin Translation Society, 1845.

———. *Institutio Religionis Christianae*. Robert Stephanus, 1559.

———. *Institutio Totius Christianiae Religionis*. Jean Girard, 1550.

———. *Inventory of Relics*. In *Tracts and Treatises*, vol. 1. Translated by Henry Beveridge. Eerdmans, 1958.

———. *Leges Academiae Genevensis*. In *Ioannis Calvini Opera Quae Supersuent Omnia*, edited by Guilielmus Baum, Eduardus Cunitz, and Eduardus Reuss, vol. 10/1. A. Schwetscke and Sons, 1871.

———. *Treatise on Relics*. 2nd ed. Translated by Valerian Krasinski. Johnstone, Hunter, & Co., 1870.

Carson, D. A. *Divine Sovereignty and Human Responsibility: Biblical Perspectives in Tension*. Baker, 1994.

———. *The Gagging of God: Christianity Confronts Pluralism*. Zondervan, 1996.

Cavanaugh, William T. *Migration of the Holy: God, State, and the Political Meaning of the Church*. Eerdmans, 2011.

Chadwick, Owen. *The Secularization of the European Mind in the 19th Century*. Cambridge University Press, 1975.

Chambers, Whittaker. *Witness: A True Story of Soviet Spies in America and the Trial That Captivated the Nation*. Regnery History, 1997.

Charnock, Stephen. *The Existence and Attributes of God*. 2 vols. Edited by Mark Jones. Crossway, 2022.

Chen, Gina Masullo. *Nasty Talk: Online Incivility and Public Debate*. Palgrave Macmillan, 2017.

Chesterton, G. K. *Orthodoxy*. John Lane, 1909.

Chow, Simon. *The Sign of Jonah Reconsidered: A Study of Its Meaning in the Gospel Traditions*. Almquist & Wiksell Intl., 1995.

Cicero. *De Amicitia*. In *De Senectute, De Amicitia, De Divinatione*, translated by William Armistead Falconer. Loeb Classical Library. Harvard University Press, 1964.

———. *De Natura Deorum et Academica*. Loeb Classical Library. Translated by H. Rackham. Harvard University Press, 1951.

———. *De Senectute, De Amicitia, De Divinatione*. Translated by William Armistead Falconer. Loeb Classical Library. Harvard University Press, 1964.

———. *Letters to His Friends*. 3 vols. Translated by W. Glynn Williams. Loeb Classical Library. Harvard University Press, 1953–1960.

———. *On the Nature of the Gods Academics*. Translated by H. Rackham. Loeb Classical Library. Harvard University Press, 1951.

Clarke, Arthur C. *Profiles of the Future: An Inquiry into the Limits of the Possible.* Rev. ed. Harper & Row, 1973.

Cleanthes. *The Hymn of Cleanthes.* Translated by E. H. Blakeney. SPCK, 1921.

Cline, Ernest. *Ready Player One.* Ballantine Books, 2011.

Clines, David J. A. *Job 1–20.* WBC 17. Word Books, 1989.

———. *Job 21–37.* WBC 18a. Thomas Nelson, 2006.

Cogan, Mordechai. *1 Kings.* AB. Doubleday, 1964.

Collins, Robin. "The Teleological Argument: An Exploration of the Fine-Tuning of the Universe." In *The Blackwell Companion to Natural Theology*, edited by William Lane Craig and J. P. Moreland. Wiley-Blackwell, 2012.

Committee on Nomenclature and Statistics of the American Psychiatric Association. *Diagnostic And Statistical Manual of Mental Disorders.* 5th ed. American Psychiatrist Association Publishing, 2022.

Conger, George Perrigo. *Theories of Macrocosms and Microcosms in the History of Philosophy.* Columbia University Press, 1922.

Corey, Michael A. *The God Hypothesis: Discovering Design in Our "Just Right" Goldilocks Universe.* Rowman & Littlefield, 2001.

Cosper, Mike. *Recapturing the Wonder: Transcendent Faith in a Disenchanted World.* IVP Books, 2017.

Craig, William Lane. "Design and the Anthropic Fine-Tuning of the Universe." In *God and Design: The TA and Modern Science*, edited by Neil A. Manson. Routledge, 2003.

———. *Did Jesus Rise from the Dead?* Impact 360 Institute, 2019.

Crenshaw, Kimberlé. "Mapping the Margins: Intersectionality, Identity Politics, and Violence Against Women of Color." *Stanford Law Review* 43/6 (1991): 1241–99.

Critchley, Simon. *Faith of the Faithless: Experiments in Political Theology.* Verso, 2014.

Davies, Paul. *The Cosmic Blueprint.* Unwin Ltd., 1989.

———. *The Goldilocks Enigma: Why Is the Universe Just Right for Life?* Allen Lane, 2006.

Davis, Erik. *TechGnosis: Myth, Magic and Mysticism in the Age of Information.* North Atlantic Books, 2015.

Davison, Andrew. *Participation in God: A Study in Christian Doctrine and Metaphysics.* Cambridge University Press, 2019.

Dawkins, Richard. *The Blind Watchmaker: Why the Evidence of Evolution Reveals a Universe Without Design.* Norton, 2015.

———. *The God Delusion.* Random House, 2006.

Delgado, Richard, and Jean Stefancic. *Critical Race Theory: An Introduction.* 3rd ed. New York University Press, 2017.

Dembski, William. *Intelligent Design: The Bridge Between Science and Theology*. IVP Academic, 2002.

DePoe, John M. "The Heavens Declaring the Glory of God: Contemporary TAs." *Review and Expositor* 111/3 (2014): 244–58.

Descartes, René. *Discourse on Method and Meditations on First Philosophy*. 4th ed. Translated by Donald A. Cress. Hackett Publishing Co., 1998.

———. "To Queen Christina, 20 November 1647." In *The Philosophical Writings of Descartes*, vol. 3, *Correspondence*, edited by John Cottingham, Robert Stoothoff, Dugald Murdoch, and Anthony Kenny. Cambridge University Press, 1991.

Dibelius, Martin. *Studies in the Acts of the Apostles*. SCM Press, 1956.

Dickinson, Emily. *The Complete Poems of Emily Dickinson*. Edited by Thomas H. Johnson. Little, Brown and Company, 1961.

Dolezal, James. "Agency, Concurrence, and Evil: A Study in Divine Providence." *Journal of IRBS Theological Seminary* (2019): 61–89.

Donne, John. *Poems and Prose*. Alfred A. Knopf, 1995.

Dooyeweerd, Herman. *In the Twilight of Western Thought*. Collected Works, Series B, vol. 16. Edited by D. F. M. Strauss. Paideia Press, 2012.

———. *Reformation and Scholasticism in Philosophy*. 3 vols. Collected Works, Series A, vols. 5/1–3. Edited by D. F. M. Strauss. Translated by Ray Togtmann. Paideia Press, 2012.

Dostoyevsky, Fyodor. *Crime and Punishment*. Translated by Constance Garnett. Barnes and Noble, 1994.

DuMoulin, Pierre. *The Anatomie of Arminianisme, or The Opening of the Controversies of These Times (Formerly Handled in the Low-Countries), Concerning the Doctrine of Providence, Predestination, and the Death of Christ, of Nature and Grace, etc.* Nathanael Newberry, 1635.

Dunn, James D. G. *Jesus Remembered: Christianity in the Making*. Vol. 1. Eerdmans, 2003.

Durkheim, Émile. *The Elementary Forms of Religious Life*. Translated by Carol Cosman. Oxford University Press, 2001.

Ebeling, Florian. *The Secret History of Hermes Trismegistus: Hermeticism from Ancient to Modern Times*. Cornell University Press, 2011.

Eco, Umberto. *Six Walks in the Fictional Woods*. Harvard University Press, 1994.

Einstein, Albert. "Introduction to Lucretius, *De Rerum Natura*." In *The Collected Papers of Albert Einstein*, vol. 14. Princeton University Press, 2015.

Engelbrecht, Edward. *Friends of the Law: Luther's Use of the Law for the Christian Life*. Concordia Publishing, 2011.

Evans, C. Stephen. *Faith Beyond Reason: A Kierkegaardian Account*. Eerdmans, 1998.

Everitt, Anthony. *Cicero: The Life and Times of Rome's Greatest Politician*. Random House, 2002.

Feser, Edward. *Scholastic Metaphysics: A Contemporary Introduction*. Editiones Scholasticae, 2014.

Fesko, J. V. *Arminius and the Reformed Tradition: Grace and the Doctrine of Salvation*. Reformation Heritage Books, 2022.

———. *Reforming Apologetics: Retrieving the Classic Reformed Approach to Defending the Faith*. Baker Academic, 2019.

Fesko, J. V., and Guy Richard. "Natural Theology and the Westminster Confession of Faith." In *The Westminster Confession into the 21st Century*, vol. 3, edited by J. Ligon Duncan. Mentor, 2009.

Foucault, Michel. *The History of Sexuality*. Vol. 1, *An Introduction*. Translated by Robert Hurley. Vintage Books, 1990.

Frame, John. *Cornelius Van Til: An Analysis of His Thought*. P&R, 1995.

———. *A History of Western Philosophy and Theology*. P&R, 2015.

France, R. T. *The Gospel of Mark*. NIGTC. Eerdmans, 2002.

Frank, Anne. *The Diary of a Young Girl: The Definitive Edition*. Edited by Otto M. Frank and Mirjam Presler. Translated by Susan Massotty. Bantam Books, 1997.

French, David. "The Ferocious Religious Faith of the Campus Social-Justice Warrior." *National Review*, November 23, 2015. https://www.nationalreview.com/2015/11/religious-zealots-campus-social-justice-warriors/.

Freud, Sigmund. *The Interpretation of Dreams*. In *The Basic Writings of Sigmund Freud*, translated by A. A. Brill. The Modern Library, 1995.

———. *Totem and Taboo: Resemblances of the Psychic Lives of Savages and Neurotics*. Translated by A. A. Brill. Moffat, Yard and Co., 1918.

Gaffin, Richard B., Jr. "Some Epistemological Reflections on 1 Cor 2:6–16." *Westminster Theological Journal* (1995): 123–24.

Galen. *De Usu Partium Corporis Humani Libri XVII*. Christiani Wechelis, 1538.

———. *Galen on the Usefulness of the Parts of the Body*. 2 vols. Cornell University Press, 1968.

García-Acero, Mary, Olga Moreno, Fernando Suárez, and Adriana Rojas. "Disorders of Sexual Development: Current Status and Progress in the Diagnostic Approach." *Current Urology* 13/4 (2020): 169–78.

Gay, Peter. "Rhetoric and Politics in the French Revolution." *The American Historical Review* 66/3 (1961): 664–76.

Geehan, E. R., ed. *Jerusalem and Athens: Critical Discussions on the Theology and Apologetics of Cornelius Van Til*. P&R, 1971.

Goldblatt, Mark. *I Feel, Therefore I Am: The Triumph of Woke Subjectivism*. Bombardier Books, 2022.

Goodrick-Clarke, Nicholas. *The Occult Roots of Nazism*. Tauris Park, 2004.

Gootjes, Nicolaas H. "Calvin on Epicurus and the Epicureans: Background to a Remark in Article 13 of the Belgic Confession." *Calvin Theological Journal* 40 (2005): 33–48.

Gottschall, Jonathan. *The Storytelling Animal: How Stories Make Us Human*. Mariner Books, 2012.

Grabill, Stephen J. *Rediscovering the Natural Law in Reformed Theological Ethics*. Eerdmans, 2006.

Green, William Henry. *Conflict and Triumph: The Argument of the Book of Job Unfolded*. Banner of Truth Trust, 1999.

Greenblatt, Stephen. *The Swerve: How the World Became Modern*. Norton, 2011.

Gregory, Brad. *The Unintended Reformation: How a Religious Revolution Secularized Society*. The Belknap Press, 2015.

Gregory of Nazianzus. *On God and Christ: The Five Theological Orations and Two Letters to Cledonius*. St. Vladimir's Seminary Press, 2002.

———. *On God and Man: The Theological Poetry of Gregory of Nazianzus*. Translated by Peter Gilbert. St. Vladimir's Seminary Press, 2001.

Grislis, Egil. "Calvin's Use of Cicero in the Institutes I:1–5—a Case Study in Theological Method." *Archiv für Reformationsgeschicte* 62/1 (1971): 5–37.

Guillen, Michael. *Believing Is Seeing: A Physicist Explains How Science Shattered His Atheism and Revealed the Necessity of Faith*. Tyndale Refresh, 2021.

Guthrie, Donald. *Hebrews: An Introduction and Commentary*. TNTC. Inter-Varsity Press, 1983.

Guyer, Paul. "Introduction: The Starry Heavens and the Moral Law." In *The Cambridge Companion to Kant*, edited by Paul Guyer. Cambridge University Press, 1992.

Habermas, Gary R. "The Case for Christ's Resurrection." In *To Everyone an Answer: A Case for the Christian Worldview*, edited by Francis J. Beckwith, William Lane Craig, and J. P. Moreland. IVP Academic, 2004.

———. "Explaining Away Jesus' Resurrection: the Recent Revival of Hallucination Theories." *Christian Research Institute* 23/4 (2001). http://www.garyhabermas.com/articles/crj_explainingaway/crj_explainingaway.htm.

———. "The Minimal Facts Approach to the Resurrection of Jesus: The Role of Methodology as a Crucial Component in Establishing Historicity." *Southeastern Theological Review* 3/1 (2012): 15–26.

———. *On the Resurrection*. Vol. 1. *Evidences*. B&H Academic, 2024.

———. "Resurrection Research from 1975 to the Present: What Are Critical Scholars Saying?" *Journal for the Study of the Historical Jesus* 3/2 (2005): 135–53.

Habermas, Gary R., and Michael R. Licona. *The Case for the Resurrection of Jesus*. Kregel, 2004.

Hall, Alexander W. "Natural Theology in the Middle Ages." In *The Oxford Handbook of Natural Theology*, edited by Russell Re Manning. Oxford University Press, 2013.

Hamilton, Edith. *Mythology*. Little, Brown and Co., 2013.

Hancock, Ange-Marie. *Intersectionality: An Intellectual History*. Oxford University Press, 2016.

Hansen, Collin, ed. *Our Secular Age: Ten Years of Reading and Applying Charles Taylor*. The Gospel Coalition, 2017.

Harari, Yuval Noah. *Homo Deus: A Brief History of Tomorrow*. Vintage, 2016.

Harrison, Peter. "'I Believe Because It Is Absurd': The Enlightenment Invention of Tertullian's Credo." *Church History* 86/2 (2017): 339–64.

Hawking, Stephen, and Leonard Mlodinow. *The Grand Design*. Bantam Books, 2012.

Hendriksen, William. *More Than Conquerors: An Interpretation of the Book of Revelation*. Baker Book House, 1967.

Herbert, T. Walter, Jr. "Calvinist Earthquake: *Moby-Dick* and Religious Tradition." In *New Essays on Moby-Dick, or The Whale*, edited by Richard H. Brodhead. Cambridge University Press, 1986.

Hitler, Adolf. *Mein Kampf*. Translated by Ralph Manheim. Houghton Mifflin Co., 1999.

Hofius, Otfried. "The Fourth Servant Son in the New Testament Letters." In *The Suffering Servant: Isaiah 53 in Jewish and Christian Sources*, edited by Bernd Janowski and Peter Stuhlmacher. Eerdmans, 2004.

Holmes, Michael W., ed. *The Apostolic Fathers: Greek Texts and English Translations*. 3rd ed. Baker Academic, 2007.

Homer. *Odyssey*. Vol. 1. Translated by A. T. Murray. Loeb Classical Library. Harvard University Press, 1945.

Hopkins, Gerard Manley. "As Kingfishers Catch Fire." In *Hopkins: Poems and Prose*. Alfred A. Knopf, 1995.

Hornblower, Simon, and Anthony Spawforth, eds., *The Oxford Classical Dictionary: The Ultimate Reference Work on the Classical World*. 3rd ed. Oxford University Press, 1996.

Huiskes, Katherine. "Timeline: The September 11 Terrorist Attacks." Miller Center. https://millercenter.org/remembering-september-11/september-11-terrorist-attacks.

Hume, David. *Dialogues Concerning Natural Religion*. 2nd ed. Edited by Richard H. Popkin. Hackett Publishing Co., 1998.

Hutton, Ronald. *The Triumph of the Moon: A History of Modern Pagan Witchcraft*. 2nd ed. Oxford University Press, 2019.

Israel, Jonathan I. *The Enlightenment that Failed: Ideas, Revolution, and Democratic Defeat*. Oxford University Press, 2020.

Jacobs, Alan. *A Theology of Reading: The Hermeneutics of Love*. Westview Press, 2001.

Jagose, Annamarie. *Queer Theory: An Introduction*. New York University Press, 1997.

Jastrow, Robert. *God and the Astronomers*. Norton, 1978.

Jerome. *Jerome's Commentary on Daniel*. Translated by Gleason L. Archer Jr. Baker Book House, 1958.

John of Damascus. *On Heresies*. In *Writings*, The Fathers of the Church, vol. 37, translated by Frederic H. Chase Jr. The Catholic University of America Press, 1958.

———. *On the Orthodox Faith*. Translated by Norman Russell. St. Vladimir's Seminary Press, 2022.

Johnson, Dennis E. *Triumph of the Lamb*. P&R, 2001.

Johnson, Jeffrey D. *The Failure of Natural Theology: A Critical Appraisal of the Philosophical Theology of Thomas Aquinas*. Free Grace Press, 2021.

Johnson, John J. *Currents in Twenty-First Century Christian Apologetics: Challenges Confronting the Faith*. Wipf & Stock, 2008.

Jonas, Hans. *The Gnostic Religion: The Message of the Alien God and the Beginnings of Christianity*, 3rd ed. Beacon Press, 2001.

Josephson-Storm, Jason Ā. *The Myth of Disenchantment: Magic, Modernity, and the Birth of the Human Sciences*. The University of Chicago Press, 2017.

Josephus. *The Works of Flavius Josephus: Comprising the Antiquities of the Jews; A History of the Jewish Wars; and Life of Flavius Josephus*. Translated by William Whiston. The S. S. Scranton Co., 1905.

Joyce, Helen. *Trans: When Ideology Meets Reality*. One World, 2021.

Kagan, Donald. "Introduction to Ancient Greek History." https://oyc.yale.edu/classics/clcv-205/lecture-3.

Kant, Immanuel. *The Cambridge Edition of the Works of Immanuel Kant*. Edited by Allen W. Wood. Translated by Mary J. Gregor. Cambridge University Press, 1999.

———. *Critique of Practical Reason*. In *Practical Philosophy*, translated and edited by Mary J. Gregor. Cambridge University Press, 1999.

———. *Groundwork of the Metaphysics of Morals*. Rev. ed. Translated and edited by Mary Gregor and Jens Timmerman. Cambridge University Press, 2012.

———. *Religion Within the Boundaries of Mere Reason and Other Writings*. Rev. ed. Edited by Allen Wood and George di Giovanni. Cambridge University Press, 2018.

Kapic, Kelly. *Embodied Hope: A Theological Meditation on Pain and Suffering*. IVP Academic, 2017.

Kass, Leon R. *Toward a More Natural Science: Biology and Human Affairs*. The Free Press, 1985.

Kempis, Thomas à. *The Imitation of Christ: A Spiritual Commentary and Reader's Guide*. Christian Classics, 2005.

Kidner, Derek. *Proverbs*. TOTC. IVP Academic, 2008.

———. *Psalms 73–150: A Commentary*. TOTC. Inter-Varsity Press, 1973.

Kirkpatrick, Sidney D. *Hitler's Holy Relics: A True Story of Nazi Plunder and the Race to Recover the Crown Jewels of the Holy Roman Empire*. Simon & Schuster, 2010.

Klausner, Joseph. *Jesus of Nazareth: His Life, Times, and Teaching*. Translated by Herbert Danby. The Macmillan Company, 1925.

Knight, A. H. J. "Nietzsche and Epicurean Philosophy." *Philosophy* 8/32 (1933): 431–45.

Knudsen, Robert D. "The Transcendental Perspective of Westminster's Apologetic." *Westminster Theological Journal* 48 (1986): 223–39.

Kraus, Hans-Joachim. *Psalms 1–59*. Fortress, 1993.

Krüger, Thomas. "Did Job Repent?" In *Das Buch Hiob unde seine Interpretationen: Beiträge sum Hiob-Symposium auf dem Monte Verità vom 14–19 August 2005*, edited by Thomas Krüger, Manfred Oeming, Konrad Schmid, and Christoph Uehlinger. Theologischer Verlag Zürich, 2007.

Kurlander, Eric. *Hitler's Monsters: A Supernatural History of the Third Reich*. Yale University Press, 2018.

Kuyper, Abraham. "The Natural Knowledge of God." Translated by Harry Van Dyke. *Bavinck Review* 6 (2015): 73–112.

———. *Principles of Sacred Theology*. Translated by J. Henrik de Vries. Eerdmans, 1963.

Laertius, Diogenes. *Lives of Eminent Philosophers*. Loeb Classical Library. Diogenes Laertius, vol. 2, translated by R. D. Hicks. G. P. Putnam's Sons, 1925.

Lane, William. *The Gospel According to Mark*. NICNT. Eerdmans, 1974.

Lang, August. "The Reformation and Natural Law." In *Calvin and the Reformation: Four Studies*. Fleming H. Revell Co., 1909.

Lanier, Greg. "'It Was Made to Appear Like That to Them:' Islam's Denial of Jesus' Crucifixion." *Reformed Faith & Practice* 1 (2016): 39–55.

Le Bon, Gustave. *The Crowd: A Study of the Popular Mind*. The Macmillan Co., 1896.

Lecavalier, Michel S. "Religious Criticism in Voltaire's *Candide*." MA Thesis, McMaster University, 1970.

Legaspi, Michael C. *The Death of Scripture and the Rise of Biblical Studies*. Oxford University Press, 2011.

Leibniz, G. W. *Theodicy: Essays on the Goodness of God the Freedom of Man and the Origin of Evil*. Edited by Austin Farrer. Translated by F. M. Uggard. Open Court, 1985.

Levering, Matthew. *Did Jesus Rise from the Dead? Historical and Theological Reflections*. Oxford University Press, 2019.

———. *Proofs of God: Classical Arguments from Tertullian to Barth*. Baker Academic, 2016.

Lewis, C. S. *The Abolition of Man*. HarperOne, 2015.

———. *The Chronicles of Narnia*. Harper Collins, 2004.

———. *An Experiment in Criticism*. Cambridge University Press, 2013.

———. *The Four Loves*. HarperOne, 1960.

———. *Mere Christianity*. HarperOne, 2017.

———. *Poems*. Edited by Walter Hooper. Harcourt Brace Jovanovich, 1964.

———. *The Space Trilogy*. Harper Collins, 2013.

———. *Till We Have Faces: A Myth Retold*. HarperOne, 2017.

Lewis, Geraint F., and Luke A. Barnes. *A Fortunate Universe: Life in a Finely Tuned Cosmos*. Cambridge University Press, 2016.

Lucretius. *On the Nature of Things*. Translated by W. H. D. Rouse. Loeb Classical Library. Harvard University Press, 1975.

———. *On the Nature of Things*. Translated by W. H. D. Rouse. Edited by Martin F. Smith. Loeb Classical Library. Harvard University Press, 1992.

Luther, Martin. *The Basic Theological Writings*. 2nd ed. Edited by Timothy F. Lull. Fortress, 2005.

———. *Martin Luther's Basic Theological Writings*. 3rd ed. Edited by Timothy F. Lull and William R. Russell. Fortress, 2012.

Machen, J. Gresham. *Christianity and Liberalism*. Eerdmans, 1923.

———. *Christianity and Liberalism*. Eerdmans, 1999.

———. "Religion, Science and Philosophy." *Princeton Theological Review* 24/1 (1926): 38–66.

Marshall, Wallace W. *Puritanism and Natural Theology*. Pickwick Publications, 2016.

Martin, Francis, and William M. Wright IV. *The Gospel of John*. Catholic Commentary on Sacred Scripture. Baker Academic, 2015.

Marx, Karl, and Friedrich Engels. *On Religion*. Dover Publications, 2008.

McAffee, Matthew. "Creation and the Role of Wisdom in Proverbs 8: What Can We Learn?" *Southeastern Theological Review* 10/2 (2019): 31–57.

McCarraher, Eugene. *The Enchantments of Mammon: How Capitalism Became the Religion of Modernity*. The Belknap Press, 2019.

McDowell, Josh. *Evidence That Demands a Verdict*. Vol. 1, *Historical Evidences for the Christian Faith*. Thomas Nelson, 1979.

McGrath, Alister E. *A Fine-Tuned Universe: The Quest for God in Science and Theology*. Westminster John Knox, 2009.

———. *Luther's Theology of the Cross*. Blackwell, 1993.

McWhorter, John. *Woke Racism: How a New Religion Has Betrayed Black America*. Portfolio/Penguin, 2021.

Medina, José. "Varieties of Hermeneutical Injustice." In *The Routledge Handbook of Epistemic Injustice*, edited by Ian James Kidd, José Medina, and Gaile Pohlhaus Jr. Routledge, 2017.

Melville, Herman. *Moby Dick*. In *Redburn, White-Jacket, and Moby Dick, or The Whale*. The Library of America, 1983.

Moberly, R. W. L. *The Bible in a Disenchanted Age: The Enduring Possibility of Christian Faith*. Baker Academic, 2020.

Moo, Douglas J. *The Letter to the Romans*. 2nd ed. NICNT. Eerdmans, 2018.

Motyer, Alec. *Isaiah: An Introduction and Commentary*. TOTC. Inter-Varsity Press, 1999.

Muller, Richard A. *Dictionary of Latin and Greek Theological Terms: Drawn Principally from Protestant Scholastic Theology*. 2nd ed. Baker Academic, 2017.

———. *Divine Will and Human Choice: Freedom, Contingency, and Necessity in Early Modern Reformed Thought*. Baker Academic, 2017.

———. "'*Duplex cognition dei*' in the Theology of Early Reformed Orthodoxy." *Sixteenth Century Journal* 10/2 (1979): 51–62.

———. *Grace and Freedom: William Perkins and the Early Modern Reformed Understanding of Free Choice and Divine Grace*. Oxford University Press, 2020.

———. "Kuyper and Bavinck on Natural Theology." *Bavinck Review* 10 (2019): 5–35.

———. "Neither Libertarian nor Compatibilist: A Response to Paul Helm." *Journal of Reformed Theology* 13 (2019): 267–86.

———. *Post-Reformation Reformed Dogmatics*. Vol. 1, *Prolegomena to Theology*. 2nd ed. Baker Academic, 2003.

———. "Reading Aquinas from a Reformed Perspective: A Review Essay." *Calvin Theological Journal* 53/2 (2018): 255–88.

———. *The Unaccommodated Calvin: Studies in the Foundation of a Theological Tradition*. Oxford University Press, 2001.

———. "Was It Really Viral? Natural Theology in the Early Modern Reformed Tradition." In *Crossing Traditions: Essays on the Reformation and Intellectual History*, edited by Maria-Cristina Pitassi and Danieal Solfaroli Camillocci. Brill, 2017.

Murphy, Roland E. "Wisdom and Creation." *Journal of Biblical Literature* 104/1 (1985): 3–11.

Murray, Douglas. *The Madness of Crowds: Gender, Race and Identity*. Bloomsbury Continuum, 2019.

Nagel, Thomas. *Mind and Cosmos: Why the Materialist Neo-Darwinian Conception of Nature Is Almost Certainly False*. Oxford University Press, 2012.

Newton, William. "A Case of Mistaken Identity: Aquinas's Fifth Way and Arguments of Intelligent Design." *New Blackfriars* (2014): 569–78.

Nietzsche, Friedrich. *The Anti-Christ*. Translated by H. L. Mencken. Alfred A. Knopf, 1931.

———. *Beyond Good and Evil: Prelude to a Philosophy of the Future*. Edited by Rolf-Peter Horstmann and Judith Norman. Translated by Judith Norman. Cambridge University, 2003.

———. *The Gay Science*. Translated by Walter Kaufman. Vintage Books, 1974.

———. *The Will to Power*. Translated by Walter Kaufmann and R. J. Hollingdale. Edited by Walter Kaufmann. Vintage Books, 1967.

Notaro, Thom. *Van Til and the Use of Evidence*. P&R, 1980.

Obama, Barack. *A Promised Land*. Crown, 2020.

O'Conner, Flannery. *Spiritual Writings*. Edited by Robert Ellsberg. Orbis Books, 2003.

Oliphint, K. Scott. *Thomas Aquinas*. P&R, 2017.

Origen. *Homilies on Genesis and Exodus*. The Fathers of the Church. Translated by Ronald E. Heine. The Catholic University of America Press, 1982.

Orr, James. *The Christian View of God and the World: As Centering in the Incarnation*. Eerdmans, 1947.

Ortlund, Dane C. "What Does It Mean to Fall Short of the Glory of God? Romans 3:23 in Biblical-Theological Perspective." *Westminster Theological Journal* 80 (2018): 121–40.

Owen, John. *Communion with God*. In *The Works of John Owen*, vol. 2. Banner of Truth, 1966.

———. *A Display of Arminianism*. In *The Works of John Owen*, vol. 10. Banner of Truth, 1993.

Paley, Vivian Gussin. *Boys and Girls: Superheroes in the Doll Corner*. University of Chicago Press, 2014.

Paley, William. *Natural Theology, or Evidence of the Existence and Attributes of the Deity, Collected from the Appearances of Nature*. Edited by Matthew D. Eddy and David Knight. Oxford University Press, 2006.

———. *Natural Theology: or, Evidences of the Existence and Attributes of the Deity Collected from the Appearances of Nature*. Sheldon & Company, 1879.

Pardigon, Flavien. *Paul Against the Idols: A Contextual Reading of the Areopagus Speech*. Pickwick Publications, 2019.

Pascal, Blaise. *Pensées*. Translated by A. J. Krailsheimer. Penguin Books, 1995.

Pelikan, Jaroslav, and Valerie Hotchkiss, eds. *Creeds and Confessions of Faith in the Christian Tradition*. 3 vols. Yale University Press, 2003.

Perdue, Leo G. *Wisdom and Creation: The Theology of Wisdom Literature*. Abingdon Press, 1994.

Perkins, William. *The Works of William Perkins*. 10 vols. Edited by Joel Beeke and Derek Thomas. Reformation Heritage Books, 2020.

Persson, Erik. *Sacra Doctrina: Reason and Revelation in Aquinas*. Translated by Ross MacKenzie. Fortress, 1970.

Peterson, Brian Neil. *John's Use of Ezekiel: Understanding the Unique Perspective of the Fourth Gospel*. Fortress, 2015.

Picasso, Pablo. "To Statements by Picasso." In *Picasso on Art: A Selection of Views*, edited by Dore Ashton. The Viking Press, 1972.

Pinker, Steven. *How the Mind Works*. Norton, 1997.

Piper, John. *Let the Nations Be Glad*. 3rd ed. Baker Academic, 2010.

Pitre, Brant. *The Case for Jesus: The Biblical and Historical Evidence for Christ*. Image, 2016.

Plantinga, Alvin. "The Reformed Objection to Natural Theology." In *Philosophy of Religion: Selected Readings*, edited by Michael Peterson, William Hasker, Bruce Reichenbach, and David Basinger. Oxford University Press, 2001.

Plato. *Five Dialogues: Euthyphro, Apology, Crito, Meno, Phaedo*. 2nd ed. Translated by G. M. A. Grube. Edited by John M. Cooper. Hackett Publishing Co., 2002.

Pliny the Younger. *Pliny: Letters*. Vol. 2. Edited by W. M. L. Hutchinson. Loeb Classical Library. The Macmillan Co., 1915.

Pluckrose, Helen, and James Lindsay. *Cynical Theories: How Activist Scholarship Made Everything About Race, Gender, and Identity—and Why This Harms Everybody*. Pitchstone Publishing, 2020.

Polkinghorne, John. *Quarks, Chaos, and Christianity: Questions to Science and Religion*. Rev. ed. The Crossroad Publishing Company, 2005.

Polyander, Johannes, et al. *Synopsis Purioris Theologiae / Synopsis of a Purer Theology*. Vol. 1. Edited by Dolf te Velde et al. Brill, 2014.

Powell, Doug. *Holman QuickSource Guide to Christian Apologetics*. Holman Reference, 2006.

Price, Joseph L. "From Sabbath Proscriptions to Super Sunday Celebrations: Sports and Religion in America." In *From Season to Season: Sports as American Religion*, edited by Joseph L. Price. Mercer University Press, 2001.

Prior, Karen Swallow. *On Reading Well: Finding the Good Through Great Books*. Brazos Press, 2018.

Pseudo-Dionysius. *On the Divine Names*. In *The Complete Works*, translated by Colm Luibheid. Paulist Press, 1987.

Raymond of Sabunde. *Theologica Naturalis, sive Liber creaturarum specialiter de homine et de natura eius in quantum homo et de his que sunt ei necessaria ad cognoscendum seipsum et Deum et omne debitum ad quod hom tenetur et obligatum tam Deo quam primo*. Martinus, 1496.

Rees, Martin. *Just Six Numbers: The Deep Forces That Shape the Universe*. Basic Books, 2000.

Reid, Thomas. *Essays on the Intellectual Powers of Man*. John Bartlett, 1852.

Roberts, Alexander, and James Donaldson. *The Ante-Nicene Fathers: Translations of the Writings of the Fathers Down to A.D. 325*. 10 vols. Charles Scribner's Sons, 1885–1887.

Robinson, Brett T. *Appletopia: Media Technology and the Religious Imagination of Steve Jobs*. Baylor University Press, 2013.

Rooney, James Dominic. "Evolutionary Biology and Classical TAs for God's Existence." *Heythrop Journal* 54 (2013): 617–30.

Ross, Hugh. *The Creation and the Cosmos: How the Latest Scientific Discoveries Reveal God*. RTB Press, 2018.

Saito, Mari. "Ten Years on, Grief Never Subsides for some Survivors of Japan's Tsunami." *Reuters*, March 10, 2021. https://www.reuters.com/investigates/special-report/japan-tsunami-survivors/.

Sayers, Dorothy. *Letters to a Diminished Church: Passionate Arguments for the Relevance of Christian Doctrine*. Thomas Nelson, 2004.

———. *The Mind of the Maker*. Harper Collins, 1987.

Schaff, Phillip, ed. *Nicene and Post-Nicene Fathers*. 14 vols. Eerdmans, 1994.

Schleiermacher, Friedrich. *Christian Faith: A New Translation and Critical Edition*. 2 vols. Translated by Terrence N. Tice, Catherine L. Kelsey, and Edwina Lawler. Westminster John Knox Press, 2016.

Schmidt, T. C. *Josephus and Jesus*. Oxford University Press, 2025.

Selderhuis, Herman J., ed. *The Calvin Handbook*. Eerdmans, 2009.

Seneca. *De Clementia*. Edited by Susanna Braund. Oxford University Press, 2011.

———. *De Providentia*. In *Moral Essays*, vol. 1, translated by John W. Basore. Loeb Classical Library. Harvard University Press, 1928.

Shakespeare, William. *Hamlet*. Edited by Jeff Dolven. Barnes and Noble, 1994.

Shatzer, Jacob. *Transhumanism and the Image of God: Today's Technology and the Future of Christian Discipleship*. IVP Academic, 2019.

Shenvi, Neil, and Pat Sawyer. *Critical Dilemma: The Rise of Critical Theories and Social Justice Ideology—Implications for Church and Society*. Harvest House Publishers, 2023.

Shrier, Abigail. *Irreversible Damage: The Transgender Craze Seducing Our Daughters*. Regnery Publishing, 2020.

Smith, James K. A. *How (Not) to Be Secular: Reading Charles Taylor*. Eerdmans, 2014.

———. *Imagining the Kingdom: How Worship Works*. Baker Academic, 2013.

———. *You Are What You Love: The Spiritual Power of Habit*. Brazos, 2016.

Smith, Justin E. H. *Irrationality: A History of the Dark Side of Reason*. Princeton University Press, 2019.

Stark, Rodney. *The Triumph of Faith: Why the World Is More Religious Than Ever*. ISI Books, 2015.

Strauss, David Friedrich. *The Life of Jesus Critically Examined*. 4th ed. Translated by George Eliot. Swan Sonnenschein & Co., 1902.

Steinbeck, John. *The Grapes of Wrath*. In *The Grapes of Wrath and Other Writings, 1936–41*. The Library of America, 1996.

Stuart, Douglas. *Hosea–Jonah*. WBC. Word Books, 1987.

Suetonius. *Lives of the Caesars*. In *Suetonius II*. Translated by John Carew Rolfe. Loeb Classical Library. Harvard University Press, 1979.

Sutanto, Nathaniel Gray. "From Antithesis to Synthesis: A Neo-Calvinistic Theological Strategy in Herman Bavinck and Cornelius Van Til." *Journal of Reformed Theology* 9 (2015): 348–74.

Tacitus. *The Annals of Tacitus: Books XI–XVI*. Edited by George Gilbert Ramsay. John Murray, 1909.

Tanenhaus, Sam. *Whittaker Chambers: A Biography*. Random House, 1998.

Tanner, Michael. *Nietzsche: A Very Short Introduction*. Oxford University Press, 1996.

Taylor, Charles. *A Secular Age*. The Belknap Press, 2007.

———. *Sources of the Self: Making of the Modern Identity*. Harvard University Press, 1989.

Thomas, Keith. *Religion and the Decline of Magic*. Penguin, 1991.

Thorndike, Lynn. "The Attitude of Origen and Augustine Toward Magic." *The Monist* 18/1 (1908): 46–66.

Thunberg, Lars. *Microcosm and Mediator: The Theological Anthropology of Maximus the Confessor*. C. W. K. Gleerup Lund, 1965.

Tolkien, J. R. R. "On Fairy Stories." In *The Monsters and the Critics and Other Essays: The Essays of J. R. R. Tolkien*. Harper Collins, 1983.

Tosi, Justin, and Brandon Warmke. *Grandstanding: The Use and Abuse of Moral Talk*. Oxford University Press, 2020.

Troeltsch, Ernst. *Protestantism and Progress: The Significance of Protestantism for the Rise of the Modern World*. Translated by W. Montgomery. G. P. Putnam's Sons, 1912.

Troy, Frank. *Herman Melville's Genius: The Author of Moby-Dick on How to Think About Religion and Other Ideologies*. Cave Canem Press, 2012.

Trueman, Carl R. *The Rise and Triumph of the Modern Self: Cultural Amnesia, Expressive Individualism, and the Road to Sexual Revolution*. Crossway, 2020.

Turner, Steve. "Chance." In *Up to Date: Poems 1968–1982*. Hodder and Stoughton, 1982.

Turretin, Francis. *Institutes of Elenctic Theology*. Translated by George Musgrave Giger. Edited by James T. Dennison Jr. P&R, 1992–1997.

Ursinus, Zacharias. *The Commentary of Dr. Zacharias Ursinus on the Heidelberg Catechism*. Translated by G. W. Williard. P&R, 1992.

VanDrunen, David. "Thomistic Natural Theology and Its Implications: A Review Article of Jeffrey Johnson's *The Failure of Natural Theology*." *Journal of the International Reformed Baptist Seminary* (2023): 109–26.

Vanhoozer, Kevin. *Remythologizing Theology: Divine Action, Passion, and Authorship*. Cambridge University Press, 2010.

Van Til, Cornelius. *Common Grace and the Gospel*. P&R, 1972.

———. *The Defense of the Faith*. P&R, 1967.

———. *Defense of the Faith*. 3rd ed. P&R, 1966.

———. *Essays on Christian Education*. P&R, 1979.

———. *Herman Dooyeweerd and Reformed Apologetics*. 3 Parts. Westminster Theological Seminary, 1972.

———. *An Introduction to Systematic Theology*. P&R, 1974.

———. *The Protestant Doctrine of Scripture*. In Defense of Biblical Christianity 1. Den Dulk Christian Foundation, 1967.

———. *The Reformed Pastor and Modern Thought*. P&R, 1980.

Viret, Pierre. *A Verie Familiare and Fruitful Exposition of the Christian Faith Contaeined in the Common Crede, Called the Apostles Crede*. London: n.d.

Voltaire. *Candide and Other Stories*. Alfred A. Knopf, 1992.

———. "The Lisbon Earthquake." In *The Works of Voltaire*, vol. 36. E. R. DuMont, 1901.

Von Humboldt, Alexander. *Cosmos: A Sketch of a Physical Description of the Universe*. 2 vols. Edited by E. C. Otté. George Bell & Sons, 1901.

Vos, Geerhardus. "Christian Faith and the Truthfulness of Bible History." *Princeton Theological Review* 4/3 (1906): 304–5.

———. "The Eschatological Aspect of the Spirit." In *Biblical and Theological Studies by the Members of the Faculty of Princeton Theological Seminary*. Charles Scribner's Sons, 1912.

———. *Lectures on Natural Theology*. Edited by J. V. Fesko. Translated by Albert Gootjes. Reformation Heritage Books, 2022.

———. *Reformed Dogmatics*. 5 vols. Edited by Richard B. Gaffin Jr. Lexham, 2015–2016.

Wahlberg, Mats. *Revelation as Testimony: A Philosophical-Theological Study*. Eerdmans, 2014.

Waldstein, Michael. "Introduction." In John Paul II, *Man and Woman He Created Them: A Theology of the Body*, translated by Michael Waldstein. Pauline Books & Media, 2006.

Walsham, Alexandra. "The Reformation and 'The Disenchantment of the World' Reassessed." *The Historical Journal* 51/2 (2008): 497–528.

Waltke, Bruce K. "The Book of Proverbs and Ancient Wisdom Literature." *Bibliotheca Sacra* 136 (1979): 211–38.

———. *The Book of Proverbs: Chapters 1–15*. NICOT. Eerdmans, 2004.

———. *The Book of Proverbs: Chapters 15–31*. NICOT. Eerdmans, 2005.

Ware, Kalistos. *The Orthodox Way*. St. Vladimir's Seminary Press, 1993.

Warfield, B. B. "The Emotional Life of Our Lord." In *Biblical and Theological Studies*. Charles Scribner's Sons, 1912.

———. *The Inspiration and Authority of the Bible*. P&R, 1948.

———. "Introduction." In Francis R. Beattie, *Apologetics: or The Rational Vindication of Christianity*. The Presbyterian Committee of Publication, 1903.

Waters, Guy Prentiss. *Acts: EP Study Commentary*. Evangelical Press, 2014.

Weber, Max. *The Vocation Lectures*. Translated by Rodney Livingstone. Edited by David Owen and Tracy B. Strong. Hackett Publishing Co., 2004.

Webster, John. "'Love Is Also a Lover of Life': *Creatio ex Nihilo* and Creaturely Goodness." *Modern Theology* 29/2 (2013): 156–71.

Weems, Ann. *Psalms of Lament*. Westminster John Knox Press, 1995.

Weinandy, Thomas. *Does God Suffer?* University of Notre Dame Press, 2000.

Weinberg, Steven. *The First Three Minutes: A Modern View of the Origins of the Universe*. Updated ed. Basic Books, 1988.

Wenham, Gordon J. "Sanctuary Symbolism in the Garden of Eden Story." In *I Studied Inscriptions from Before the Flood: Ancient Near Eastern, Literary, and Linguistic Approaches to Genesis 1–11*, edited by Richard S. Hess and David Toshio Tsumura. Sources for Biblical and Theological Study, vol. 4. Eisenbrauns, 1994.

Whealey, Alice. *Josephus on Jesus: The Testimonium Flavianum Controversy from Late Antiquity to Modern Times*. Peter Lang, 2003.

Winter, Bruce W. "Theological and Ethical Responses to Religious Pluralism—1 Corinthians 8–10." *Tyndale Bulletin* 41/2 (1990): 209–26.

Wolf, Maryanne. *Reader, Come Home: The Reading Brain in a Digital World*. Harper, 2018.

Wright, N. T. *The Resurrection of the Son of God*. Fortress, 2003.

———. *Surprised by Scripture: Engaging Contemporary Issues*. HarperOne, 2015.

Young, E. J. *A Prophecy of Daniel: A Commentary*. Eerdmans, 1949.

Zachman, Randall. "The Universe as the Living Image of God: Calvin's Doctrine of the Universe Reconsidered." *Concordia Theological Quarterly* 61/4 (1997): 299–313.

Zanchi, Girolamo. *De Natura Dei, seu De Divnis Attributis*. Wilhelm Harnis, 1598.

Zugibe, Frederick T. *The Crucifixion of Jesus: A Forensic Inquiry*. 2nd ed. M. Evans and Company, 2005.

Index